Race and Ethnicity

perspectives

Race and Ethnicity

Academic Editor
Amber Ault
Oakland University

coursewise
publishing
inc.

Bellevue • Boulder • Dubuque • Madison • St. Paul

Our mission at **Coursewise** is to help students make connections—linking theory to practice and the classroom to the outside world. Learners are motivated to synthesize ideas when course materials are placed in a context they recognize. By providing gateways to contemporary and enduring issues, **Coursewise** publications will expand students' awareness of and context for the course subject.

For more information on **Coursewise,** visit us at our web site: http://www.coursewise.com

To order an examination copy: Houghton Mifflin Sixth Floor Media 800-565-6247 (voice); 800-565-6236 (fax)

Coursewise Publishing Editorial Staff

Thomas Doran, ceo/publisher: Environmental Science/Geography/Journalism/Marketing/Speech
Edgar Laube, publisher: Political Science/Psychology/Sociology
Linda Meehan Avenarius, publisher: **Courselinks™**
Sue Pulvermacher-Alt, publisher: Education/Health/Gender Studies
Victoria Putman, publisher: Anthropology/Philosophy/Religion
Tom Romaniak, publisher: Business/Criminal Justice/Economics
Kathleen Schmitt, publishing assistant
Gail Hodge, executive producer

Coursewise Publishing Production Staff

Lori A. Blosch, permissions coordinator
Mary Monner, production coordinator
Victoria Putman, production manager

Note: Readings in this book appear exactly as they were published.
Thus, inconsistencies in style and usage among the different
readings are likely.

Cover photo: Copyright © 1997 T. Teshigawara/Panoramic Images, Chicago, IL. All Rights Reserved.

Interior design and cover design by Jeff Storm

Library of Congress Catalog Card Number: 99-64020

ISBN 0-395-97304-X

Printed in the United States of America by Coursewise Publishing, Inc.
7 North Pinckney Street, Suite 346, Madison, WI 53703

10 9 8 7 6 5 4 3 2 1

from the
Publisher

Edgar Laube
Coursewise Publishing

Do you remember the first time you ate pizza? Where was it? What type of pizza? How much did you like it? Here are my answers to these questions: yes, a bowling alley in LaCrosse, Wisconsin, pepperoni, and VERY MUCH. I remember thinking that Italian food was a great discovery and that my world had expanded significantly.

That was forty years ago, when I was twelve. "Pizza pie" was unknown in my hometown in Iowa. Elvis was just getting his start. John and Paul knew each other, but they didn't know George and certainly not Ringo, who still dreamed of becoming a hairdresser. "Ethnic" was usually a type of exotic food. Most families had single incomes, and Mom stayed home. Michael Jordan had not been born yet. White people referred to black people as "Negroes."

Well, it's forty years later. Elvis has morphed into a hundred impersonators, and Paul has been knighted. "Ethnic" connotes a lot more than food, and Mom often works a double shift (home and work). Michael Jordan is retired. The color lines in our society have blurred significantly. It's incredible how much things have changed. Yet, that expanding world that pizza symbolized to me still seems a long way off. In part, it's because I, like many others, confuse change with progress.

"Change" has many definitions, but one that is relevant here is simply "the replacing of one thing with another." Typewriters have become computers, black rotary phones have become cell phones, highways have become freeways. But, are we better writers, communicators, or drivers because of it? "Progress," on the other hand, means movement toward a goal, or improvement. Change can contribute to progress, of course—look at the field of medicine—but change and progress are certainly not the same thing. This is especially true in the areas of race, ethnicity, and gender. We've witnessed an enormous amount of change regarding these issues, but I wonder how much progress we've made as a society.

I like the way that Amber Ault has framed these issues for you. Her perspective, and that of most sociologists, is that issues of race, ethnicity, and gender are socially constructed; they are social systems that derive from society—and not from genetics or philosophy. Given that society is a collection of individuals, only change in the attitudes of individuals can change the overarching systems and produce progress. So, Amber, thanks for your hard work and patience. I've learned something from reading through this work, and I'm confident that others will as well.

Students, check out the rich resources supporting this project at the **Courselinks**™ site for Race and Ethnicity (http://www.courselinks.com). While you're there, please let Amber and me know how you're doing and what you think.

I commend you for your interest in these important issues. You're taking an important step in attempting to inform yourselves, which means change and, just maybe, progress. Good luck!

from the
Academic Editor

Amber Ault
Oakland University

Amber Ault recently finished a postdoctoral fellowship in mental health services research at the University of Wisconsin and is now an assistant professor of sociology and director of women's studies at Oakland University in Rochester, Michigan. With graduate education in both anthropology and sociology, her interdisciplinary scholarship focuses on issues of identity construction and negotiation, the scientific construction of identity categories, and conflicts among identity-based groups. She teaches in the areas of gender, race, and sexuality, and is grateful for all that her students have taught her.

To study race relations in the United States requires courage, a willingness to risk, and an openness to the possibility of change. Having seen in my sociology classrooms that no topic proves more provocative, more sensitive, or more transformative than that of "race," I enthusiastically accepted an invitation from **Coursewise Publishing** to edit a reader on race and ethnicity. I hope that this first edition of *Perspectives: Race and Ethnicity* will make an interesting contribution to the course for which it has been selected.

As the Academic Editor of this reader, I set out to create a volume different from most existing readers on race and ethnicity in a number of important ways. First, I organized this collection by issues, instead of by racialized groups. I chose this strategy to highlight the structural and socially constructed nature of racial systems. My hope is that you will learn that the racial categories we use in the United States (and the world beyond) today are not rooted in biology but, instead, in society. Second, I included themes that reflect common topics in courses on race and ethnicity, as well as in other courses, like "Introduction to Sociology" and "Introduction to Cultural Anthropology." As a result, this reader can reinforce your coursework in other classes and can even be used to supplement materials in such courses. Third, because the reader focuses on race and ethnicity as social systems, I sought to include as many articles as possible on how social institutions create racial categories, and on interactions and intersections between racialized groups. Finally, because scholars are increasingly aware that systems of gender, sexuality, and race mutually reinforce one another, I included a number of articles that make the connections between sexism, homophobia, and racism, as well as several readings that explicitly examine the experiences of one sex or the other within particular racialized groups. Because the approach of this reader is different from that of other readers on race and ethnicity, I hope that the final effect is to encourage you to think both critically and systemically—that is, sociologically—about the racializing of the world in which we all live.

I am indebted to **Coursewise** publisher Ed Laube for understanding and supporting from the outset my vision for the project. I am extremely grateful to the members of my Editorial Board, who supported my approach to the reader with enthusiasm and facilitated its production with wonderful article nominations. In addition, I am grateful to the authors who allowed their work to be included in this volume, and to the students whose participation in my courses influenced the final shape of the reader. I offer special personal thanks to MaryLou Ault, whose early teachings inspired my passion about race relations, to Eve Sandberg for connecting me with **Coursewise,** to Michele Besant, Carla Corroto, Nora Jacobson, Tamara Hamlish, and Linda Sturtz for their support of the reader and my writing process, and to A. B. Orlik for both her practical assistance and her patiently impractical acceptance of the extended demands of this project.

Editorial Board

We wish to thank the following instructors for their assistance. Their many suggestions not only contributed to the construction of this volume, but also to the ongoing development of our Race and Ethnicity web site.

WiseGuide Introduction

Critical Thinking and Bumper Stickers

Question Authority

The bumper sticker said: Question Authority. This is a simple directive that goes straight to the heart of critical thinking. The issue is not whether the authority is right or wrong; it's the questioning process that's important. Questioning helps you develop awareness and a clearer sense of what you think. That's critical thinking.

Critical thinking is a new label for an old approach to learning—that of challenging all ideas, hypotheses, and assumptions. In the physical and life sciences, systematic questioning and testing methods (known as the scientific method) help verify information, and objectivity is the benchmark on which all knowledge is pursued. In the social sciences, however, where the goal is to study people and their behavior, things get fuzzy. It's one thing for the chemistry experiment to work out as predicted, or for the petri dish to yield a certain result. It's quite another matter, however, in the social sciences, where the subject is ourselves. Objectivity is harder to achieve.

Although you'll hear critical thinking defined in many different ways, it really boils down to analyzing the ideas and messages that you receive. What are you being asked to think or believe? Does it make sense, objectively? Using the same facts and considerations, could you reasonably come up with a different conclusion? And, why does this matter in the first place? As the bumper sticker urged, question authority. Authority can be a textbook, a politician, a boss, a big sister, or an ad on television. Whatever the message, learning to question it appropriately is a habit that will serve you well for a lifetime. And in the meantime, thinking critically will certainly help you be course wise.

Getting Connected

This reader is a tool for connected learning. This means that the readings and other learning aids explained here will help you to link classroom theory to real-world issues. They will help you to think critically and to make long-lasting learning connections. Feedback from both instructors and students has helped us to develop some suggestions on how you can wisely use this connected learning tool.

WiseGuide Pedagogy

A wise reader is better able to be a critical reader. Therefore, we want to help you get wise about the articles in this reader. Each section of *Perspectives* has three tools to help you: the WiseGuide Intro, the WiseGuide Wrap-Up, and the Putting It in *Perspectives* review form.

WiseGuide Intro

In the WiseGuide Intro, the Academic Editor introduces the section, gives you an overview of the topics covered, and explains why particular articles were selected and what's important about them.

Also in the WiseGuide Intro, you'll find several key points or learning objectives that highlight the most important things to remember from this section. These will help you to focus your study of section topics.

At the end of the WiseGuide Intro, you'll find questions designed to stimulate critical thinking. Wise students will keep these questions in mind as they read an article (we repeat the questions at the start of the articles as a reminder). When you finish each article, check your understanding. Can you answer the questions? If not, go back and reread the article. The Academic Editor has written sample responses for many of the questions, and you'll find these online at the **Courselinks**™ site for this course. More about **Courselinks** in a minute. . . .

WiseGuide Wrap-Up

Be course wise and develop a thorough understanding of the topics covered in this course. The WiseGuide Wrap-Up at the end of each section will help you do just that with concluding comments or summary points that repeat what's most important to understand from the section you just read.

In addition, we try to get you wired up by providing a list of select Internet resources—what we call R.E.A.L. web sites because they're **R**elevant, **E**nhanced, **A**pproved, and Linked. The information at these web sites will enhance your understanding of a topic. (Remember to use your Passport and start at http://www.courselinks.com so that if any of these sites have changed, you'll have the latest link.)

Putting It in *Perspectives* Review Form

At the end of the book is the Putting It in *Perspectives* review form. Your instructor may ask you to complete this form as an assignment or for extra credit. If nothing else, consider doing it on your own to help you critically think about the reading.

Prompts at the end of each article encourage you to complete this review form. Feel free to copy the form and use it as needed.

The Courselinks™ Site

The **Courselinks** Passport is your ticket to a wonderful world of integrated web resources designed to help you with your course work. These resources are found at the **Courselinks** site for your course area. This is where the readings in this book and the key topics of your course are linked to an exciting array of online learning tools. Here you will find carefully selected readings, web links, quizzes, worksheets, and more, tailored to your course and approved as connected learning tools. The ever-changing, always interesting **Courselinks** site features a number of carefully integrated resources designed to help you be course wise. These include:

http://www.courselinks.com

- **R.E.A.L. Sites** At the core of a **Courselinks** site is the list of R.E.A.L. sites. This is a select group of web sites for studying, not surfing. Like the readings in this book, these sites have been selected, reviewed, and approved by the Academic Editor and the Editorial Board. The R.E.A.L. sites are arranged by topic and are annotated with short descriptions and key words to make them easier for you to use for reference or research. With R.E.A.L. sites, you're studying approved resources within seconds—and not wasting precious time surfing unproven sites.

- **Editor's Choice** Here you'll find updates on news related to your course, with links to the actual online sources. This is also where we'll tell you about changes to the site and about online events.

- **Course Overview** This is a general description of the typical course in this area of study. While your instructor will provide specific course objectives, this overview helps you place the course in a generic context and offers you an additional reference point.

- **www.orksheet** Focus your trip to a R.E.A.L. site with the www.orksheet. Each of the 10 to 15 questions will prompt you to take in the best that site has to offer. Use this tool for self-study, or if required, email it to your instructor.

- **Course Quiz** The questions on this self-scoring quiz are related to articles in the reader, information at R.E.A.L. sites, and other course topics, and will help you pinpoint areas you need to study. Only you will know your score—it's an easy, risk-free way to keep pace!

- **Topic Key** The online Topic Key is a listing of the main topics in your course, and it correlates with the Topic Key that appears in this reader. This handy reference tool also links directly to those R.E.A.L. sites that are especially appropriate to each topic, bringing you integrated online resources within seconds!

- **Web Savvy Student Site** If you're new to the Internet or want to brush up, stop by the Web Savvy Student site. This unique supplement is a complete **Courselinks** site unto itself. Here, you'll find basic information on using the Internet, creating a web page, communicating on the web, and more. Quizzes and Web Savvy Worksheets test your web knowledge, and the R.E.A.L. sites listed here will further enhance your understanding of the web.

- **Student Lounge** Drop by the Student Lounge to chat with other students taking the same course or to learn more about careers in your major. You'll find links to resources for scholarships, financial aid, internships, professional associations, and jobs. Take a look around the Student Lounge and give us your feedback. We're open to remodeling the Lounge per your suggestions.

Building Better Perspectives!

Please tell us what you think of this *Perspectives* volume so we can improve the next one. Here's how you can help:

1. Visit our **Coursewise** site at: http://www.coursewise.com

2. Click on *Perspectives*. Then select the Building Better *Perspectives* Form for your book.

3. Forms and instructions for submission are available online.

Tell us what you think—did the readings and online materials help you make some learning connections? Were some materials more helpful than others? Thanks in advance for helping us build better *Perspectives*.

Student Internships

If you enjoy evaluating these articles or would like to help us evaluate the **Courselinks** site for this course, check out the **Coursewise** Student Internship Program. For more information, visit:

http://www.coursewise.com/intern.html

Brief Contents

Contents

At **Coursewise,** we're publishing connected learning tools. That means that the book you are holding is only a part of this publication. You'll also want to harness the integrated resources that **Coursewise** has developed at the fun and highly useful **Courselinks**™ web site for *Perspectives: Race and Ethnicity*. If you purchased this book new, use the Passport that was shrink-wrapped to this volume to obtain site access. If you purchased a used copy of this book, then you need to buy a stand-alone Passport. If your bookstore doesn't stock Passports to **Courselinks** sites, visit http://www.courselinks.com for ordering information.

section 1
The Scientific Construction of Race

section 2
Race, Representation, and Popular Culture

section 3

Race, Ethnicity, and Immigration

section 4

Racial and Ethnic Identities

**section
5**

Race and Gender

**section
6**

Family

section 7

Crime and Criminal Justice

section 8

Challenging Racism

Topic Key

This Topic Key is an important tool for learning. It will help you integrate this reader into your course studies. Listed below, in alphabetical order, are important topics covered in this volume. Below each topic you'll find the reading numbers and titles, and R.E.A.L. web site addresses, relating to that topic. Note that the Topic Key might not include every topic your instructor chooses to emphasize. If you don't find the topic you're looking for in the Topic Key, check the index or the online topic key at the **Courselinks**™ site.

African-Americans

5 Michael Jordan's Family Values: Marketing, Meaning, and Post-Reagan America
15 Subordinating Masculinities/Racializing Masculinities: Writing White Supremacist Discourse on Men's Bodies
16 The Mind That Burns in Each Body: Women, Rape, and Racial Violence
17 Sister Acts: Resisting Men's Domination in Black and White Fraternity Little Sister Programs
18 Sleeping with the Enemy? Talking about Men, Race, and Relationships
19 Constructing Amniocentesis: Maternal and Medical Discourses
20 Black Teenage Mothers and Their Mothers: The Impact of Adolescent Childbearing on Daughters' Relations with Mothers
21 Crime Control and Ethnic Minorities: Legitimizing Racial Oppression by Creating Moral Panics
22 The Code of the Streets
23 The Fort Bragg Swastika
25 An American Litany: Diary of a Mad Law Professor
26 When Justice Kills: After Years of Decline, Police Brutality Is on the Rise, Sparking a Reform Movement

Death by Discrimination? A Paper by Professor Joe Feagin
http://curry.edschool.virginia.edu/go/multicultural/papers/joe.html

National Association for the Advancement of Colored People
http://www.naacp.org/

American Indians

3 Postwar Photographic Histories of Race and Gender in *National Geographic* Magazine
13 Desperately Seeking Redemption: Rise of Native American Neo-shamanic Books and Workshops

American Indian Sports Team Mascots
http://members.tripod.com/~earnestman/1indexpage.htm

Anti-Racist Movements

16 The Mind That Burns in Each Body: Women, Rape, and Racial Violence
24 Anti-Racist Ad Fuels Debate on Strategy: Advertisement Sponsored by the Anti-Racist Alliance

Anti-Racist Mentality Education Page
http://www.externet.hu/arm/educate.htm

Anti-Semitism

6 Hatemongering on the Data Highway
15 Subordinating Masculinities/Racializing Masculinities: Writing White Supremacist Discourse on Men's Bodies
23 The Fort Bragg Swastika
25 An American Litany: Diary of a Mad Law Professor

Anti-Defamation League Online
http://www.adl.org/

Asian-Americans

7 The Transnationals: Status of Immigrants in the U.S.
8 The Ordeal of Immigration in Wausau
18 Sleeping with the Enemy? Talking about Men, Race, and Relationships

Asian History, Chinese History, Chinese-Americans, Asians
http://www.abetterbigtoy.com/lk-ahsty.htm

Childhood Socialization

11 The Meanings of Macho: Changing Mexican Male Identities
19 Constructing Amniocentesis: Maternal and Medical Discourses
20 Black Teenage Mothers and Their Mothers: The Impact of Adolescent Childbearing on Daughters' Relations with Mothers
28 Confessions of a Skinhead: After 15 Years in the Movement, T. J. Leyden Jr. Renounces Life As White-Supremacist, Neo-Nazi Brawler

Economics

4 We Said We Wanted a Revolution: Race, Ethnicity, and the Political Economics of Marketing/Representation by Nike
5 Michael Jordan's Family Values: Marketing, Meaning, and Post-Reagan America
9 The New Politics of Immigration: "Balanced-Budget Conservatism" and the Symbolism of Proposition 187
16 The Mind That Burns in Each Body: Women, Rape, and Racial Violence
20 Black Teenage Mothers and Their Mothers: The Impact of Adolescent Childbearing on Daughters' Relations with Mothers
22 The Code of the Streets

A Crusader Makes Celebrities Tremble
http://www.nlcnet.org/Press/Newsclip/greenhou.htm

European-Americans

13 Desperately Seeking Redemption: Rise of Native American Neo-shamanic Books and Workshops
14 Promise Keepers: Patriarchy's Second Coming As Masculine Renewal
15 Subordinating Masculinities/Racializing Masculinities: Writing White Supremacist Discourse on Men's Bodies
16 The Mind That Burns in Each Body: Women, Rape, and Racial Violence
17 Sister Acts: Resisting Men's Domination in Black and White Fraternity Little Sister Programs
27 Apologize for Slavery? Facing Up to the Living Past
28 Confessions of a Skinhead: After 15 Years in the Movement, T. J. Leyden Jr. Renounces Life As White-Supremacist, Neo-Nazi Brawler

Language of Closet Racism: An Illustration
http://curry.edschool.virginia.edu/go/multicultural/papers/langofracism2.html

section
1

Key Points

- Racial classification schemes are rooted in social systems, not biological systems.

- Sociologists conceive of race and racism as features of social structures instead of as features of individuals.

The Scientific Construction of Race

 **WiseGuide Intro**

What is race? What is ethnicity?

While nearly everyone shares an understanding of ethnicity as the cultural traditions of particular groups of people, definitions of race vary. If we were to ask a variety of United States citizens how they define race, most people—including many doctors, lawyers, educators, and politicians—would tell us that biology determines race and that racial categories are fixed and immutable. If there were a sociologist, an anthropologist, or an historian within our random sample, however, she or he would likely offer a different definition and would tell us that race is not biologically determined but socially constructed; that racial categories change as a function of history, politics, and cultural contact; and that, instead of speaking of different "races," we should speak of racialized groups—groups that our society defines by attaching social significance to particular biological traits, such as skin color. What are the origins of these two divergent understandings of race? What are their politics? Which is most useful to us in the study of race and ethnicity? For answers to these questions, we turn to the scientific construction of race.

Most cultures and many religions around the world have offered explanations for the diversity within humanity. In Western culture, from the period of The Enlightenment forward, the dominant voice defining, describing, and explaining race and racial and cultural differences has been that of modern science. Adopting methods originally used to classify plants and animals, European scientists attempted to classify human beings according to selected biological traits—traits often chosen because they accentuated apparent physical differences between European populations and people from other parts of the world. Practitioners of modern European science devised a number of systems for classifying the world's people according to "race," with a great deal of variation in the number of races thought to exist, as well as in the assignment of populations to particular categories. Despite this variety, most classification schemes had in common an implicit evaluation of each racialized group's status within the human family, and most placed white Europeans at the pinnacle of human biological and cultural evolution. Such classification systems bolstered European rationalizations for the colonization of many parts of the world inhabited by the racialized groups which European science deemed inferior. Such typologies encouraged in some Europeans a "moral obligation" to spread "civilization" to other continents; this "moral obligation" allowed others to regard the lives of people they considered "savages" as worthless and without any of the rights common in European societies.

The scientific construction of race clearly was not simply a benign academic pursuit in Enlightenment Europe. The racialization that resulted from scientific conceptualizations reinforced cultural and social stereotypes and helped solidify social hierarchies, both among Europeans and between Europeans and the peoples of other continents. Throughout the past 200 years, the world has witnessed the use of science in the maintenance of "racial" hierarchies in any number of circumstances. In the United States, as in Europe, the scientific study of race often reported "biological" differences between whites and Blacks as a way of explaining and justifying social differences between these groups. In Germany, Nazi scientists constructed "biological" differences between Jews and non-Jews in order to justify the persecution, internment, and murder of Jewish people, who were seen as a race apart from other Germans and as "polluting" the so-called Aryan gene pool. Science, as a human pursuit, reflects the interests of its practitioners. It should not be surprising that the science of those who benefit from racial or ethnic privilege produces "findings" that reinforce the dominant racial hierarchy of a given society, or that such science is welcomed by members of dominant racialized groups in societies that rely on science as an arbiter of truth.

In this section, physical anthropologist Stephen Jay Gould explores the origins of Enlightenment scientific conceptions of racial categories, calling the emergence of the dominant racial classification scheme "one of the most fateful transitions in the history of Western science." Gould encourages us to think about how this system of classification affected the American democracy that was emerging at the same time and to imagine how the world might have been different had science conceived of racial categories differently. Sociologist Eduardo Bonilla-Silva explores how social science conceives of racism, which, of course, depends on understandings of race. Bonilla-Silva argues that we must see race, racialization, and racism as features of social structure, the relatively stable patterns that organize a society and serve as a "roadmap" for its members.

What are the implications of Gould's revelation that race is "scientifically constructed"? Why is the emergence of a "scientific" typology of race "one of the most fateful transitions in the history of Western science"?

The Geometer of Race

In the eighteenth century, a disastrous shift occurred in the way Westerners perceived races. The man responsible was Johann Friedrich Blumenbach, one of the least racist thinkers of his day.

Stephen Jay Gould

Interesting stories often lie encoded in names that seem either capricious or misconstrued. Why, for example, are political radicals called "left" and their conservative counterparts "right"? In many European legislatures, the most distinguished members sat at the chairman's right, following a custom of courtesy as old as our prejudices for favoring the dominant hand of most people. (These biases run deep, extending well beyond can openers and scissors to language itself, where dexterous stems from the Latin for "right," and sinister from the word for "left.") Since these distinguished nobles and moguls tended to espouse conservative views, the right and left wings of the legislature came to define a geometry of political views.

Among such apparently capricious names in my own field of biology and evolution, none seems more curious, and none elicits more questions after lectures, than the official designation of light-skinned people in Europe, western Asia, and North Africa as Caucasian. Why should the most common racial group of the Western world be named for a mountain range that straddles Russia and Georgia? Johann Friedrich Blumenbach (1752–1840), the German anatomist and naturalist who established the most influential of all racial classifications, invented this name in 1795, in the third edition of his seminal work, *DeGeneris Humani Varietate Nativa (On the Natural Variety of Mankind)*. Blumenbach's definition cites two reasons for his choice—the maximal beauty of people from this small region, and the probability that humans were first created in this area.

Caucasian variety. I have taken the name of this variety from Mount Caucasus, both because its neighborhood, and especially its southern slope, produces the most beautiful race of men, I mean the Georgian; and because . . . in that region, if anywhere, it seems we ought with the greatest probability to place the autochthones [original forms] of mankind.

Blumenbach, one of the greatest and most honored scientists of the Enlightenment, spent his entire career as a professor at the University of Gottingen in Germany. He first presented De Generis Humani Varietate Nativa as a doctoral dissertation to the medical faculty of Gottingen in 1775, as the minutemen of Lexington and Concord began the American Revolution. He then republished the text for general distribution in 1776, as a fateful meeting in Philadelphia proclaimed our independence. The coincidence of three great documents in 1776—Jefferson's Declaration of Independence (on the politics of liberty), Adam Smith's Wealth of Nations (on the economics of individualism), and Blumenbach's treatise on racial classification (on the science of human diversity)—records the social ferment of these decades and sets the wider context that makes Blumenbach's taxonomy, and his subsequent decision to call the European race Caucasian, so important for our history and current concerns.

The solution to big puzzles often hinges upon tiny curiosities, easy to miss or to pass over. I suggest that the key to understanding Blumenbach's classification, the foundation of much that continues to influence and disturb us today,

Stephen Jay Gould, "The Geometer of Race," *Discover:* 15(11), 1994. Stephen Jay Gould/© 1994. Reprinted with permission of *Discover* Magazine.

lies in the peculiar criterion he used to name the European race Caucasian—the supposed superior beauty of people from this region. Why, first of all, should a scientist attach such importance to an evidently subjective assessment; and why, secondly, should an aesthetic criterion become the basis of a scientific judgment about place of origin? To answer these questions, we must compare Blumenbach's original 1775 text with the later edition of 1795, when Caucasians received their name.

Blumenbach's final taxonomy of 1795 divided all humans into five groups, defined both by geography and appearance—in his order, the Caucasian variety, for the light-skinned people of Europe and adjacent parts of Asia and Africa; the Mongolian variety, for most other inhabitants of Asia, including China and Japan; the Ethiopian variety, for the dark-skinned people of Africa; the American variety, for most native populations of the New World; and the Malay variety, for the Polynesians and Melanesians of the Pacific and for the aborigines of Australia. But Blumenbach's original classification of 1775 recognized only the first four of these five, and united members of the Malay variety with the other people of Asia whom Blumenbach came to name Mongolian.

We now encounter the paradox of Blumenbach's reputation as the inventor of modern racial classification. The original four-race system, as I shall illustrate in a moment, did not arise from Blumenbach's observations but only represents, as Blumenbach readily admits, the classification promoted by his guru Carolus Linnaeus in the founding document of taxonomy, the *Systema Naturae of 1758*. Therefore, Blumenbach's only original contribution to racial classification lies in the later addition of a Malay variety for some Pacific peoples first included in a broader Asian group.

This change seems so minor. Why, then, do we credit Blumenbach, rather than Linnaeus, as the founder of racial classification? (One might prefer to say "discredit," as the enterprise does not, for good reason, enjoy high repute these days.) But Blumenbach's apparently small change actually records a theoretical shift that could not have been broader, or more portentous, in scope. This change has been missed or misconstrued because later scientists have not grasped the vital historical and philosophical principle that theories are models subject to visual representation, usually in clearly definable geometric terms.

By moving from the Linnaean four-race system to his own five-race scheme, Blumenbach radically changed the geometry of human order from a geographically based model without explicit ranking to a hierarchy of worth, oddly based upon perceived beauty, and fanning out in two directions from a Caucasian ideal. The addition of a Malay category was crucial to this geometric reformulation—and therefore becomes the key to the conceptual transformation rather than a simple refinement of factual information within an old scheme. (For the insight that scientific revolutions embody such geometric shifts, I am grateful to my friend Rhonda Roland Shearer, who portrays these themes in a forthcoming book, *The Flatland Hypothesis*.)

Blumenbach idolized his teacher Linnaeus and acknowledged him as the source of his original fourfold racial classification: "I have followed Linnaeus in the number, but have defined my varieties by other boundaries" (1775 edition). Later, in adding his Malay variety, Blumenbach identified his change as a departure from his old mentor in the most respectful terms: "It became very clear that the Linnaean division of mankind could no longer be adhered to; for which reason I, in this little work,

ceased like others to follow that illustious man."

Linnaeus divided the species *Homo sapiens* into four basic varieties, defined primarily by geography and, interestingly, not in the ranked order favored by most Europeans in the racist tradition—Americanus, Europaeus, Asiaticus, and Afer, or African. (He also alluded to two other fanciful categories: ferus for "wild boys," occasionally discovered in the woods and possibly raised by animals—most turned out to be retarded or mentally ill youngsters abandoned by their parents—and monstrosus for hairy men with tails, and other travelers' confabulations.) In so doing, Linnaeus presented nothing original; he merely mapped humans onto the four geographic regions of conventional cartography.

Linnaeus then characterized each of these groups by noting color, humor, and posture, in that order. Again, none of these categories explicitly implies ranking by worth. Once again, Linnaeus was simply bowing to classical taxonomic theories in making these decisions. For example, his use of the four humors reflects the ancient and medieval theory that a person's temperament arises from a balance of four fluids (humor is Latin for "moisture")—blood, phlegm, choler (yellow bile), and melancholy (black bile). Depending on which of the four substances dominated, a person would be sanguine (the cheerful realm of blood), phlegmatic (sluggish), choleric (prone to anger), or melancholic (sad). Four geographic regions, four humors, four races.

For the American variety, Linnaeus wrote "rufus, cholericus, rectus" (red, choleric, upright); for the European, "albus, sanguineous, torosus" (white, sanguine, muscular); for the Asian, "luridus, melancholicus, rigidus" (pale yellow, melancholy, stiff); and for the African, "niger, phlegmaticus, laxus" (black, phlegmatic, relaxed).

I don't mean to deny that Linnaeus held conventional beliefs about the superiority of his own European variety over others. Being a sanguine, muscular European surely sounds better than being a melancholy, stiff Asian. Indeed, Linnaeus ended each group's description with a more overtly racist label, an attempt to epitomize behavior in just two words. Thus the American was regitur consuetudine (ruled by habit); the European, regitur ritibus (ruled by custom); the Asian, regitur opinionibus (ruled by belief); and the African, regitur arbitrio (ruled by caprice). Surely regulation by established and considered custom beats the unthinking rule of habit or belief, and all of these are superior to caprice—thus leading to the implied and conventional racist ranking of Europeans first, Asians and Americans in the middle, and Africans at the bottom.

Nonetheless, and despite these implications, the overt geometry of Linnaeus's model is not linear or hierarchical. When we visualize his scheme as an essential picture in our mind, we see a map of the world divided into four regions, with the people in each region characterized by a list of different traits. In short, Linnaeus's primary ordering principle is cartographic; if he had wished to push hierarchy as the essential picture of human variety, he would surely have listed Europeans first and Africans last, but he started with native Americans instead.

The shift from a geographic to a hierarchical ordering of human diversity must stand as one of the most fateful transitions in the history of Western science—for what, short of railroads and nuclear bombs, has had more practical impact, in this case almost entirely negative, upon our collective lives? Ironically, Blumenbach is the focus of this shift, for his five-race scheme became canonical and changed the geometry of human order from Linnaean cartography to linear ranking—in short, to a system based on putative worth.

I say ironic because Blumenbach was the least racist and most genial of all Enlightenment thinkers. How peculiar that the man most committed to human unity, and to inconsequential moral and intellectual differences among groups, should have changed the mental geometry of human order to a scheme that has served racism ever since. Yet on second thought, this situation is really not so odd—for most scientists have been quite unaware of the mental machinery, and particularly of the visual or geometric implications, lying behind all their theorizing.

An old tradition in science proclaims that changes in theory must be driven by observation. Since most scientists believe this simplistic formula, they assume that their own shifts in interpretation record only their better understanding of newly discovered facts. Scientists therefore tend to be unaware of their own mental impositions upon the world's messy and ambiguous factuality. Such mental impositions arise from a variety of sources, including psychological predisposition and social context. Blumenbach lived in an age when ideas of progress, and the cultural superiority of European ways, dominated political and social life. Implicit, loosely formulated, or even unconscious notions of racial ranking fit well with such a world view—indeed, almost any other organizational scheme would have seemed anomalous. I doubt that Blumenbach was actively encouraging racism by redrawing the mental diagram of human groups. He was only, and largely passively, recording the social view of his time. But ideas have consequences, whatever the motives or intentions of their promoters.

Blumenbach certainly thought that his switch from the Linnaean four-race system to his own five-race scheme arose only from his improved understanding of nature's factuality. He said as much when he announced his change in the second (1781) edition of his treatise: "Formerly in the first edition of this work, I divided all mankind into four varieties; but after I had more actively investigated the different nations of Eastern Asia and America, and, so to speak, looked at them more closely, I was compelled to give up that division, and to place in its stead the following five varieties, as more consonant to nature." And in the preface to the third edition, of 1795, Blumenbach states that he gave up the Linnaean scheme in order to arrange "the varieties of man according to the truth of nature." When scientists adopt the myth that theories arise solely from observation, and do not grasp the personal and social influences acting on their thinking, they not only miss the causes of their changed opinions; they may even fail to comprehend the deep mental shift encoded by the new theory.

Blumenbach strongly upheld the unity of the human species against an alternative view, then growing in popularity (and surely more conductive to conventional forms of racism), that each major race had been separately created. He ended his third edition by writing: "No doubt can any longer remain but that we are with great probability right in referring all . . . varieties of man . . . to one and the same species."

As his major argument for unity, Blumenbach noted that all supposed racial characteristics grade continuously from one people to another and cannot define any separate and bounded group. "For although there seems to be so great a difference between widely separate nations, that you might easily take the inhabitants of the Cape of Good Hope, the Greenlanders, and the Circassians for so many different species of man, yet when the matter is thoroughly considered, you see that all do so run into one another, and that one variety of mankind does so sensibly pass into the other, that you cannot mark out the limits between them." He particularly refuted the common racist claim that black Africans bore unique features of their inferiority: "There is no single character so peculiar and so universal among the Ethiopians, but what it may be observed on the one hand everywhere in other varieties of men."

Blumenbach, writing 80 years before Darwin, believed that Homo sapiens had been created in a single region and had then spread over the globe. Our racial diversity, he then argued, arose as a result of this spread to other climates and topographies, and to our adoption of different modes of life in these various regions. Following the terminology of his time, Blumenbach referred to these changes as "degenerations"—not intending the modern sense of deterioration, but the literal meaning of departure from an initial form of humanity at the creation (de means "from," and genus refers to our original stock).

Most of these degenerations, Blumenbach argued, arose directly from differences in climate and habitat—ranging from such broad patterns as the correlation of dark skin with tropical environments, to more particular (and fanciful) attributions, including a speculation that the narrow eye slits of some Australian aborigines may have arisen in response to "constant clouds of gnats . . . contracting the natural face of the inhabitants." Other changes, he maintained, arose as a consequence of customs adopted in different regions. For example, nations that compressed the

heads of babies by swaddling boards or papoose carriers ended up with relatively long skulls. Blumenbach held that "almost all the diversity of the form of the head in different nations is to be attributed to the mode of life and to art."

Blumenbach believed that such changes, promoted over many generations, could eventually become hereditary. "With the progress of time," Blumenbach wrote, "art may degenerate into a second nature." But he also argued that most racial variations, as superficial impositions of climate and custom, could be easily altered or reversed by moving to a new region or by adopting new behavior. White Europeans living for generations in the tropics could become dark-skinned, while Africans transported as slaves to high latitudes could eventually become white: "Color, whatever be its cause, be it bile, or the influence of the sun, the air, or the climate, is, at all events, an adventitious and easily changeable thing, and can never constitute a diversity of species," he wrote.

Convinced of the superficiality of racial variation, Blumenbach defended the mental and moral unity of all peoples. He held particularly strong opinions on the equal status of black Africans and white Europeans. He may have been patronizing in praising "the good disposition and faculties of these our black brethren," but better paternalism than malign contempt. He campaigned for the abolition of slavery and asserted the moral superiority of slaves to their captors, speaking of a "natural tenderness of heart, which has never been benumbed or extirpated on board the transport vessels or on the West India sugar plantations by the brutality of their white executioners."

Blumenbach established a special library in his house devoted exclusively to black authors, singling out for special praise the po-

etry of Phillis Wheatley, a Boston slave whose writings have only recently been rediscovered: "I possess English, Dutch, and Latin poems by several black authors, amongst which however above all, those of Phillis Wheatley of Boston, who is justly famous for them, deserves mention here." Finally, Blumenbach noted that many Caucasian nations could not boast so fine a set of authors and scholars as black Africa has produced under the most depressing circumstances of prejudice and slavery: "It would not be difficult to mention entire well-known provinces of Europe, from out of which you would not easily expect to obtain off-hand such good authors, poets, philosophers, and correspondents of the Paris Academy."

Nonetheless, when Blumenbach presented his mental picture of human diversity in his fateful shift away from Linnaean geography, he singled out a particular group as closest to the created ideal and then characterized all other groups by relative degrees of departure from this archetypal standard. He ended up with a system that placed a single race at the pinnacle, and then envisioned two symmetrical lines of departure away from this ideal toward greater and greater degeneration.

We may now return to the riddle of the name Caucasian, and to the significance of Blumenbach's addition of a fifth race, the Malay variety. Blumenbach chose to regard his own European variety as closest to the created ideal and then searched for the subset of Europeans with greatest perfection —the highest of the high, so to speak. As we have seen, he identified the people around Mount Caucasus as the closest embodiments of the original ideal and proceeded to name the entire European race for its finest representatives.

But Blumenbach now faced a dilemma. He had already affirmed the mental and moral equality of all peoples. He therefore could not use these conventional criteria of racist ranking to establish degrees of relative departure from the Caucasian ideal. Instead, and however subjective (and even risible) we view the criterion today, Blumenbach chose physical beauty as his guide to ranking. He simply affirmed that Europeans were most beautiful, with Caucasians as the most comely of all. This explains why Blumenbach, in the first quote cited in this article, linked the maximal beauty of the Caucasians to the place of human origin. Blumenbach viewed all subsequent variation as departures from the originally created ideal—therefore, the most beautiful people most live closest to our primal home.

Blumenbach's descriptions are pervaded by his subjective sense of relative beauty, presented as though he were discussing an objective and quantifiable property, not subject to doubt or disagreement. He describes a Georgian female skull (found close to Mount Caucasus) as "really the most beautiful form of skull which . . . always of itself attracts every eye, however little observant." He then defends his European standard on aesthetic grounds: "In the first place, that stock displays . . . the most beautiful form of the skull, from which, as from a mean and primeval type, the others diverge by most easy gradations. . . . Besides, it is white in color, which we may fairly assume to have been the primitive color of mankind, since . . . it is very easy for that to

degenerate into brown, but very much more difficult for dark to become white."

Blumenbach then presented all human variety on two lines of successive departure from this Caucasian ideal, ending in the two most degenerate (least attractive, not least morally unworthy or mentally obtuse) forms of humanity— Asians on one side, and Africans on the other. But Blumenbach also wanted to designate intermediary forms between ideal and most degenerate, especially since even gradation formed his primary argument for human unity. In his original four-race system, he could identify native Americans as intermediary between Europeans and Asians, but who would serve as the transitional form between Europeans and Africans?

The four-race system contained no appropriate group. But inventing a fifth racial category as an intermediary between Europeans and Africans would complete the new symmetrical geometry. Blumenbach therefore added the Malay race, not as a minor, factual refinement but as a device for reformulating an entire theory of human diversity. With this one stroke, he produced the geometric transformation from Linnaeus's unranked geographic model to the conventional hierarchy of implied worth that has fostered so much social grief ever since.

I have allotted the first place to the Caucasian . . . which makes me esteem it the primeval one. This diverges in both directions into two, most remote and very different from each other; on the one side, namely, into the Ethiopian, and on the other into the Mongolian.

The remaining two occupy the intermediate positions between that primeval one and these two extreme varieties; that is, the American between the Caucasian and Mongolian; the Malay between the same Caucasian and Ethiopian.

—From Blumenbach's third edition.

Scholars often think that academic ideas must remain at worst, harmless, and at best, mildly amusing or even instructive. But ideas do not reside in the ivory tower of our usual metaphor about academic irrelevance. We are, as Pascal said, a thinking reed, and ideas motivate human history. Where would Hitler have been without racism, Jefferson without liberty? Blumenbach lived as a cloistered professor all his life, but his ideas have reverberated in ways that he never could have anticipated, through our wars, our social upheavals, our sufferings, and our hopes.

I therefore end by returning once more the extraordinary coincidences of 1776—as Jefferson wrote the Declaration of Independence while Blumenbach was publishing the first edition of his treatise in Latin. We should remember the words of the nineteenth-century British historian and moralist Lord Acton, on the power of ideas to propel history:

It was from America that . . . ideas long locked in the breast of solitary thinkers, and hidden among Latin folios, burst forth like a conqueror upon the world they were destined to transform, under the title of the Rights of Man.

 Article Review Form at end of book.

How should sociologists study racism, if it is a structural feature of society? How might strategies for challenging racism vary, depending on how *race, racialization,* and *racism* are defined?

Rethinking Racism:

Toward a Structural Interpretation

Eduardo Bonilla-Silva

Eduardo Bonilla-Silva is Assistant Professor of Sociology and African American Studies at the University of Michigan. He is working on two books, one titled Squatters, Politics, and State Responses: The Political Economy of Squatters in Puerto Rico, *and the other* The New Racism: Toward an Analysis of the U.S. Racial Structure, 1960s–1990s. *Currently he is exploring post-civil rights White ideology in an article titled " 'I Am Not a Racist But . . .': An Examination of White Racial Attitudes in the Post-Civil Rights Period."*

The study of race and ethnic conflict historically has been hampered by inadequate and simplistic theories. I contend that the central problem of the various approaches to the study of racial phenomena is their lack of a structural theory of racism. I review traditional approaches and alternative approaches to the study of racism, and discuss their limitations. Following the leads suggested by some of the alternative frameworks, I advance a structural theory of racism based on the notion of racialized social systems.

"The habit of considering racism as a mental quirk, as a psychological flaw, must be abandoned."

—Frantz Fanon (1967:77)

The area of race and ethnic studies lacks a sound theoretical apparatus. To complicate matters, many analysts of racial matters have abandoned the serious theorization and reconceptualization of their central topic: racism. Too many social analysts researching racism assume that the phenomenon is self-evident, and therefore either do not provide a definition or provide an elementary definition (Schuman, Steeh, and Bobo 1985; Sniderman and Piazza 1993). Nevertheless, whether implicitly or explicitly, most analysts regard racism as a purely ideological phenomenon.

Although the concept of racism has become the central analytical category in most contemporary social scientific discourse on racial phenomena, the concept is of recent origin (Banton 1970; Miles 1989, 1993). It was not employed at all in the classic works of Thomas and Znaniecki (1918), Edward Reuter (1934), Gunnar Myrdal (1944), and Robert Park (1950).[1] Benedict (1945) was one of the first scholars to use the notion of racism in her book, *Race and Racism.* She defined racism as "the dogma that one ethnic group is condemned by nature to congenital inferiority and another group is destined to congenital superiority" (p. 87). Despite some refinements, current use of the concept of racism in the social sciences is similar to Benedict's. Thus van den Berghe (1967) states that racism is "any *set of beliefs* that organic, genetically transmitted differences (whether real or imagined) between human groups are intrinsically associated with the presence or the absence of certain socially relevant abilities or characteristics, hence that such differences are a legitimate basis of invidious distinctions between groups socially defined as races" (p. 11, emphasis added). Schaefer (1990) provides a more concise definition of racism: ". . . a *doctrine* of racial supremacy, that one race is superior" (p. 16).

This idealist view is still held widely among social scientists. Its narrow focus on ideas has reduced the study of racism mostly to social psychology, and this perspective has produced a schematic view of the way racism operates in society. First, racism is defined as a set of ideas or beliefs. Second, those beliefs are regarded as having the potential to lead individuals to develop prejudice, defined as "negative attitudes towards an entire group of people" (Schaefer 1990: 53). Finally, these prejudicial attitudes may induce individuals to real actions or discrimination against racial minorities. This conceptual framework, with minor modifications, prevails in the social sciences.

"Rethinking Racism: Toward a Structural Interpretation," *American Sociological Review,* 62, June 1997, pp. 465–480. Reprinted by permission of the American Sociological Association, and the author.

Some alternative perspectives on racism have closely followed the prevailing ideological conceptualization in the social sciences. For example, orthodox Marxists (Cox 1948; Perlo 1975; Szymanski 1981, 1983), who regard class and class struggle as the central explanatory variables of social life, reduce racism to a legitimating ideology used by the bourgeoisie to divide the working class. Even neo-Marxists (Bonacich 1980a, 1980b; Carchedi 1987; Cohen 1989; Hall 1980; Miles 1989, 1993; Miles and Phizacklea 1984; Solomos 1986, 1989; Wolpe 1986, 1988) share to various degrees the limitations of the orthodox Marxist view: the primacy of class, racism viewed as an ideology, and class dynamics as the real engine of racial dynamics. For example, although Bonacich's work provides an interesting twist by regarding race relations and racism as products of a split labor market, giving theoretical primacy to divisions within the working class, racial antagonisms are still regarded as byproducts of class dynamics.

Other scholars have advanced nonideological interpretations of racism but have stopped short of developing a structural conceptualization of racial matters. From the institutionalist perspective (Alvarez et al. 1979; Carmichael 1971; Carmichael and Hamilton 1967; Chesler 1976; Knowles and Prewitt 1969; Wellman 1977), racism is defined as a combination of prejudice and power that allows the dominant race to institutionalize its dominance at all levels in a society. Similarly, from the internal colonialism perspective (Barrera 1979; Blauner 1972; Moore 1970), racism is viewed as an institutional matter based on a system in which the White majority "raises its social position by exploiting, controlling, and keeping down others who are categorized in racial or ethnic terms" (Blauner 1972:22). The main

difference between these two perspectives is that the latter regards racial minorities as colonial subjects in the United States; this view leads unequivocally to nationalist solutions.[2] Both perspectives contribute greatly to our understanding of racial phenomena by stressing the social and systemic nature of racism and the structured nature of White advantages. Furthermore, the effort of the institutionalist perspective to uncover contemporary mechanisms and practices that reproduce White advantages is still empirically useful (e.g., Knowles and Prewitt 1969). Yet neither of these perspectives provides a rigorous conceptual framework that allows analysts to study the operation of racially stratified societies.

The racial formation perspective (Omi and Winant 1986, 1994; Winant 1994) is the most recent theoretical alternative to mainstream idealist approaches. Omi and Winant (1994) define racial formation as "the sociohistorical process by which racial categories are created, inhabited, transformed, and destroyed" (p. 55). In their view, race should be regarded as an organizing principle of social relationships that shapes the identity of individual actors at the micro level and shapes all spheres of social life at the macro level.

Although this perspective represents a breakthrough, it still gives undue attention to ideological/cultural processes,[3] does not regard races as truly social collectivities, and overemphasizes the racial projects (Omi and Winant 1994; Winant 1994) of certain actors (neoconservatives, members of the far right, liberals), thus obscuring the social and general character of racialized societies.

In this paper I point out the limitations of most contemporary frameworks used to analyze racial issues and suggest an alternative structural theory built on some of

the ideas and concepts elaborated by the institutionalist, the internal colonial, and the racial formation perspectives. Although "racism" has a definite ideological component, reducing racial phenomena to ideas limits the possibility of understanding how it shapes a race's life chances. Rather than viewing racism as an all-powerful ideology that explains all racial phenomena in a society, I use the term *racism* only to describe the racial ideology of a racialized social system. That is, racism is only part of a larger racial system.

Limitations of Mainstream Idealist Views and of Some Alternative Frameworks

I describe below some of the main limitations of the idealist conception of racism. Because not all limitations apply to the institutionalist, the internal colonialist, and the racial formation perspectives, I point out the ones that do apply, and to what extent.

Racism is excluded from the foundation or structure of the social system. When racism is regarded as a baseless ideology ultimately dependent on other, "real" forces in society, the structure of the society itself is not classified as racist. The Marxist perspective is particularly guilty of this shortcoming. Although Marxists have addressed the question of the historical origin of racism, they explain its reproduction in an idealist fashion. Racism, in their accounts, is an ideology that emerged with chattel slavery and other forms of class oppression to justify the exploitation of people of color and survives as a residue of the past. Although some Marxists have attempted to distance their analysis from this purely ideological view (Solomos 1986; Wolpe 1988) and to ground racial phenomena in social relations, they do so by ultimately subordinating racial matters to class matters.

Even though the institutionalist, internal colonialism, and racial formation perspectives regard racism as a structural phenomenon and provide some useful ideas and concepts, they do not develop the theoretical apparatus necessary to describe how this structure operates.

Racism is ultimately viewed as a psychological phenomenon to be examined at the individual level. The research agenda that follows from this conceptualization is the examination of individuals' attitudes to determine levels of racism in society (Schuman et al. 1985; Sears 1988; Sniderman and Piazza 1993). Given that the constructs used to measure racism are static—that is, that there are a number of standard questions which do not change significantly over time—this research usually finds that racism is declining in society. Those analysts who find that racist attitudes are still with us usually leave unexplained why this is so (Sniderman and Piazza 1993).

This psychological understanding of racism is related to the limitation I cited above. If racism is not part of a society but is a characteristic of individuals who are "racist" or "prejudiced"—that is, racism is a phenomenon operating at the individual level—then (1) social institutions cannot be racist and (2) studying racism is simply a matter of surveying the proportion of people in a society who hold "racist" beliefs.

Orthodox Marxists (Cox 1948; Perlo 1975; Szymanski 1983) and many neo-Marxists (Miles 1993; Miles and Phizaclea 1984; Solomos 1986) conceive of racism as an ideology that may affect members of the working class. Although the authors associated with the institutionalist, internal colonialist, and

racial formation perspectives focus on the ideological character of racism, they all emphasize how this ideology becomes enmeshed or institutionalized in organizations and social practices.

Racism is treated as a static phenomenon. The phenomenon is viewed as unchanging; that is, racism yesterday is like racism today. Thus, when a society's racial structure and its customary racial practices are rearticulated, this rearticulation is characterized as a decline in racism (Wilson 1978), a natural process in a cycle (Park 1950), an example of increased assimilation (Rex 1973, 1986), or effective "norm changes" (Schuman et al. 1985). This limitation, which applies particularly to social psychologists and Marxist scholars, derives from not conceiving of racism as possessing an independent structural foundation. If racism is merely a matter of ideas that has no material basis in contemporary society, then those ideas should be similar to their original configuration, whatever that was. The ideas may be articulated in a different context, but most analysts essentially believe that racist ideas remain the same. For this reason, with notable exceptions (Kinder and Sears 1981; Sears 1988), their attitudinal research is still based on responses to questions developed in the 1940s, 1950s, and 1960s.

Analysts defining racism in an idealist manner view racism as "incorrect" or "irrational thinking"; thus they label "racists" as irrational and rigid. Because racism is conceived of as a belief with no real social basis, it follows that those who hold racist views must be irrational or stupid (Adorno 1950; Allport 1958; Santa Cruz 1977; Sniderman and Piazza 1993; for a critique see Blauner 1972 and Wellman 1977). This view allows for a tactical distinction between individuals with the "pathology" and social actors who

are "rational" and racism-free. The problem with this rationalistic view is two-fold. First, it misses the rational elements on which racialized systems originally were built. Second, and more important, it neglects the possibility that contemporary racism still has a rational foundation. In this account, contemporary racists are perceived as Archie Bunker-type individuals (Wellman 1977).

Among the alternative frameworks reviewed here, only orthodox Marxism insists on the irrational and imposed character of racism. Neo-Marxists and authors associated with the institutionalist, internal colonialist, and racial formation perspectives insist, to varying degrees, on the rationality of racism. Neo-Marxists (e.g., Bonacich, Wolpe, Hall) and authors in the racial formation tradition (e.g., Omi and Winant) acknowledge the short-term advantages that workers gain from racism; the institutionalist and internal colonial paradigms emphasize the systematic and long-term character of these advantages.

Racism is understood as overt behavior. Because the idealist approach regards racism as "irrational" and "rigid," its manifestations should be quite evident, usually involving some degree of hostility. This does not present serious analytical problems for the study of certain periods in racialized societies when racial practices were overt (e.g., slavery and apartheid), but problems in the analysis of racism arise in situations where racial practices are subtle, indirect, or fluid. For instance, many analysts have suggested that in contemporary America racial practices are manifested covertly (Bonilla-Silva and Lewis 1997; Wellman 1977) and racial attitudes tend to be symbolic (Pettigrew 1994; Sears 1988). Therefore it is a waste of time to attempt to detect "racism" by asking questions such as, "How strongly would you object if a member of your family wanted to bring a Black friend home to dinner?"[4] Also, many such questions were developed to measure the extent of racist attitudes in the population during the Jim Crow era of race relations; they are not suitable for the post-1960s period.

Furthermore, this emphasis on overt behavior limits the possibility of analyzing racial phenomena in other parts of the world such as Brazil, Cuba, and Puerto Rico where race relations do not have an overt character. The form of race relations—overt or covert—depends on the pattern of racialization that structures a particular society (Cox 1948; Harris 1964; Rex 1983; van den Berghe 1967) and on how the process of racial contestation and other social dynamics affects that pattern (see the following section).

Contemporary racism is viewed as an expression of "original sin"—as a remnant of past historical racial situations. In the case of the United States, some analysts argue that racism preceded slavery and/or capitalism (Jordan 1968; Marable 1983; Robinson 1983). Others regard racism in the United States as the result of slavery (Glazer and Moynihan 1970). Even in promising new avenues of research, such as that presented by Roediger (1991) in *The Wages of Whiteness*, contemporary racism is viewed as one of the "legacies of white workerism" (p. 176). By considering racism as a legacy, all these analysts downplay the significance of its contemporary materiality or structure.

Again the Marxist perspective shares this limitation. Marxists believe that racism developed in the sixteenth century and has been used since then by capitalists or workers to further their own class interests. All other models recognize the historical significance of this "discovery," but associate contemporary racial ideology with contemporary racially based inequalities.

Racism is analyzed in a circular manner. "If racism is defined as the behavior that results from a belief, its discovery becomes ensnared in a circularity—racism is a belief that produces behavior, which is itself racism" (Webster, 1992:84). Racism is established by racist behavior, which itself is proved by the existence of racism. This circularity results from not grounding racism in social relations among the races. If racism, viewed as an ideology, were seen as possessing a structural[5] foundation, its examination could be associated with racial practices rather than with mere ideas and the problem of circularity would be avoided.

Racialized Social Systems: An Alternative Framework for Understanding Racial Phenomena

Because all kinds of racial matters have been explained as a product of racism, I propose the more general concept of *racialized social systems* as the starting point for an alternative framework. This term refers to societies in which economic, political, social and ideological levels are partially structured by the placement of actors in racial categories or races. Races typically are identified by their phenotype, but (as we see later) the selection of certain human traits to designate a racial group is always socially rather than biologically based.

These systems are structured partially by race because modern social systems articulate two or more forms of hierarchical patterns (Hall 1980; Williams 1990; Winant 1994).[6] Although processes of racialization are always embedded in other structurations (Balibar and Wallerstein 1991), they acquire autonomy and have "pertinent effects" (Poulantzas 1982) in the social system. This implies that the phenomenon which is coded as racism and is regarded as a free-floating ideology in fact has a structural foundation.

In all racialized social systems the placement of people in racial categories involves some form of hierarchy[7] that produces definite social relations between the races. The race placed in the superior position tends to receive greater economic remuneration and access to better occupations and/or prospects in the labor market, occupies a primary position in the political system, is granted higher social estimation (e.g., is viewed as "smarter" or "better looking"), often has the license to draw physical (segregation) as well as social (racial etiquette) boundaries between itself and other races, and receives what DuBois (1939) calls a "psychological wage" (Marable 1983; Roediger 1991).[8] The totality of these racialized social relations and practices constitutes the racial structure of a society.

Although all racialized social systems are hierarchical, the particular character of the hierarchy, and thus of the racial structure, is variable. For example, domination of Blacks in the United States was achieved through dictatorial means during slavery, but in the post-civil rights period this domination has been hegemonic (Omi and Winant 1994; Winant 1994).[9] Similarly, the racial practices and mechanisms that have kept Blacks subordinated changed from overt and eminently racist to covert and indirectly racist (Bonilla-Silva and Lewis 1997). The unchanging element throughout these stages is that Blacks' life chances are significantly lower than those of Whites, and ultimately a racialized social order is distinguished by this difference in life chances. Generally, the more dissimilar the races' life chances, the more racialized the social system, and vice versa.

Insofar as the races receive different social rewards at all levels, they develop dissimilar objective interests, which can be detected in their struggles to either transform or maintain a particular racial order. These interests are collective rather than individual, are based on relations between races rather than on particular group needs, and are not structural but practical; that is, they are related to concrete struggles rather than derived from the location of the races in the racial structure. In other words, although the races' interests can be detected from their practices, they are not subjective and individual but collective and shaped by the field of real practical alternatives, which is itself rooted in the power struggles between the races.[10] Although the objective general interests of races may ultimately lie in the complete elimination of a society's racial structure, its array of alternatives may not include that possibility. For instance, the historical struggle against chattel slavery led not to the development of race-free societies but to the establishment of social systems with a different kind of racialization. Race-free societies were not among the available alternatives because the nonslave populations had the capacity to preserve some type of racial privilege. The historical "exceptions" occurred in racialized societies in which the nonslaves' power was almost completely superseded by that of the slave population.[11]

A simple criticism of the argument advanced so far would be that it ignores the internal divisions of the races along class and gender lines. Such criticism, however, does not deal squarely with the issue at hand. The fact that not all members of the superordinate race receive the same level of rewards and (conversely) that not all members of the subordinate race or races are at the bottom of the social order does not negate the fact that races, as social groups, are in either a superordinate or a subordinate position in a social system. Historically the racialization of social systems did not imply the exclusion of other forms of oppression. In fact, racialization occurred in social formations also structured by class and gender. Hence, in these societies, the racial structuration of subjects is fragmented along class and gender lines.[12] The important question—which interests move actors to struggle?—is historically contingent and cannot be ascertained a priori (Anthias and Yuval-Davis 1992; Wolpe 1988). Depending on the character of racialization in a social order, class interests may take precedence over racial interests as they do in contemporary Brazil, Cuba, and Puerto Rico. In other situations, racial interests may take precedence over class interests as in the case of Blacks throughout U.S. history.

In general, the systemic salience of class in relation to race increases when the economic, political, and social distance between races decreases substantially. Yet this broad argument generates at least one warning: The narrowing of within-class differences between racial actors usually causes more rather than less racial conflict, at least in the short run, as the competition for resources increases (Blalock 1967; Olzak 1992). More significantly, even when class-based conflict becomes more salient in a social order, the racial component survives until the races' life chances are equalized and the mechanisms and social practices that produce those differences are eliminated. Hence societies in which race has declined in significance, such as Brazil, Cuba, and Mexico, still have a racial problem insofar as the racial groups have different life chances.

Because racial actors are also classed and gendered, analysts must control for class and for gender to ascertain the material advantages enjoyed by a dominant race. In a racialized society such as ours, the independent effects of race are assessed by analysts who (1) compare data between Whites and non-White in the same class and gender positions, (2) evaluate the proportion as well as the general character of the races' participation in some domain of life, and (3) examine racial data at all levels—social, political, economic, and ideological—to ascertain the general position of racial groups in a social system.

The first of these procedures has become standard practice in sociology. No serious sociologist would present racial statistics without controlling for gender and class (or at least the class of persons' family of origin). By doing this, analysts assume they can measure the unadulterated effects of "discrimination" manifested in unexplained "residuals" (Farley 1984, 1993; Farley and Allen 1987). Despite its usefulness, however, this technique provides only a partial account of the "race effect" because (1) a significant amount of racial data cannot be retrieved through surveys and (2) the technique of "controlling for" a variable neglects the obvious—why a group is over- or underrepresented in certain categories of the control variables in the first place (Whatley and Wright 1994). Moreover, these analysts presume that it is possible to analyze the amount of discrimination in one domain (e.g., income, occupational status) "without analyzing the extent to which discrimination also affects the factors they hold constant" (Reich 1978:383). Hence to evaluate "race effects" in any domain, analysts must attempt to make sense of their findings in relation to a race's standing on other domains.

But what is the nature of races or, more properly, of racialized social groups? Omi and Winant (1986;

also see Miles 1989) state that races are the outcome of the racialization process, which they define as "the extension of racial meaning to a previously racially unclassified relationship, social practice or group" (p. 64). Historically the classification of a people in racial terms has been a highly political act associated with practices such as conquest and colonization, enslavement, peonage, indentured servitude, and, more recently, colonial and neocolonial labor immigration. Categories such as "Indians" and "Negroes" were invented (Allen 1994; Berkhoffer 1978; Jordan 1968) in the sixteenth and seventeenth centuries to justify the conquest and exploitation of various peoples. The invention of such categories entails a dialectical process of construction; that is, the creation of a category of "other" involves the creation of a category of "same." If "Indians" are depicted as "savages," Europeans are characterized as "civilized"; if "Blacks" are defined as natural candidates for slavery, "Whites" are defined as free subjects (Gossett 1963; Roediger 1991, 1994; Todorov 1984). Yet although the racialization of peoples was socially invented and did not override previous forms of social distinction based on class or gender, it did not lead to imaginary relations but generated new forms of human association with definite status differences. After the process of attaching meaning to a "people" is instituted, race becomes a real category of group association and identity.[13]

Because racial classifications partially organize and limit actors' life chances, racial practices of opposition emerge. Regardless of the form of racial interaction (overt, covert, or inert), races can be recognized in the realm of racial relations and positions. Viewed in this light, races are the effect of racial practices of opposition ("we" versus "them") at the economic, political, social, and ideological levels.[14]

Races, as most social scientists acknowledge, are not biologically but socially determined categories of identity and group association.[15] In this regard, they are analogous to class and gender (Amott and Matthaei 1991). Actors in racial positions do not occupy those positions because they are of X or Y race, but because X or Y has been socially defined as a race. Actors' phenotypical (i.e., biologically inherited) characteristics, such as skin tone and hair color and texture, are usually, although not always (Barth 1969; Miles 1993), used to denote racial distinctions. For example, Jews in many European nations (Miles 1989, 1993) and the Irish in England have been treated as racial groups (Allen 1994). Also, Indians in the United States have been viewed as one race despite the tremendous phenotypical and cultural variation among tribes. Because races are socially constructed, both the meaning and the position assigned to races in the racial structure are always contested (Gilroy 1991). What and who is to be Black or White or Indian reflects and affects the social, political, ideological, and economic struggles between the races. The global effects of these struggles can change the meaning of the racial categories as well as the position of a racialized group in a social formation.

This latter point is illustrated clearly by the historical struggles of several "White ethnic" groups in the United States in their efforts to become accepted as legitimate Whites or "Americans" (Litwack 1961; Roediger 1991; Saxton 1990; Williams 1990). Neither light-skinned—nor, for that matter, dark-skinned—immigrants necessarily came to this country as members of race X or race Y. Light-skinned Europeans, after brief periods of being "not-yet White" (Roediger 1994), became "White," but they did not lose their "ethnic" character. Their struggle for inclusion had specific implications: racial inclu-

sion as members of the White community allowed Americanization and class mobility. On the other hand, among dark-skinned immigrants from Africa, Latin America, and the Caribbean, the struggle was to avoid classification as "Black." These immigrants challenged the reclassification of their identity for a simple reason: In the United States "Black" signified a subordinate status in society. Hence many of these groups struggled to keep their own ethnic or cultural identity, as denoted in expressions such as "I am not Black; I am Jamaican," or "I am not Black; I am Senegalese" (Kasinitz and Freidenberg-Herbstein 1987; Rodríquez 1991; Sutton and Makiesky-Barrow 1987). Yet eventually many of these groups resolved this contradictory situation by accepting the duality of their social classification as Black in the United States while retaining and nourishing their own cultural or ethnic heritage—a heritage deeply influenced by African traditions.

Although the content of racial categories changes over time through manifold processes and struggles, race is not a secondary category of group association. The meaning of Black and White, the "racial formation" (Omi and Winant 1986), changes within the larger racial structure. This does not mean that the racial structure is immutable and completely independent of the action of racialized actors. It means only that the social relations between the races become institutionalized (forming a structure as well as a culture) and affect their social life whether individual members of the races want it or not. In Barth's words (1969), "Ethnic identity implies a series of constraints on the kinds of roles an individual is allowed to play [and] is similar to sex and rank, in that it constrains the incumbent in all his activities" (p. 17). For instance, free Blacks during the slavery period struggled to change the meaning of "blackness," and specifically to dissociate it from slavery. Yet they could not escape the larger racial structure that restricted their life chances and their freedom (Berlin 1975; Franklin 1974; Meir and Rudwick 1970).

The placement of groups of people in racial categories stemmed initially[16] from the interests of powerful actors in the social system (e.g., the capitalist class, the planter class, colonizers). After racial categories were used to organize social relations in a society, however, race became an independent element of the operation of the social system (Stone 1985).

Here I depart from analysts such as Jordan (1968), Robinson (1983), and Miles (1989, 1993), who take the mere existence of a racial discourse as manifesting the presence of a racial order. Such a position allows them to speak of racism in medieval times (Jordan) and to classify the antipeasant views of French urbanites (Miles) or the prejudices of the aristocracy against peasants in the Middle Ages (Robinson) as expressions of racism. In my view, we can speak of racialized orders only when a racial discourse is accompanied by social relations of subordination and superordination between the races. The available evidence suggests that racialized social orders emerged after the imperialist expansion of Europe to the New World and Africa (Boggs 1970; Cox 1948; Furnivall 1948; Magubane 1990; E. Williams [1944] 1961; R. Williams 1990).

What are the dynamics of racial issues in racialized systems? Most important, after a social formation is racialized, its "normal" dynamics always include a racial component. Societal struggles based on class or gender contain a racial component because both of these social categories are also racialized; that is, both class and gender are

constructed along racial lines. In 1922, for example, White South African workers in the middle of a strike inspired by the Russian revolution rallied under the slogan "Workers of the world unite for a White South Africa." One of the state's "concessions" to this "class" struggle was the passage of the Apprenticeship Act of 1922, "which prevented Black workers acquiring apprenticeships" (Ticktin 1991:26). In another example, the struggle of women in the United States to attain their civil and human rights has always been plagued by deep racial tensions (Caraway 1991; Giddings 1984).

Nonetheless, some of the strife that exists in a racialized social formation has a distinct racial character; I call such strife "racial contestation"—the struggle of racial groups for systemic changes regarding their position at one or more levels. Such a struggle may be social (Who can be here? Who belongs here?), political (Who can vote? How much power should they have? Should they be citizens?), economic (Who should work, and what should they do? They are taking our jobs!), or ideological (Black is beautiful! The term designating people of African descent in the United States has changed from Negro to Black to African American).

Although much of this contestation is expressed at the individual level and is disjointed, sometimes it becomes collective and general, and can effect meaningful systemic changes in a society's racial organization. The form of contestation may be relatively passive and subtle (e.g., in situations of fundamental overt racial domination, such as slavery and apartheid) or more active and more overt (e.g., in quasi-democratic situations such as the contemporary United States). As a rule, however, fundamental changes in racialized social systems are accompanied by struggles that

reach the point of overt protest.[17] This does not mean that a violent racially based revolution is the only way of accomplishing effective changes in the relative position of racial groups. It is a simple extension of the argument that social systems and their supporters must be "shaken" if fundamental transformations are to take place.[18] On this structural foundation rests the phenomenon labeled racism by social scientists.

I reserve the term *racism* (racial ideology) for the segment of the ideological structure of a social system that crystallizes racial notions and stereotypes. Racism provides the rationalizations for social, political, and economic interactions between the races (Bobo 1988). Depending on the particular character of a racialized social system and on the struggles of the subordinated races, racial ideology may be developed highly (as in apartheid), or loosely (as in slavery), and its content can be expressed in overt or covert terms (Bobo and Smith forthcoming; Jackman 1994; Kinder and Sears 1981; Pettigrew 1994; Sears 1988).

Although racism or racial ideology originates in race relations, it acquires relative autonomy in the social system and performs practical functions.[19] In Gilroy's (1991) words, racial ideology "mediates the world of agents and the structures which are created by their social praxis" (p. 17; also see Omi and Winant 1994; van Dijk 1984, 1987, 1993). Racism crystallizes the changing "dogma" on which actors in the social system operate (Gilroy 1991), and becomes "common sense" (Omi and Winant 1994); it provides the rules for perceiving and dealing with the "other" in a racialized society. In the United States, for instance, because racial notions about what Blacks and Whites are or ought to be pervade their encounters, Whites still have difficulty in dealing with Black bankers, lawyers, professors, and doctors (Cose 1993; Graham 1995). Thus, although racist ideology is ultimately false, it fulfills a practical role in racialized societies.

At this point it is possible to sketch the elements of the alternative framework presented here. First, racialized social systems are societies that allocate differential economic, political, social and even psychological rewards to groups along racial lines; lines that are socially constructed. After a society becomes racialized, a set of social relations and practices based on racial distinctions develops at all societal levels. I designate the aggregate of those relations and practices as the racial structure of a society. Second, races historically are constituted according to the process of racialization; they become the effect of relations of opposition between racialized groups at all levels of a social formation. Third, on the basis of this structure, there develops a racial ideology (what analysts have coded as racism). This ideology is not simply a "superstructural" phenomenon (a mere reflection of the racialized system), but becomes the organizational map that guides actions of racial actors in society. It becomes as real as the racial relations it organizes. Fourth, most struggles in a racialized social system contain a racial component, but sometimes they acquire and/or exhibit a distinct racial character. Racial contestation is the logical outcome of a society with a racial hierarchy. A social formation that includes some form of racialization will always exhibit some form of racial contestation. Finally, the process of racial contestation reveals the different objective interests of the races in a racialized system.

Conclusion

My central argument is that racism, as defined by mainstream social scientists to consist only of ideas, does not provide adequate theoretical foundation for understanding racial phenomena. I suggest that until a structural framework is developed, analysts will be entangled in ungrounded ideological views of racism. Lacking a structural view, they will reduce racial phenomena to a derivation of the class structure (as do Marxist interpreters) or will view these phenomena as the result of an irrational ideology (as do mainstream social scientists). Although others have attempted to develop a structural understanding of racial matters (such as authors associated with the institutionalist, internal colonial, and racial formation perspectives) and/or to write about racial matters as structural (Bobo and Smith forthcoming; Cose 1993; Essed 1991; Feagin and Feagin 1993; Page 1996; van Dijk 1993), they have failed to elaborate a framework that extends beyond their critique of mainstream views.

In the alternative framework developed here, I suggest that racism should be studied from the viewpoint of racialization. I contend that after a society becomes racialized, racialization develops a life of its own.[20] Although it interacts with class and gender structurations in the social system, it becomes an organizing principle of social relations in itself (Essed 1991; Omi and Winant 1986; Robinson 1983; van Dijk 1987). Race, as most analysts suggest, is a social construct, but that construct, like class and gender, has independent effects in social life. After racial stratification is established, race becomes an independent criterion for vertical hierarchy in society. Therefore different races experience positions of subordination and superordination in society and develop different interests.

The alternative framework for studying racial orders presented here has the following advantages over traditional views of racism:

Racial phenomena are regarded as the "normal" outcome of the racial structure of a society. Thus we can account for all racial manifestations. Instead of explaining racial phenomena as deriving from other structures or from racism (conceived of as a free-floating ideology), we can trace cultural, political, economic, social, and even psychological racial phenomena to the racial organization of that society.

The changing nature of what analysts label "racism" is explained as the normal outcome of racial contestation in a racialized social system. In this framework, changes in racism are explained rather than described. Changes are due to specific struggles at different levels among the races, resulting from differences in interests. Such changes may transform the nature of racialization and the global character of racial relations in the system (the racial structure). Therefore, change is viewed as a normal component of the racialized system.

The framework of racialization allows analysts to explain overt as well as covert racial behavior. The covert or overt nature of racial contacts depends on how the process of racialization is manifested; this in turn depends on how race originally was articulated in a social formation and on the process of racial contestation. This point implies that rather than conceiving of racism as a universal and uniformly orchestrated phenomenon, analysts should study "historically-specific racisms" (Hall 1980:336). This insight is not new; Robert Park (1950) and Oliver Cox (1948) and Marvin Harris (1964) described varieties of "situations of race relations" with distinct forms of racial interaction.

Racially motivated behavior, whether or not the actors are conscious of it, is regarded as "rational"—that is, as based on the races' different interests.[21] This framework accounts for Archie Bunker-type racial behavior as well as for more "sophisticated" varieties of racial conduct. Racial phenomena are viewed as systemic; therefore all actors in the system participate in racial affairs. Some members of the dominant racial group tend to exhibit less virulence toward members of the subordinated races because they have greater control over the form and the outcome of their racial interactions. When they cannot control that interaction—as in the case of revolts, general threats to Whites, Blacks moving into "their" neighborhood—they behave much like other members of the dominant race.

The reproduction of racial phenomena in contemporary societies is explained in this framework, not by reference to a long-distant past, but in relation to its contemporary structure. Because racism is viewed as systemic (possessing a racial structure) and as organized around the races' different interests, racial aspects of social systems today are viewed as fundamentally related to hierarchical relations between the races in those systems. Elimination of the racialized character of a social system entails the end of racialization, and hence of races altogether. This argument clashes with social scientists' most popular policy prescription for "curing" racism, namely education. This "solution" is the logical outcome of defining racism as a belief. Most analysts regard racism as a matter of individuals subscribing to an irrational view, thus the cure is educating them to realize

that racism is wrong. Education is also the choice "pill" prescribed by Marxists for healing workers from racism. The alternative theorization offered here implies that because the phenomenon has structural consequences for the races, the only way to "cure" society of racism is by eliminating its systemic roots. Whether this can be accomplished democratically or only through revolutionary means is an open question, and one that depends on the particular racial structure of the society in question.

A racialization framework accounts for the ways in which racial/ethnic stereotypes emerge, are transformed, and disappear. Racial stereotypes are crystallized at the ideological level of a social system. These images ultimately indicate (although in distorted ways) and justify the stereotyped group's position in a society. Stereotypes may originate out of (1) material realities or conditions endured by the group, (2) genuine ignorance about the group, or (3) rigid, distorted views on the group's physical, cultural, or moral nature. Once they emerge, however, stereotypes must relate—although not necessarily fit perfectly—to the group's true social position in the racialized system if they are to perform their ideological function. Stereotypes that do not tend to reflect a group's situation do not work and are bound to disappear: For example, notions of the Irish as stupid or of Jews as athletically talented have all but vanished since the 1940s, as the Irish moved up the educational ladder and Jews gained access to multiple routes to social mobility. Generally, then, stereotypes are reproduced because they reflect the group's distinct position and status in

society. As a corollary, racial or ethnic notions about a group disappear only when the group's status mirrors that of the dominant racial or ethnic group in the society.

The framework developed here is not a universal theory explaining racial phenomena in societies. It is intended to trigger a serious discussion of how race shapes social systems. Moreover, the important question of how race interacts and intersects with class and gender has not yet been addressed satisfactorily. Provisionally I argue that a nonfunctionalist reading of the concept of social system may give us clues for comprehending societies "structured in dominance" (Hall 1980). If societies are viewed as systems that articulate different structures (organizing principles on which sets of social relations are systematically patterned), it is possible to claim that race—as well as gender—has both individual and combined (interaction) effects in society.

To test the usefulness of racialization as a theoretical basis for research, we must perform comparative work on racialization in various societies. One of the main objectives of this comparative work should be to determine whether societies have specific mechanisms, practices, and social relations that produce and reproduce racial inequality at all levels—that is, whether they possess a racial structure. I believe, for example, that the persistent inequality experienced by Blacks and other racial minorities in the United States today is due to the continued existence of a racial structure (Bonilla-Silva and Lewis 1997). In contrast to race relations in the Jim Crow period, however, racial practices that reproduce racial inequality in contemporary America (1) are increasingly covert, (2) are embedded in normal operations of institutions, (3) avoid direct racial terminology, and (4) are invisible to most Whites. By examining whether other countries have practices and mechanisms that account for the persistent inequality experienced by their racial minorities, analysts could assess the usefulness of the framework I have introduced.

Notes

1. Yet they employed the very similar notion of ethnocentrism as developed by William Graham Sumner (1906). According to Sumner (1906) ethnocentrism was the belief that "one's own group is at the center of everything, and all others are scaled and rated with reference to it" (p. 13).

2. Carmichael and Hamilton (1967) also advocate nationalist strategies. Unlike other institutionalists, however, they insist on the colonial relationship of minorities to the majority in the United States.

3. In the most recent edition of *Racial Formation in the United States,* Omi and Winant (1994) move closer to a structural view, but they still retain the ideological and juridico-political focus that characterizes the original edition.

4. This question is used by NORC and has been employed by Schuman et al. (1985).

5. By *structure* I mean, following Whitmeyer (1994), "the networks of (interactional) relationships among actors as well as the distributions of socially meaningful characteristics of actors and aggregates of actors" (p. 154). For similar but more complex conceptions of the term, which are relational and incorporate the agency of actors, see Bourdieu (1984) and Sewell (1992). I reserve the term *material* to refer to the economic, social, political, or ideological rewards or penalties received by social actors for their participation (whether willing, unwilling, or indifferent) in social structural arrangements.

6. Some potentially useful conceptions about the interaction of race, class, and gender (the primary axes of social hierarchy in modern societies) are Segura's (1990) "triple oppression" and Essed's (1991) analysis of "gendered racism." Also see Andersen and Hill Collins (1995) and Fraser 1989).

7. This argument applies only to racialized social systems. In contrast, *ethnic* situations need not be based on relations between superiors and subordinates, as is the case between the Fur and the Baggara in western Sudan (Barth 1969), and various ethnic groups in Switzerland (Hunt and Walker 1974), the Tungus and the Cossacks in Siberia (Berry 1965), the Lake Zwai Laki and the Arsi in Ethiopia (Knutson 1969), and certain mountain tribes and the Thai in Laos (Izikowitz 1969). Certainly, ethnic situations can be conflictual and hierarchical, as illustrated by the Tutsis and the Hutus in Rwanda or the conflict between Serbians, Croatians, and Bosnians in what was once Yugoslavia. The point is that ethnicity and race are different bases for group association. Ethnicity has a primarily sociocultural foundation, and ethnic groups have exhibited tremendous malleability in terms of who belongs (Barth 1969; Leach [1954] 1964); racial ascriptions (initially) are imposed externally to justify the collective exploitation of a people and are maintained to preserve status differences. Hence scholars have pointed out that despite the similarities between race and ethnicity, they should be viewed as producing different types of structurations (Balibar and Wallerstein 1991; Cox 1948; Rex 1973; van den Berghe 1967; Wilson 1973). On this point see Horowitz (1985), Schermerhorn (1970), and Shibutani and Kwan (1965).

8. Herbert Blumer was one of the first analysts to make this argument about systematic rewards received by the race ascribed the primary position in a racial order. Blumer (1955) summarized these views in his essay "Reflections on Theory of Race Relations." Also see the works of Blalock (1967), Schermerhorn (1970), Shibutani and Kwan (1965), and van den Berghe (1967).

9. *Hegemonic* means that domination is achieved more through consent than by coercion.

10. *Power* is defined here as a racial group's capacity to push for its racial interests in relation to other races.

11. I am referring to cases such as Haiti. Nonetheless, recent research has suggested that even in such places, the abolition of slavery did not end the racialized character of the social formation (Trouillot 1990).

12. Some authors have developed notions combining racial/ethnic positions with class. Gordon (1964) developed the concept of "ethclass" but assumed that this was a temporary phenomenon. Geschwender (1977) transformed the notion into the concept of race-class, defined as "a social collectivity comprised of persons who are simultaneously members of the same class and the same race" (p. 221; also see Barrera 1979:174–279). Geschwender, however, views racial interests as somewhat less "objective" and less "fundamental" than class interests.

13. This point has been stressed by many social analysts since Barth's (1969) crucial work conceiving of ethnicity as a form of social organization.

14. This last point is an extension of Poulantzas's view on class. Races (as classes) are not an "empirical thing"; they denote racialized social relations or racial practices at all levels (Poulantzas 1982:67).

15. Weber ([1920] 1978) made one of the earliest statements of this view. He regarded race and ethnicity as "presumed identities" in which the actors attached subjective meanings to so-called common traits. Leach ([1954] 1964), in his study of the Kachin in highland Burma, was one of the first social scientists to illustrate the malleability of ethnic boundaries.

16. The motivation for racializing human relations may have originated in the interests of powerful actors, but after social systems are racialized, all members of the dominant race participate in defending and reproducing the racial structure. This is the crucial reason why Marxist analysts (Cos 1948; Reich 1981) have not been successful in analyzing racism. They have not been able to accept the fact that after the phenomenon originated with the expansion of European capitalism into the New World, it acquired a life of its own. The subjects who were racialized as belonging to the superior race, whether or not they were members of the dominant class, became zealous defenders of the racial order.

17. This argument is not new. Analysts of the racial history of the United States have always pointed out that most of the significant historical changes in this country's race

relations were accompanied by some degree of overt violence (Button 1989; Cruse 1968; Franklin 1974; Marable 1983).

18. This point is important in literature on revolutions and democracy. On the role of violence in the establishment of bourgeois democracies, see Moore 1966). On the role of violence in social movements leading to change, see Piven and Cloward (1979) and Tilly (1978).

19. The notion of relative autonomy comes from the work of Poulantzas (1982) and implies that the ideological and political levels in a society are partially autonomous in relation to the economic level; that is, they are not merely expressions of the economic level.

20. Historian Eugene Genovese (1971) makes a similar argument. Although he still regards racism as an ideology, he states that once it "arises it alters profoundly the material reality and in fact becomes a partially autonomous feature of that reality" (p. 340).

21. Actions by the Ku Klux Klan have an unmistakably racial tone, but many other actions (choosing to live in a suburban neighborhood, sending one's children to a private school, or opposing government intervention in hiring policies) also have racial undertones.

References

Adorno, Theodore W. 1950. *The Authoritarian Personality.* New York: Harper and Row.

Allen, Theodore W. 1994. *The Invention of the White Race.* Vol. 1, *Racial Oppression and Social Control.* London, England: Verso.

Allport, Gordon W. 1958. *the Nature of Prejudice.* New York: Doubleday Anchor Books.

Alvarez, Rodolfo, Kenneth G. Lutterman, and Associates. 1979. *Discrimination in Organizations: Using Social Indicators to Manage Social Change.* San Francisco, CA: Jossey-Bass.

Amott, Theresa and Julie A. Matthaei. 1991. *Race, Gender, and Work: A Multicultural Economic History of Women in the United States.* Boston, MA: South End Press.

Andersen, Margaret and Patricia Hill Collins. 1995. *Race, Class, and Gender: An Anthology.* Belmont, NY: Wadsworth.

Anthias, Floya and Nira Yuval-Davis. 1992. *Racialized Boundaries: Race, Nation, Gender, Colour and Class and the Anti-Racist Struggle.* London, England: Routledge.

Balibar, Etienne and Immanuel Wallerstein. 1991. *Race, Nation, Class: Ambiguous Identities.* New York: Verso.

Banton, Michael. 1970. "The Concept of Racism." Pp. 17–34 in *Race and Racialism,* edited by S. Zubaida. London, England: Tavistock.

Barrera, Mario. 1979. *Race and Class in the Southwest: A Theory of Racial Inequality.* Notre Dame, IN: University of Notre Dame Press.

Barth, Fredrik. 1969. "Introduction." Pp. 9–38 in *Ethnic Groups and Boundaries: The Social Organization of Culture Difference,* edited by F. Barth. Bergen, Norway: Universitetsforlaget.

Benedict, Ruth F. 1945. *Race and Racism.* London, England: Routledge and Kegan Paul.

Berkhoffer, Robert E. 1978. *The White Man's Indian: Images of the American Indian from Columbus to the Present.* New York: Vintage.

Berlin, Ira. 1975. *Slaves without Masters: The Free Negro in Antebellum South.* New York: Pantheon.

Berry, Brewton. 1965. *Race and Ethnic Relations.* Boston, MA: Houghton Mifflin.

Blalock, Hubert M., Jr. 1967. *Toward a Theory of Minority-Group Relations.* New York: John Wiley and Sons.

Blauner, Robert. 1972. *Racial Oppression in America.* New York: Harper and Row.

Blumer, Herbert G. 1955. "Reflections on Theory of Race Relations." Pp. 3–21 in *Race Relations in World Perspective,* edited by A. W. Lind, Honolulu, HI: University of Hawaii Press.

Bobo, Lawrence. 1988. "Group Conflict, Prejudice and the Paradox of Contemporary Racial Attitudes." Pp. 85–114 in *Eliminating Racism: Profiles in Controversy,* edited by P. A. Katz and D. A. Taylor. New York: Plenum.

Bobo, Lawrence and Ryan Smith. Forthcoming. "From Jim Crow Racism to Laissez-Faire Racism: An Essay on the Transformation of Racial Attitudes in America." In *Beyond Pluralism,* edited by W. Katchin and A. Tyree. Urbana, IL: University of Illinois Press.

Boggs, James. 1970. *Racism and the Class Struggle: Further Pages from a Black Worker's Notebook.* New York: Monthly Review Press.

Bonacich, Edna. 1980a. "Advanced Capitalism and Black/White Relations in the United States: A split Labor Market Interpretation." Pp. 341–62 in *The Sociology of Race Relations: Reflection and Reform,* edited by T. Pettigrew. New York: Free Press.

———. 1980b. "A Theory of Ethnic Antagonism: The Split Labor Market." *American Sociological Review* 37:547–59.

Bonilla-Silva, Eduardo and Amanda Lewis. 1997. "The 'New Racism': Toward an Analysis of the U.S. Racial Structure, 1960s–1990s." Department of Sociology, University of Michigan. Ann Arbor, MI. Unpublished manuscript.

Bourdieu, Pierre. 1984. *Distinction: A Social Critique of the Judgement of Taste.* Cambridge, MA: Harvard University Press.

Button, James, W. 1989. *Blacks and Social Change: Impact of the Civil Rights Movement in Southern Communities.* Princeton, NJ: Princeton University Press.

Caraway, Nancy. 1991. *Segregated Sisterhood: Racism and the Politics of American Feminism.* Knoxville, TN: The University of Tennessee Press.

Carchedi, Guglielmo. 1987. *Class Analysis and Social Research.* Oxford, England: Basil Blackwell.

Carmichael, Stokely. 1971. *Stokely Speaks: Black Power Back to Pan-Africanism.* New York: Vintage Books.

Carmichael, Stokely and Charles Hamilton. 1967. *Black Power: The Politics of Liberation in America.* New York: Vintage Books.

Chesler, Mark. 1976. "Contemporary Sociological Theories of Racism." Pp. 21–71 in *Towards the Elimination of Racism,* edited by P. A. Katz. New York: Pergamon.

Cohen, Gerry A. 1989. "Reconsidering Historical Materialism." Pp. 88–104 in *Marxist Theory,* edited by A. Gallinicos. Oxford, England: Oxford University Press.

Cose, Ellis. 1993. *The Rage of a Privileged Class: Why Are Middle Class Blacks Angry? Why Should America Care?* New York: Harper Collins.

Cox, Oliver, C. 1948. *Caste, Class, and Race.* New York: Doubleday.

Cruse, Harold. 1968. *Rebellion or Revolution.* New York: William Morrow.

Dubois, William E. B. 1939. *Black Folk, Then and Now: An Essay in the History and Sociology of the Negro Race.* New York: Henry Holt.

Essed, Pilomena. 1991. *Understanding Everyday Racism: An Interdisciplinary Approach.* London, England: Sage.

Fanon, Frantz. 1967. *Black Skin, White Masks.* New York: Grove.

Farley, Reynolds. 1984. *Blacks and Whites: Narrowing the Gap?* Cambridge, MA: Harvard University Press.

———. 1993. "The Common Destiny of Blacks and Whites: Observations about the Social and Economic Status of the Races." Pp. 197–233 in *Race in America: The Struggle for Equality,* edited by H. Hill and J. E. Jones, Jr. Madison, WI: University of Wisconsin Press.

Farley, Reynolds and Walter R. Allen. 1987. *The Color Line and the Quality of Life in America.* New York: Russell Sage.

Feagin, Joe R. and Clarence Booher Feagin. 1993. *Racial and Ethnic Relations.* Upper Saddle River, NJ: Prentice Hall.

Franklin, John Hope. 1974. *From Slavery to Freedom: A History of Negro Americans.* New York: Alfred A. Knopf.

Fraser, Nancy. 1989. *Unruly Practices: Power, Discourse and Gender in Contemporary Social Theory.* Minneapolis, MN: University of Minnesota Press.

Furnivall, J. S. 1948. *Colonial Policy and Practice: A Comparative Study of Burma and Netherlands India.* Cambridge, England: Cambridge University Press.

Genovese, Eugene. 1971. *In Red and Black: Marxian Explorations in Southern and Afro-American History.* New York: Pantheon.

Geschwender, James A. 1977. *Class, Race, and Worker Insurgency: The League of Revolutionary Black Workers.* Cambridge, England: Cambridge University Press.

Giddings, Paula. 1984. *When and Where I Enter: The Impact of Black Women on Race and Sex in America.* New York: Bantam.

Gilroy, Paul. 1991. *"There Ain't No Black in the Union Jack": The Cultural Politics of Race and Nation.* Chicago, IL: the University of Chicago Press.

Glazer, Nathan and Daniel P. Moynihan. 1970. *Beyond the Melting Pot: The Negroes, Puerto Ricans, Jews, Italians, and Irish of New York City.* Cambridge, MA: MIT Press.

Gordon, Milton M. 1964. *Assimilation in American Life.* New York: Oxford University Press.

Gossett, Thomas. 1963. *Race: The History of an Idea in America.* Dallas, TX: Southern Methodist University Press.

Graham, Otis Lawrence. 1995. *Member of the Club: Reflections on Life in a Racially Polarized World.* New York: Harper Collins.

Hall, Stuart. 1980. "Race Articulation and Societies Structured in Dominance." Pp. 305–45, in *Sociological Theories: Race and Colonialism,* edited by UNESCO. Paris, France: UNESCO.

Harris, Marvin. 1964. *Patterns of Race in the Americas.* New York: Walker.

Horowitz, Donald. 1985. *Ethnic Groups in Conflict.* Berkeley, CA: University of California Press.

Hunt, Chester L. and Lewis Walker. 1974. *Ethnic Dynamics: Patterns of Intergroup Relations in Various Societies.* Homewood, IL: Dorsey.

Izikowitz, Karl G. 1969. "Neighbors in Laos." Pp. 135–44 in *Ethnic Groups and Boundaries: The Social Organization of Culture Difference,* edited by F. Barth. Bergen, Norway: Universitetsforlaget.

Jackman, Mary R. 1994. *Velvet Glove: Paternalism and Conflict in Gender, Class, and Race Relations.* Berkeley, CA: University of California Press.

Jordan, Winthrop. 1968. *White Over Black: American Attitudes toward the Negro, 1550–1812.* New York: W.W. Norton.

Kasinitz, Philip and Judith Freidenberg-Herbstein. 1987. "The Puerto Rican Parade and West Indian Carnival: Public Celebrations in New York City." Pp. 305–25 in *Caribbean Life in New York City: Sociocultural Dimensions,* edited by C. R. Sutton and E. M. Channey. New York: Center for Migration Studies of New York.

Kinder, Donald R. and David O. Sears. 1981. "Prejudiced and Politics: Symbolic Racism versus Racial Threats to the Good Life." *Journal of Personality and Social Psychology* 40: 414–31.

Knowles, Louis L. and Kenneth Prewitt. 1969. *Institutional Racism in America.* Patterson, NJ: Prentice Hall.

Knutson, Eric. 1969. "Dichotomization and Integration." Pp. 86–100 in *Ethnic Groups and Boundaries: The Social Organization of Culture Difference,* edited by F. Barth. Bergen, Norway: Universitetsforlaget.

Leach, Edmund R. [1954] 1964. *Political Systems of Highland Burma: A Study of Kachin Social Structure.* London, England: G. Bell and Sons.

Litwack, Lenn F. 1961. *North of Slavery: The Negro in the Free States.* Chicago, IL: University of Chicago Press.

Magubane, Bernard M. 1990. *The Political Economy of Race and Class in South Africa.* New York: Monthly Review Press.

Marable, Manning. 1983. *How Capitalism Underdeveloped Black America.* Boston, MA: South End.

Meir, August and Elliot Rudwick. 1970. *From Plantation to Ghetto.* New York: Hill and Wang.

———. 1989. *Racism.* London, England: Routledge.

———. 1993. *Racism after "Race Relations."* London, England: Routledge.

Miles, Robert and Annie Phizacklea. 1984. *White Man's Country.* London, England: Pluto

Moore, Barrington, Jr. 1966. *Social Origins of Dictatorship and Democracy.* Boston, MA: Beacon Press.

Moore, Joan W. 1970. "Colonialism: The Case of the Mexican-Americans." *Social Problems* 17:463–72.

Myrdal, Gunnar. 1944. *An American Dilemma: The Negro Problem and Modern Democracy.* New York: Harper and Brothers.

Olzack, Susan. 1992. *The Dynamics of Ethnic Competition and Conflict.* Stanford, CA: Stanford University Press.

Omi, Michael and Howard Winant. 1986. *Racial Formation in the United States: From the 1960s to the 1980s.* New York: Routledge and Kegan Paul.

———. 1994. *Racial Formation in the United States: From 1960s to 1980s.* 2d ed. New York: Routledge.

Page, Clarence. 1996. *Showing My Color: Impolite Essays on Race and Identity,* New York: Harper Collins.

Park, Robert Ezra. 1950. *Race and Culture.* Glencoe, IL: Free Press.

Perlo, Victor. 1975. *Economics of Racism U.S.A.: Roots of Black Inequality.* New York: International Publishers.

Pettigrew, Thomas. 1994. "New Patterns of Prejudice: The Different Worlds of 1984 and 1964." Pp. 53–59 in *Race and Ethnic Conflict,* edited by F. L. Pincus and H. J. Erlich. Boulder, CO: Westview.

Piven, Frances Fox and Richard A. Cloward. 1979. *Poor People's Movements: Why They Succeed, How They Fail.* New York: Vintage.

Poulantzas, Nicos. 1982. *Political Power and Social Classes.* London, England: Verso.

———. 1978. "The Economics of Racism." Pp. 381–88 in *The Capitalist System: A Radical Analysis of American Society,* edited by R. Edwards, M. Reich, and T. Weisskopf. Englewood Cliffs, NJ: Prentice Hall.

———. 1981. *Racial Inequality: A Political-Economic Analysis*. Princeton, NJ: Princeton University Press.

Reuter, Edward B. 1934. "Introduction: Race and Culture Contacts." Pp. 1–12 in *Race and Culture Contacts*, edited by E. B. Reuter. New York: McGraw Hill.

Rex, John. 1973. *Race, Colonialism and the City*. London, England: Routledge and Kegan Paul.

———. 1983. *Race Relations in Sociological Theory*. London, England: Weidenfeld and Nicolson.

———. 1986. *Race and Ethnicity*. Philadelphia. PA: Open University Press.

Robinson, Cedric J. 1983. *Black Marxism: The Making of the Black Radical Tradition*. London, England: Zed.

Rodríguez, Clara. 1991. *Puerto Ricans: Born in the U.S.A.* Boulder, CO: Westview.

Roediger, David. 1991. *The Wages of Whiteness: Race and the Making of the American Working Class*. London, England: Verso.

———. 1994. *Towards the Abolition of Whiteness: Essays on Race, Politics, and Working Class History*. London, England: Verso.

Santa Cruz. Hernán. 1977. *Racial Discrimination: Special Rapporteur of the Sub-Commission on Prevention of Discrimination and Protection of Minorities*. New York: United Nations.

Saxton, Alexander. 1990. *The Rise and Fall of the White Republic: Class Politics and Mass Culture in Nineteenth-Century America*. London, England: Verso.

Schaefer, Richard T. 1990. *Racial and Ethnic Groups*. 4th ed. CITY, IL: Scott Foresman/Little Brown Higher Education.

Schermerhorn, Richard A. 1970. *Comparative Ethnic Relations: A Framework for Theory and Research*, New York: Random House.

Schuman, Howard, Charlotte Steeh, and Lawrence Bobo. 1985. *Racial Attitudes in America: Trends and Interpretations*. Cambridge, MA: Harvard University Press.

Sears, David O. 1988. "Symbolic Racism." Pp. 53–84 in *Eliminating Racism: Profiles in Controversy*, edited by P. A. Katz and D. A. Taylor. New York: Plenum.

Segura, Denise. 1990. "Chicanas and the Triple Oppression in the Labor Force." Pp. 47–65 in *Chicana Voices: Intersection of Class, Race, and Gender*, edited by National Association for Chicano Studies. Albuquerque, NM: University of New Mexico Press.

Sewell, William H., Jr. 1992. "A Theory of Structure: Duality, Agency, and Transformation." *American Journal of Sociology* 98:1–29.

Shibutani, Tamotsu and Kian Kwan. 1965. *Ethnic Stratification*. New York: MacMillan.

Sniderman, Paul M. and Thomas Piazza, 1993. *The Scar of Race*. Cambridge, MA: Harvard University Press.

Solomos, John. 1986. "Varieties of Marxist Conceptions of 'Race,' Class and the State: A Critical Analysis." Pp. 84–109 in *Theories of Race and Ethnic Relations*, edited by J. Rex and D. Mason. Cambridge, England: Cambridge University Press.

———. 1989. *Race and Racism in Contemporary Britain*. London, England: MacMillan.

Stone, John. 1985. *Racial Conflict in Contemporary Society*. Cambridge, England: Cambridge University Press.

Sumner, William Graham. 1906. *Folkways*. New York: Ginn.

Sutton, Constance R. and Susan R. Makiesky-Barrow. 1987. "Migration and West Indian Racial and Ethnic Consciousness." Pp. 86–107 in *Caribbean Life in New York City: Sociocultural Dimensions*, edited by C. R. Sutton and E. M. Channey. New York: Center for Migration Studies of New York.

Szymanski, Albert. 1981. "The Political Economy of Racism." Pp. 321–46 in *Political Economy: A Critique of American Society*, edited by S. G. McNall. Dallas, TX: Scott Foresman.

———. 1983. *Class Structure: A Critical Perspective*. New York: Praeger Publishers.

Thomas, William I. and Florian Znaniecki. 1918. *The Polish Peasant in Europe and America*. Vol. 1. New York: Knopf.

Ticktin, Hillel. 1991. *The Politics of Race: Discrimination in South Africa*. London, England: Pluto.

Tilly, Charles. 1978. *From Mobilization to Revolution*. Reading, MA: Addison-Wesley.

Todorov, Tzevetan. 1984. *The Conquest of America: The Question of the Other*. New York: Harper Colophon.

Trouillot, Michel-Rolph. 1990. *Haiti, State Against Nation: Origins and Legacy of Duvalierism*. New York: Monthly Review Press.

van den Berghe, Pierre. 1967. *Race and Racism: A Comparative Perspective*. New York: John Wiley and Sons.

van Dijk, Teun A. 1984. *Prejudice in Discourse: An Analysis of Ethnic Prejudice in Cognition and Conversation*. Amsterdam, The Netherlands: John Benjamins.

———. 1987. *Communicating Racism: Ethnic Prejudice in Thought and Talk*. Newbury Park, CA: Sage.

———. 1993. *Elite Discourse and Racism*. Newbury Park, CA: Sage.

Weber, Max. [1920] 1978. *Economy and Society*. Vol. 1. Edited by G. Roth and C. Wittich. Berkeley, CA. University of California Press.

Webster, Yehudi O. 1992. *The Racialization of America*. New York: St. Martin's.

Willman, David. 1977. *Portraits of White Racism*. Cambridge, England: Cambridge University Press.

Whatley, Warren and Gavin Wright. 1994. *Race, Human Capital, and Labour Markets in American History*. Working Paper #7, Center for Afroamerican and African Studies. University of Michigan, Ann Arbor, MI.

Whitmeyer, Joseph. 1994. "Why Actors Are Integral to Structural Analysis." *Sociological Theory* 12:153–65.

Williams, Eric. [1944] 1961. *Capitalism and Slavery*. New York: Russell and Russell.

Williams, Richard. 1990. *Hierarchical Structures and Social Value: The Creation of Black and Irish Identities in the United States*. Cambridge, England: Cambridge University Press.

Wilson, William J. 1973. *Power, Racism, and Privilege: Race Relations in Theoretical and Sociohistorical Perspectives*. New York: MacMillan.

———. 1978. *The Declining Significance of Race: Blacks and Changing American Institutions*. Chicago, IL: The University of Chicago Press.

Winant, Howard. 1994. *Racial Conditions: Politics, Theory, Comparisons*. Minneapolis, MN: University of Minnesota Press.

———. 1986. "Class Concepts, Class Struggle and Racism." Pp. 110–30 in *Theories of Race Relations*, edited by J. Rex and D. Mason. Cambridge, England: Cambridge University Press.

———. 1988. *Race, Class and the Apartheid State*. Paris, France: UNESCO Press.

Article Review Form at end of book.

WiseGuide Wrap-Up

- Racial categories have been created and reinforced by science, which often reflects the social inequalities of the society from which scientists come. Most physical scientists now recognize that there are no biological bases for racialization; race is socially constructed.

- The fact that race is socially constructed does not deny the reality of racialization or its consequences for society. Sociologists must adopt structural approaches in their analyses of race and racism.

R.E.A.L. Sites

This list provides a print preview of typical **Coursewise** R.E.A.L. sites. (There are over 100 such sites at the **Courselinks**™ site.) The danger in printing URLs is that web sites can change overnight. As we went to press, these sites were functional using the URLs provided. If you come across one that isn't, please let us know via email to: webmaster@coursewise.com. Use your Passport to access the most current list of R.E.A.L. sites at the **Courselinks** site.

Site name: Victorian Science: An Overview

URL: http://www.stg.brown.edu/projects/hypertext/landow/victorian/science/sciov.html

Why is it R.E.A.L.? Although science presents itself as "objective," its theories often reinforce the social hierarchies of the society in which it is produced. Modern U.S. notions of racial categorization are rooted in Victorian Europe's "science," as the essays at this site demonstrate.

Key topics: scientific construction of race, racial categories

Try this: From the "Victorian Science" homepage, select the button for "Anthropology: Race in Victorian Science." From there, choose "Race and Class Overview: Parallels in Racism and Class Prejudice," written by Vassar historian Dr. Anthony S. Wohl. Read the essays contained in the links, so that you can write an essay about how British Victorians conceived of Africans and their descendants as having racial similarities with the Irish, and the implications of this for your understanding of the "science" of race.

Site name: Discoveries Challenge Idea of Race

URL: http://staff.uwsuper.edu/hps/mjohnson/ETHART/Race.htm

Why is it R.E.A.L.? Most physical scientists, anthropologists, and sociologists agree that racial categories reflect social inequalities, not biological differences. Still, some scholars hang on to the notion of race as a biological reality—as do many members of the general public. This article takes a closer look at this phenomenon.

Key topics: scientific construction of race, scientific legitimation of racism

Try this: Read Robert S. Boyd's paper on the science of biological "race." Relate this article to Reading 1 by Gould and to the "Victorian Science" web page. Taken together, what implications do these papers have for your sense of yourself as a "racialized" person? What implications do they have for historical and contemporary public policy? Write a brief reaction paper commenting on these questions.

section 2

Key Points

- Media images that communicate messages about race and racialized cultures reflect the power and politics of the people manufacturing those images.

- Corporate advertising strategies may communicate messages that support racial and sexual equality, while corporate practices undermine the sincerity of those messages.

- Cultural constructions of Black masculinity establish the contexts and conditions that determine which Black male celebrities will be acceptable to white audiences.

- The Internet provides safe haven for neo-Nazis, Holocaust deniers, and hatemongers, whose online messages may be invitations to violence.

Race, Representation, and Popular Culture

 **WiseGuide Intro**

Popular culture offers us much useful and interesting material for the study of race and ethnicity in contemporary industrialized societies. Media images, rap lyrics, advertising pitches, movie plot-lines, television programs, baseball cards, action figures, Barbie dolls, and a host of other symbolic and material sources daily convey to the public many messages about race and ethnicity and about various groups with racialized identities. To what extent do these messages reflect reality? To what extent do these images create reality? To what degree do these messages reflect the interests of the most privileged groups in our society? To what degree might such images disrupt the prevailing racial hierarchy? These are the questions with which we grapple in thinking about the representation of race in popular culture.

In the United States, children now spend more time each week in front of televisions than in front of teachers. What do they see there? How much of what they see do they believe? Critical studies of television suggest that it provides us with "education" as well as entertainment, and that this "education" reflects the interests of some people more than others: the wealthy more than the middle or working classes, European-Americans more than people of color, men more than women. If you were the proverbial historian or sociologist from the future trying to piece together a picture of our society from only the old television reruns shown on "Nick at Night," what would your description of this society include? What would it exclude? How accurate would it be? Would the picture change if you used only episodes of "Melrose Place," "Beverly Hills 90210," or the television coverage of the O. J. Simpson trial? Using only the images from one week's viewing of this medium, how would you describe the racial composition of the United States? Using only its messages, what would you believe about the social locations, roles, and interrelationships of people from different racial and ethnic groups in this society? Would you correctly discern the percentage of people in this society who identify themselves as belonging to a racial minority? Would you be able to assess accurately the percentages of white people who commit crimes and the percentages of poor people who are white?

Television programming, advertising, children's books, and other forms of popular culture fail to represent the statistical realities of our multiracial heritage as a nation but succeed in reinforcing racial stereotypes and perpetuating the racial privileging of whites. In a critical commentary on the impact of racism in the mass media, comedian Whoopie Goldberg once conveyed the experience of receiving these messages as an outsider in a character sketch about a five-year-old Black girl who longs for "long, luxurious blonde hair" because that's all she sees in the media; she has painfully learned that only long, straight, blonde hair is "beautiful" by the standards of the dominant culture.

White Americans who live in areas with a great degree of racial homogeneity may encounter images of people of other races only in magazines, movies, and television. In the absence of genuine human relationships across the lines of racial difference, people may believe the extremes and stereotypes often encountered in these media: that all people of color are jovial and living lives unconstrained by racism or that all people of color are poor and living on welfare or drug money. Such images may leave people from dominant groups unaware of and unconcerned over racism as a social problem or, alternatively, terrified of interacting with people from different ethnic or racial groups. In either case, the effect is similar: to reinforce racial stratification and white privilege while communicating that racial discrimination is not a problem about which European-Americans should be concerned.

The readings assembled in this section provide a sample of issues and approaches in the study of the representation of race in popular culture. Jane Collins and Catherine Lutz write about the racial imagery contained in a popular journal many students have encountered, *National Geographic*. In "Postwar Photographic Histories of Race and Gender in *National Geographic* Magazine," these authors explore the messages conveyed about race in the United States and in the world through the apparently objective lenses of *National Geographic* photographers. Ruth Goldman explores other visual images in "We Said We Wanted a Revolution: Race, Ethnicity, and the Political Economies of Marketing/Representation by Nike," an article on the political economy of race and gender as it relates to an advertising campaign by Nike and the company's production practices in the Third World. Mary McDonald analyzes the valorization of Michael Jordan in "Michael Jordan's Family Values: Marketing, Meaning, and Post-Reagan America" by asking why white America has been so receptive to this Black athlete. Finally, Richard Chesnoff takes us to the Internet, where he examines the "virtual" racism embedded in the words and images of cyberspace in an article called "Hatemongering on the Data Highway."

As you read these articles, pay attention to how their authors use the representations of race and ethnicity they find in popular culture—music, television, print media, sports, and the Internet—as data to analyze. Think, too, about how they position their analyses of their "data" within the context of a wider society that organizes hierarchies by reinforcing racial differentiation. Reflect on how you may have experienced these materials before reading these articles and on how they seem different after you've read these analyses. Because we live in a world increasingly shaped by popular culture, it is important that we become "media literate," a process that allows us to think critically about the consumption-driven popular culture around us. Perhaps these readings will help you to identify and evaluate more easily the messages you're receiving about race and ethnicity from the symbolic world around you.

? Questions ?

Reading 3. How did changes in the content of National Geographic's photos of people in other countries reflect changing debates on race in the United States? How are gender issues connected to racial issues through the lens of *National Geographic*?

Reading 4. How does Nike's advertising strategy involve global discourses on race, ethnicity, and gender?

Reading 5. How does the "marketing of Michael Jordan" reinforce the profamily discourses of the New Right? How does this idealization/idolization obscure social realities?

Reading 6. Why is the Internet, as a medium, easily exploited by hate groups? How might Internet users best use the medium to challenge racism and anti-Semitism, as well as homophobia and sexism?

How did changes in the content of *National Geographic*'s photos of people in other countries reflect changing debates on race in the United States? How are gender issues connected to racial issues through the lens of *National Geographic?*

Postwar Photographic Histories of Race and Gender in *National Geographic* Magazine

**Catherine A. Lutz
and Jane L. Collins**

Race is, as Henry Gates has said, "a trope of ultimate, irreducible difference between cultures, linguistic groups, or adherents of specific belief systems that—more often than not—also have fundamentally opposed economic interests" (1985: 5). It is a trope that is particularly dangerous because it "pretends to be an objective term of classification." Gates points to the profoundly social nature of racial classification. Social groups engaged in struggle define racial boundaries in the contexts of that struggle; powerful groups then invoke biology in a post-hoc justification of the boundaries they have drawn. Those in power elaborate observable physical differences—no matter how subtle—into explanations, affirmations, and justifications for inequality and oppression. Once this work is done, and the boundaries are intact, racist theory produces full-

blown descriptions of culture and personality that juxtapose powerful ego and degraded/dangerous alter, "lending the sanction of God, biology or the natural order to presumably unbiased descriptions of cultural tendencies and differences" (Gates 1985: 5).

As Gates and others have so eloquently pointed out, racial difference—and its supposed cultural concomitants—is thus not the *source* of the many contemporary conflicts where it is said to be at issue. It is never a simple matter of two groups in contact finding themselves so physically and culturally different that they just cannot get along. Rather, racial and cultural difference become coded ways of talking about other differences that matter—differences in power and in interests.[1] For this reason—however absolute and intransigent they may seem—racial/racist theories must retain flexibility and are frequently ambiguous. As Omi and Winant (1986: x) have said, race is an inherently

unstable "complex of social meanings, constantly being transformed by political struggle." To work to uncover the social arrangements that give rise to and reproduce racism is to place its analysis in realms of human agency and to emphasize the specificity of its historical forms.

Tranquil Racial Spaces

National Geographic magazine is the product of a society deeply permeated with racism as a social practice and with racial understandings as ways of viewing the world. It sells itself to a reading public that—while they do not consider themselves racist—turn easily to race as an explanation for culture and for social outcome. The Geographic headquarters itself has had few black employees up to the present, despite the predominantly African American citizenry of Washington, D.C. It is not surprising, therefore, that while race is rarely addressed directly in the magazine, white

American racial categories powerfully structure the images contained in its pages.

One of the most powerful (and distinctive) tenets of racism in the United States is the idea that "blackness" is an all-or-nothing phenomenon. Racial law through the period of the Civil War, and after, held that any "black" ancestry was sufficient to define one as black. As recently as 1983, this type of reasoning was upheld by the State Supreme Court of Louisiana, when it refused to allow a woman descended from an eighteenth-century white planter and a black slave to change the classification on her birth certificate from "colored" to "white" (Omi and Winant 1986: 57). The laws in question, and the cultural preconceptions upon which they were based, insistently denied the reality of interracial sexual relations or of the sexual exploitation that so frequently accompanied the master/slave relation. They insisted on pure and unequivocal categories with which to reason about difference. Such airtight categories were viewed as necessary to guard the privileges of "whites" as absolute, and to justify the denial of equality to "blacks" as an impossibility.

Nevertheless, when Euramericans turned their eyes outside the borders of their own country, other forms of reasoning prevailed. Evolutionist thought dominated attempts to understand the human diversity of the non-European world. Such thinking needed a continuum, and one that was grounded in nature. Skin color is obviously highly variable, only with some difficulty made to accommodate the simple binary classification "black"/"white" in the United States. A continuum of skin color was thus a perfect biological substratum on which to graft stories of human progress or cultural evolution.

Late nineteenth-century fairs and expositions frequently organized the world cultures they presented along an evolutionary scale. These almost always corresponded to a racial continuum as Rydell (1984) has noted, from the "savagery" of the dark-skinned Dahomeyans, to the Javanese "Brownies," to the "nearly-white" Chinese and Japanese. As evolutionary trajectories were reproduced over the course of the twentieth century, in anthropological theory and in white popular consciousness, they almost always were connected to a scale of skin color, which was then construed, in many cases, as an independent form of verifying their correctness.

As we examined *National Geographic* photographs, we hypothesized that it was this more differentiated scale—rather than the simple binary opposition called into play for analyzing American culture—that would inform the ways *National Geographic* would portray, and readers would interpret, images of the third world. Distinctions in popular stereotypes of the peoples of Northern and sub-Saharan Africa, or of Melanesia and Polynesia, indicated that Euramericans drew conclusions about others based on the *degree* of darkness of skin color. As we analyzed constructions of race in *National Geographic* photographs, we thus coded them in a way that would allow us to determine whether "bronze" peoples were portrayed different from those who would be more commonly seen as "black"; to see, in other words, if simply binary constrictions informed the images, or if more complex evolutionary schema structured their messages.[2]

The period for which we analyzed photographs—1950–86—encompassed times of great turmoil in racially defined relationships in the United States. The late 1950s and early sixties saw struggles to overturn racial codes that were more intense than any since the Civil War era. Participants in the civil rights movement sought to obtain basic civil liberties for African Americans; they used the egalitarian verbiage of federal law to challenge the restrictive laws and practices of states and municipalities. Such changes did not simply require a change in the legal codes and their implementation, however; they also demanded, as Omi and Winant have argued, "a paradigm shift in established systems of racial meanings and identities" (1986: 90).

Nonviolent tactics such as freedom rides, marches, attempts to desegregate key southern school districts and universities, and sit-ins at segregated lunchrooms characterized the period up until the passage of the 1964 Civil Rights Act and the voting rights legislation of 1965. By the mid-sixties, however, many who had worked and hoped for these changes were disillusioned. Changes in legislation had profound symbolic value, and materially benefitted a small number of middle-class African Americans. But they did not alter the economic circumstances of the vast majority of blacks living in poverty, and they did not adequately challenge the tremendous and continuing burden of institutional racism. This led to an increasing radicalization of key branches of the civil rights movement and to angry rioting in places like Watts and Newark (Harding 1981; Carson 1981).

The civil rights movement contested white privilege and its counterpart, the institutionalized oppression of black Americans. It also contested the very meaning of race in American culture. As white Americans were deprived of one of the master tropes explaining their privileged position in the world, race became an uncomfortable topic for them. This discomfort was reflected in the pages of *National Geographic*. Clearly the magazine did not cover the turmoil in U.S. cities during the period. At the same time, it sought to ease anxieties in its portrayal of the third world. As late as the early 1950s, the Euramerican reading public could comfortably view Asian and African peoples attending white explorers and photographers— carrying them across rivers, pulling them in rickshaws, carrying their packs and bags. By the late sixties, however, these images were too disturbing, the possibility of rebellion and anger was too present. White travelers simply disappeared from the pictures, removing the possibility of conflictual relationships.

With this action, third world spaces were cleared for fantasy. Black and bronze peoples of Africa, Asia, and Latin America were shown going about their daily lives—happy, poor but dignified, and attuned to basic human values. The photographs themselves were not all that different from those of previous decades; however, in the racially charged context of the fifties and sixties, their meaning had changed. The implicit contrast with Watts and Newark, or even with Selma and Montgomery, operated behind the scenes. The third world was constituted as safe, comfortable space, where race was not an issue and where white people did not have to re-evaluate the sources of their privilege.

Apparently, though, in the minds of *National Geographic* editors, too much of even a reassuring fantasy could be disturbing. Until 1961, the numbers of white, black, or bronze people occurring in any given issue of *National Geographic* was variable. In 1952, for example, only about 15 percent of people depicted in articles on the Third World were dark-skinned; in 1958, the figure was about 46 percent. Beginning in 1961, however, a re-

markably stable pattern began to appear. For the next twenty-five years the percentage of dark-skinned people in any issue held very constant at about 28 percent. People who could be categorized as bronze formed a fairly regular 60 percent of the total, with the remaining 12 percent constituted by light or white-skinned third world peoples. The intense stability of this pattern, and particularly the almost invariant proportion of dark-skinned people represented, suggests that editorial attention may have been focused on the issue.

This is admittedly indirect evidence. We did not find anyone at *National Geographic* who was willing to say that skin color per se was a consideration in putting together issues (although conversations in planning meetings suggest that it may well be). We do know, however, that *National Geographic*'s marketing department gathered significant amounts of data on the popularity of different kinds of articles and that Africa was by far the least popular world region. By marketing definitions, African peoples constituted a difficult topic; to the extent that market concerns drive content, one would thus expect some sort of regulation of their coverage.

In photographs where dark-skinned peoples were portrayed, there were interesting regularities—contributing to an overall image of contentment, industriousness, and simplicity. The activity level of individuals portrayed in the photographs, for example, clearly sorted out on an evolutionary scale marked by skin color. Individuals coded as black were most likely to be depicted in high levels of activity—engaged in strenuous work or athletics. People coded white were most likely to be engaged in low-level activity— seated or reclining, perhaps manipulating something with their hands, but rarely exerting them-

selves. Those coded bronze were most likely to be found engaged in activities that fell somewhere between the two extremes, such as walking or herding animals. In keeping with this pattern, people of color (both black and bronze) were most likely to be portrayed at work in the photographs we examined, while people with white skin were most likely to be found at rest.

Portraying people at work is in keeping with an editorial policy that demands a focus on the positive as construed in the United States, that is, the work ethic. It is possible to imagine that editors sought to counter images of the laziness of non-white peoples (in the Euramerican imagination) by deliberately presenting an alternative view. At the same time, in the contradictory manner that is characteristic of colonial/neocolonial mentality (see Bhabha 1983)—it is also possible that deeply ingrained notions of racial hierarchy made it seem more "natural" for dark-skinned peoples to be at work and engaged in strenuous activity. White ambivalence around the black male seems often to center around issues of strength: while vigor is good for the worker to have, it also has the threatening connotations of potential rebelliousness, and so some hobbling often follows the rendition of strength.

Few topics have occupied as much space in colonial discourse as the relationship of blacks to labor. As Euramericans sought to build wealth on the backs of colonized peoples and slaves, they sought to continually refine methods of maximizing the labor they were able to extract. Colonial administrators and plantation bosses continually reported on the successes and failures of innovations in the process. The double mentality reflected in the reports was plain—while people of color were inherently suited to labor, they never wanted to work hard enough in the fields of their white masters. The image of a tremendous capacity to work, coupled with an unwillingness to do so, gave rise to contradictory stereotypes. The heritage of these stereotypes and the labor relations that gave rise to them can be traced in the strenuously employed black bodies portrayed in the pages of *National Geographic.*

In equally regular ways, black and bronze peoples were more likely to be portrayed as poor and technologically backward. Individuals coded as white were more likely to be wealthy and less likely to be poor than other categories. Still, only 21 percent of black and 16 percent of bronze people were photographed in contexts of poverty. Fully 70 percent of the former and 72 percent of the latter were shown without any markers of wealth or poverty, and some of each group were portrayed as wealthy. There is clearly a tension at work in the photographs. The greater poverty of darker-skinned individuals may, in part, be empirically determined; it is also in keeping with popular Euramerican stereotypes of the degraded status of dark-skinned peoples. On the other hand, *National Geographic*'s policy of focusing on the positive and avoiding advocacy precludes too heavy an emphasis on impoverishment. Dark-skinned peoples have a somewhat greater tendency to be poor—one might construe the statistical weight of the photographs as saying—but, in general, they live well.

Individuals coded white were most likely to be depicted with machines of one kind or another; black and bronze individuals were most likely to be shown with simple tools of local manufacture. Not surprisingly, people of color were more often depicted as engaged in ritual. This variable also sorted out along an evolutionary/skin color continuum: the darker the skin color, the more likely to engage in ritual practices. In classic evolutionist terms, superstition (represented by ritual) and science (represented by technology) were counterposed. Similarly, the darker the skin color of an individual, the less likely he or she was to be depicted in Western-style clothing. The darker the skin of the people portrayed, the less they were associated with things European, and the more exotic they were rendered.

Given these trends, it was somewhat surprising to find that dark-skinned peoples were not photographed in natural settings (that is, in landscapes or greenery) more often than their lighter-skinned counterparts. They were, however, more likely to appear in settings where surroundings were not clearly discernible. Such portrayals tend to aestheticize the materials upon which they focus. In this case, they force attention to the lines, shapes and colors of the bodies themselves, rather than providing information about the context in which the bodies appear. Because such photos were relatively numerous, dark-skinned people consequently appeared in *social* surroundings less frequently.

People coded black or bronze were more likely to be photographed in large groups than those coded white. They were less likely to be portrayed alone or in small intimate groups. People of color were therefore less often the subject of individualized photographic accounts, attentive to "biographic" features and life circumstances. They were more often portrayed as part of a mass, perhaps thereby suggesting to readers that they had relatively undifferentiated feelings, hopes, or needs. Individuals coded as black and bronze were far more likely to be photographed gazing into the camera than individuals coded white—a stance that, while complex and sometimes ambiguous— frequently suggests availability and compliance.

Despite some Euramerican stereotypes, dark skin was not associated with evidence of aggression in the pages of *National Geographic* through most of the period we have examined. Aggression is generally taboo as a topic for *National Geographic* photographs, except in the highly specific case of depicting U.S. military power. Additionally, however, to retain its status as a place where white U.S. readers go to assuage their fears about race and cultural difference, *National Geographic* must studiously avoid photographs that might suggest a potential threat from colonized and formerly colonized peoples. To depict anger, violence, or the presence of weapons is to evoke the fear that they might be turned to retaliation. They serve as an uncomfortable reminder of a world given to struggles for independence, revolutions, and rebellions.

In the marketplaces of images, *National Geographic* relies on two intertwined strategies. It relies on recognition—on offering readers what they already know and believe, in new and appealing ways. Its reputation and sales also turn on the classic humanism with which it portrays the world. In its depictions of "nonwhite" peoples, the humanist mission—to portray all humans as basically the same "under the skin"[3]—comes into conflict with Western "commonsense knowledge" about the hierarchy of races.

The organization of photographs into stories about cultural evolution (couched in more "modern" terms of progress and development) provides the partial resolution of this contradiction. These stories tell the Euramerican public that their race prejudice is not so wrong; that at one point people of color *were* poor, dirty, technologically backward, and, superstitious—and some still are. But this is not due to intrinsic or insuperable characteristics. With guidance and support from the West, they can in fact overcome these problems, acquire the characteristics of civilized peoples and take their place alongside them in the world. In the context of this story, the fact that bronze peoples are portrayed as slightly less poor, more technologically adept, serves as proof that progress is possible and fatalistically links progress to skin color.

At the same time, the "happy-speak" policies of *National Geographic* have meant that for people of color—as for others—the overall picture is one of tranquility and well-being. We are seldom confronted with historical facts of racial or class violence, with hunger as it unequally affects black and white children, or with social movements that question established racial hierarchies. One photographer expressed this poignantly, pointing to a photograph of an African family in a 1988 issue on population. "The story is about hunger," he said, "but look at these people. It's a romantic picture."

This is not to say that no one at the National Geographic Society is attentive to these issues. Dedicated photographers and editors worked hard in the 1970s to produce and push into print two deeply disturbing accounts of apartheid. And while this attempt engendered a repressive movement within the Society's Board of Trustees, an article critical of South African black homelands appeared in February 1986.

The same strategies, however, pursued in different epochs, can have different meanings and consequences. The humanist side of *National Geographic* in the 1950s and 1960s denied social problems; it also provided images of people of color living their lives in relatively dignified ways. It gave short shrift to poverty and disharmony, but it

permitted a certain amount of identification across racial boundaries. In a period when racial boundaries were highly visible and when African Americans were struggling for equal rights under the law, these images could be read, at least in part, as subtle arguments for social change.

The 1970s have been characterized as a period of "racial quiescence," when social movements waned and conflicts receded (Omi and Winant 1986: 2). Racial oppression did not cease, but it was not as openly contested. In turn, the 1980s saw a backlash in undisguised attempts to dismantle legislation protecting civil rights and nondiscriminatory practices. These moves did not require—and, in fact, assiduously avoided—an explicitly racial discourse. Busing, originally implemented to desegregate schools, was overturned under banners of "community control" and "parental involvement." Rejections of racially balanced textbooks were couched in terms of battles against "secular humanism" and "political correctness." And in the 1988 presidential campaign, movements of people of color were recast as "special interests" (Oni and Winant 1986: 125).

In such a context, classic humanism takes on pernicious overtones. The denial of race as a *social* issue, in a society with a profoundly racist history and where institutional racism still exists, forecloses dialogue on the issues. *National Geographic* has not intentionally contributed to this foreclosure; it goes on producing pictures in much the same way it has for years. And yet the message that we are all alike under the skin takes on new meaning in a social context that denies that discrimination exists or that race has been used to consolidate the privilege of some and oppress others. The racism of the 1980s was not confrontational and defiant; it simply turned its back on the issues. The tranquil

racial spaces of *National Geographic* can only contribute to this willed ignorance.

The Women of the World

National Geographic photographs of the women of the world tell a story about the women of the United States over the post–World War II period. It is to issues of gender in white American readers' lives, such as debates over women's sexuality or whether women doing paid labor can mother their children adequately, that the pictures refer as much as to the lives of third world women. Seen in this way, the *National Geographic*'s women can be placed alongside the other women of American popular culture: the First Lady, the woman draped over an advertisement's red sports car, the Barbie doll, the woman to whom the Hallmark Mother's Day card is addressed. Rather than treating the photos as simply images of women, we can set them in the context of a more complex cultural history of the period, with the sometimes radical changes it brought to the lives of the women who are the readers (or known to the male readers) of the magazine.

The photographs of *National Geographic* are indispensable to understanding issues of gender because the magazine is one of the very few popular venues trafficking in large numbers of images of black women. While the photographs tell a story about cultural ideals of femininity, the narrative threads of gender and race are tightly bound up with each other. In the world at large, race and gender are clearly not separate systems, as Trinh (1989), Moore (1988), Sacks (1989), and others have reminded us.

For the overwhelmingly white readers of the *Geographic*, the dark-skinned women of distant regions serve as touchstones, giving lessons both positive and negative about what women are and should be (compare Botting 1988). Here, as elsewhere, the magazine plays with possibilities of the other as a flexible reflection—even a sort of funhouse mirror—for the self. The women of the world are portrayed in sometimes striking parallel to popular images of American womanhood of the various periods of the magazine's production—for instance, as mothers and beautiful objects. At certain times, with certain races of women, however, the Geographic's other women provide a contrast to stereotypes of white American women—they are presented as hard-working breadwinners in their communities.

As with American women in popular culture, Third World women are portrayed less frequently than men: one-quarter of the pictures we looked at focus primarily on women.[4] The situation has traditionally not been that different in the anthropological literature covering the non-Western world, and it may be amplified in both genres where the focus is on cultural difference or exoticism. Given the association between women and the natural world, men and things cultural (Ortner 1974), a magazine that aspires to describe the distinctive achievements of civilizations might be expected to highlight the world of men. But like the "people of nature" in the Fourth World, women have been treated as all the more precious for their nonutilitarian, nonrationalistic qualities. Photographs of women become one of the primary devices by which the magazine depicts "universal human values," and these include the values of family love and the appreciation of female beauty itself.[5] We turn to these two issues now, noting that each of them has had a consistent cultural content through the postwar period, during historical changes that give the images differ-

ent emphases and form through the decades.

The motherhood of man. There is no more romantic set of photographs in the Geographic than those depicting the mothers of the world with their children. There is the exuberant picture showing the delight of a Kurd mother holding her infant. Filling much space, as an unusually high percentage of the magazine's mother-child pictures do, the photograph covers two pages despite the relative lack of information in it. Its classical composition and crisp, uncluttered message are similar to those in many such photos. They often suggest the Western tradition of madonna painting, and evoke the Mother's Day message: this relationship between mother and child, they say, is a timeless and sacred one, essentially and intensely loving regardless of social and historical context—the foundation of human social life rather than cultural difference. The family of man, these pictures might suggest, is first of all a mother-child unit, rather than a brotherhood of solidarity between adults.[6]

For the magazine staff and readers of the 1950s, there must have been even more power in these images than we see in them today. The impact of the photos would have come from the intense cultural and social pressures on middle-class women to see their most valued role as that of mother (Margolis 1984). The unusually strong pressure of this period is often explained as motivated by desires to place returning World War II veterans (and men in general) in those jobs available and by anxieties about the recent war horror and the future potential for a nuclear conflagration, which made the family seem a safe haven (May 1988). As a new cult of domesticity emerged, women were told—through both science and popular culture—that biology, morality, and

the psychological health of the next generation required their commitment to full-time mothering. This ideological pressure persisted through the 1950s despite the rapid rise in female employment through the decade.

The idealization of the mother-child bond is seen in everything from the warm TV relationships of June Clever with Wally and the Beaver to the cover of a *Life* magazine issue of 1956 devoted to "The American Woman" showing a glowing portrait of a mother and daughter lovingly absorbed in each other; all of this is ultimately and dramatically reflected in the period's rapidly expanding birth rate. This idealization had its counterpoint in fear of the power women were given in the domestic domain. In both science and popular culture, the mother was criticized for being smothering, controlling, oversexualized, and, a bit later, overly permissive (Ehrenreich and English 1978, 1988).

The *National Geographic*'s treatment of children can be seen as an extension of these ideologies of motherhood and the family. As the "woman question" came to be asked more angrily in the late 1950s, there was a gradual erosion of faith in the innocence of the mother-infant bond and even in the intrinsic value of children (Ehrenreich and English 1978), centered on fears of juvenile delinquency and the later 1960's identification of a "generation gap." The *National Geographic*, however, continued to print significant numbers of photographs of children, perhaps responding to their increasingly sophisticated marketing information which indicated that photographs of children and cute animals were among their most popular pictures.

In the *National Geographic*'s pictures of mother and child, it often appears that the nonwhite mother is backgrounded, with her gaze and the gaze of the reader focused on the infant. The infant may in fact be an even more important site for dealing with white racial anxieties, by virtue of constituting an acceptable black love object. A good number of pictures in the postwar period have the form of these two: one a Micronesian and the other an Iraqi infant, from 1974 and 1976 respectively, each peacefully asleep in a cradle with the mother visible behind. The peacefulness constitutes the antithesis of the potentially threatening differences of interest, dress, or ritual between the photographed adult and the reader.

Women and their breasts. The "nude" woman sits, stands or lounges at the salient center of *National Geographic* photography of the non-Western world. Until the phenomenal growth of mass circulation pornography in the 1960s, the magazine was known as the only mass culture venue where Americans could see women's breasts. Part of the folklore of Euramerican men, stories about secret perusals of the magazine emerged time after time in our conversations with *National Geographic* readers. People vary in how they portray the personal or cultural meaning of this nakedness, some noting it was an aid to masturbation, others claiming it failed to have the erotic quality they expected. When white men tell these stories about covertly viewing black women's bodies, they are clearly not recounting a story about a simple encounter with the facts of human anatomy or customs; they are (perhaps unsuspectingly) confessing a highly charged—but socially approved—experience in this dangerous territory of projected, forbidden desire and guilt. Such stories also exist (in a more charged, ironic mode) in the popular culture of African Americans—

for example, in Richard Pryor's characterization of *National Geographic* as the black man's *Playboy.*

The racial distribution of female nudity in the magazine conforms, in pernicious ways, to Euramerican myths about black women's sexuality. Lack of modesty in dress places black women closer to nature. Given the pervasive tendency to interpret skin color as a marker of evolutionary progress, it is assumed that white women have acquired modesty along with other characteristics of civilization. Black women remain backward on this scale, not conscious of the embarrassment they should feel at their nakedness (Gilman 1985: 114–15, 193). Their very ease unclothed stigmatizes them.

In addition, black women have been portrayed in Western art and science as both exuberant and excessive in their sexuality. While their excess intrigues, it is also read as pathological and dangerous. In the texts produced within white culture, Haraway writes, "Colored women densely code sex, animal, dark, dangerous, fecund, pathological" (1989:154). Thus for the French surrealists of the 1930s, the exotic, unencumbered sexuality of non-Western peoples—and African women in particular—represented an implicit criticism of the repression and constraint of European sexuality. The Africanism of the 1930s, like an earlier Orientalism, evidenced both a longing for—and fear of—the characteristics attributed to non-Western peoples (Clifford 1988: 61). The sexuality of black women that so entertained French artists and musicians in cafes and cabarets, however, had fueled earlier popular and scientific preoccupation with the Hottentot Venus and other pathologized renditions of black women's bodies and desires (Gilman 1985).

The *Geographic*'s distinctive brand of cultural relativism, however, meant that this aspect of black sexuality would be less written in by the institution than read in by readers, particularly in comparison with other visual venues such as Hollywood movies. One can see the distinctive *Geographic* style in comparison with *Life* photography of non-Western women. A stronger cultural viewpoint on race is at work in a 1956 *Life* article on "other women," which ran next to an article on American women of various regions of the country. The two articles read as a kind of beauty pageant, with all the photographs emphasizing the sitter's appearance, sexuality, and passivity. Ultimately, the magazine's editors judged American women the better-looking set (many captions also noted the "natural," "healthy," wholesome—non-perverted?—quality of the American women), but the adjectives they used to caption the non-Western women describe their sense of the more passive and sexually explicit stance of the other women. So they are variously praised for their "fragility," "great softness," "grace," "languorous" qualities, and eagerness "to please"; "the sensuous quality often seen in women of the tropics" was found in one Malayan woman. The hypersexual but passive woman here replicates the one found by many Westerners in their imaginary African travels throughout the last century (Hammond and Jablow 1977). In the *Life* article, all of the non-Western women except the one Chinese "working girl" (and many of the American women), touch themselves, their clothes, or fans in the usual pose for characterizing female self-involvement (Goffman 1979).

If *National Geographic* trades in the sexuality of black women, it is less comfortable with that of black men. Men coded black were far more likely than those coded white to appear bare-chested in the pages of the magazine—often in poses that drew attention to musculature and strength. The *National Geographic* has apparently tried to include pictures of "handsome, young men" (Abramson 1987: 143). The magazine has been extremely skittish, however, about portraying male genitals. A respect for the facts has not inhibited the careful erasure of all evidence of male penises from photographs. In cultures where men do not customarily wear pants, the magazine has relied on careful extensions of loin clothes, the drawing in of shorts, or simply air-brushing away body parts to avoid offending the white reading public. The fear of—and desire to erase—black male sexuality has a long tradition in Euramerican culture. It reached its fullest and most heinous development in the paranoid fantasies of organizations such as the Ku Klux Klan and in the castrations and lynchings of southern black men for real or imputed advances toward white women (Carby 1985: 307–308). Haraway (1989) and Torgovnick (1990) offer vivid examples and analyses of the evidence of miscegenation and black abduction anxieties in American popular culture materials, such as the Tarzan stories and movies. Masquerading as taste or propriety, however, the underlying anxiety also finds its place in the pages of *National Geographic*.

Like the nude and its role in Western high art painting (Hess and Nochlin 1972; Betterton 1987; Nead 1990), nudity in *Geographic* photographs has had a potential sexual, even pornographic, interpretation. Such interpretations would obviously threaten the magazine's legitimacy and sales, achieved through its self-definition

as a serious, relatively high-brow, family magazine. Pornography represents just the opposite values: "disposability, trash," the deviant, the unrespectable, the low class (Nead 1990: 325). Like fine art, science attempts to frame the nude female body as devoid of pornographic attributes. While art aestheticizes it, science dissects, fragments, and otherwise desexualizes it. The *National Geographic* nude has at times done both of these contradictory things.

Two important stylistic changes can be identified in photos of women's bodies in the magazine, one related to changes in commercial photography of women and the other to the growing tolerance of "aesthetic" pictures in the *Geographic* of the eighties. Beginning in the late fifties, certain changes in the way women were photographed in commercials began to be reflected in *National Geographic* images. In early advertisements of the period, women are shown directly involved in the use of a product, as when a woman with a fur stole is shown being helped into her 1955 Chrysler by the doorman of an obviously upscale building. By contrast, a 1966 Chevrolet ad depicts a woman lying on the roof of the car putting on lipstick, with a small inset photo that shows her sitting on the roof being photographed by a man. The ads of the 1950s show women as domestic royalty; the later ads place them in more straightforwardly sexual roles and postures.

In *National Geographic* documentary images as well, we find a shift, coming some years after that in commercial photography; the naked woman moves from being just an ethnographic fact ("this is the way they dress as they go about their lives") to presentation as in part an aesthetic and sexual object. After 1970, naked women are less often shown framed with men, less

often mothering, more often dancing or lounging.[7] The erotic connotations of the horizontal woman (known and drawn on by advertisers [Goffman 1979]), and of the woman absorbed in dance, combine with more romantic, aesthetic styles to create photos which follow the inflation of sexualized images of women in the culture at large (Wolf 1991).

A second explanation for changes in the rendering of the nude woman is found in the increasing tolerance of a more aesthetic rendering of all subjects in the *Geographic*. Aesthetic style, however, has special implications and nuances when the photos are of women. What arises after the fifties in the *Geographic* is not just a more self-consciously aesthetic style, but also a style whose uses elsewhere in the culture were centered on photography of women, as in fashion and other commercial work.

The cultural debate (however minor in scale and impact) over whether the nudity in the *Geographic* was or is appropriate follows shifting and conflicting definitions of acceptable portrayals of women's bodies (Nead 1990). At issue is not simply whether women's bodies are displayed, but what the cultural context of those images is (Myers 1987; Vance 1990); that context includes the sexualization of the breasts, the objectification of women, the racist understanding of black femininity, and the shame that inheres in American culture to sexuality itself.[8] Nonetheless, the still heavily white male photographic and editorial staff at the *Geographic* appears relatively unaffected by feminist critiques of the use of women's bodies or the critique of colonial-looking relations (Gaines 1988) that prompt both the frequent inclusion and a particular distorted reading by subscribers of the nude black woman's body.

The kitchen debates in Africa: Woman's place in the march of progress. In a subtly nuanced analysis of the genre of 1980s Hollywood success movies, Traube (1989) details the influence of the Reagan years and a particular moment of labor demography and consumer capitalism in the construction of the films' plots and styles. These films describe, among other things, the gender-specific dangers and possibilities of the world of managerial work for the middle-class youth who view these movies on their way to corporate work lives. Specifically, they include "warning of the feminizing effects of deference on men and, conversely, the masculinizing effects of ambition on women" (1989: 291). The *National Geographic*'s women do not provide as easy an identificatory anchor for the magazine's readers as do these movie's characters, but their image, too, has responded to changes in the politics and rate of American women's labor force participation. They have also played a role in articulating longstanding cultural notions about the role of women in socioeconomic development overseas.

Against the indolent native of colonialist discourse, the *Geographic*'s industrious native toils in response to an editorial policy which calls for a sympathetic other. Women's work is portrayed, however, as less intellectually demanding and more toilsome than that of men. Take the Melanesian man and woman set up on opposite pages (April 1969: 574–75). A male archer on the left is labeled, "man, the hunter" and, on the right, a photo of a woman with child in netbag carrying a large load of firewood, "woman, the laborer." The woman smiles under her burden, perhaps thereby evoking images long in circulation in Western culture: these are images which romanticize the hard-working black woman, often ignoring the difference between her endur-

ing and enjoying (much less opposing) oppression (hooks 1981: 6). In this latter cultural discourse, the black woman could endure what no lady could and therefore revealed her more natural, even animal nature (81–82). For many readers of the *Geographic,* it may be an easy step from the celebration of the strong, working woman to her dehumanization as someone with less than human abilities to withstand those burdens.[9]

Cultural ambivalence toward women working outside the home has been profound during the postwar period, when women's waged employment grew from 25 percent in 1940 to 40 percent in 1960. More of this is accounted for by African American women, half of whom were employed in 1950, with their waged work continuing at high rates in the following decades. The ideological formulation of the meaning of women's work has changed. Working women in the fifties were defined as helpmates to their husbands. Only much later did women's work come to be seen by some as a means to goals of independence and self-realization (Chafe 1983), although even here, as Traube (1989) points out, messages were widely available that women's success in work was threatening to men. This ambivalence occasionally shows up in the *Geographic* when the laboring woman is presented as a drudge or when her femininity, *despite her working,* is emphasized. An example of the latter is found in a photograph of a Burmese woman shown planting small green shoots in a garden row (June 1974: 286). Retouching has been done both to her line of plants and to the flowers which encircle her hair. The sharpening and coloring of these two items lets the picture much more clearly tell a narrative about her femininity and her productivity and about how those two things are not mutually exclusive.

More often, however, the labor of women as well as other aspects of their lives are presented by the *Geographic* as central to the march of progress in their respective countries. Women are constructed as the vanguard of progress in part through the feminizing of the developing nation state itself (Kabbani 1986; cf. Shaffer 1988). How does this work? In the first instance, those foreign states are contrasted, in some Western imaginations, with a deeply masculine American national identity (Krasniewitz 1990; Jeffords 1989), a gendering achieved through the equation of the West (*in* the West, of course) with strength, civilization, rationality, and freedom, its other with vulnerability, primitivity, superstition, and the binds of tradition. Once this equation has been made, articles can be titled as in the following instance where progress is masculinized and the traditional nation feminized: "Beneath the surge of progress, old Mexico's charm and beauty lie undisturbed" (October 1961).

Fanon (1965: 39) pointed out in his analysis of French colonial attitudes and strategies concerning the veil in Algeria that the colonialists' goal, here as elsewhere in the world, was "converting the woman, winning her over to the foreign values, wrenching her free from her status" as a means of "shaking up the [native] man" and gaining control of him. With this and other motives, those outsiders who would "develop" the Third World have often seen the advancement of non-Western women as the first goal to be achieved, with their men's progress thought to follow rather than precede it. In the nineteenth century, evolutionary theory claimed that the move upward from savagery to barbarism to civilization was indexed by the treatment of women, in particular by their liberation "from the burdens of overwork, sexual abuse, and male violence" (Tiffany and Adams 1985: 8). It "saw women in non-Western societies as oppressed and servile creatures, beasts of burden, chattels who could be bought and sold, eventually to be liberated by 'civilization' or 'progress,' thus attaining the enviable position of women in Western society" (Etienne and Leacock 1980: 1), who were then expected to be happy with their place.[10] The *Geographic* has told a much more upbeat version of this story, mainly by presenting other women's labors positively.

The continuation of these ways of thinking into the present can be seen in how states defined as "progressive" have been rendered by both Western media like the *National Geographic* and the non-Western state bureaucrats concerned. Graham-Brown (1988) and Schick (1990) describe how photographic and other proof of the progress or modernity of states like Turkey and pre-revolutionary Iran has often been found primarily in the lives of their women, and particularly in their unveiling.[11] Indeed, as Schick points out, "a photograph of an unveiled woman was not much different from one of a tractor, an industrial complex, or a new railroad; it merely symbolized yet another one of men's achievements" (1990: 369).

Take the example from the *Geographic*'s January 1985 article on Baghdad. Several photographs show veiled women walking through the city's streets. One shot shows women in a narrow alley. The dark tones of the photograph are a function of the lack of sunlight reaching down into the alley, but they also reproduce the message of the caption. Playing with the associations between veil and past that are evoked for most readers, it says, "In the shadows of antiquity, women in long black

abayas walk in one of the older sections of the city." A few pages earlier, we learn about the high-rise building boom in the city and the changing roles of women in a two-page layout that shows a female electrical engineer in a hard hat and jeans organizing a building project with a male colleague. The caption introduces her by name and goes on: "Iraqi women, among the most progressive in the Arab world, constitutes 25 percent of the country's work force and are guaranteed equality under Baath Party doctrine." On the opposite page, the modern buildings they have erected are captioned, "New York on the Tigris." The equation of the end point (Manhattan) with the unveiled woman is neatly laid out.

The celebration of simultaneous women's liberation and national progress is not the whole story, of course. The magazine also communicates—in a more muted way through the fifties and into the sixties—a sense of the value of the "natural," Gemeinshaft-based life of the people without progress. Progress can be construed as a socially corrosive process as it was in the late nineteenth century, when non-Western women were seen as superior to their Western counterparts because too much education had weakened the latter (Ehrenreich and English 1978: 114), sapping vitality from their reproductive organs. The illiterate woman of the non-Western world still lives with this cultural inheritance, standing for the woman "unruined" by progress.

An example of the contradictory place of progress is found in two photographs that draw attention to housewives. In the first, an Inuit woman wearing a fur trimmed parka stands in front of a washing machine: "Unfamiliar luxury" the caption says, "a washing machine draws a housewife to the new 'Tuk' laundromat, which also

offers hot showers" (July 1968). This picture is explicitly structured around the contrast between the premodern and the modern, with the evaluative balance falling to the luxurious present. It might have still resonated for readers with the image from 1959 of Nixon and Khrushchev arguing over the benefits of capitalism next to a freshly minted washing machine and dryer at the American National Exhibition in Moscow. In those debates, Nixon could argue that the progress of American society under capitalism is found in its ability to provide labor-saving devices to women. "I think that this attitude toward women is universal. What we want is to make easier the life of our housewives," he said. In the gender stories told during the cold war, family life and commodities provided what security was to be found in the post-Hiroshima, post-Holocaust world (May 1988). The non-Western woman, too, could be deployed as proof of capitalism's value, of the universal desire for these goods, and of the role of women in the evolution of society.

From January 1971, however, an article titled "Housewife at the End of the World" documents the adventures of an Ohio woman settling in Tierra del Fuego, and congratulates her on adapting to local norms of self-sufficiency and simplicity. The last photo's caption articulates the theme of the whole article: "Life in this remote land spurs inventiveness. . . . My special interests keep me so busy I have little time to miss the conveniences I once knew." The North American woman chooses to forgo the benefits of progress in search of an authentically simple place, as her "younger sister" climbs the ladder in the other direction.

In stories of progress and/or decline, Western and non-Western women have often been played off of one another in this way, each used to critique the other in line with different purposes and in the end leaving each feeling inadequate. The masculine writer/image maker/consumer thereby asserts his own strength, both through his right to evaluate and through his completeness in contrast to women. Although non-Western men cannot be said to fare well in these cultural schemes, they are used less frequently and in other ways (Honour 1989) to either critique or shore up white men's masculinity.

In sum, the women of the non-Western world represent a population aspiring to the full femininity achieved in Western cultures, and, in a more secondary way, they are a repository for the lost femininity of "liberated" Western women. Both an ideal and thus a critique of modern femininity, they are also a measure to tell the Western family how far it has advanced. They are shown working hard and as key to their countries' progress toward some version of the Western consumer family norm. The sometimes contradictory message these pictures can send to middle class women is consistent with cultural ideologies in the United States that both condemn and affirm the woman who would be both mother and wage laborer. We can see the women of the *National Geographic* playing a role within a social field where the Cold War was being waged and where social changes in kinship structures and gender politics were precipitated by the entrance of white women into the paid labor force in larger and larger numbers.

Notes

1. This is not to deny that there are complex correspondences between culture and racial categories as socially deployed. Once race has been used to marginalize and isolate social groups, shared experiences of oppression, coping and resistance may give rise to shared cultural premises. The "culture" or "cultures" that result, however, are at least partly a consequence of the deployment of racial categories and not evidence of the validity of the categories themselves.

2. The authors and an anthropology graduate student coded the photographs. Intercoder agreement occurred for 86 percent of all decisions. We resolved disagreements through discussion between coders. The photographic features coded included world location, gender, age, activity type, surroundings, dress style, wealth or poverty indicators, nudity, presence of technology, vantage, and camera gaze. A complete description of these features may be found in Lutz and Collins (1993: 285).

3. In part because of its focus on everyday life, *National Geographic* does not trade in the standardized images of black people that have been common in western art— some of which have been characterized by Honour (1989) as "heroes and martyrs," "the benighted," "the defiant," and "the pacified."

4. This proportion is based on those photos in which adults of identifiable gender are shown (N = 510). Another 11 percent show women and men together in roughly equal numbers, leaving 65 percent of the photos depicting mainly men.

5. The popularity of this notion in American culture, which *National Geographic* relies on as much as feeds, is also one wellspring for American feminism's focus on universal sisterhood, that is, its insistence, particularly in the 1970s, that Western and non-Western women will easily see each other as similar or sharing similar experiences.

6. Edward Steichen's *Family of Man* exhibition, first displayed in the United States in 1955, also included a substantial section devoted to mothers and infants, nicknamed "Tits and Tots" by the staff of photographers who organized it (Meltzer 1978). This exhibit was immensely popular when it toured, and the catalogue became a bestselling book.

7. This is based on the twenty photos in our sample of 592, where women are shown without shirts on; half of that number occurred from 1950 to 1969 and the other half from 1970 to 1986 (one would, of course, expect there to be somewhat fewer such photos as urbanization and change in dress styles spread across the globe). Some of the same phenomena noted here have been found in advertising in American family magazines (that is, a decrease in images of married women shown in child care and an increase in those showing them at recreation), although in the latter ads the trends begin earlier, in the later 1940s (Brown 1981).

8. The *Geographic*'s breasts should be seen against the broader background of the social changes in the industrial West around sexuality. Foucault (1978) has noted that those changes have been mistakenly associated with a "liberation" of sexuality. In fact, he suggests, with the emergence of the modern state and its regulatory needs has come an obsession with "talking" about and managing sex—through science, state policy, clinical medicine, and now photography.

9. That step may have been taken by white feminism as well, hooks points out: "When the women's movement was at its peak and white women were rejecting the role of breeder, burden bearer, and sex object, black women were celebrated for their unique devotion to the task of mothering; for their 'innate' ability to bear tremendous burdens; and for their ever-increasing availability as sex object. We appeared to have been unanimously elected to take up where white women were leaving off" (1981: 6). See Hammond and Jablow 1977 for an analysis of the particular strength of the notion of non-white women as beasts of burden in the case of African women; see also Collins (1991).

10. Western feminism in the 1970s may have simply transformed rather than fundamentally challenged the terms of this argument as well when it argued that the women of the world were oppressed by men and to be liberated by feminism as defined in the West (see Amos and Parmar 1984).

11. Although feminist anthropology has analyzed and critiqued these kinds of assumptions, it has

nonetheless often continued a basic evolutionary discourse in the assumption that Ong has identified: "Although a common past may be claimed by feminists, Third World women are often represented as mired in it, ever arriving at modernity when Western feminists are already adrift in postmodernism" (1988: 87).

References

Abramson, Howard S. 1987. *National Geographic: Behind America's Lens on the World.* New York: Crown.

Amos, V., and Prathiba Parmar. 1984. Challenging Imperial Feminism. *Feminist Review* 17: 3–20.

Betterton, Rosemary, ed. 1987. *Looking On: Images of Femininity in the Visual Arts and Media.* London: Pandora.

Bhabha, Homi K. 1983. The Other Question—Homi K. Bhabha Reconsiders the Stereotype and Colonial Discourse. *Screen* 24(6): 18–36.

Botting, Wendy. 1988. *Posing for Power/Posing for Pleasure: Photographies and the Social Construction of Femininity.* Binghamton, NY. University Art Gallery.

Brown, Bruce W. 1981. *Images of Family Life in Magazine Advertising: 1920–1978.* New York: Praeger.

Canaan, Joyce. 1984. Building Muscles and Getting Curves: Gender Differences in Representations of the Body and Sexuality among American Teenagers. Paper Presented at the Annual Meeting of the American Anthropological Association, Denver.

Carby, Hazel. 1985. "On the Threshold of Woman's Era": Lynching, Empire and Sexuality in Black Feminist Theory. In *Race, Writing and Difference,* ed. H. Gates, pp. 301–16. Chicago: University of Chicago Press.

Carson, Claybourne. 1981. In *Struggle: SNCC and the Black Awakening of the 1960s.* Cambridge: Harvard University Press.

Chafe, William. 1983. Social Change and the American Woman, 1940–70. In *A History of Our Time: Readings on Postwar America,* ed. William Chafe and Harvard Sitkoff, pp. 147–65. New York: Oxford University Press.

Clifford, James. 1988. *The Predicament of Culture: Twentieth-Century Ethnography, Literature and Art.*

Cambridge, Mass.: Harvard University Press.

Collins, Patricia Hill. 1991. *Black Feminist Thought.* Boston: Unwin Hyman.

Ehrenreich, Barbara and Deirdre English. 1978. *For Her Own Good: 150 Years of the Experts' Advice to Women.* Garden City, NY: Anchor Press/Doubleday.

Etienne, Mona, and Eleanor Leacock. 1980. *Women and Colonization: Anthropological Perspectives.* New York: Praeger.

Fanon, Frantz. 1965. *A Dying Colonialism.* New York: Grove Press.

Foucault, Michel. 1978. *The History of Sexuality.* Vol. 1, trans. R. Hurley. New York: Random House.

Gaines, Jane. 1988. White Privilege and Looking Relations: Race and Gender in Feminist Film Theory. *Screen* 29 (4): 12–27.

Gates, Henry Louis, Jr. 1985. Writing "Race" and the Difference it Makes. In *"Race," Writing, and Difference,* ed. H. L. Gates, pp. 1–20. Chicago: University of Chicago Press.

Gilman, Sander. 1985. *Difference and Pathology: Stereotypes of Sexuality, Race, and Madness.* Ithaca: Cornell University Press.

Goffman, Erving. 1979. *Gender Advertisements.* New York: Harper and Row.

Graham-Brown, Sarah. 1988. *Images of Women: The Portrayal of Women in Photography of the Middle East, 1860–1950.* London: Quartet Books.

Hammond, Dorothy and Alta Jablow. 1977. *The Myth of Africa.* New York: Library of Social Science.

Haraway, Donna. 1989. *Primate Visions: Gender, Race, and Nature in the World of Modern Science.* New York: Routledge.

Harding, Vincent. 1981. *There Is a River: The Black Struggle for Freedom in America.* New York: Harcourt Brace Jovanovich.

Hess, Thomas B., and Linda Nochlin. 1972. *Women as Sex Object: Studies in Erotic Art, 1730–1970.* New York: Newsweek Books.

Honour, Hugh. 1989. The Image of the Black in Western Art. Vol. 4, *From the American Revolution to World War I.* New York: Morrow.

hooks, bell. 1981. *Ain't I a Women? Black Women and Feminism.* Boston: South End.

Jeffords, Susan. 1989. *The Remasculinization of America: Gender and the Vietnam War.* Bloomington: Indiana University Press.

Kabbani, Rana. 1986. *Europe's Myths of the Orient.* Bloomington: Indiana University Press.

Krasniewicz, Louise. 1990. Desecrating the Patriotic Body: Flag Burning, Art Censorship, and the Powers of "Protoypical Americans." Paper presented at the Annual Meeting of the American Anthropological Association, New Orleans.

Lutz, Catherine A. and Jane L. Collins. 1993. *Reading National Geographic.* Chicago: University of Chicago Press.

Margolis, Maxine. 1984. *Mothers and Such.* Berkeley and Los Angeles: University of California Press.

May, Elaine Tyler. 1988. *Homeward Bound: American Families in the Cold War Era.* New York: Basic Books.

Meltzer, Milton. 1978. *Dorothea Lange: A Photographer's Life.* New York: Farrar Straus Giroux.

Moore, Henrietta. 1988. *Feminism and Anthropology.* Cambridge: Cambridge University Press.

Myers, Kathy. 1987. Towards a Feminist Erotica. In *Looking On,* ed. R. Betterton, pp. 189–202. London: Pandora.

Nead, Lynda. 1990. The Female Nude: Pornography, Art, and Sexuality. *Signs* 15: 323–35.

Omi, Michael, and Howard Winant. 1986. *Racial Formation in the United States: From the 1960s to the 1980s.* New York: Routledge.

Ong, Aihwa. 1988. Colonialization and Modernity: Feminist Representation of Women in Non-Western Societies. *Inscriptions* 3/4: 79–93.

Ortner, Sherry. 1974. Is Female to Male as Nature is to Culture? In *Woman, Culture and Society,* ed. M. Rosaldo and L. Lamphere, pp. 67–88. Stanford: Stanford University Press.

Rydell, Robert. 1984. *All the World's a Fair: Visions of Empire at American International Expositions, 1876–1916.* Chicago: University of Chicago Press.

Sacks, Karen. 1989. Toward a Unified Theory of Class, Race and Gender. *American Ethnologist* 16: 534–50.

Schaffer, Kay. 1988. *Women and the Bush: Forces of Desire in the Australian Cultural Tradition.* Cambridge: Cambridge University Press.

Schick, Irvin Cemil. 1990. Representing Middle Eastern Women: Feminism and Colonial Discourse. *Feminist Studies* 16(2): 345–80.

Tiffany, Sharon, and Kathleen Adams. 1985. *The Wild Woman: An Inquiry into the Anthropology of an Idea.* Cambridge, Mass.: Schenkman.

Torgovnick, Marianna. 1990. *Gone Primitive: Savage Intellects, Modern Lives.* Chicago: University of Chicago Press.

Traube, Elizabeth G. 1989. Secrets of Success in Postmodern Society. *Cultural Anthropology* 4: 273–300.

Trinh Minh-Ha. 1989. *Woman, Native, Other: Writing Postcoloniality and Feminism.* Bloomington: Indiana University Press.

Vance, Carol. 1990. The Pleasures of Looking: The Attorney General's Commission on Pornography versus Visual Images. In *The Critical Image,* ed. Carol Squires, pp. 38–58. Seattle: Bay Press.

Wallace, Michele. 1990. *Invisibility Blues: From Pop to Theory.* London: Verso.

Wolf, Naomi. 1991. *The Beauty Myth: How Images of Beauty Are Used Against Women.* New York: Morrow.

Young, Iris Marion. 1990. Breasted Experience. In *Throwing Like a Girl and Other Essays in Feminist Philosophy and Social Theory,* ed. I. M. Young. Bloomington: Indiana University Press.

 Article Review Form at end of book.

How does Nike's advertising strategy involve global discourses on race, ethnicity, and gender?

We Said We Wanted a Revolution:

Race, Ethnicity, and the Political Economics of Marketing/Representation by Nike

Ruth Goldman

There Is a Girl Being Born in America*

There is a girl being born in America,
And somebody will tell her she is
    beautiful,
and somebody will tell her she is strong.
Somebody will tell her she is precious,
and somebody will tell her she is tough.
There is a girl being born in America,
and someone will give her a doll,
and someone will give her a ball,
and then someone will give her
    a chance.

> —Nike Corporation's "Women's
> Empowerment Campaign" (1997).

The visuals that accompany this text constitute an advertisement that is not your standard commercial network television fare. The young female narrator stares intently into the camera and her voice is strong, sincere, and packed with emotion. The images that flash before your eyes all feature girls, from a variety of racial and age groups, playing, learning, or simply, boldly, staring into the camera. The camera angles are seductively empowering. The emphasis is on action: the camera lingers only for a moment to caress a face, to capture a goalie diving for a ball, or to highlight a forward surging

*Taken from Nike's "Women's Empowerment Campaign," courtesy of Nike Inc.

upward for a shot at the basket. These active, empowered, multicultural girls play for Nike, and in addition to playing with dolls and balls, they play, quite simply, with our heartstrings.

But they also play with our conscience; the underlying political message is that girls of all races don't yet have a *fair* chance, and it is up to us—the "someone" of the text—to give them that chance. Obviously then, this neither sounds nor looks like your average product advertisement. And it isn't; according to Dan Wieden, a partner in Wieden & Kennedy, Nike's primary advertisement agency:

> The process of creating brands and relationships is also the process by which you create the values our culture operates on, so it has a huge ethical component. The ethical dimension makes our work seem like much more than the movement of goods and services. (Wieden in Willigan, 1992: 97)

For Nike then, the emphasis is on much more than just selling athletic products. Nike is also selling cultural values and a particular brand of social issues.

Such emotionally captivating and profoundly empowering advertising has become emblematic of Nike. Nike strives to be different.

Nike wants to provoke thought. As Wieden explains, "Being provocative is ultimately more important than being pleasant." (Ibid.) Through such advertising techniques, Nike strives to "build emotional ties"[1] with its audience, and judging from its ad campaigns and philanthropic practices, Nike is particularly interested in capturing the attention of marginalized groups like women and people of color.

The women's empowerment ad campaign was conceptualized in the late 1980s when Nike realized that a key to growth lay in capturing the blossoming women's fitness market. Therefore, Nike mounted a sort of grassroots campaign, speaking with hundreds of women throughout the U.S. in order to find out what women really wanted to see in advertising. Not surprisingly, the original women's empowerment print ads were phenomenally popular from the moment they appeared. Just eight weeks after their introduction, Nike had received more than 50,000 phone calls requesting reprints and offering support for both the ads and the company. In that same year, Nike had a "40% increase in women's business." (Savan, 1993: 44)

Ruth Goldman, "We Said We Wanted a Revolution." Reprinted with permission.

But this is only a small part of an incredibly innovative, unique, and popular advertising campaign that Nike has been waging for the past ten years. And this campaign, along with others employing progressive rhetoric, helped Nike pocket a whopping $9.2 billion dollars in 1997—to which many people from the marginalized groups—especially people of color—represented in the ads no doubt contributed. Nike CEO Philip Knight explains Nike's advertising campaigns in this way, "what really matters in the long run is that the message means something. . . . You have to convey what the company is really all about, what it is that Nike is really trying to do." (Knight in Willigan, 1992: 100)

But what is it that Nike is really trying to do? Although Nike commercials offer stunningly empowering images of athletes, women and men of color, physically disabled people, older people, white women and girls, and people with HIV, Nike's corporate image as a progressive multinational corporation deserves further interrogation. As we shall see, Nike's history is full of contradictions characterized by savvy, risky, and, some would argue, unethical business practices that have made it the unquestionable leader in the sport shoe industry. But most important for my purposes here, the history of this phenomenally popular corporation inextricably involves global discourses of race, ethnicity, and gender. By illustrating the ways in which Nike's women's empowerment advertising campaign employs feminist discourses that implicitly critique the system through which Nike exploits women of color in their labor and production practices, I intend to prove that the two spheres of advertising and production are not only intricately related but that Nike's phenomenal success and progressive reputation depends on that in-

terrelation. In doing so, I hope to present a political economy of representations which illustrates that Nike employs dualistic, or two-tiered, strategies in both production and marketing practices, in order to maintain what amounts to an insidiously duplicitous and ultimately typical type of hegemony for a corporation operating in a late capitalist and increasingly global economy.

In the early part of this decade, Nike ran a controversial commercial for its new product, Visible Air, that featured the Beatle's song "Revolution." According to Philip Knight, Nike began the "Revolution Campaign" (aka "Just Do It") because, "[w]e wanted to communicate not just a radical departure in shoes but a revolution in the way Americans felt about fitness, exercise, and wellness." (Knight in Willigan, 1992: 99) Judging from the popular and press reception, Nike's "Just Do It" advertising campaign, whether addressing athletes in general or any of the socially disempowered groups often featured, represents a revolution in terms of advertising and network commercial television representations. The controversy surrounding Nike's use of the Beatles' song stemmed from Nike's choice to use a song that was part of the 1960s and 1970s progressive movement for social change to advertise a shoe, apparently undermining the original intent of the song. As we shall see, however, stripping the movement from the message is a strategy with which Nike is quite comfortable.

In discussing the economic and political conditions that led to a move to control labor in the 1970s, David Harvey argues that "to the degree that collective action was thereby made more difficult . . . so rampant individualism fits into place as a necessary . . . condition for the transition from Fordism to flexible accumulation." (Harvey, 1990: 171) Since rampant

individualism has also fueled the increase in the consumption of goods, it seems to me that it's possible to apply a related argument to the corporate co-optation of counter-cultural values and practices which stress collective action. For example, as any of their socially progressive ads illustrate, Nike's use of social change movement rhetoric to sell its products neatly preserves the rhetoric while effectively obscuring any collective movement that might have accompanied such a message. In fact, one could even argue that Nike is, on some level, trying to insert itself as the movement.

One recent example from their women's empowerment advertising campaign is an ad called "If You Let Me Play." This ad features close-ups of a racially mixed collection of young girls, who one after the other, stare solemnly into the camera and make a plea for equal rights for girls—at least on the playing field. Their first person narrative, detailing benefits of playing sports like increases in self-esteem and decreases in risk of breast cancer and early pregnancy, is nothing less than haunting. Its script reads:

If You Let Me Play*

I will like myself more
I will have more self-confidence
I will suffer less depression
I will be 60% less likely to get breast cancer
I will be less likely to get pregnant before I want to
I will be more likely to leave a man who beats me
I will learn what it means to be strong.
If you let me play sports.

Like Nike's other empowerment ads, this analysis of sexism and discrimination against women includes only the signature Swoosh at the end, giving the ad the feel of a Public Service Announcement rather than an advertisement for a product. This stylistic tactic is in accordance with Nike's advertising strategy, which, if you remember, is

*Taken from Nike's "Women's Empowerment Campaign," courtesy of Nike Inc.

less about "goods and services," and more about "emotional ties."

But what makes this particular ad stand out is its consciously political stance. In fact, *Adweek* writer Debra Goldman calls "If You Let Me Play," "[t]he most effective political ad I've seen in the last 12 months"—quite a feat for a shoe company! According to Goldman, Nike's ad surpasses current political advertising because, "What this ad does that conventional political ads do not even attempt is to create a constituency. The response of consumers who warm to its message is coherent; one can actually deduce something about their values from their reaction." (Goldman, 1996)

Indeed, by producing ads such as "If You Let Me Play," as well as ads featuring men of color, like the Ric Munoz ad that draws attention to the lives of people with HIV disease, Spike Lee ads targeting racism, and Tiger Woods ads tackling segregation in the golfing world, Nike is clearly, if sometimes indirectly, setting itself up as an ally in the movement for progressive social change. But if the business of advertising is ultimately sales, as Goldman notes, Nike is not only aligning itself with, but is in fact, *selling* a particular left-of-center *brand of values*. In fact, what Nike is doing—indirectly—is highlighting systemic imperfections, and thus, as Goldman notes, trying to further strengthen "emotional ties" with a particular group, or constituency— in this case, a constituency that has historically been disenfranchised.

The fact that Nike's followers *do* have emotional—and one could argue quasi-political—ties to Nike[2], illustrates Nike's revolutionary potential; they appear to be addressing not simply specialized niche market segments, but actual individuals. One prime example is Nike's popularity in the African-American community. According to a number of African-American scholars and activists, due to Nike's endorsements of African-American athletes, empowering media representations, and apparent respect for Black street culture, Nike is perceived as a company that cares about Black youth. According to political analyst Earl Ofari Hutchinson, "Young African-American males are so marginalized, and so devalued, and here you've got a corporation that's saying, 'Hey, we not only value your dollar, but we also value you as a person.' " (quoted in Alexander, 1997) And thus Nike successfully transcends what is rapidly becoming the out-moded model of the rigid, monolithic corporation, and instead represents more of a progressive community or political organization: something one joins or supports. In other words, we can experience and participate in the revolution—or a revolution— simply by buying athletic products and supporting the Nike global (counter)cultural nation.

However, as I have hope I have begun to make clear, Nike's use of counter-cultural rhetoric is characteristic of post-Fordist aesthetics. As Harvey explains, "[t]he relatively stable aesthetic of Fordist modernism has given way to all the ferment, instability and fleeting qualities of a postmodernist aesthetic that celebrates difference, ephemerality, spectacle, fashion, and the commodification of cultural forms." (Harvey, 1990: 156) Nike, therefore, is taking part in a strategy that, if revolutionary, is simply part of a regime of corporate practices—a new sleight of hand from the same bag of corporate tricks. A similar practice is Nike's use of strategic philanthropy. The majority of Nike's corporate donations involve athletics in some way; their P.L.A.Y. (Participate in the Lives of America's Youths) campaign is the most obvious and well publicized example.[3] By choosing and publicizing philanthropic goals related to their mission, corporations like Nike hope to enhance their corporate image, which, as Harvey reminds us, is essential to the success of today's corporations. As Phil Knight himself explains,

I've always believed that businesses should be good citizens . . . But the thing I was missing until recently is the issue of visibility . . . It's not enough to do good things. You have to let people know what you're doing." (quoted in Willigan, 1992: 101)

Practices like Nike's strategic philanthropy combined with its adoption of counter-cultural rhetoric and endorsements of prominent athletes of color and white female athletes function to deflect criticism away from Nike's internal corporate sexism and racism as well as its exploitative production practices. Ultimately, the promotion of equal opportunity in athletics strengthens their consumer base while posing no concrete threat to the system that sustains them.

From a business perspective, the success of Nike's revolutionary campaign is undeniable. Even with its recent slump, Nike continues to post a hefty profit and command an astounding 47% share of the athletic footwear market. Based on the fact that Nike and Reebok "sell more than half the athletic footwear in the U.S., and control over 40% of the global market," *Fortune* magazine represents the company's success using a pie chart with the caption: "Pursuing Hegemony at Home and Abroad." (Labich, 1995: 97-98) Although it seems likely that *Fortune* is referring to Nike's and Reebok's struggle to maintain control over the global shoe market, Stuart Hall explains, "we must take note of the multi-dimensional, multi-arena character of hegemony . . . It represents mastery over a whole series of different 'positions' at once . . . Effectively, it results from winning a substantial degree of popular consent." (Hall, 1996: 424) If we apply this concept to Nike, what we find is the maintenance of economic hegemony in the athletic shoe market, as well as a type of (counter)cultural hegemony amongst groups of consumers. However, as we shall see, Nike's particular brand of hegemony is inherently duplicitous.

Nike is building economic and (counter)cultural hegemony by strengthening emotional ties with consumers through strategic philanthropy and cutting-edge advertising that targets social issues like racism and sexism. In the meantime, however, Nike's gaining an increasing stronghold on the sports industry through sponsorship of major sports events, high school and college athletic programs, and individual professional athletes, while simultaneously exploiting hundreds of thousands of young Asian workers, most of whom are women.

The sphere of production is where Nike, the good company, the "brand that cares," the corporation that declares, "NIKE has always valued the global diversity of our employees, our athletes, and our customers, and we are committed to a work place based upon performance and respect" begins to look even more hypocritical. ("Nike" WWW) If, as Dan Wieden indicates, Nike's current advertising campaign is quite consciously designed to deflect attention away from "goods and services," and onto the (counter)cultural values the corporation seems to be selling, then it is essential to examine the production practices that have enabled Nike to become such a celebrated global entity.

Nike began producing shoes under a different name in the early 1970s and from the start, Philip Knight figured out that the key to profit was to move the production of Nikes out of this country and into industrially developing countries—mostly populated by people of color— where wages were lower and labor unions were either weak or illegal. In fact, as

Harvey points out, Nike was at the forefront of another revolution that involved women:

The transition to flexible accumulation has . . . been marked by a revolution (by no means progressive) in the role of women in labour markets and labour processes during a period when the women's movement has fought for both greater awareness and improved conditions for what is now more than 40 per cent of the labour force in many of the advanced capitalist countries. (Harvey, 1990: 155)

In the 1980s, scholars began to note the existence of a global trend toward what economist Guy Standing calls "the feminization of labor." Standing and others have argued that it is supply-side economics, which emphasizes export-oriented manufacturing, that "has led to a series of changes in women's economic roles, increasing their use as workers but weakening their income and employment security in both low-income industrializing and industrialized countries." (Standing, 1989: 1077) And Nike's dependence on cheap, temporary, and non-unionized labor is not limited to Asia. Like a number of other large corporations, Nike has begun to replace permanent salaried workers in the U.S. with temporary workers, most of whom are women. According to Ann Crittenden, writing in *Working Woman* magazine,

In companies like General Electric, Johnson & Johnson and Nike, where some regular employees have been replaced by lower-paid temps and contract workers, a de facto two-tier wage system has emerged. At Nike's distribution center in Memphis, for example, dozens of temporaries earn $6.50 an hour, with no health benefits, for the same work done by permanent employees earning at least $13 an hour in wages and benefits. (Crittenden, 1994: Lexis/Nexis)

Thus, what the *Far Eastern Economic Review* refers to as "The New Nike Economy" is beginning to emerge in this country as well.

The abolition of protectionist policies like international trade tariffs and the establishment of Free

Trade Zones (FTZs)[4] within industrially developing countries has enabled United States manufacturing corporations, like Japanese corporations, to participate in a flexible labor system which relies on low-cost labor situated in developing countries. Thus, U.S. based multinational corporations now use contract workers, temporary workers (the majority of whom are women and many of whom are women of color), and out-sourcing instead of the salaried (and often unionized) full-time workers employed in the U.S. manufacturing industry before the 1980s.

Furthermore, Nike has taken full advantage of relaxations of tariffs and the growth of free trade as well as the shift from centralized to diversified systems of production. In fact, according to the *Far Eastern Economic Review*, one Nike shoe is made up of as many as 52 different components from five different countries. Furthermore, "A single pair of Nike shoes is touched by more than 120 pairs of hands during production." ("The New Nike," 8/29/96: 5) Many of those hands are hands of people of color. By diversifying the production process, Nike is able to minimize costs and maximize profits. In a nutshell, according to Bennett Harrison:

The Nike production system is organized into two broad tiers. In the first of these tiers, 'developed partners' located mainly in Taiwan and South Korea work closely with the R&D [research & design] personnel in Oregon to make the firm's most expensive, high-end footwear . . . The second tier . . . consists of the many material, component, and subassembly sources. (Harrison, 1994: 492-3)

Ultimately, according to Harrison, this two-tiered system "remains a dualistic system, combining high-wage and low-wage, specialized and standardized production, core and periphery." (Ibid: 493) For Nike, the core is mainly white, American, and male, while the periphery is mainly female and Asian. Furthermore, unlike previous centralized, rigid—or Fordist—systems of production, this diversification allows Nike to be flexible; as Michael Donaghu and Richard Barff explain, "Nike has a history of shifting production between factories and countries. It has opened plants and begun contracts only to end them within a matter of a year or two." (Donaghu & Barff, 1990: 547) In reality, what this has meant is that Nike, which began producing shoes in Japan and the United States in the early 1970s, has subcontracted factories in a total of thirteen countries over the past eighteen years. They ended production in the U.S. in 1986, have subcontracted facilities in a number of Asian and European countries, and now produce about 75% of their shoes in China, Indonesia, and Vietnam.

Nike's been lauded by the financial press as being at the forefront of yet another type of revolution, by taking advantage of strategies of flexible production and predicting the economic growth of late industrializing countries like Indonesia. According to Tony Tassell of *The Financial Times,* "now the Nike trainer has been adapted as a gauge of economic performance for developing countries in Asia." (Tassell, 1997: 22) A recent study by broker Robert Fleming proclaims that, " '[w]here Nike produces, economies roar . . . So far every country that Nike has produced sneakers in has seen high, long-term economic growth." (Ibid.) Furthermore, the *Far Eastern Economic Review* devoted a series of five editorials to "the new Nike economy," ultimately proclaiming, "the future looks a lot like Nike." ("The New Nike, " 1996) Not surprisingly, Nike has been quick to take credit for rising wages and increases in GNPs in countries where it produces.

Although per capita incomes and GNPs have risen in many Southeast Asian NICs (newly industrialized countries) and industrially developing countries, income distribution is by no means equitable.[5] In fact, these gross gains and averages mask micro-level realities. For example in the case of Indonesia, *Chicago Tribune* writer Merrill Goozner explains that "the distribution of this new wealth is wildly skewed. While tens of millions of workers . . . live on $60 a month, a U.S. marketing executive estimated there are four million households in Indonesia earning more than $50,000 a year" (Goozner, 1994).

However, wages *have* risen considerably since 1987, when Nike began subcontracting in Indonesia. For example, in April of 1995, the minimum wage was $1.89 per day, while one year later it was $2.37 per day. Nike has consistently claimed credit for the rise in wages. But according to the Indonesian government, the latter amount still only covered 93% of subsistence needs. Furthermore, John Cavanaugh and Robin Broad explain that the rise in wages is a direct result of pressure from labor-rights activists who filed a petition with the U.S. government's trade office, "charging that Indonesia allows systematic violation of workers' rights" and recommending that the U.S. government should move to revoke "special trade privileges under a 1984 law that conditions the privileges on countries' respect for those rights." The result was that the Indonesian government, fearing trade restrictions, raised the minimum wage by 29%, and thus, "Nike and other manufacturing companies have been *forced* to raise wages."[my italics] (Cavanaugh & Broad, 1996) However, even despite such government intervention, many Nike factories were able to obtain exemptions from paying minimum wage. (Manning, 1997C; O'Rourke, 1998)

But how does all of this affect individual women in countries where Nike produces? Let's look a little more closely at the situation in Indonesia, where Nike maintains four to six subcontractors, on an as-needed basis. (Gargan, 35) From all accounts, young women of color who comprise 80% of the work force in Nike's Indonesian factories feel that factory work is beneficial in a number of different ways. In particular, it frees them from long hours of work at home or in the fields, gives them a certain amount of independence from their parents and families, and provides them with individual wages.

But the overall picture is not so encouraging. In fact, working women in industrially developing countries historically have been paid less than subsistence wages—that is, less than they need to survive.[6] For example, in Central Java, Indonesia, anthropologist Diane Wolf found that male factory workers were paid 50% more than females with the underlying justification that male factory work was more difficult, and that males would have families to support. However, in reality, the tasks that males performed were not more difficult than those of their female counterparts and most of the male factory workers did not yet have families to support (Wolf, 1992: 118). Furthermore, since young women are often expected to continue to contribute financially to the rural families they've left behind, Standing questions the validity of "earnings or income data" as "valid measures of women's net disposable income," arguing that, "taking account of deductions by intermediaries, including relatives, it is likely that large and growing proportions of women workers receive much lower net incomes . . . " (Standing, 1989: 1093)

But low wages aren't the only problems facing these young women. Other problems include high incidences of physical and sexual harassment and abuse and prolonged exposure to toxic chemicals and unsafe working conditions. Some of the most sensational incidents of abuse in Nike factories have taken place in Vietnam where Korean or Chinese supervisors, with their strict notions of discipline, often clash horribly with workers not used to working for private employers under stressful conditions. For example, Schwartz relates an incident that took place in a Vietnamese factory in March of 1996: South Korean supervisor Jang Mi Baek, "[a]ngered by the quality of work in her sewing department . . . lined up 15 female workers and beat them about the face and hands with an unfinished shoe." (Schwartz, 63: 1996) Vietnamese-American businessman Thuyen Nguyen conducted his own investigation of Nike factories in Vietnam and reported shocking incidents such as workers forced to stand out in the sun until they passed out and had to be rushed to the emergency room, or workers forced to run laps around the factory as punishment for infractions like wearing the wrong shoes to work. (Herbert, 1997A & 1997B) Furthermore, Manning reports that Vo Thi Oanh, a young Vietnamese woman, was fired for spending too much time in the bathroom. (Manning, 1997B)

And the problems aren't just limited to Vietnam. The majority of Nike's subcontracting facilities are located in China and Indonesia, both of which have notoriously repressive governments. Most of the facilities sound like they're run like boot camps, with training consisting in partly of marching around the factory. (Manning, 1997A) In Indonesia, countless Nike workers have been fired, harassed, arrested, and held without charges for striking or trying to organize workers. (INGI, 1991; Clifford, 1996)

Ironically, conditions in Nike's factories are clearly some of the best in all of these countries—even observers critiquing the company note that the factories are much newer and are nicer looking than their counterparts in the U.S.—but by all accounts, health

and safety conditions are still substandard. An internal report submitted to Nike by Ernst & Young, an accounting company Nike hired to inspect its factories, indicates that at one factory in Vietnam, workers "were exposed to carcinogens that exceeded local legal standards by 177 times in parts of the plant and that 77 percent of the employees suffered from respiratory problems." (Greenhouse, 1997B) Furthermore, according to Australian researcher Anita Chan, "In many Chinese footwear factories . . . workers . . . are exposed to extremely toxic glue solvents . . . without protective gear or proper ventilation." (Chan, 1997) And Community Aid Abroad reports that in Indonesia workers routinely lost fingers in the machinery and that workers handling chemicals suffered from respiratory and skin diseases. (Community Aid Abroad, 1996) A report from the Asia Monitor Resource Centre and the Hong Kong Christian Industrial Committee lists similar problems within Chinese factories. (AMRC & HKCIC, 1997) Nike's response to criticisms of such conditions has been typically nonchalant. According to reporter Jeff Manning, "Dusty Kidd, manager of Nike's labor practices department, downplayed the danger, saying most workers' exposure is limited because they don't stay more than two or three years in the factories." (Manning, 1997C)

Of course, this is probably the only benefit of the short-term employment Nike guarantees for many of its subcontracted employees; because of a sharp decline in demand for its products this past fall, Nike canceled all orders to four subcontracting facilities, effectively laying off more than 50,000 workers. Although Nike often deflects criticisms of conditions in its factories by citing the "hope" these jobs bring to workers in industrially developing countries, in reality while some workers do hold jobs long

enough to save some of their earnings and increase their standard of living, others make barely enough to survive. (Gargan, 1996; Manning, 1997C) Furthermore, because of its flexible strategies of production, Nike can easily—and routinely does—close up one factory and open another.

Indeed, although Knight loves to take responsibility for rising wages in countries in which Nike produces, when those wages get too high, Nike leaves. As Fleming's study reports, "While rising production of Nike trainers in a country may indicate growth prospects, a fall could signify a maturing of its economy." (Tassell, 1997: 22) What happens to the workers abandoned by Nike is never discussed though. And as we have already seen, rising GNPs and per capita incomes do not benefit populations equally. In fact, although the "revolution for women" or new "feminization of the economy" I mentioned earlier, provides women with limited new opportunities, it also carries with it some serious problems. One of these problems involves the flexibility of the new system that allows corporations much greater mobility but leaves the mainly female workforce, extremely vulnerable to fluctuations in foreign markets or local economies, as recent events in Asia illustrate all too well.

The main reason that development strategies that target young, single, poor women of color for factory jobs in multinational industrial manufacturing plants featuring low wages, few benefits, and poor working conditions have been so successful is that they draw upon and replicate existing patriarchal power structures that construct women as inferior to men. These ideologies are forged and reinforced locally, nationally, and globally through a combination of state policies (with international and especially Western influences)[7], local and cultural norms, and capitalist transnational discourses.

Although state policies are normally characterized as top-down, Aihwa Ong, in her study of factory workers in Malaysia explains that the system is much more insidious:

Ideological domination operated not necessarily as a coherent system of statements issued from above, but rather through a complex series of mechanisms whereby meaning was coded and mobilized in the daily activities of the *Kampung* folk: in development projects, school programs, welfare services, party politicking, and religious practice. (Ong, 1987: 218)

This is consistent with the findings of a number of ethnographers in Java; patriarchal control is maintained through structural development programs which recognize men as heads of households and primary wage-earners, state policies which recognize women only in domestic and reproductive roles,[8] Islamic religious tenets which affirm the superiority of men over women, and hierarchical structures within factories which replicate cultural norms in featuring males in positions of authority (owners, managers. etc.) and women in positions of inferiority (workers) (Mather, 1983; Wolf, 1992; Blackwood, 1995). Furthermore, as mentioned before, women themselves prefer factory work to their other, albeit severely limited, options.

In addition, according to Aiwha Ong, there is a discourse produced by transnational capitalism which "naturalize[s] the subordination of women in industrial enterprises." (Ong, 1991: 291) Racist and sexist representations of Asian women as docile and diligent workers add another layer to this discourse. Wolf found that according to factory owners and managers in rural Java, female workers were preferable to male workers because "[f]emales were thought to be easier to control . . . quicker, and more diligent" (Wolf, 1992: 116). And Dara O'Rourke, a consultant to the United

Nations Industrial Development Organization (UNIDO) who in 1997 conducted an independent audit of a Tae Kwang Vina, a Korean owned Nike subcontracting facility in Vietnam, was given similar justifications from managers when questioned about their preference for women workers. (O'Rourke, 1998)

But if at this point it seems like we've entered a world far from the one represented by Nike's advertising, we are deceived. Those socially progressive Nike ads are in fact critiquing—if indirectly—the very system that Nike itself supports through its global and diverse manufacturing practices. According to Nike's own figures in 1995, labor accounted for $1.66 or 2.4 *per cent* of the entire cost of a $70 Pegasus shoe, while Nike's cut accounted for $22.95 or 33 *per cent* of the entire cost of the shoe. (cited in Enloe, 1995: 12) In 1996, Nike spent only $216 million, or 2.3 *per cent* of its sales on capital costs and $978 million, or 10.7 *percent*—three times as much—on advertising. (Manning, 1997A) The irrefutable fact is that the denial of livable wages for young women of color laborers in Southeast Asia ensures ample amounts of money for Nike advertisements which promote young women of color in this country.

Ironically, Nike's highly successful advertising campaign has also been one of the key elements in the process that has rendered the company vulnerable to criticism. Nike has spent years and considerable amounts of money building an image, and the particular image it has cultivated has made the company even more vulnerable than some of its competitors. Because the corporation has marketed itself almost as a movement for social change that dares to be different by confronting incredibly entrenched systemic problems like racism and sexism, it is no small wonder that activists and consumers alike, upon realizing the hypocrisy of Nike's

position, have lashed back with a vengeance, again and again demanding that Nike "Just Do It" when it comes to improving labor conditions.

Nike's strategy for combating this problem is complex and has changed significantly over time. At first, Nike's management was more than willing to ignore reports of problems, advocating a "hands off" policy for its subcontracting facilities. For example, in 1991, Nike's Indonesian general manager was asked about incidents of abuse in the factories. His reply was, "It's not within our scope to investigate" (quoted in Cavanaugh & Broad, 1996) However, as accusations of problems multiplied, management began to respond to problems more directly. For example, in response to an article by Bob Herbert of *The New York Times*, Phil Knight writes, "Nike has paid, on average, double the minimum wage as defined in countries where its products are produced under contract. This in addition to free meals, housing and health care and transportation subsidies." (Knight, 1996) But although Nike continues to trot out similar statistics, as we have already seen, there is a growing amount of evidence to contradict its claims. Reporter Jeff Manning explains that, according to Nike officials themselves, "through much of the 1990s, Nike-aligned apparel and footwear factories in Indonesia received government exemptions from paying even the minimum wage." (Manning, 1997A) Furthermore, although many workers have made more than minimum wage, this is because they are forced to work many hours of overtime. (Ballinger, 1992; Clifford, 1996; AMRC & HKCIC, 1997) And finally, although Nike does provide their workers with meals, often they are not "free" at all—at some factories, workers' checks are docked for each meal they eat. (Goodman, 1993)

As some of my earlier examples illustrate, Nike has also appealed to a logic clearly drawn from modernization theory to justify its production practices: third world countries must follow the first world model along the path to industrialization in order to successfully develop. According to Philip Knight, "A country like Indonesia is converting from farm labor to semiskilled—an industrial transition that has occurred throughout history. There's no question that we're giving these people hope." (quoted in Katz, 1994: 190) The same sort of paternalistic attitude emanates from Andrew Young's report on conditions in Nike factories. (Young, 1997) But such discourses that posit (white) Western corporations as saviors for their (brown) Eastern workers echo an age-old colonial—and fundamentally racist—discourse.

In defense of Nike, sportswriter Bob Baum argues that, "[f]ar from being an exploiter, Nike sees itself as helping struggling countries emerge in the industrialized world." (Knight in Baum, 1996:Lexis/Nexis) Furthermore, in an interview in April of 1996, Phil Knight told Baum: "We have thousands of people in line for the jobs that we have . . . and they're the best shoe factories in the world, the best conditions." (Knight in Baum, WWW) However, what does it mean to be "the best" within a highly exploitative system structured around gender, racial, and class iniquities?

In fact, current market-oriented development strategies are based on individual and not collective gains. According to a case study on the impacts of industrialization on local communities in central Java, Sudharto Hadi found that "large scale, export oriented and externally controlled industries in Central Java do not benefit local people. The industrial growth centre is economically causing poverty,

socially creating disharmony and environmentally harming the amenities." (Hadi, 1993: 208–9) And it is far from clear to what extent the young women employed in factories like Nike's benefit from their short-term employment. Theoretically, after working in a factory they would gain new skills and be able to advance to the next level—but the reality may be different. As Neoleen Hayzer of the Asian and Pacific Development Center points out, women "are integrated into the lowest ranks of industrial work, and assigned the most monotonous and most mechanized processes on the production line . . . Women are offered little training and therefore have little prospect of upward mobility." (Heyzer, 1989: 1118) Finally, the long term effects of exposure to the types of toxic chemicals these women are exposed to are not yet known; their short-term health is certainly impaired and working in these factories may actually shorten their life spans.

The fact is, although Nike seems willing to take on any issue in their advertising campaigns, they are less than willing to tackle difficult issues in the real world. For example, in 1993 Nike executive Dave Taylor was quoted as saying: "To say that Nike can go into a country like Indonesia with 170 million people, or to China with 1.4 billion, and make a huge impact on what happens there, in labor or human rights or industrialization, is ridiculous." (quoted in Katz, 191: 1994) But let's juxtapose this to Nike's claim that, "When Nike enters a country to manufacture products, wages increase and poverty decreases." ("So You Think . . . " Nike web page) Such a claim undoubtedly derives from studies like Fleming's, which posit Nike as the knight in shining armor for industrially developing countries. However, Fleming's study also points out that "Nike's choice of production locations was an in-

dicator of countries' development, as it was made not just on labour costs but also on criteria such as political stability, staff quality, infrastructure, government 'openness,' duties, and quotas." (Tassel, 1997: 22) And, in the cases of China and Indonesia, where Nike maitains 70% of its production facilities, "political stability" and "government openness" come at the expense of workers' and human rights. Therefore, although Nike is all too willing to take responsibility for rising wages and declining poverty, it, like the majority of other MNCs, has absolutely no desire to take responsibility for addressing these systemic problems. In its 1997 annual report Nike answers such charges by glibly concluding, "We are not here to eliminate poverty and famine or lead the war against violence and crime . . . We are here to inspire and motivate the athlete in all of us and advocate the love of sports."

If a global powerhouse like Nike doesn't think it can effect tangible change in countries like China or Indonesia, it seems peculiar that are they willing to use their advertising campaigns to challenge incredibly entrenched systemic problems like sexism and racism in a big country like the U.S.A. As I've illustrated in the first part of my paper, the truth of the matter is that by using counter-cultural rhetoric Nike has tapped into a discourse that suggests the systemic need for change, but by focusing on one narrow aspect—increased opportunities for minorities in sports—and targeting individual consumers they've successfully elided a systemic critique. Furthermore, the use of progressive rhetoric helps deflect attention away from the corporate regime of practices that sustains Nike's involvement in highly exploitative labor and production practices.

Gramsci's multi-faceted concept of hegemony is useful here because Nike, while supporting a hegemonic economic paradigm that favors unrestricted global trade and a system that centralizes capital amongst an elite few corporations and management personnel, simultaneously publicly opposes a hegemonic social paradigm which denies marginalized groups empowerment through representation, access to leisure time, and presumably greater economic opportunities. Thus, we might say that Nike has achieved a sort of (counter)cultural hegemony that, in fact, would seem to contradict the type of "class-corporate" hegemony through which it participates in the global economic realm. The end product is a duplicitous and ultimately dangerous hegemonic strategy.

The fact that "[t]echnically, Nike doesn't own any factories," ("The New Nike," 8/29/96) has allowed Nike for many years to defer responsibility for the politics and labor practices of the countries in which its shoe production is centralized. As Nike executive Dave Taylor said, "We don't pay anybody at the factories and we don't set policy within the factories; it is their [subcontractors'] business to run." (quoted in Katz, 1994:191) Furthermore, the incredible popularity of Nike products among youth, women, and other subaltern groups, has strengthened Nike's cultural power, and continues to help defer criticisms. Thus, like its production and labor strategies "outside the berm,"[9] whether deliberate or not, Nike employs a two-tiered strategy at the level of representation.

As the editors of the *Far Eastern Economic Review* explain, "What gives Nike sports shoe its value . . . is the stunning combination of factors—design, marketing, delivery, etc. —that together allow a pair of Nikes to command a premium. In other words, it is the process, not the product." ("The New Nike . . . " 10/31/96) But part of this process involves a two-

tiered wage structure and skillful management of the press, as Knight himself attests. And in fact, once you begin to juxtapose Michael Jordan's $20 million dollar a year endorsement contract for part-time work, to factory workers' pathetically small salaries for 60 hour work-weeks, or campaigns that promote women's empowerment to the support of governments or practices which involve the systematic and systemic disempowerment of women workers, another two-tiered system emerges. In this one Nike puts social issues at the top in its advertising and philanthropic campaign/strategy while placing them at the bottom in its economic global production practices.

If, as the financial press and Nike advertisements seem to suggest, Nike is leading a revolution, then it is a revolution made possible only through the logic of a postmodern, transnational capitalist condition. And though the most obvious conclusion would be to call for increased responsibility and ethics on the part of Nike, it is clear that the problem I've presented here is much bigger than Nike. Nike's practices cannot stand alone but must be placed within a corporate regime of practices forged and reinforced at local, national, and global levels. The recent agreement to end sweatshop labor is a step in the right direction, but does nothing to address racial and gender inequities, two of the most firmly entrenched problems within this system. If we are ever to reach the level of equality that Nike's advertisements suggest is possible, serious structural changes will have to take place.

Notes

1. According to one of countless Nike web pages (created mainly by the corporation's loyal fans) this is a part of Nike's Mission Statement.
2. Nike's loyal supporters have created thousands of web sites on various aspects of Nike, some of

which clearly represent Nike as a quasi-political organization or cause that needs support. One such web site, "The Green Swoosh Campaign" adopts rhetoric traditionally associated with political campaigns.
3. In fact, print ads for P.L.A.Y. feature images from "There is a Girl . . . " and contain no reference to Nike itself.
4. According to economists Diane Elson and Ruth Pearson, FTZs are "special areas which are exempt from normal import and export regulations, and also from many other kinds of regulations, such as protective labour legislation, and taxation laws." (Elson & Pearson, 1981: 106)
5. Of course, this is the case in the U.S. as well, and the advent of transnational capitalism has only intensified the discrepancy between high and low incomes in this country.
6. Of course, working women in so-called "developed" countries like the U.S. have also been, and continue to be, underpaid.
7. The case of Indonesia provides a perfect example. Anthropologist Evelyn Blackwood explains that, "The emphasis on women's domesticity in Indonesia . . . is fueled in large part by the practices of development economics, which is a product of the historical and social conditions of Europe and America." (Blackwood, 1995: 135)
8. And in this way deny any pay iniquities; women are recognized by the state as possessing "complementary equality" through their domestic and reproductive roles. However, although women are not recognized by the state as potential wage earners, according to Diane Wolf, "often a wife's income is used for day-to-day living expenses while the male's income is more sporadic and less reliable. " (Wolf, 65) Furthermore, while almost all Indonesian women marry at some point in their lives, the divorce rate is quite high and female-headed households are not uncommon. And finally, many of the women working in the Nike factories are young, independent, single women who depend on their income to support themselves.
9. This is what employees at Nike's Beaverton, Oregon "campus" call outsiders, in reference to the dirt mound that encircles the campus.

Bibliography

Alexander, Nick, "Missing Pieces: How the Nike Campaign Fails to Engage African-Americans," *Third Force* (July/August, 1997).

Asia Monitor Resource Centre and Hong Kong Christian Industrial Committee, "Working Conditions in Sports Shoe Factories in China Making Shoes for Nike and Reebok," Hong Kong (September 1997).

Ballinger, Jeffrey, "The New Free Trade-Heel," *Harper's Magazine* (August 1992): 46–7.

Baum, Bob, "Jordan's Critics Say It Must Be the Shoes," AP (6/6/96): Lexis/Nexis.

Blackwood, Evelyn, "Senior Women, Model Mothers, and Dutiful Wives: Managing Gender Contradictions in a Minangkabau Village," in *Bewitching Women, Pious Men: Gender and Body Politics in Southeast Asia,* Aihwa Ong and Michael G. Peletz, eds. Berkeley: University of California Press (1995): 124–158.

Cavanaugh, John, and Robin Broad, "Global Reach: Workers Fight the Multinationals, *The Nation* (3/18/96): Lexis/Nexis.

Chan, Anita, "Letter to the Editor," *The Washington Post* (1997).

Clifford, Mark, "The China Connection," *Far Eastern Economic Review* (11/5/96): 60.

———, "Pangs of Conscience," *Business Week* (7/29/96) 46–7.

Community Aid Abroad, "Sweating for Nike," Briefing Paper 31 (November 1996).

Crittenden, Ann, "Temporary Solutions; Increase in Temporary and Part-Time Workers," *Working Woman* (February 1994): Lexis/Nexis.

Dolnaghu, Michael, and Richard Barff, "Nike Just Did It: International Subcontracting and Flexibility in Athletic Footwear Production," *Regional Studies* 24(6)(1990): 537–552.

Elson, Diane and Ruth Pearson, "Nimble Fingers Make Cheap Workers: An Analysis of Women's Employment in Third World Export Manufacturing," *Feminist Review* 4 (1981): 87–107.

Enloe, Cynthia, "The Globetrotting Sneaker," *Ms.* (March/April 1995): 10–15.

Gargan, Edward, "International Business: An Indonesian Asset Is Also a Liability; Low Wages Woo Business, but the Price Is Worker Poverty," *The New York Times* (3/16/96): 35.

Goldman, Debra, "Simple Politics," *Adweek* (5/13/96): Lexis/Nexis.

Goozner, Merrill, "Asian Labor: Wages of Shame; Western Firms Help to Exploit Brutal Conditions," *Chicago Tribune* (11/6/94): Lexis/Nexis.

"Green Swoosh Campaign," http://www.wsu.edu:8080/~jtwillia/gsc.html.

Greenhouse, Stephen, 1997A. "Nike Supports Women in Its Ads but Not Its Factories, Groups Say." *The New York Times* (10/26/97): Lexis/Nexus.

———, 1997B. "Nike Shoe Plant in Vietnam Is Called Unsafe for Workers," *The New York Times* (11/18/97): Lexis/Nexus.

Hall, Stuart, "Gramsci's Relevance for the Study of Race and Ethnicity," in *Critical Dialogues in Cultural Studies,* eds., David Morley and Kuan-Ilsing Chen, London: Routledge (1996): 411–440.

Harrison, Bennett, "The Dark Side of Flexible Production," *National Productivity Review* (Autumn 1994): 479–501.

Harvey, David, *The Condition of Postmodernity,* Cambridge: Blackwell (1990).

Hadi, Sudharto Prawata, "Planning for Industrialization in Central Java, Indonesia: The Process, the Impacts and the Alternatives," dissertation. University of British Columbia (1993).

Herbert, Bob, "Nike's Bad Neighborhood," (6/14/96): 29+.

———, "In America, Trampled Dreams," *New York Times* (7/12/96): 27+.

Heyzer, Noeleen, "Asian Women Wage-Earners: Their Situation and Possibilities for Donor Intervention," *World Development* 17(7) 1989: 1109–1123.

INGI (International NGO Forum on Indonesia Labour Working Group), "Unjust but Doing It! Nike Operations in Indonesia," *Inside Indonesia* 27 (1991): 7–9.

Katz, Donald, *Just Do It: The Nike Spirit in the Corporate World,* New York: Random House (1994).

Knight, Philip, "Letter to the Editor," *New York Times* (6/18/96).

Labich, Kenneth, "Nike vs. Reebok: A Battle for Hearts, Minds, and Feet," *Fortune* (9/18/95): 90–106.

Manning, Jeff, 1997A. "Critics Target Nike for Abusive Labor Practices in Third World Countries," *The Oregonian* (11/19/97): Lexis/Nexus.

Manning, Jeff, 1997B. "Nike Struggles to Monitor Its Asian Production Network," *The Oregonian* (11/19/97): Lexis/Nexus.

Manning, Jeff, "Manufacturing," *Star Tribune* (11/28/97): Lexis/Nexus.

Mather, Celia, "Industrialization in the Tangerang Regency of West Java: Women Workers and the Islamic Patriarchy," *Bulletin of Concerned Asian Scholars* 15 (2), 1983: 2–17.

"The New Nike Economy: World Without Borders" (series of six editorials) *Far Eastern Economic Review* (8/29/96–11/21/96): 5.

"NIKE General Info and History," http://www.avana.net/pages/personal/rbro/nikeinfo.htm.

"Nike," http://www.careermag.com/employers/nike/index.html.

"Nike, Inc.," http://www.infomkt.ibm.com/ht3/hepnike.htm.

"NIKE Promotes Sport and Fitness for All," *Exceptional Parent* (May 1996): 60.

Ong, Aiwha, "The Gender and Labor Politics of Postmodernity," *Annual Review of Anthropology* 20 (1991): 279–309.

———, *Spirits of Resistance and Capitalist Discipline: Factory Women in Non-Western Societies,* Albany: SUNY Press (1987).

O'Rourke, Dara, "Swooshing It Under the Rug," Havens Center presentation (4/23/98).

Schwartz, Adam, "Culture Shock," *Far Eastern Economic Review* (8/22/96): 63.

Standing, Guy, "Global Feminization Through Flexible Labor," *World Development* 17 (7): 1077–1095 (1989).

Tassell, Tony, "Nike's Trainers Track Fitness of Asian Nations," *The Financial Times* (4/2/97): 22.

Tsing, Anna, *In the Realm of the Diamond Queen: Marginality in an Out-of-the-Way Place,* Princeton: Princeton University Press (1993).

Willigan, Geraldine, "High-Performance Marketing: An Interview with Nike's Phil Knight," *Harvard Business Review* (July-August 1992): 91–101.

Wolf, Diane, *Factory Daughters: Gender, Household Dynamics, and Rural Industrialization in Java,* Berkeley: University of California Press (1992).

Young, Andrew, "Andrew Young/Goodworks International Report on Nike." http://www.digitalrelease.com/egi-shl/entry.pl?noframes1@goodworkslib.

 Article Review Form at end of book.

How does the "marketing of Michael Jordan" reinforce the profamily discourses of the New Right? How does this idealization/idolization obscure social realities?

Michael Jordan's Family Values:

Marketing, Meaning, and Post-Reagan America

Mary G. McDonald

Miami University

Michael Jordan's body offers a significant site to explore larger cultural meanings and anxieties in post-Reagan America. Informed by cultural studies sensibilities, this paper explores selected sporting and advertising accounts to suggest that representations of Jordan's athletic body are constructed by promoters in ways which rely on particular associations of Black masculinity, sexuality, and the nuclear family. The carefully crafted image of Michael Jordan offers an enticing portrait of Black masculinity, playing off notions of natural athleticism and family sentiment in ways designed to induce devotion. This public persona of Jordan participates in the moralistic "family values" climate of post-Reagan America, while simultaneously working to deny historical and stereotypical depictions of Black masculinity as overtly erotic and dangerous. Thus marketing strategies encourage a voyeuristic, albeit "safe" enjoyment of Jordan's commodified body.

Michael Jordan's body is one of the most visible and celebrated bodies of recent times. Thanks to the National Basketball Association's (NBA) clever promotion of appealing personalities, creative commercials produced by Nike and other commercial sponsors, and his own marketing savvy, Jordan's fame has translated into 1995 endorsement earnings estimated to be $40 million (Lane & McHugh, 1995). As Michael Eric Dyson (1993) and David Andrews (1993, 1996) argue, Michael Jordan represents more than a successful marketing campaign that sells Nike sneakers, the NBA, Wheaties, Hanes underwear, Coca-Cola, Gatorade, Chevrolets, and McDonald's hamburgers: Jordan's body is a culturally significant site for the commodification and subsequent consumption of Black masculinity.

The marketing appeal of Michael Jordan is worth exploring given the historically complex representations of Black masculinity. Henry Louis Gates (1994) cites critic Barbara Johnson in suggest-

ing that African American men embody an "already read text." That is, images of African American men carry historically forged racist and sexist meanings that associate African Americans with nature, animality, hypersensuality, and eroticism. Once used to legitimate slavery and White supremacy, these representations persist in the visual media and hold particular significance within the conservative, backlash climate of post-Reagan America: the bodies of African American men (and women) have been made to serve as "symbolic icons for the nation's ills" (Golden, 1994, p. 22). For example, Wilt Chamberlain stands for "perverse promiscuity," Clarence Thomas for sexual harassment, Mike Tyson for date rape, and O. J. Simpson for spousal abuse (Golden, 1994).

Given this historical legacy and current hysteria, how and why is it that Michael Jordan manages to be marketable and extremely successful as a cultural symbol? On one level, exploring the popularity

Reprinted by permission from McDonald, M., 1996, "Michael Jordan's Family Values: Marketing, Meaning, and Post-Reagan America," *Journal of the Sociology of Sport*, 13(4): 344–365.

of Michael Jordan is a seemingly simple task. Jordan offers a fresh, more tolerant, and thus, a more marketable vision of Black masculinity because he has achieved an extraordinary level of success in a culture that celebrates masculine achievements like those romanticized in sport. Off the court and in commercial endorsements, Jordan appears as an engaging, thoughtful, private family man. This portrait of Jordan apparently counters and challenges the socially constructed representations of African American men as dangerous, incompetent, and overtly hypersexualized. Still, given the unstable, contextual state of cultural meanings, Jordan's public persona as an exceptional athlete and private family man cannot be blithely celebrated as a positive portrayal of African Americans nor for that matter, simply dismissed as reactionary Reaganism. Rather, making sense of Michael Jordan's ubiquitous presence within popular media necessitates exploring the historically specific, often contradictory economic rationales, social relations, and ideologies in which Jordan and his image are embedded,

Informed by cultural studies sensibilities, in this paper I explore the public persona of Michael Jordan in selected sporting and advertising accounts to critically interrogate the image(s) we are being offered to consume. What makes representations of Michael Jordan so complex and intriguing for cultural analysis is that they offer a unique opportunity to illuminate the complicated political status of popular culture and identity. To interrogate the ideologies of race, class, masculinity, and sexuality inscribed on Michael Jordan's commodified body is to acknowledge that relations of power are always multiple and contradictory. We cannot fully understand Michael Jordan if we focus only on the socially constructed representations

of his identity as an African American, or a heterosexual, or a man, or a member of the capitalist class. While that sort of analytical compartmentalization may be appealing, its simplicity fails to provide an accurate reflection of the complex, interrelated, and fluid character of cultural meanings and power relations (Birrell & McDonald, 1993).

This analysis of Michael Jordan benefits from the concept of articulation which suggests that cultural meaning does not inhere to texts, identities, or practices; rather it is produced through their interactions (Hall, 1985; Hall, 1986a; Hall, 1986b; Hall, 1991; Howell, 1990; Grossberg, 1992). An articulation is an association or a link between distinctive ideological elements that operate in a specific historical place and time with identifiable consequences. Methodologically, this suggests that cultural analysis is an interpretive act requiring the exploration of both text(s) and context(s). The cultural process is further complicated by the incessant generation of new meanings and fresh associations.

In this paper I trace the contradictory ways in which representations of gender, race, class, and sexuality are articulated through the phenomenon of Michael Jordan within the context of post-Reagan America. Specifically, I explore the ways media accounts of Jordan's basketball talents reinforce lingering stereotypes that equate natural athleticism with men—particularly African American men—and suggest people of color have privileged access to bodily pleasures and expressions (see Harris, 1991; Birrell, 1989; Wiggins, 1989; hooks, 1992; West, 1993). Likewise, the off-court persona of Jordan as a private family man participates in contemporary popular discourses on the family, engaging a variety of racial, class, gender, sexual, and national ideologies. The definition of what

constitutes the family continues to be reformulated from a variety of positions, while dominant cultural portrayals of the nuclear family proclaim it is "in crisis," "on the decline" or just plain "broken." The alleged decline of the traditional nuclear family—a heterosexual couple with children featuring a breadwinner father and housewife mother—has been successfully deployed by the conservative New Right as the commonsense explanation for social problems ranging from crime, poverty, and sexual "promiscuity," to drug abuse (Reeves & Campbell, 1994).

Jordan and his promoters play up his seemingly natural athleticism while down playing any suggestion of excessive sensuality. An apparent devotion to "traditional family values" serves to further distance Jordan from the stereotypical portrayal of Black masculinity as hypersexual, immoral, and irresponsible, the very demonic characteristics members of the New Right claim threaten the nuclear family and, by association, the very moral fiber of America itself. In post-Reagan America where traditional family values and the public hysteria surrounding AIDS suggest sexuality is both immoral and life-threatening, Jordan's commodified body is culturally coded as natural in ways that are socially sanctioned and culturally envied.

Here Comes Mr. Jordan: The Marketing of Black Masculinity

Understanding Michael Jordan's status as a cultural and marketing icon in post-Reagan America means acknowledging the tremendous significance of both sport and advertising in the national consciousness. Mark Dyreson (1989) traces the symbiotic relationship between consumerism and sport to the 1920s, where Americans increasingly understood sport "as a vehicle of entertainment—one of the many items available for amusement in a culture which glorified consumption" (p. 261). The form and content of sport as a commodity have varied and shifted over the years, just as the crafting of Jordan as an appealing persona to be marketed and consumed has its own unique history. Exploring the convergence of the historical with the economic and biographical suggests that much of Jordan's appeal can be attributable to his athletic status: professional basketball offers a prominent site for African American men such as Jordan to be visible, culturally lauded, and clearly successful.

Michael Eric Dyson (1993) notes that Jordan represents the hope of freedom and ultimate escape from the pernicious beliefs and social structures that stand between African Americans and economic prosperity, as well as physical and psychological security. Jordan's commodified body is, therefore, the "symbolic carrier of racial and cultural desires to fly beyond limits and obstacles" . . . and thus the player's "achievements have furthered the cultural acceptance of at least the Black athletic body" (p. 71). While acknowledging Dyson's arguments about the resistant potential of the Black athletic body, cultural critic bell hooks (1994) suggests the selling of Michael Jordan is best understood as the signpost and reinforcement of overtly depoliticized times. Beginning in the late 1970s, market forces co-opted much of the subversive potential of Black masculinity while male athletes increasingly espoused politically neutral positions in an effort to secure financially lucrative endorsement deals.

Significantly, the increasing numbers of Black male athletes endorsing products parallels the ascent of the Reagan era, a unique historical epoch characterized by a shift in the national *Zeitgeist*. First emerging under the leadership of President Ronald Reagan, this shift in the national consciousness suggests movement away from the overt political activism of the 1960s toward an era of backlash politics that also served to justify economic policies favoring the wealthy. By the 1980s, conservative voices had positioned a pro-business agenda as tantamount to the emotionally cherished ideals of family, respectability, and nation (Hall, 1988; Reeves & Campbell, 1994). The underlying rationale was that corporate expansion and freedom strengthened not only the economy, but the nuclear family and, by association, the very moral fiber of America. According to key members of the New Right, economic problems, such as inflation or the budget deficit, could be traced to the "permissive" and "hedonistic" politics of big government. Bleeding heart liberalism, characterized by the expansion of the state's social entitlement programs like the New Deal, the Great Society, and the War on Poverty, merely undermine the values of hard work, family, and nation. Illegitimate birth rates, joblessness, and welfare dependency were all created and/or reinforced by "economic incentives to bear out-of-wedlock children and disincentives to work created by the Great Society" (Edsall & Edsall, 1991, p. 15).

While always contested, challenged, and resisted, increasingly socially conservative world views gained popularity among a broad segment of the American population. According to Grossberg (1992), these positions include the growing acceptance of social and economic inequalities for various subordinated groups, the attempt to impose a narrowly defined notion of morality on all of society, the justification of inequality in the name of economic competition, and the demonization of activist groups who challenge the political and conservative status quo. Distancing himself from potentially controversial issues and espousing benign views (see Cole & Andrews, 1996), Jordan fits neatly with the regressive political climate of post-Reagan America. Andrews (1996) argues that Jordan's successes on the basketball court and in the advertising world offer apparent "proof" of a racially tolerant and color-blind society. Read from this perspective, Jordan's popularity is both the product of, and reinforcement for, New Right strategies to maintain White interests by suggesting that racism has been eradicated (Andrews, 1996).

The commodification of Michael Jordan also signals the loss of political agency and the once-radical political potential of Black athletes. Michael Jordan as a spectacular athlete and willing corporate apologist stands in stark contrast to another powerful vision of yesteryear: that of African American athletes as political activists and outspoken critics of the establishment (hooks, 1994). Perhaps no one individual athlete better embodied the civil rights era and mandate for social change of the 1960s and 1970s than boxer Muhammad Ali. Ali spoke out against the war in Vietnam and in support of Black power, willingly sacrificing fame for his convictions. Ali's conversion to the Nation of Islam and refusal to serve in Vietnam war cost him the heavyweight boxing title and a prison term (Harris, 1995). While Ali no doubt embodied the sexism of professional boxing (see Sammons, 1995) and earned a tremendous amount of money, at the prime of his athletic career Ali also offered a decidedly subversive persona as an outspoken critic of the racial status quo. Othello Harris (1995) suggests that Ali countered stereotypes of African Americans while moving beyond "White limits of acceptability in his beliefs and behavior" (p. 66).

While I don't wish to oversimplify complex cultural meanings, especially in light of feminist critiques of both sport and history, suffice it to say these contrasts between Ali and Jordan exemplify distinctions between the two divergent eras: where Ali embodied the pride of Black resolve in the 1960s, the commodification of Michael Jordan in the 1980s and 1990s is a sign of increasingly reactionary times. While also commodified, Ali was among a group of African American athletes who helped publicize issues like economic stratification and racial segregation (hooks, 1994). Contrast the image of "rebellious masculinity" (hooks, 1994, p. 133) embodied by Ali to that of the genial association created by Nike in pairing Michael Jordan with Bugs Bunny in the "Hare Jordan" campaign. As hooks (1994) sees it, in those commercials where Jordan:

speaks to the cartoon figure of Bugs Bunny as though they are equals—peers—his elegance and grace of presence is ridiculed and mocked by a visual aesthetics which suggests that his body makes him larger than life, a fantasy character. This visual image, though presented as playful and comic, in fact dehumanizes. (p. 134)

Creating appealing fantasy characters also was a key strategy employed by the NBA in the 1980s in an effort to revive the once-floundering, financially strapped league of the 1970s. As Cheryl Cole and Harry Denny (1994) note, a key element of the league's resurgence lies in the ability of promoters to distance the NBA from previous racist associations conflating the predominately Black athletic labor force with an "undisciplined" style of play and the stigma of drug abuse. Cole and Denny suggest that during the 1980s marketers and an equally invested sport media promoted professional

basketball as an appealing cultural event complete with stylized play and extraordinary larger-than-life personalities like those of Earvin "Magic" Johnson of the Los Angeles Lakers and Larry Bird of the Boston Celtics. With an assist from Nike, fresh meanings were associated with Black masculinity in an effort to court White middle-class audiences. New narratives suggested that NBA athletes possessed exceptional skill, hard work, dedication, and determination. The presentation of NBA players as idealized athletic heroes committed to competition and meritocracy also suggests the New Right's understanding of a racially harmonious country (Cole & Denny, 1994).

By the time Jordan entered the league in 1984, the NBA was well on its way toward transforming games into spectacular entertainment events. Just as this time period saw the explosion of special effects in *Raiders of the Lost Ark* (1981), *ET* (1982), *Ghostbusters* (1984), *Back to the Future* (1985), *Batman* (1989), and other top-grossing blockbuster Hollywood films of the era, so too did the NBA exploit the spectacular, employing laser shows, dramatic player introductions, energizing music, half-time contests, and sideshows. The NBA changed basketball games into a unique type of athletic escapism. In doing so, NBA commissioner David Stern makes it clear that the NBA is targeting the entire family:

They have themes parks. . . . and we have theme parks, only we call them arenas. They have characters: Mickey Mouse, Goofy. Our characters are named Magic and Michael [Jordan]. Disney sells apparel; we sell apparel. They make home videos; we make home videos. (quoted in Swift, 1991, p. 84)

That Stern would choose to align the NBA with Disney, the corporate exemplar of wholesome entertainment, is particularly telling. Disney's wholesomeness, excitement, and eternal optimism are the

antithesis of the racist characterizations of "undisciplined" Blackness associated with the NBA of the 1970s. The reference to Disney also helps identify the NBA's idealized, target audience—Disney productions "relentlessly define the United States as White, middle-class, and heterosexual" (Giroux, 1994, p. 31).

By the 1990s, the NBA had been successfully "Disneyfied." The complete reversal of financial fortunes included a complete line of commodities: NBA licensed caps, jerseys, t-shirts, basketballs, videos, etc. To this day, however, the most valuable commodities continue to be the players themselves; the now-global NBA has successfully created a sense of audience identification and name recognition. Thus, the NBA has followed the long-established capitalist logic of the film and television industries. As David Lusted (1991) argues in regards to television: "A stock of recognized names acts as an assurance that audiences will return again (and again) to their role as viewers, perpetuating—via advertising or license revenue—the flow of cash to maintain the institution" (p. 251).

Still, this remaking of the NBA did not displace the themes most commonly connected to professional basketball including those of masculine prowess and competitive capitalism. Henry Giroux's (1994) analysis of Disney's sanitized aura can be applied to the NBA's complicity in what Giroux terms the "politics of innocence." Behind Disney's guise of naiveté rests a multinational conglomerate that wields enormous cultural and political power:

Disney's power and its reach into popular culture combine an insouciant playfulness and the fantastic possibility of making childhood dreams come true—yet only through the reproduction of strict gender roles, an unexamined nationalism, and a choice that is attached to the proliferation of commodities. (p. 31)

Similarly, NBA promotional strategies entice fans in ways that appear benevolent, yet mask particular relations of power. Underlying the visible space of the game is a semipublic masculinized and heterosexualized culture displayed through "a 'politics of lifestyle' marked by the semipublic sexual exchange of a conspicuously displayed network of adoring, supportive female fans, girlfriends, and/or wives: it is a masculine lifestyle meant to be embraced, admired, envied, and consumed" (Cole & Denny, 1994, p. 128). This masculinist preserve of the NBA is further complicated by the stereotypical association that equates people of color with sensuality and physicality. Thus, perceptions of hypersexuality and eroticism persist as powerful racist undercurrents within the consumer culture and the commodified space of the NBA (Cole & Denny, 1994).

Cole and Denny's (1994) contention that these racist assumptions are constantly being managed through the marketing of particular player personalities is important for understanding the cultural appeal of Jordan. The very public depiction of Michael Jordan as a wholesome family figure helps stabilize the league's hoped-for clean-cut image just as it diffuses lingering impressions of Black hypersexuality. Indeed, one of the first snapshots of Jordan in the NBA features the nuclear family: parents James and Deloris attended the 1984 press conference to witness the announcement of the $6-million contract awarded by the professional Chicago Bulls to Michael. Over the course of the next several years, even after the tragic murder of James Jordan in 1993, the pair provided affirmation of Jordan's All-American persona.

In *Michael Jordan: Come Fly With Me* (Sperling, 1989), a video produced by NBA Entertainment, basketball game footage is juxta-posed against voice-over narratives outlining Jordan's personal virtues. Accompanied by piano music and film of his own aesthetically pleasing body running and leaping on the court, Jordan states assertively that his parents' influence continues: "I was always taught never to forget where you came from. My parents, if I change as a person, they would be the first to tell me that, and they have not told me that yet. So, I'm doing well" (Sperling, 1989). This persona is an enticing portrait of Black masculinity, highlighting "natural" athleticism, and family sentiment in ways designed to provoke "desire without evoking dread" (Jackson, 1994, p. 49).

Body Language: Cultivating Michael Jordan's "Natural" Physicality

One of the most enduring and seemingly endearing aspects of the Michael Jordan phenomenon are the words and phrases coined to describe his particular type of physically expressive basketball talent. The most popular and lasting nicknames connote flight for Jordan—"Air," "Air Jordan," "His Airness," a "Flyer, who operates in either "Air Time" or "Rare Air" or is perpetually "Talking to the Air." Of course, these phrases did not originate out of thin air. References to flight are testimony to the tremendous role of advertising discourses in generating Jordan's image. "Air Jordan" is part of Nike's clever plan to market an air-sole shoe to challenge Converse, long the leader in the gym shoe segment of the market (Raissman, 1984). In 1984, Nike transferred a lion's share of their advertising budget into one preeminent multi-million dollar 5-year deal, an agreement sealed before Jordan's rookie year in the National Basketball Association (NBA). David Falk, Jordan's agent then with ProServ, explained the cultural logic of this marriage:

Because of Michael's style of play—we like to call him a flier—he fits in well with the whole line of the shoe [Air Shoe] which is high tech. That's where the upper end of Nike's marketing strategy is going. (quoted in Raissman, 1984, p. 1)

Two early Air Jordan TV commercials, first "aired" in the spring of 1985, helped construct Jordan's public persona. One commercial was created as a response to the NBA's "uniformity of uniform" clause when commissioner David Stern banned the original red-and-black Technicolor Nike Air Jordan shoes. The voice-over states: "On October 18, the NBA banned Michael Jordan from wearing these shoes. But the NBA can't stop you from buying these shoes. Air Jordan. Basketball by Nike" (Murphy, 1985, p. 34). In this commercial, Jordan is presented as a menacing figure—even angry—with a scowl, presumably in response to the authoritarian stance taken by the league in banning the Nike shoes. This portrayal of Jordan plays on racist depictions of Black men as threatening and intimidating. Significantly, it also is the last time Jordan is presented as an intimidating figure in an advertisement (Murphy, 1985). In subsequent promotional campaigns, Jordan would be represented as approachable and likable, an everyday American with extraordinary athletic talents.

The archetype that Nike, the NBA, and subsequent advertisers seized upon appeared in another early Nike commercial from the spring of 1985 entitled "Jordan Flight." It features Jordan moving across a black-topped basketball court at twilight with the Chicago skyline in the background. The sound of jet engines revving to an increasingly higher pitch reaches its zenith when Jordan slam dunks the basketball. Jordan remains in the air with his legs apart for the final 10 seconds of the commercial, an apparent testimonial to both his incredible athleticism and the power of the red-and-black Technicolor Nike athletic shoes he wears (Katz, 1994). The voice-over booms: "Who said man was not meant to fly" (Murphy, 1985, p. 34). This commercial presents an affable Jordan as the quintessential "natural athlete," for as the rather hyperbolic claim goes, he can literally fly through the air.

A quick read of this Nike commercial suggests Michael Jordan's celebrated and commodified physicality is dramatically embellished in basketball and advertising discourses through catchy narratives and phrases, slow-motion replay, and special effects. These commercials, along with video highlights and televised NBA games, use multiple camera angles, slow-motion replays, and personalized narratives to create the illusion of an intimate, revealing, and pleasurable encounter with Michael "Air" Jordan. The ways in which Jordan is represented also assist in the reconstruction, legitimation, and embellishment of larger cultural associations between natural athleticism and masculinity (especially Black masculinity) which play a significant role in the area of contemporary gender relations. "Symbolic representations of the male body as a symbol of strength, virility, and power have become increasingly important in popular culture as actual inequalities between the sexes are contested in all areas of public life" (Messner, 1988, p. 212).

Images of masculinity as powerful and "natural" on televised sporting spectacles offer men of all socioeconomic backgrounds one of the most powerful sites to collectively identify with masculinity and an ideology of male physical and cultural superiority

(Messner, 1988; Theberge, 1991). Still these representations offer contradictory meanings when connected with commonsense perceptions of African American men. Traits, such as aggression and brute strength, have been historically associated with both African American men and athleticism (Sabo & Jansen, 1992). Television sports commentary, for example, more often credits White basketball players with exhibiting "intelligence" while explaining the success of African Americans in terms of their "innate" physicality (Jackson, 1989; Harris, 1991). This seemed to be the implicit message of the 1989 NBC television special Black Athletes: Fact and Fiction, according to Laurel Davis (1990). Relying heavily on questionable bioscientific discourses, NBC focused an entire show exploring the presumed link between racial difference and athletic performance. This quest downplayed human agency and dismissed sociopolitical issues, including the very racist preoccupation with the alleged "naturalness" of African Americans (Davis, 1990). As Andrews (1996) has recently demonstrated, the media reinforce this type of pseudoscientific, essentialist logic with repeated references to Jordan as someone who was seemingly "born to dunk."

Media images, such as Nike commercials, have a powerful effect, subtly influencing our perceptions of the body. Here technology merges with ideology to reify notions of African Americans as naturally athletic. For example, slow-motion replay offers a particularly compelling dramatic aesthetic. Margaret Morse (1983) argues that the conventions of slow-motion replay allow for an analysis of "body movements which are normally inaccessible to view; this capacity has justifiably lent slow motion an aura of scientificity" (p. 49). The video Come Fly With Me (Sperling, 1989) offers

many examples of how slow-motion replay creates the dramatic, aesthetic athleticism of Jordan's athletic body. A scene near the end of the video features four different examples of Jordan dunking the basketball in slow motion, each from a dramatically different camera angle.

Slow motion's aura of scientific legitimacy helps to strengthen the illusion that Jordan can defy the laws of gravity. This presentation has proven to be persuasive. On June 13, 1991, for example, the ABC television show Primetime Live aired a segment narrated by Diane Sawyer, in which several people were asked, "Why does Michael Jordan seem to fly?" The broadcasted responses:

First Fan: Michael Jordan hangs in the air for at least 8 to 10 seconds.
Second Fan: Six seconds.
Third Fan: Ten seconds.
Fourth Fan: 4.56 seconds.
Fifth Fan: Oh, his hang time's got to be at least 8 seconds.
Sawyer: Eight seconds? Is it possible Michael Jordan is airborne that long? Is he exempt from gravity? In other words, if Michael Jordan had fallen from that apple tree, would Sir Isaac Newton still be waiting for a bop on the head? (Primetime Live, 1991)

The scene shifts to Peter Brancazio, a professor in the Department of Physics at Brooklyn College, who assures the audience that the "laws of physics apply to everyone, even Michael Jordan." Using basic physics, Brancazio concludes that a 3-foot leap leaves Jordan in "flight" not for the 3 to 10 seconds believed by the audience, but for about nine-tenths of a second.

By the time of Jordan's October 6, 1993 initial retirement from professional basketball, this reputation for flight had long been well-established: basketball and advertising discourses drawing on commonsense assumptions about athleticism repeatedly constructed

Jordan as the ultimate natural athlete. Even the nickname "air" suggests an aura of naturalness and reinforces the rather hyperbolic notion that Jordan could defy gravity via his uncanny "hang time,"[1] the seeming ability to remain suspended in space as if in flight.

Still, these characterizations of flight are far from innocent, communicating much more than Michael Jordan's great athleticism and symbolic worth. Historically, African Americans have been linked with nature in racist ways that seemingly suggest extraordinary "sexuality, sensuality, and an alternately celebrated or denigrated propensity for physical ability" (Desmond, 1994, p. 43).

These associations are rooted in the racist assumptions that Black men are "closer to nature" than White men and from Victorian notions that Africans have a different genetic makeup from their more genteel and intellectual European counterparts. Rooted in allegedly natural differences, these ideologies have helped to restrict Black men to certain occupational niches such as sports, music, and entertainment. Crucially, these ideologies operate by making the connection between sporting and sexual prowess (Jackson, 1994, p. 54).

The Black athletic body is often referenced in terms of an extraordinary physicality. According to critic Peter Jackson (1994), the dominant perspective of White heterosexual masculinity still expects superior sexual performance from people of color. The marketing strategy applied to Jordan suggests an apparent awareness of these larger issues. Under the direction of his original marketing agency ProServ and agent David Falk, and thanks partially to the promotional apparatuses of the NBA and sport media, Jordan has played up the "natural" Black athletic body while simultaneously repudiating any suggestion of culturally inappropriate sexuality.

This serves to undermine stereotypical associations of Black sexuality with destructive and predatory behavior (Jackson, 1994).

The cultural power of these depictions of Black sexuality derives from America's simultaneous obsession with sex and fear of Black sexuality (West, 1993). The "exotic" images of African American sexuality thus also speak to the paradox of sexuality and race in America. According to Cornel West (1993), behind "closed doors the dirty, disgusting, and funky sex associated with Black people is often perceived to be more intriguing and interesting, while in public spaces talk about Black sexuality is virtually taboo" (p. 120). Sexual myths about African Americans, invented during Reconstruction to maintain White cultural and financial privilege, present them as either oversexed, threatening personas or as desexed individuals committed to serving White interests. Although the former might be the most pernicious, all of these types of representations distort and dehumanize African Americans.

These myths flourish in professional sport where African American male athletes make disproportionate contributions, most notably in baseball, football, and basketball. The masculinist culture of professional sport also encourages men of all backgrounds to treat women as sexual conquests (Curry, 1991). Too often being a male athlete means that one has power over and entitlement to women's bodies. Still, the stereotypes of Black sexuality ensure that African American men disproportionately bear the pejorative label of hypersexuality (Rowe, 1994). In sport, there is a long history in which gender, race, and sexuality have been articulated to suggest depravity. For example, Jack Johnson became the heavyweight boxing champion of the world in 1908 when the pseudoscience of eu-

genics seemed to "prove" the mental and physical inferiority of African Americans. While Johnson gained a measure of material success from boxing and performing in Vaudeville, he was perhaps as much a draw (and certainly more infamous) for his sexual relations with White women (Roberts, 1983).

Lest the Johnson story seem like old history, consider also that the Associated Press named boxer Mike Tyson's rape trial and conviction as its 1992 story of the year in sport, despite considerable debate over whether a rape trial even belonged on the sports pages. Tyson was convicted of raping Desiree Washington, after the failure of a defense strategy that presented him as pathologically incapable of sexual control. While undoubtedly a White defendant would never have to bear the burden of overcoming stereotypes of hypersexuality, the strategy used by Tyson's lawyers actually played into racist and sexist world views. Tyson's trial provided a convenient link between criminality, race, sexuality, and sport (Birrell & McDonald, 1993). Angela Davis (1984) maintains the myth of the Black rapist has been historically conjured up to maintain White privilege and justify White violence and terror against the Black community. Far more African American women were raped by White men than White women by Black men, yet this idea still persists. Who better represents the stereotype of the Black rapist than Mike Tyson (Birrell & McDonald, 1993)? Alongside Willie Horton, the convicted rapist whose parole was used during the Bush presidential campaign to portray opponent Michael Dukakis as soft on crime, the Mike Tyson case has become "evidence" to justify White America's commonsense perception of violence among Blacks. This concept is especially powerful during a time when many civil rights advances have stagnated or been reversed by Reaganite economic and social policies (Birrell & McDonald, 1993).

While the Tyson case represents the most glaring association of sexual deviance and sport, representations of sexual prowess echo throughout the culture. The linkage between African American's "innate" physicality and sexuality were perhaps most crudely articulated in 1988 in the words of sportscaster Jimmy "The Greek" Snyder:

The Black is a better athlete to begin with because he's been bred to be that way because of his thigh size and big size. . . . [The advantage] goes all the way back to the Civil War, when during the slave period the slave owner would breed his big Black buck with his big woman so that they could have a big Black kid. That's where it all started. (quoted in Harris, 1991, p. 25)

These words provoked national outrage, resulting in the sportscaster's dismissal from CBS television. Rather than reflecting the words of one misinformed individual, however, the sentiment expressed by Snyder crudely represents a lingering cultural commonsense belief that African Americans are more animalistic as the very terms "bred" and "buck" suggest. The underlying message is that African Americans have privileged access to bodily expressions and pleasure (hooks, 1992).

Critic bell hooks (1992) explains the paradoxical implications of this image of Black masculinity.

It is the young Black male body that is seen as epitomizing this promise of wildness, of unlimited physical prowess and unbridled eroticism. It was this Black body that was most "desired" for its labor in slavery, and it is this body that is most represented in contemporary popular culture as the body to be watched, imitated, desired, possessed. (p. 34)

Indeed, sensuality and sexuality offer one of the few resources African American men and women have been able to parlay into wider popularity in the entertainment industries (hooks, 1992; Rowe, 1994).

African American actors, musicians, and athletes often are impelled to walk a narrow and ambiguous line between the suggestion of threat and the allure of desire, particularly in attempting to appeal to a wide range of audiences (Rowe, 1994).

The salience of the Black body has, if possible, magnified in an era where bodies have increasingly become available for inspection and comparison (see Foucault, 1978; Watney, 1989; Theberge, 1991; King, 1993). The fitness boom in the late 1970s and early 1980s, coupled with the AIDS crisis, have added to an overall obsession with the fit, healthy body and with reasserting the superiority of the heterosexual body. Male athletes, especially African American athletes, stand for the commodification of the hard body and an active heterosexuality.

Peter Jackson's (1994) analyses of British athletes Daley Thompson and John Barnes helps elucidate the ways Jordan's athletic body negotiates notions of sensuality, sexuality, and athleticism. According to Jackson, both Thompson and Barnes are presented in advertising discourses as the "acceptable face" of Black masculinity, their presumed sensual energy coupled with impeccable moral reputations and pleasing personalities. The well-known athletes' personas defuse any perceived sexual threat and defy the "conventional mapping of the mind-body dualism on to White and Black men respectively" (p. 56). Described in various media accounts as "supple and muscular" (Norment, 1991), "sexy" (Naughton, 1992), and offering basketball audiences "pleasure, sheer delight, and wonderment" (Vancil, 1992), Jordan's body offers consumers a voyeuristic encounter (see hooks, 1994). His carefully cultivated persona as a devoted son, husband, and father is a key component of this process, serving to

distance Jordan from any overt association of hypersexuality (see Jackson, 1994; Cole & Denny, 1994).

"Just Wait Until We Get Our Hanes on You"

Two commercials for Hanes underwear illustrate the ways Jordan is marketed to exploit the Black body as safely erotic. The Hanes campaign offers some of the most overtly risqué representations of Jordan. While other athletes have made a career out of revealing their bodies in underwear ads (witness the meteoric rise in popularity of baseball player Jim Palmer after he posed in scant briefs several years ago), Jordan is presented rather modestly in Hanes commercials. Maintaining Jordan's wholesome person in the Hanes campaign must have provided a bit of a challenge because sensuality and eroticism are closely aligned with advertising campaigns for underwear. Over the past 15 years, Calvin Klein has parlayed the America's uncomfortable titillation with youthful sexuality into a business empire (Ingrassia, 1995). Calvin Klein launched a controversial campaign in the mid-1980s featuring young men in their "Calvins" as the object of an erotic gaze. More recently, White rap star Marky Mark was featured in Calvin Klein ads on billboards across the country. Dressed only in a pair of lycra boxer shorts that hugged his muscular thighs and bulged provocatively at his crotch, Mark stood laughing with his baggy pants twisted around the ankles as if someone had just pulled his trousers down (Harris, 1993). His muscular body and apparently delighted reaction suggest agency, power, and approval: Mark appears as a willing and wanton accomplice in the ad's scenario.

In sharp contrast to the provocative profiles of the White entertainers, Jim Palmer and Marky

Mark, Jordan appears in Hanes television commercials fully clothed. Where Mark's image of phallic power is representative of the larger cultural trend to position men in (hetero)sexualized, yet assertive ways to sell products, Jordan's modest attire is representative of the cultural anxiety around Black masculinity and sexuality. Hanes advertisers have clearly decided to play it safe, locking into already well-established images of Jordan's athleticism and position in the nuclear family.

For example, a commercial produced in 1992, opens with a voice-over: "Michael Jordan in Hanes briefs." The camera focuses on a smiling Jordan clutching a basketball, dressed in suit coat, white (presumably Hanes) undershirt, and slacks. This casual suit reveals far less flesh than does the sleeveless jersey and long, modest baggy shorts of the Chicago Bulls uniform. Both a voice-over and graphic proclaim: "Michael Jordan in NEW IMPROVED Hanes briefs." Jordan then leaps into the air as special effects technologies produce the illusion of flight. With background noise of a jet engine, Jordan continues to "fly" through the rafters of a basketball gymnasium, which resembles an airplane hanger complete with an indoor runway. Jordan circles several times over the basket before slamming the ball through the hoop and returning to the ground. The good-natured parody of the ads implies that "New Improved" Hanes underwear can somehow improve performance.

Another Hanes commercial with Jordan alludes to the subject of sexual performance. The scene opens with the words: "Michael Jordan for Hanes fashion briefs." Wearing loafers, long casual shorts, a bright blue shirt, and a baseball cap, Jordan dribbles a basketball into a tastefully, expensively decorated room, apparently his own house. Jordan shoots the basketball into a laundry basket and sits down next to his father. James Jordan puts down his newspaper, reaches into the laundry basket, and picks up a pair of red bikini briefs from a pile of blander underwear. The elder Jordan asks, "Michael, are these your Hanes? Son, is there a reason why you wear them?" At this point Michael's wife, Juanita, enters the room, embraces her husband, and with a firm kiss on Michael's cheek says, "Definitely." Given this feminine approval, James Jordan asks his son, "Do you think mom would like me in these?" Michael replies hesitantly, "Maybe," at which point the word "definitely" flashes across the screen. The commercial concludes with slow-motion footage of Jordan bashfully smiling as the familiar Hanes jingle rings the sexually suggestive words: "Just wait until we get our Hanes on you."

This father-and-son bonding episode, complete with Michael Jordan's shy, sheepish expressions and repeatedly raised eyebrows, distances Jordan from both the overtly sexist views of many professional athletes and the racist vision of hypersexuality. Rather, this commercial promotes the notion of sexual restraint and a stable family relationship with James Jordan as a strong, sensitive father figure. This sets Michael Jordan apart from the homogenized and simplistic media portrayal of African American families in post-Reagan America which suggest that strong men and father figures are nowhere to be found, having "vanished," abdicating their responsibility and abandoning their own families.

In contrast, James and Michael's conversation about Hanes is reminiscent of father-son talks about responsible sexuality. The generational signs are carefully crafted and are readily displayed in the divergent ways in which the two men are dressed. Michael Jordan's attire suggests boyhood and innocence, especially the casual shorts, loafers, and a baseball cap without any professional team affiliation. This ensemble sharply contrasts with James Jordan's clothing, which evokes the adult business world: a button-down, lightly colored Oxford shirt and nicely creased slacks. Their short dialogue suggests awkwardness and modesty. The younger Jordan appears uncomfortable with this parental query into his underwear choice and the resulting unspoken association of his own sexuality and his father's sexuality.

However modest, this short discussion represents a twist on intergenerational male bonding over female sexuality. Each man is looking for ways to dress in order to please a woman. Juanita is portrayed as the most actively sexual of the three, with the embrace and approval of a boyish and innocent, albeit sexy, Michael Jordan. Yet, even this portrayal is tempered by the white, long-sleeved, high-necked blouse and white slacks she wears. The white color suggests virginal restraint, or perhaps even a sanitized presence. The affectionate embrace and brief kiss on the cheek are devoid of any obvious reference to unbridled passion. Rather, intimacy is suggested as both Michael and Juanita knowingly raise their eyebrows, give each other sideways glances and, thus, allude to excitement and heterosexual intimacy (apparently thanks to the racy red bikini Hanes underwear). The unspoken suggestion is that sexual passion is a personal issue and, thus, any tantalizing detail beyond innuendo is not for public discussion; rather it is best expressed and experienced in private.

Placed within the nuclear family, Jordan offers quite a different aura than does Marky Mark and professional (male) sport. The presence of Michael Jordan's wife and father evoke the socially constructed sentimental images often associated with the family, including warmth, emotional support, respectability, love, and sexual restraint. This blissful restraint between Juanita and Michael Jordan promotes what has, in the age of AIDS, become the ideological bastion of safe sex: the presumably monogamous heterosexual marriage. Magic Johnson's revelation of his HIV status no doubt adds to the common sense of this connection (see Cole & Denny, 1994). Johnson's public announcement occurred in November 1991, ironically the very month in which *Ebony* magazine featured a cover shot of Michael and Juanita Jordan embracing happily under the headline: "Michael and Juanita Jordan on Marriage, Love, and Life after Basketball." In this piece, Juanita speaks at length about the loving support husband Michael gives to her and their children (Norment, 1991).

Still, the contrast between the two basketball players may be diminishing. After revealing that he acquired HIV through unprotected sex in the effort to "accommodate" many women, Johnson is now increasingly referenced from a position within the nuclear family (see King, 1993; Cole & Denny, 1994; Rowe, 1994). In an effort to deflect criticism away from queries about Johnson's sexual identity, his wife Cookie has become increasingly visible.

Frequent images of Johnson and family in the media and statements like, "Cookie is a very strong woman. Marrying her is the smartest thing I've ever done," have cemented the public respectability, which was undermined by his HIV status. Anchoring Johnson inside the family immediately temporizes his promiscuity, with his "bachelor's life" safely consigned to the past. (Rowe, 1994, p. 16)

Jordan has been repeatedly referenced within the nuclear family and pictured off-the-court with children throughout his basketball career. Early in his career Deloris and James Jordan praised Michael as a loving, moral son, as the elder

Jordan's wholesome appeal seems to explain their son's success. The Jordans embody the seemingly lost ideal of family values. Consider, for example, the words of sportswriter Curry Kirkpatrick (1991):

Jordan takes his sense of humor from his dad, who used to work around the house with his tongue hanging out (sound familiar?), his sense of business from his mom, and his work ethic from both. "The Jordans are from the old school where education and teachers and administration meant something to parents," says Laney High principal Kenneth McLaurin. (p. 72)

It is not widely known that Jordan and his wife, Juanita Vanoy, transgressed one of American society's moral rules in 1989 by having their first child out of wedlock. Jordan suffered relatively little adverse media publicity in this matter; he was reportedly urged by several business associates to marry Vanoy in order to protect his carefully cultivated moral image (Naughton, 1992). Even the source of this cynical assessment assures us that, once married, Jordan matured thanks to wife Juanita's influence (Naughton, 1992). Once married, the Jordan familial bliss means partaking in the good life afforded by the consumer culture and in the promise of greater material rewards: In the *Ebony* piece there is discussion of a dream home to be constructed for Michael and Juanita Jordan and their children, with six bedrooms, a guest house, an indoor/outdoor swimming pool (with Jacuzzi and sauna), and ample parking space for the Jordan's dozen or so cars including Porsches, Mercedes-Benzes, Testarossas, and a Jeep or two (Norment, 1991).

The Black Family As Contested Terrain

Nowhere is an image of harmonious family life more obviously represented than in a recent adver-

tisement for Ball Park Franks.[2] In that ad, a casually dressed Michael and Juanita Jordan stand with a small child (presumably one of their young sons), all smiling gleefully at the camera while clutching hot dogs. Reminiscent of a family portrait, Jordan has one arm draped over Juanita's shoulder; she similarly places a light touch on the shoulder of the child. The headline reads: Michael's Family Values. The scripted text proclaims: "Enjoy Ball Park Franks, Fat Free Classics, and kid-size Fun Franks, all with the delicious Ball Park taste that your family values."

In this advertisement, the Jordans lend support to one of the most ubiquitous themes of post-Reagan America: a vocal rhetoric that calls for a return to "traditional" family values. While never explicitly defined, the word "values" suggests a link between morality and responsibility; the entire phrase advises Americans to hearken back to bygone eras when family life was presumably simpler, purer, and more enjoyable. This emphasis on "pro-family" issues and traditional values can be partially seen as conservative backlash aimed at advances of women and other political minorities, and the perceived challenge to hegemony of heterosexual love and marriage. Returning to the past means returning to the rigid gender role conformity and racial segregation reasserted in the wake of World War II (Reeves & Campbell, 1994). By aligning himself with the term "family values," Michael Jordan joins a whole host of individuals who have exploited a storybook fantasy of family, hearth, and home. Realizing the powerful emotions and sentiment that could be mobilized around appeals to a mythical nuclear family, Ronald Reagan co-opted images of harmonious domesticity as the presumed ideal American way of life. Despite the recent numerical decline of the nuclear family and Reagan's tumultuous relationship with his own children, as well as his status as the only divorcee to serve as president, appeals to a nostalgic, conflict-free family life proliferated throughout the Reagan-Bush era (Jeffords, 1994; Fiske, 1994). The 1990s continued to be fraught with nostalgic depictions of the family as the ultimate refuge of the traditional American values of hard work, discipline, and self-denial.

The conservative political agenda of the New Right, developed under the tenure of presidents Reagan and Bush and continuing through the 1990s under the direction of Newt Gingrich, politicized notions of family in particular ways. The presumed breakdown of the seemingly stable family unit with the never-divorced breadwinner/husband and housewife/mother continues to be used by conservatives to explain many of the social ills exacerbated by a rapidly deindustrializing economy and conservative political policies which privilege a corporate world view (Fiske, 1994). Ironically, the profile of the ideal nuclear family celebrated by Reagan might best be described as representing "the way we never were" to borrow Stephanie Coontz's (1992) phrase. Until the 19th century in Western industrializing countries, both women and men worked inside or around the home. Only during the Industrial Revolution did "men's work" move outside the home while middle-class White women remained confined and enshrined within the domestic sphere. By the early portion of the 20th century, consumerism, a developing youth culture and women's suffrage all contributed to the contestation of the extended family as the dominate norm. According to Elaine Tyler May (1988), only in the wake of World War II did cold war fears, increased prosperity, new technolo-

gies, and fears over women's emancipation help fuel conformity to the suburban family ideal. Thus, this much-debated nuclear unit has only recently come into existence and has almost never been experienced by the vast majority of poor and disenfranchised people at any time. Furthermore, the romanticized ideal of the nuclear family, with the breadwinner husband/father and the wife/mother who does not work outside the home, now accounts for only 7% of American families (Hoff & Farnham, 1992).

Despite these numbers, the nuclear family continues to serve as the beacon of presumed morality in an era fraught with all sorts of changes and challenges. Under the guise of morality, fairness and a commitment to family values, a whole host of regressive social policies have been enacted. For example, women's access to legal abortions has been greatly curbed, civil rights legislation has been rolled back, and antipornography campaigns have been waged against artists, while corporate freedom and capital expand (Clarke, 1991; Reeves & Campbell, 1994; Faludi, 1991). The New Right's claim of declining family values can thus be seen as a way to legitimize a series of policy changes enacted to expand capital as well as a way to remain staunchly antiwelfare, antiabortion, antiaffirmative action, and antigay (Reeves & Campbell, 1994). The classic example of this type of reductive reasoning is found in the statements made after the Los Angles riots in 1992 by then Vice President Dan Quayle, who noted that "the anarchy and lack of structure in our inner cities are testament to how quickly civilization falls apart when the family foundation cracks" (quoted in Hoff & Farnham, 1992). This isolated focus on the family renders invisible political, economic, and cultural issues, which all continue to have

enormous impact on the poor, people of color and White women.

Images of Jordan within the nuclear family contrast strikingly with the suggestion of the Black family's decline and destruction. The well-publicized "decline" of the African American family is a notion that itself is class-based, a strategy used by conservatives and liberals alike to marginalize the increasingly large number of people of color who find themselves in poverty. Rather than blaming poverty on larger economic changes—such as deindustrialization, a rapidly globalizing economy, or continuing political issues, including institutional racism and the gendered division of labor—the rhetoric returned to a classic blame-the-victim scenario. In post-Reagan America, renewed attacks were launched against the Black family as pathologically weak, indicative of what then Vice President Dan Quayle would call "a poverty of values" (Fiske, 1994).

These politicized notions of the family reinforced the conservative moralism of Reaganism that operates on the assumption of a binary logic privileging those who espoused the "traditional" virtues of hard work, determination, and loyalty while demonizing those who need legal, social, or financial assistance. Susan Jeffords (1994) argues that this dialogical reasoning of Reaganism positions individual Americans in two fundamentally different camps, separating the privileged "hard bodies" from the errant bodies. These "soft" and undesirable bodies are those which are infected—containing sexually transmitted diseases, immorality, laziness, and illegal chemicals. In a culture marked by race and gender, the soft body usually belonged to a female or person of color, whereas the prototype hard body was invariably male and White. According to Jeffords (1994), the classic example of the Reaganite hard body can be seen in some of the most popular Hollywood films of the era. The action film hero Rambo is the quintessential success story of the period: a muscular hard body—White, male, heterosexual—committed to military strength while fighting against the ineptitude of excessive governmental regulation and other bureaucracies (Jeffords, 1994). Jordan's hard body masculinity is much more consistent with the "kinder, gentler" version which Jeffords (1994) argues attracted popular appeal during the Bush presidency and continues into the 1990s. This prototype offers a twist on the classic masculine "hard body" of Rambo, a shift not toward softness but toward an increased commitment to self-reflection, the nuclear family, and intimacy. This "gentler" version of masculinity is less intimidating and, thus, partially explains how an African American man could gain mainstream support without much White uneasiness.

By contrast, the mythical profile of the welfare mother represents the iconic soft body of Reaganism, a site where pro-family discourses intersect with racism, sexism, and classism. This depiction rests on stereotypical racist and sexist images of the (assumed) Black matriarch, domineering, castigating, and lazy, who robs a husband or lover of his "rightful" role as head of the family while depending on welfare for sustenance (Reeves & Campbell, 1994). According to Black feminist Patricia Hill Collins (1989), gender plays an important role in the commonsense depiction of poverty. Poor African American women, the quintessential soft bodies of post-Reagan America, are often portrayed as overly masculine, apparently "choosing" to head the household in domineering ways. This inappropriate gender socialization is then passed on to their impressionable offspring who repeat the cycle by marginalizing the importance of the traditional male

provider. The result, according to both conservative and many liberal voices, is a life of welfare dependency (Collins, 1989). Thus, by appealing to circular reasoning, the absence of patriarchal power relations in these families is offered as the apparent "proof" of Black cultural deficiency (Baca Zinn, 1989; Collins, 1989). Or in the words of then Vice President Dan Quayle, "for those concerned about the children growing up in poverty, marriage is probably the best anti-poverty program of all" (quoted in Hoff & Farnham, 1992, p. 8).

The Jordan family serves as the moral obverse of this stereotypical vision of the Black family. This portrait is readily apparent in one *Newsweek* account, published in March of 1995 just as Jordan was contemplating a return to professional basketball after a brief sabbatical/retirement. A picture of Jordan holding his daughter Jasmine as he raises his retired jersey to the rafters is juxtaposed against a text that records reactions of young Jordan fans from "the beleaguered" Houston projects where teens stand around "drinking malt liquor from brown paper sacks" (Leland, 1995, p. 54). In addressing the issue of what Jordan meant to them,

a few of the players cited Jordan's game. But all talked about his life off the court: about his character, his family, and especially about his relationship with his father, James Jordan, who was murdered in 1993. "He's got a good attitude, he don't smoke, he don't drink," says Robert Taylor, 11, who considers Jordan his hero. "He's got two kids—*and* a wife." (p. 54)

As this passage suggests, the ideological salience of the Jordan familial bliss lies in the enticing depictions of harmony built on the traditional gender roles that middle-class men and women have been encouraged to follow when married. Juanita raises the children with love while Michael takes his role as the family's provider very seriously: "I've got to do more for

her, because this is what she expects of her husband—to be taken out to dinner, to movies, on vacations. . . . From a husband's point of view, I've got to improve" (quoted in Norment, 1991, p. 70).

While Jordan's position within the nuclear family represents an ideal that only a tiny minority of Americans can achieve, the image of Jordan as a private family man articulates a conservative moral agenda. The visibility of the African American family, such as the Jordans, reinforces the desirability of consumer comfort, patriarchal privilege, and familial bliss—all hallmarks of America, especially post-Reagan America (McDonald, 1995). The Jordans offer a particularly powerful image masking what Reeves and Campbell (1994) identify as the perils of "reverse Robin Hoodism." Despite significant challenges, post-Reagan America has seen budget cuts, program changes, and reorganizations in social programs coupled with increased public opposition to welfare, affirmative action, and civil rights laws. These changes and challenges have disproportionately and adversely affected people of color (Shull, 1993). As Andrews (1993, 1996) also has argued in an era increasingly committed to corporate freedom and individualism, the happiness of the Jordan family seemingly offers "proof" that the American Dream is available to those people of color who are apparently committed enough to pull themselves up by their bootstraps.

Concluding Remarks: Family Matters

In discussing representations of Michael Jordan, I have attempted to highlight some of the historically specific economic rationales and dominant cultural beliefs that constitute and are reciprocally reinforced through these depictions. Michael

Jordan is popular precisely because his commodified persona negotiates historically specific and complex gendered, racialized and sexualized meanings in ways that are socially accepted and culturally envied by mainstream audiences. The appealing persona of Jordan suggests that Black masculinity, which historically has been viewed as inappropriate to White and middle-class America, is represented in an attractive, albeit still highly ideologically charged, way. Given the intense focus on Jordan's "natural body," representations of the nuclear family serve a key role in this process. Jordan's status as a family man assists in suppressing the socially constructed portrait of a threatening Black sexuality. This idealized vision of Jordan within the nuclear family also reinforces the pro-family discourses of the New Right.

Cultural analysis suggests that particular popular figures are linked to a variety of discourses, suggesting multiple, often contradictory meanings, and the need to explore representations within a variety of contexts. Given this insight, it is possible to acknowledge both politically progressive and regressive elements within the phenomenon of Michael Jordan. Indeed, representations of Jordan defy racist sexual stereotypes just as these depictions assist in furthering a reactionary agenda in regard to U.S. families. Still, because cultural processes are fluid, there is no guarantee a specific version and vision of Michael Jordan will remain etched in history forever. Meanings are never essential for all time; rather they have to be constantly renewed and remade. Fresh associations will be forged as the "text" of Jordan is a boundless one, subject to rearticulation in accordance with a variety of historically specific needs and individual circumstances, including Jordan's own human agency. To locate representations within the realm of the historical and political also is to locate the commonsense meanings circulating in the wider culture within the realm of construction, contestation, and change. From this critical perspective, to interrogate representations of Michael Jordan is to offer cultural criticism as a strategy of intervention in the politicized terrain of commodified popular culture. This conceptualization alerts us to the contested character of social relations, so that we can envision alternative forms of cultural practices as well as the insight necessary to engage critically in the practice of social change.

References

Andrews, D. (1993). *Deconstructing Michael Jordan: Popular culture, politics, and postmodern America.* Unpublished doctoral dissertation, University of Illinois, Urbana-Champaign.

Andrews, D. (1996). The fact(s) of Michael Jordan's Blackness: Excavating a floating racial signifier. *Sociology of Sport Journal, 13*(2), 125–158.

Baca Zinn, M. (1989). Family, race, and poverty in the eighties. *Signs: Journal of Women in Culture and Society, 14*(41), 856–874.

Birrell, S. (1989). Racial relations theories and sport: Suggestions for a more critical analysis. *Sociology of Sport Journal, 6*(3), 212–227.

Birrell, S., & McDonald, M. (1993, February). *Privileged assault: The representation of violence and the inadequacy of segmented category analysis.* Paper presented at the meeting of the National Girls and Women in Sport Symposium, Slippery Rock, PA.

Calo, B. (Segment Producer). *Primetime Live.* (1991, June 13). *The puzzle of Michael Jordan: Why does he seem to fly?* [Transcript # 197]. Journal Graphics, Denver, CO.

Clarke, J. (1991). *New Times and old enemies: Essays on cultural studies and America.* London: Harper Collins Academic.

Cole, C., & Andrews, D. (1996). Look—it's NBA's *ShowTime*!: Visions of race in the popular imaginary. *Cultural Studies: A Research Annual, 1*(1), 141–181.

Cole, C, & Denny, D. (1994). Visualizing deviance in post-Reagan America: Magic Johnson, AIDS, and the promiscuous world of professional sport. *Critical Sociology, 20*(3), 123–147.

Collins, P. H. (1989). A comparison of two works on Black family life. *Signs: The Journal of Women in Culture and Society, 14*(41), 875–879.

Coontz, S. (1992). *The way we never were: American families and the nostalgia trap.* New York: Basic.

Curly, T. J. (1991). Fraternal bonding in the locker room: A profeminist analysis of talk about competition and women. *Sociology of Sport Journal, 8,* 119–135.

Davis, A. (1984). Rape, racism, and the myth of the Black rapist. In A. Jaggar & P. Rothenberg, (Eds.), *Feminist frameworks: Alternative accounts of the relations between women and men* (2nd ed., pp. 428–431). New York: McGraw-Hill.

Davis, L. (1990). The articulation of difference: White preoccupation with the question of racially linked genetic differences among athletes. *Sociology of Sport Journal, 7*(2), 179–187.

Desmond, J. (1994). Embodying difference: Issues in dance and cultural studies. *Cultural Critique, 26,* 33–62.

Dyreson, M. (1989). The emergence of consumer culture and the transformation of physical culture: American sport in the 1920s. *Journal of Sport History, 16*(3), 261–281.

Dyson, M. (1993). Be like Mike?: Michael Jordan and the pedagogy of desire. *Cultural Studies, 7*(1), 64–72.

Edsall, T., & Edsall, M. (1991). *Chain reaction: The impact of race, rights, and taxes on the American public.* New York: W. W. Norton.

Faludi, S. (1991). *Backlash: The undeclared war against American women.* New York: Anchor.

Fiske, J. (1994). *Media matters: Everyday culture and political change.* Minneapolis, MN: University of Minnesota.

Foucault, M. (1978). *History of sexuality: An introduction.* New York: Vintage Books.

Gates, H. L. (1994). Preface. In T. Golden (Ed.), *Black male: Representations of masculinity in contemporary art* (pp. 11–14). New York: Whitney Museum of American Art.

Giroux, H. (1994). *Disturbing pleasures.* New York: Routledge.

Golden, T. (1994). My brother. In T. Golden (Ed.), *Black male: Representations of masculinity in contemporary art* (pp. 19–43). New York: Whitney Museum of American Art.

Grossberg, L. (1992). *We gotta get out of this place: Popular conservatism and postmodern culture.* New York: Routledge.

Hall, S. (1985). Signification, representation, and ideology: Althusser and the post-structuralist debates. *Critical Studies in Mass Communication, 2,* 91–114.

Hall, S. (1986a). The problem of ideology: Marxism without guarantees. *Journal of Communication Inquiry,* **10**(2), 28–44.

Hall, S. (1986b). On postmodernism and articulation: An interview. *Journal of Communication Inquiry,* **10**(2), 45–60.

Hall, S. (1988). *The hard road to renewal: Thatcherism and the crisis of the left.* London: Verso.

Hall, S. (1991). Signification, representation and ideology: Althusser and the post-structuralist debates. In R. Avery & D. Eason (Eds.), *Critical perspectives on media and society* (pp. 88–113). New York: Guilford.

Harris, D. (1993). The current crisis in men's lingerie: Notes on the belated commercialization of a noncommercial product. *Salmagundi,* **100**, 131–139.

Harris, O. (1991). The image of the African American in psychological journals, 1825–1923. *The Black Scholar,* **21**(4), 25–29.

Harris, O. (1995). Muhammad Ali and the revolt of the Black athlete. In E. Gorn (Ed.), *Muhammad Ali: The people's champ* (pp. 54–69). Urbana, IL: The University of Illinois.

Hoff, J., & Farnham, C. (1992). Sexist and racist: The postcold war world's emphasis on family values. *Journal of Women's History,* **4**(2), 6–9.

hooks, b. (1992). *Black looks: Race and representation.* Boston: South End.

hooks, b. (1994). Feminism inside: Toward a Black body politic. In T. Golden (Ed.), *Black male: Representations of masculinity in contemporary art* (pp. 127–140). New York: Whitney Museum of American Art.

Howell, J. (1991). A revolution in motion: Advertising and the politics of nostalgia. *Sociology of Sport Journal,* **8**(3), 258–271.

Ingrassia, M. (1995). Calvin's world. *Newsweek,* **126**(11), 60–66.

Jackson, D. (1989, January 22). Calling the plays in black and white. *The Boston Globe,* pp. A30–A33.

Jackson, P. (1994). Black male: Advertising and the cultural politics of masculinity. *Gender, Place, and Culture,* **1**(1), 49–59.

Jeffords, S. (1994). *Hard bodies: Hollywood masculinity in the Reagan era.* New Brunswick, NJ: Rutgers University.

Katz, D. (1994). *Just do it: The Nike spirit in the corporate world.* New York: Random House.

King, S. (1993). The politics of the body and the body politic: Magic Johnson and the ideology of AIDS. *Sociology, of Sport Journal,* **10**, 270–285.

Kirkpatrick, C. (1991, December 23). The unlikeliest homeboy. *Sports Illustrated,* **75**(27), 70–75.

Lane, R., & McHugh, J. (1995, December 18). A very green 1995. *Forbes,* **156**(14), 212–232.

Leland, J. (1995, March 20). Hoop dreams: Will Michael Jordan return to basketball? *Newsweek,* **125**(12),48–55.

Lusted, D. (1991). The glut of personality. In C. Gledhill (Ed.), *Stardom: The industry of desire* (pp. 251–258). London: Associated University.

May, E. T. (1988). *Homeward bound: American families in the cold war era.* New York: Basic Books.

McDonald, M. (1995). *Clean "air": Representing Michael Jordan in the Reagan-Bush era.* Unpublished doctoral dissertation, University of Iowa, Iowa City.

Messner, M. (1988). Sport and male domination: The female athlete as contested terrain. *Sociology of Sport Journal,* **5**, 197–211.

Morse, M. (1983). Sport on television: Replay and display. In A. Kaplan (Ed.), *Regarding television: Critical approaches—an anthology* (pp. 44–66). Los Angeles: American Film Institute.

Murphy, T. (1985, June). On the rebound. *Madison Avenue,* **27**, 28–34.

Naughton, J. (1992). *Talking to the air: The rise of Michael Jordan.* New York: Warner.

Norment, L. (1991, November). Michael and Juanita Jordan talk about love, marriage, and life after basketball. *Ebony,* **47**, 68–76.

Raissman, R. (1984, October 18). Jordan soars for Nike deal: New strategy seen. *Advertising Age,* **1**, 58.

Reeves, J., & Campbell, R. (1994). *Cracked coverage: Television news, the anticocaine crusade, and the Reagan legacy.* Durham, NC: Duke University.

Roberts, R. (1983). *Papa Jack: Jack Johnson and the era of white hopes.* New York: Free Press.

Rowe, D., (1994). Accommodating bodies: Celebrity, sexuality, and "tragic Magic." *Journal of Sport and Social Issues,* **18**(2), 6–26.

Sabo, D., & Jansen, S. (1992). Images of men in the sport media: The social reproduction of the gender order. In S. Craig (Ed.), *Men, masculinity, and the media: Research on men and masculinities* (pp. 169–184). Newbury Park, CA: Sage.

Sammons, J. (1995). Rebel with a cause: Muhammad Ali as sixties protest symbol. In E. Gorn (Ed.), *Muhammad Ali: The people's champ* (pp. 154–180). Champaign: University of Illinois Press.

Shull, S. (1993). *A kinder gentler racism? The Reagan-Bush civil rights legacy.* Armonk, NY: M. E. Sharpe.

Sperling, D. (Executive Producer). (1989). *Michael Jordan: Come fly with me.* New York: CBS/Fox.

Swift, E. M. (1991, June 3). From corned beef to caviar. *Sports Illustrated,* **74**(27), 54–58.

Theberge, N. (1991). Reflections on the body in the sociology of sport. *Quest,* **43**, 123–134.

Vancil, M. (1992, May). Playboy interview: Michael Jordan. *Playboy,* 51–64.

Watney, S. (1989). *Policing desire: Pornography, AIDS, and the media* (2nd ed.) Minneapolis, MN: University of Minnesota.

West, C. (1993). *Race matters.* Boston: Beacon Press.

Wiggins, D. (1989). Great speed but little stamina: The historical debate over Black athletic superiority. *Journal of Sport History,* **16**(2), 158–185.

Notes

1. It is interesting to note the ironic rearticulation of "hang time" to describe Michael Jordan's athletic talents. In this country's sordid history of race relations to speak of hanging, especially in relationship to African American men, is to suggest lynching. That an African American man is marketed for his "hang time" complete with a protruding tongue is ironic given the historical lethal power of lynching to reinforce ideologies of White dominance.

2. I would like to thank Laurel Davis for bringing this ad to my attention.

 Article Review Form at end of book.

Why is the Internet, as a medium, easily exploited by hate groups? How might Internet users best use the medium to challenge racism and anti-Semitism, as well as homophobia and sexism?

Hatemongering on the Data Highway

Bigotry carves out a niche in cyberspace.

Richard Z. Chesnoff

Chicago computer buff Bob Arbetman was happily surfing through cyberspace one night when his attention was drawn to a bulletin board offering titled HOLOHOAX.TXT. Tapping in, Arbetman found himself in touch with a professional Holocaust denier whose message, he says, was rabidly antisemitic. "It was straight neo-Nazi propaganda," recalls the 37-year-old electrical engineer.

Outraged by what he was downloading, Arbetman alerted the Simon Wiesenthal Center, the Los Angeles-based institute that exposes neo-Nazis and other bigots. His tip and calls from others who had encountered similar online, often violent, antiblack, antigay, antisemitic hate messages triggered an extensive three-year investigation by Wiesenthal researcher Rick Eaton. The result, U.S. News has learned, is a massive dossier of cyberspace hatemongering that the Wiesenthal Center has just submitted to FCC Chairman Reed Hundt. "It may be time for the FCC to place a cop on the superhighway of information," says Rabbi Abraham Cooper, Wiesenthal Center associate dean.

A right to hate. But any attempt to police cyberspace is fraught with practical and legal issues. The FCC, which oversees the nation's airwaves, has no jurisdiction over the Internet, the sprawling computer network of more than a million computers in universities, research institutions, private companies and homes around the world. Like the international telephone system, there is no overall governing body that checks on the system's estimated 25 million users.

Controlling Internet traffic would not necessarily be legal, even if it were possible. "This is strictly a First Amendment issue," says Mike Godwin, a lawyer with the Electronic Frontier Foundation, a Washington-based public interest group devoted to cyberspace freedom. The question is whether the Internet is more like a public broadcast system such as television or radio, and so subject to control, or more like the telephone system or the mail, which have greater freedoms over the content of the messages. Unless hate mail directly interferes with civil liberties, insists Godwin, "I can't conceive of any constitutional controls." Net users who do not want to view the material can simply block it, he says.

The very strengths of the Internet—its broad accessibility, open-minded discussions and anonymity—can be used to advantage by hatemongers. Sophisticated bigots often infiltrate otherwise legitimate discussion groups on the Net that deal with history or sociology. Cooper is especially alarmed because cyberspace provides hatemongers with far easier access to two things they never have had before: a mass audience and the attention of young, unsuspecting users. "It's the natural venue for peddling their wares to computer age kids," says Cooper.

Some of the offerings are frightening invitations to violence and hate. A file called HOMOBASH describes shooting a gay person in the face with a handgun. A graphic titled MONKEY pictures blacks copulating with animals and suggests this was the start of the AIDS epidemic. Another shows a bare-chested, hooknosed Jew holding a bloody knife and standing in a sea of gentile blood.

Some commercial networks, such as Prodigy, say they have taken steps to ban the use of their systems by propagandists of bias. Vinton Cerf, president of the Internet Society, a user organization, says he and his colleagues are preparing a set of voluntary norms they hope will put restraints on racists and other objectionable E-mailers. But guidelines may have little effect in a freewheeling venue such as the Internet. The FCC, for its part, turned the Wiesenthal Center dossier over to the Justice Department last week.

The most effective protection against bigotry on the Net, argue many enthusiasts, lies in the freedom that has characterized the culture from the start. Cyberhate so enraged 53-year-old Vancouver resident Ken McVay, for instance, that he established his own server list that already provides thousands of carefully documented responses to the odious claims of extremists and Holocaust deniers. "It's the only way to answer these liars," says McVay. "Every time we knock down one of these guys, it's there forever in the computer."

 Article Review Form at end of book.

WiseGuide Wrap-Up

- "Pop culture" images reflect and perpetuate the ethnic, racial, and gendered hierarchies of the societies in which they are produced; they also sometimes challenge those hierarchies.

- Sociologists and anthropologists, among others, analyze popular culture for clues about the values and structures of contemporary societies.

- U.S. popular culture often reflects the U.S. position within a larger global system; thinking critically about popular culture allows us to situate the images and messages we receive from the media within broader systems of inequality and to assess our own participation in those systems.

R.E.A.L. Sites

This list provides a print preview of typical **Coursewise** R.E.A.L. sites. (There are over 100 such sites at the **Courselinks**™ site.) The danger in printing URLs is that web sites can change overnight. As we went to press, these sites were functional using the URLs provided. If you come across one that isn't, please let us know via email to: webmaster@coursewise.com. Use your Passport to access the most current list of R.E.A.L. sites at the **Courselinks** site.

Site name: Ethnic Images in the Comics

URL: http://www.libertynet.org/balch/comics/comics.html

Why is it R.E.A.L.? Popular culture reflects social biases and challenges them. Characters from the comics have influenced American popular understandings of African-Americans, Jewish people, and people of various nationalities, as the readings assembled at this site indicate.

Key topics: popular culture, stereotyping, changing images of ethnic groups

Try this: Review the papers here and write a brief report on how the comics have both reinforced and undermined popular stereotypes about particular racial and ethnic groups.

Site name: Popular Culture and the Rise of the Mass Media

URL: http://www.middlebury.edu/~ac400/index.html

Why is it R.E.A.L.? As your readings in this section indicate, athletes and the athletics industry are closely linked to global and national discourses on race. At this site you'll find, among other papers, one devoted to Nike and Michael Jordan, written by a Middlebury College undergraduate studying with Professor Timothy Spears.

Key topics: mass media, Michael Jordan and Nike, Harlem Renaissance

Try this: Click on the "Advertising and Popular Culture" button and then choose Josh Bonifa's paper "Nike and Michael Jordan." How does this paper relate to Readings 4 and 5, by Goldman and McDonald, respectively? Choose an object or issue from popular culture that's interesting to you and draw a diagram of how this object or issue is linked to local, national, and international patterns of racial and ethnic stratification.

section

3

Key Points

- Globalization and technological innovation affect the processes of immigration and the possibilities of assimilation in the United States.

- When immigrants from a dissimilar culture come to constitute 10 percent of a small town's population, the long-time residents become uneasy.

- Nativism resurges in anti-immigrant sentiment which diverts popular focus from problems with the economy.

- New immigrants still see the United States as a land of opportunity but face many challenges in realizing the "American Dream."

Race, Ethnicity, and Immigration

 **WiseGuide Intro**

Most people in the United States today can trace their ancestry to people who came from other nations. Nearly 11 percent of the people living in the United States were themselves born in other countries, while most of those born into U.S. citizenship are descendants of people who arrived here as slaves or indentured servants, as immigrants or refugees. Many who identify as Native American can also trace parts of their heritage to Europe, Asia, or Africa. The history of immigration to this country, which has been long seen as a land of opportunity and possibility, serves as the foundation for its unique racial and ethnic diversity. Pride in the United States as the great "melting pot" of humanity is instilled in many citizens, who believe that the Statue of Liberty's directive to "Send [me] your tired, your poor, your huddled masses yearning to breathe free" accurately reflects public policy on immigration.

However, despite—or perhaps because of—the importance of immigration in the history of this country, the United States as a state and U.S. citizens as a people display a noteworthy ambivalence around immigration issues. On the one hand, people believe that immigrants built this superpower nation and embrace the strength wrought by the diversity immigration patterns created; on the other hand, they worry about "protecting" the country from immigrants and the impact of immigration processes. This ambivalence appears in the history of federal policy on immigration. In 1783, George Washington declared that this is a country "whose bosom is open to receive the persecuted and oppressed of all nations," although actual practice made some "persecuted and oppressed" people more welcome than others. A little more than 200 years later, Ronald Reagan made no pretense of receiving the oppressed with open arms when he authorized the Immigration Reform and Control Act, which was designed to rid the country of so-called illegal aliens, many of whom are people of color. Popular sentiment against legal and undocumented immigrants alike appears to be on the rise at the end of the century, despite the immigrant legacies of most U.S. citizens.

U.S. history includes a wide range of policies and practices that have linked immigration rights to nationality, race, ethnicity, IQ scores, language, education, occupation, and the specific politics of any given period. While many Western European immigrants have enjoyed quick access to legal citizenship throughout the country's history, foreign-born Chinese-Americans could not hold citizenship in the United States until 1943, and foreign-born Japanese-Americans were granted citizenship rights only in 1952, though immigrants from both countries had long made important contributions to settling the country and building its infrastructure. After World War I, the United States strictly limited the immigration of people from Eastern European countries. This practice continued through World War II and effectively barred the immigration of many Eastern European Jews, whom the U.S. government returned to their countries of origin to face very uncertain futures. In ensuing decades, when Eastern Europe came under communist rule, the United States became eager to accept as refugees people who had left the same Eastern bloc countries, which had become Cold War enemies of the United States. In the aftermath of the fall of communism in this area, Eastern Europeans once again find it difficult to immigrate to the United States.

Should the United States limit immigration? What might be the impact of various strategies to do so? Some critics of President Reagan's 1986 Immigration Reform and Control Act claim that its impact has been to establish a permanent underclass of exploited and exploitable undocumented workers—mostly people of color—who have no hope of ever achieving the American Dream, let alone citizenship or fair treatment in work, housing, and the legal system. How should the United States restrict immigration, if it should be restricted? To what extent should race and nationality be factors in admitting applicants for citizenship? What might be the social and economic impact of lifting immigration restrictions? How does the United States benefit from immigration, both legal and illegal?

The articles in this section are designed to provide a range of perspectives on this complex issue. In "The Transnationals: Status of Immigrants in the U.S.," anthropologist Nancy Foner compares and contrasts the experiences of people in the "current wave" of immigration with those of people in the last great wave, which peaked before World War I. Journalist Roy Beck's article examines the resentments of white people in Wausau, Wisconsin, as they struggle with the social impact of Hmong immigration to their community. Sociologist Kitty Calavita provides an important framework for analyzing anti-immigrant sentiments as she explores nativism in "The New Politics of Immigration: 'Balanced Budget Conservatism' and the Symbolism of Proposition 187."

? Questions ?

Reading 7. How are the experiences of contemporary immigrants to the United States similar to those of immigrants of earlier generations? How are they different? How do changes in the immigrant experience reflect global changes?

Reading 8. What are the sources of the resentment that white citizens of Wausau, Wisconsin, harbor against their Hmong neighbors? How might this community resolve its problems?

Reading 9. What is "balanced-budget conservatism," and how is it connected to rising anti-immigrant sentiment among California voters? Why does the author argue that California citizens are using their votes "symbolically"?

How are the experiences of contemporary immigrants to the United States similar to those of immigrants of earlier generations? How are they different? How do changes in the immigrant experience reflect global changes?

The Transnationals:

Status of Immigrants in the U.S.

Nancy Foner

Nancy Foner is a professor of anthropology at the State University of New York at Purchase.

America's last great wave of immigration began more than a hundred years ago and peaked before World War I. A new wave, only decades old, is transforming the nation today. In 1997, an all-time-record 29 million foreign-born persons were living in the United States—the proportion of immigrants, at 11 percent, is inching up toward the 1910 figure of 15 percent. And these new arrivals are moving beyond the gateway cities into the heartland. Hmong refugees from Laos, to pick one example, are now more than 10 percent of the population of Wausau, Wisconsin.

Immigrants who came through Ellis Island in the last wave were overwhelmingly from southern and eastern Europe; today's arrivals are far more diverse. They come from Mexico, the Philippines, Vietnam, the Dominican Republic, and China—to name the top five source countries for legal immigrants in 1995. Where once there were Jewish pushcart peddlers, now there are Korean greengrocers and Indian newsstand dealers. Mexican gardeners and busboys are also a familiar part of the urban landscape.

A century ago, immigrants were generally poor and low skilled; today, too, many reach America with little more than the shirts on their backs. Still, according to the 1990 census, a third of all those who arrived in the previous five years were college graduates. The West African driving your cab in New York City could well turn out to be studying engineering at City College. The Korean greengrocer may have a master's degree. Many are practicing their professions and trades here—in medicine, engineering, and computers. And some are bringing with them substantial amounts of capital that give them a start in business.

In what seems like a timeless feature of immigrant settlement, today's newcomers often cluster in enclaves near kinfolk and friends, finding comfort and security in an environment of shared languages and institutions. But new polyethnic neighborhoods, with no parallel in previous waves of immigration, have also emerged. New York's Elmhurst section, in the borough of Queens, now has the distinction of welcoming more people from more places than any other ZIP code in the United States. Between 1991 and 1995, nearly 13,000 immigrants from a stunning 123 countries moved there. Among better-educated and more prosperous immigrants, a new kind of suburban existence is developing in the nation's bedroom communities. Monterey Park, California, only eight miles east of downtown Los Angeles, has been dubbed the first suburban Chinatown.

Another dramatic difference is that most of today's immigrants are people of color, while those in the last great wave were, in the main, phenotypically white. Most newcomers enter racially polarized cities, where they often live among—and are victims of the same kind of prejudice as—native-born blacks and Hispanics. Bear in mind, however, that race was an issue in the last wave as well. Jews and Italians, thought to belong to inferior races, faced outspoken prejudice.

Some reasons that immigrants are drawn to America do not change. Today's newcomers are often escaping oppressive governments and poverty. In 1991, the minimum monthly salary for full-time work in the United States was thirteen times higher than the minimum wage in the Dominican Republic; a Brazilian baby-sitter in New York makes more in one week than she made in a month as a head nurse back home. Government policies have also influenced the flow of migrants. Some countries, like China, have relaxed their exit restrictions. In the United States, the liberalization of immigration laws after 1965, along with new refugee policies, opened the gates to millions (most notably, Asians) who had been shut out before.

Once the immigrants settle here, modern transportation and communications change the context in which they live out their lives. Some social scientists even think a new term needs to be invented - "transnational"—to characterize the way many people now forge ties across national borders. Even before they arrive, their exposure to a new, global consumer culture and economy means that today's immigrants are more culturally attuned to the United States than their predecessors were. Once, letters spread the word about America; now, movies and television bring vivid, up-close views of American popular culture to the remotest villages in the developing world.

A century ago, the trip back to Italy took about two weeks, and more than a month elapsed between sending a letter home and receiving a reply. Today's immigrants can hop on a plane or make a phone call to check out how things are going at home. They can participate in weddings of scattered relatives by watching videotapes sent by mail and maintain business involvement in more than one country through modern telecommunications. And the technology is not all that's changed. New, dual-nationality provisions in a growing number of countries allow immigrants who become United States citizens to vote in their home country as well as here. The Dominican Republic will soon allow its citizens to cast their ballots in polling places abroad, making New York's Dominican community the second largest constituency in Dominican elections— exceeded only by Santo Domingo.

The newcomers are a force to be reckoned with. In California, the Republican Party worries about alienating the growing Hispanic vote; Miami already has a Cuban American mayor. By 1990, Asians were 15 percent of the entering class at Harvard and almost 25 percent at MIT. Although the Chinese were once vilified as the "yellow peril" and Japanese Americans were imprisoned in internment camps not so long ago, Asian Americans now have a new image; some even call them the "model minorities."

Will the new immigrants follow the path of those who went before? How will their children respond to the American scene? Who among them will become our leaders? All we can say with certainty is that this new wave of immigration, like its predecessor, will profoundly change the way we live.

 Article Review Form at end of book.

What are the sources of the resentment that white citizens of Wausau, Wisconsin, harbor against their Hmong neighbors? How might this community resolve its problems?

The Ordeal of Immigration in Wausau

Roy Beck

It all began simply enough, when a few churches and individuals in Wausau, Wisconsin, decided to resettle some Southeast Asian refugees during the late 1970s. To most residents, it seemed like a nice thing to do. Nobody meant to plant the seeds for a social transformation. But this small and private charitable gesture inadvertently set into motion events that many residents today feel are spinning out of control. Wausau—the county seat of the nation's champion milk-producing county—has learned that once the influx starts, there's little chance to stop it. Regardless of how many newcomers failed to find jobs in this north-central Wisconsin city of 37,500, or how abraded the social fabric became, the immigrant population just kept growing.

In little more than a decade the immigrant families' children have come to make up almost a quarter of the elementary schools' enrollment, crowding facilities past their limits—and there's no peak in sight. The majority of immigrant students are Southeast Asians, and most of these are from the nomadic Hmong mountain tribes of Laos, which unsuccessfully tried to prevent a Communist takeover of their homeland some twenty years ago. Seventy percent of the immigrants

and their descendants are receiving public assistance, because the local labor market has not been able to accommodate them. Religious and other private agencies—which, through federal agreements, create most of the refugee streams into American communities—are pledged to care for the newcomers for only thirty days.

Native-born taxpayers must shoulder most of the rising costs of providing more infrastructure, public services, teachers, and classrooms for the burgeoning community of immigrants, who make up relatively little of the tax base. In 1992 alone the Wausau school district's property-tax rate rose 10.48 percent—three times as much as taxes in an adjoining school district with few immigrants.

"At first, most saw the new residents as novel and neat; people felt good about it," Fred Prehn, a dentist and the father of two school-age children, told me during a visit I made to Wausau some months ago. At the time we spoke, he was the senior member of Wausau's school board. "Now we're beginning to see gang violence and guns in the schools. Immigration has inspired racism here that I never thought we had." Prehn accused religious agencies of swelling the immigrant population without regard to the city's capac-

ity for assimilation. He said that the numbers and concentration of newcomers had forced the school board into a corner from which busing was the only escape. English was becoming the minority spoken language in several schools. Many native-born parents feared that their children's education was being compromised by the language-instruction confusion; many immigrant parents complained that their children couldn't be assimilated properly in schools where the immigrant population was so high. For two years citizens were polarized by the prospect of busing—something that would have been inconceivable in 1980. Divisions deepened last September, when the school board initiated the busing, and again in December, when voters recalled Prehn and four other board members, replacing them with a slate of anti-busing candidates. Community divisions are likely to persist, since busing supporters threaten lawsuits if the new board ends the busing.

Even more of a shock has been the emergence of organized gang activity. Wausau Detective Sergeant Paul Jicinsky told me that Asian gangs of thieves, centered in St. Paul and Milwaukee, have recruited immigrant youths in Wausau. Most small Wisconsin cities started Asian-refugee resettlement programs at

Roy Beck, "The Ordeal of Immigration in Wausau," *The Atlantic,* April 1994, Vol. 273, No. 4, p. 84. Reprinted by permission of the author.

the prodding of government and religious leaders a decade or so ago, and most are now part of a Crime Information Exchange that, Jicinsky said, had been established almost exclusively to keep track of Asian gang activity in Minnesota and Wisconsin. Hmong parents, lamenting that their difficulty with English impedes their exercise of authority over their children, were at the forefront of those asking the police to combat gang activity. The cycle of community tensions spins round as native youths link up with outside white gangs to respond to Asian gangs. Compared with the urban core of many big cities, Wausau remains quite a peaceful place. But the comparison that matters for most residents is with the Wausau that used to be. "We don't want to become another California," a Wausau businessman told me. It's a fear often expressed as residents grapple with the problems familiar to America's congested coastal urban areas after nearly three decades of federally sponsored mass immigration and refugee resettlement.

At the same time, frustration grows among immigrants whose economic assimilation is dramatically incomplete. That frustration, in combination with resentment among natives over taxes and busing, seems to be the cause of interethnic violence among the young. The violence takes varied forms. A dance at Wausau East High School, for instance, had to be canceled just as it was starting because of a fight between immigrant and native girls which was serious enough that an ambulance had to be called. Mayor John D. Hess, in a newsletter to all residents, wrote, "Is there a problem with groups/gangs of school age kids in Wausau? Emphatically, yes. The number of incidents involving group violence leads all of us to believe that groups of school age kids are organizing for whatever reasons. . . . Is there a problem relating to racial tensions in Wausau? Emphatically, yes."

The 1980 U.S. Census found Wausau to be the most ethnically homogeneous city in the nation, with less than one percent of the population other than white. "This was a very nice thriving community; now immigration problems have divided the town and changed it drastically," Sandy Edelman, a mother of preschool-age children, told me. "Neighborhood is pitted against neighborhood. When we were moving here, a few years ago, I had this image of children walking to school. It was paradise, we thought. We never thought it was possible there ever could be busing in these schools."

A Middle-Class Dream

Although Wausau is not marked by splashy displays of wealth, the word "paradise" crops up in wistful descriptions of the recent past by all types of residents, including immigrants. They obviously aren't talking about some idyllic South Seas utopia. What they have in mind seems to be a kind of pragmatic middle-class American dream, in which labor produced a comfortable standard of living in a community that was under the control of its residents and where there existed a safe, predictable domestic tranquility in which to rear children and nearby open spaces for north-country recreation. It was a way of life created by the descendants of German and Polish immigrants and New England Yankee migrants, who by 1978 had spent roughly a century getting used to one another and creating a unified culture.

On my visit to Wausau, I found some anger. But the overwhelming emotion seemed to be sadness about a social revolution that the community as a whole had never requested or even discussed. While most residents spoke well of the immigrants as individuals, they thought that the volume of immigration had crossed some kind of social and economic

threshold. Many sensed that their way of life is slipping away, overwhelmed by outside forces they are helpless to stop.

Wausau leaders describe their city prior to 1978 as one with no social tensions and only traces of crime. Residents enjoyed a long tradition of progressive politics, education, and business. A healthy match between the labor force and well-paying jobs was the result of a diverse economy heavily reliant on the Wausau Insurance Companies and the manufacture of windows, paper, cheese, electric motors and generators, fast-food-outlet exhaust fans, and garden tools.

In the eyes of some residents, though, this "paradise" may well have been boring. "This was a rather sterile community, and we needed ethnic diversity," says Phyllis A. Bermingham, the director of the county department that administers the jobs program for welfare recipients. "I'm glad Wausau had major refugee resettlement. It has added so much variety." Sue Kettner, who is in charge of refugee services at a family-planning agency, says, "I have a dream that Wausau will become uniquely cosmopolitan and take advantage of its diversity." The until-recently "sterile" and homogeneous Wausau-area schools now enroll students from Laos, Cambodia, Thailand, Vietnam, China, the Philippines, Korea, Japan, Norway, Albania, Egypt, the former East Germany, the former Yugoslavia, and the former Czechoslovakia.

The idea of a moratorium on immigration comes up often in discussions in Wausau. But many people told me that they don't raise the idea in public, because they believe that religious, media, and government leaders would readily label any kind of criticism of immigration a manifestation of racism. From 1924 until 1965 the nation's immigration laws prevented foreign migration from reshaping the social landscape of American communities. The laws no longer do. Wausau is but one example of the results of radically modified laws, and many residents are astonished at the rapidity and relentlessness of change.

From a few dozen refugees in 1978, Wausau's immigrant community grew to 200 by 1980, doubled from there by 1982, and doubled again by 1984. Since then it has more than quintupled, to reach roughly 4,200. Even if the influx slows, Southeast Asians may become the majority population in Wausau well within the present residents' lifetimes. In this, Wausau is not unique but only an indicator of the demographic effects of current immigrant streams in the nation as a whole.

First Stream: Refugee Resettlement

When they agreed to become local resettlement sponsors, in the late 1970s, Wausau congregations did not simply provide refuge for a few Hmong, Lao, and Vietnamese families; they also inadvertently created a channel through which the federal government could send a continuing stream of refugees. "In the beginning we had no concept of what this would turn into," says Jean Russell, a county official who helps administer public assistance to some 2,900 local immigrants.

Wausau residents discovered that the refugees invited to stay in their home town soon began issuing their own invitations and serving as local sponsors for their relatives. (Around the same time, the congregations ceased serving as formal sponsors.) The cost of inviting was low, since government agencies paid nearly all the new arrivals' expenses. And for the same reason the lack of jobs was no deterrent to invitations. The first wave of refugees thus sent for more.

The resettlement stream shows no sign of drying up. The main source of Hmong immigrants is refugee camps in Thailand that were set up nineteen years ago, after the long Indochina wars. But there are still roughly 20,000 Hmong in the Thai camps today. Thailand insists that it should not have to continue to provide refuge.

United Nations workers continue to move people out of the camps. Inasmuch as there are already more than 40 million refugees and displaced persons worldwide, the primary UN solution has to be repatriation to the refugees' original home country. UN officials consider permanent resettlement in another country to be a last resort. And they and others say that it is now safe for the Hmong to return home. According to a State Department spokeswoman, "The United States believes the Hmong can go back to Laos. We have been watching repatriations all along. Our people investigate. There never has been one verifiable story of anybody being persecuted for having been repatriated."

But that does not mean that the Hmong resettlement into the United States will stop. The spokeswoman explains that current U.S. policy leaves the decision up to the Hmong in the camps. If they decide they don't want to go back home to Laos, they will be put into a pool for American resettlement, even though there is no reasonable suspicion that they face the threat of persecution in Laos. (This is not unusual: the majority of refugees coming into the United States do not meet a "last resort" criterion for resettlement.) If most of the Hmong decide against returning to Laos, one U.S. official estimates, 19,000 may be put into U.S. resettlement channels. That may not sound like much when compared with the number of immigrants into the United States as a whole, but for a community like

Wausau, where refugees have already settled and where future refugees will surely go, the potential impact of 19,000 is great.

Second Stream: Secondary Migration

Cities where refugees were resettled tend to be rewarded with a secondary migration of refugees who have first been settled elsewhere in the United States. "They heard how good it was here and moved from big cities, mostly from California, because of the crime, unemployment, and overcrowding," Yi Vang, who was first settled in Memphis and moved to Wausau in 1983, told me. Jean Russell, of the county welfare department, emphasized in our conversation that "they are really nice people," but nonetheless shook her head in consternation at the additional burden that secondary migration puts on the social-service system. "Why do so many come here?" she asked, and answered her own question: "This is sort of the right-sized city. It is a wonderful place to live." Wisconsin's generous welfare system is a big draw. A study by the Wisconsin Policy Research Institute found that when the federal government began to cut back its relief benefits to refugees, in 1982, large numbers of refugees sought out the states that provided the best Aid to Families with Dependent Children payments. Wisconsin became a popular destination.

One branch of the secondary-migration stream that provides just a trickle now will potentially add a considerable flow: As the refugees become citizens, the 1965 Immigration Act and its successors give them the right to bring in members of their extended families through regular immigration channels. A continuous chain of immigration can ensue, as it already has among many nationalities, particularly in several coastal states.

Third Stream: High Immigrant Fertility

Natives in Wausau complain about the size of Hmong families. John Weeks, the director of the International Population Center, at San Diego State University, and a colleague have studied the Hmong and believe that their birth rate in this country may be one of the highest of any ethnic group in the world.

Unremarkable in Wausau would be a twenty-two year old Hmong woman with five kids who comes to Family Planning Health Services for a pregnancy test and contraceptive advice, Sue Kettner says. She says that part of the reason for the big families is the terrible misery and high death rate the Hmong suffered during their long fight with Communists. "I talked to one man whose parents and four brothers and sisters were dead," Kettner told me. "He was having ten children. He wasn't willing to contracept."

Life in America boosts Hmong infant-survival rates beyond what they were in Asia, Weeks says, and the Hmongs have lower infant-mortality rates than African-American natives because they have better access to social services and their culture encourages positive prenatal behavior. "They don't smoke, drink, or get fat during pregnancy," he says.

"We find the girls' periods start as early as the third grade," says Lynell Anderson, the coordinator of the Wausau schools' English as a Second Language program. "We've had pregnant sixth-graders." Pregnancies in junior high school are not uncommon. Although such cultural patterns would not be so noticeable in Los Angeles or New York City, they are conspicuous and jarring to many Wausau parents concerned about the future of the Hmong girls and about the effects on their own children. Marilyn Fox, an ESL teacher, was quoted in the local newspaper in 1992 lamenting pregnancies in her junior high. The article pointed out that such pregnancies conflict directly with Wisconsin law, which invalidates the consent to intercourse given by anyone under sixteen. And anyone sixteen or older who impregnates an underage girl is guilty of a felony. Fox and a colleague complained that none of the Hmong men or boys impregnating the girls were being prosecuted. But many communities find it difficult to impose American standards of behavior on people who claim membership in another culture.

At one point Anderson sat down with some other teachers to take an informal look at the list of Hmong girls in high school. They calculated that 35 percent were pregnant or already had children. That, of course, didn't include the Hmong mothers who had dropped out of school. Few kids marry without having children immediately, and the Hmong culture of arranged marriages ensures that pregnant girls get married to somebody. Single-parent families—which some officials identify as a growing social problem among Wausau natives—are virtually nonexistent among the Hmong. The availability of infant formula may also contribute to the high fertility: "We've heard the Hmong in Laos have kids three years apart, because of breast feeding. But here it is every one or one and a half years, because women have moved to formula to be more modern," Kettner says. All the various factors add up to substantial population growth. The Wausau Daily Herald cited a striking statistic from the 1990 Census which illustrates the widely disparate fertility rates: 7.7 percent of European-American natives in Wausau were under the age of six, as were 30 percent of residents of Southeast Asian origin.

Both Weeks and Kettner see signs that the fertility rate is likely to come down. "The Hmong Association has a very positive view of family planning," Kettner says, "because it sees the economic need for women to work." Tou Yang, a young case manager for the county program that finds jobs for people on welfare, says that high fertility forces some people to stay on public assistance because a low-wage job won't replace lost welfare benefits, which can be sizable for large families. Total public assistance (AFDC, food stamps, Medicaid, and housing and energy subsidies) for a Hmong family can be worth more than $20,000 a year, according to local officials. The welfare-use rate for immigrants in the county is sixteen times as high as it is for natives.

Yang says that some of the Hmong talk about having small families, but their idea of small is generally four children. That is a bit higher than what the demographer Leon Bouvier, in his book *Fifty Million Californians?*, says is the Latino fertility rate, which is such an important contributor to that state's rapid population growth. At four the population will still soar. A couple in a four-child culture has eight times as many great-grandchildren as a couple in a two-child culture.

Population and Taxes

In 1978 Wausau taxpayers were beginning to enjoy the fruits of the replacement-level fertility that Americans had adopted during the emergence of modern environmentalism and feminism, early in the decade. Gone were the days of the Baby Boom and a perpetual need to build lots more schools, sewers, streets, and so on. Government could direct its energy toward maintaining and improving the quality of existing institutions. The student population had stabilized and even declined some.

But in 1994 the Wausau public school system is struggling to handle an increase of more than 1,500 students in less than a decade, nearly all of them children of immigrants. Although some schools were closed in the late 1970s, according to Berland Meyer, the assistant superintendent of schools, everything available is in use now, and classrooms are bursting at their proverbial seams. Taxpayers at first refused to get back on the building treadmill, rejecting tax increases in 1990. But they later approved one that led to the opening of a $15 million middle school last fall. A $4.5 million addition to the old middle school has just been completed as well. Meyer says that taxpayers still need to provide another $3.5–$4.5 million for a new elementary school. Unfortunately, all this construction will handle only immediate population growth.

Wausau's experience, although relatively uncommon in the Midwest, is quite common among American communities of the 1980s and 1990s. The majority of U.S. population growth since 1970 has come from immigrants and their descendants. They will probably contribute two thirds of the growth during this decade and nearly all of it after the turn of the century if federal policies remain the same.

False Promises

On a main road into downtown, an ALL-AMERICAN CITY sign reminds residents and visitors alike that Wausau is not inherently incapable of rising to the challenge of assimilating new residents. It was doing a fine job in 1984, when it won the award commemorated by the sign.

Nearby is another sign. WELCOME HOME TO WAUSAU, this one says, in the homespun way of small cities. It is more than a cliche to say that many natives no longer feel at home here, even as newcomers feel less than welcome. It is noteworthy, however, that when natives told me longingly of a lost "home," most seemed to refer not to the Wausau of 1978, before the refugee influx, but to the Wausau of 1984, when the influx was at a level that still constituted a delightful spice and community relations were harmonious.

John Robinson, who was the mayor of Wausau from 1988 to 1992, acknowledges that no government entity at any stage of Wausau's transformation talked to residents about immigration rates or developed community-wide planning for projecting future changes or deciding whether current trends should be allowed to continue. "The Southeast Asian evolution in Wausau was not a planned process," Robinson told me. "It was sort of a happening. Could the city have planned differently? Yes. But until there is a real need staring you in the face, you don't always reach out and address it." Robinson, who was a young city councilman from 1974 to 1981 and a member of the legislature from 1981 to 1988, says he isn't sure the city could have changed anything even if officials had spoken out against continuing federal refugee resettlement.

In 1984 Wausau's welcome of Southeast Asians was still bighearted enough, and its relations between cultures congenial enough, for Wausau to be designated an All-American City. Youa Her, an educated, articulate leader of the early wave of Hmong settlers, made one of Wausau's presentations to the national panel of judges. The thirty-four-year-old woman's description of Wausau's generosity reportedly left the panelists with tears in their eyes.

Nobody is exactly sure when and how everything started to go sour. But it was probably around the time of the award—certainly before Youa Her's tragic death, in January of 1986, of tubercular meningitis. Newspapers from those years reveal a community increasingly sobered by the realization that what had appeared to be a short-term, private charitable act had no apparent end and was starting to entail a lot of local public costs. Many natives resent that nobody ever leveled with them about costs or where trends would lead, and they feel they were misled by the local media and by federal, state, and religious leaders.

During the late 1970s residents had assumed that the congregations would cover any costs of caring for the refugees they were sponsoring. After all, it was their project. One sponsor reinforced that notion, telling a reporter, "Sponsorship is not something that will last three days or three months or three years. It can be something to last a lifetime."

But the churches' financial commitment was actually rather shallow and short-lived, as Jean Russell, of the county welfare department, explains it. "At the beginning it was good Christian people wanting to do something for somebody. What they did was pick the refugees up at the airport and drive them to our office. The churches did help some, but the Hmong couldn't make it without social services." (The Hmong are not unusual in this regard. A 1991 U.S. Department of Health and Human Services study indicated that nationwide about two-thirds of all Southeast Asian refugees who have arrived since 1986 remain on public assistance.)

Wausau residents were assured, though, that they had no reason to worry about increased welfare costs. In 1979 Susan G. Levy, the coordinator for the state's resettlement assistance office, explained that local taxpayers would not be adversely affected by private sponsors' generosity in inviting refugees, because the federal government would pick up the welfare tab.

As long as the flow was meager, Wausau's economy did fairly well at providing jobs to keep the immigrants off the welfare rolls. "Refugees Are Very Adaptable, State Officials Say" was one 1979 headline in the local paper. In June of 1980 the paper reported that 80 percent of the city's refugees became self-supporting within about three years: "Wausau's 200 Asian refugees doing well, more sponsors needed."

Promoters seemed certain that anything that was good and worked on one scale would be even better on a larger scale. Milton Lorman, a state representative from Fort Atkinson, urged Wisconsin to speed the flow of refugees. "The Statue of Liberty symbolizes the historic support of this country for immigrant rights," he said. "Wisconsin, as a state settled by immigrants, proves that this dream works."

But by May of 1982 an important threshold of danger had been crossed. One headline read, "Most refugees now receiving AFDC, relief aid." The immigrant population in Wausau had doubled since 1980, and the nation was in recession. That spring the federal government cut back its welfare assistance to new refugees. In the years that followed, federal and state governments—having enticed communities to take in immigrants—withdrew more and more support, leaving local taxpayers to bear most of the cost. "The federal government was a silent partner and then became a nonexistent partner," John Robinson laments.

Youa Her in late 1984 accepted the idea of economic limita-

tions. "Anybody that calls," she said, "we'll tell them to think it over and not to be so hurried to move to Wausau." Choj Hawj, who was the elected leader of the Hmong Association at the time, said, "When I look to the economy and the population of Wausau city, we don't want any more to come until things look up."

The former school-board member Fred Prehn recalls that Youa Her was also concerned about proportionality and the effect of continued immigration on social relationships. He says she thanked city leaders for how well Wausau had provided for her people. But she warned them not to let the Hmong become more than five percent of the population, Prehn says; if their numbers went much higher, the natives might start to resent the immigrants, and hostility would begin to replace hospitality.

A month after Her's death Robert Nakamaru, a college professor, addressed the proportionality issue at an event that was intended in part to soothe emerging ethnic tensions. "When there are just a handful, they are seen as quaint," Nakamaru said of the immigrants. "But there is a point where a minority reaches a critical mass in the perception of the majority. Wausau is getting close to that point." Since then the city's immigrant population has quadrupled.

Who Is Responsible?

Nobody involved, apparently, has the authority to stop the refugee- resettlement process if it becomes harmful to a community. Once a week representatives of twelve voluntary agencies sit around a table in a New York office and divide up some 2,000 refugees' names. The Administration has determined the overall number in consultation with Congress. The U.S. Immigration and Naturalization Service has determined the eligibility of each

refugee, and the refugees wait in other countries until a voluntary agency picks up their names at the weekly meeting and begins the process of resettlement.

Federal officials say that refugees cannot be brought into the country unless a voluntary agency is willing to settle them. The agencies sign an agreement—voluntarily—with the State Department to resettle everybody the government wants to bring in. At the time of the annual agreement could the agencies pledge smaller numbers than the government wants to bring in? "That is hypothetical; it never occurs," a State Department spokeswoman says. Actually, the voluntary agencies tend to lobby the government to bring in many more refugees nationwide than it chooses to each year. They receive compensation for each refugee.

Critics in Wausau say that the national Lutheran and Catholic refugee agencies should refuse to help place anybody else in Wausau. Back when problems got serious there, says Jack Griswold, of the Lutheran Immigration and Refugee Service, the LIRS did stop sending refugees who were not joining relatives. But 80 percent of refugees entering the United States today are joining relatives. And that, Griswold says, is why the LIRS continues to settle refugees in Wausau, which he acknowledges has an overloaded infrastructure reminiscent of California's: "If we insisted on settling them somewhere else, then they'd be on the bus for Wausau the next day." The message to communities considering sponsoring refugees for the first time is that once they create the channel, voluntary-agency and federal officials have no way to restrict the flow—unless all the agencies refuse to sign the agreement. But if the agencies did that, they would be out of the business of settling refugees—which is, after all, their reason for being.

One remedy might be to take the decisions away from the voluntary agencies and federal officials and put them in the hands of the local and regional entities that pay most of the bills. A variation might be for Congress to poll cities every year about how many immigrants and refugees they wanted and then offer various incentives and controls to ensure that new arrivals settled in the cities doing the inviting. This would democratize the process, allowing communities to decide much of their own demographic fate.

Nothing in the recent past suggests that Congress, the President, or federal bureaucrats take American communities into consideration at all when setting immigration numbers and policies. The U.S. Bureau of the Census has issued a report projecting that given current immigration patterns, another 134 million people will be added to the United States by 2050. No other factor in American life is likely to have such a large effect on all the other factors. Yet not a single congressional committee or presidential task force has shown any interest in considering whether the nation should become what the Census Bureau projects it will become given current policies. The outcome of those policies, however, has been more accidental than deliberate. Eugene McCarthy recently said that he and other Senate sponsors of the 1965 law that set mass immigration into motion never intended to open the floodgates. The quadrupling of annual immigration numbers has been an inadvertent and harmful result. Yet over the past two decades the federal government has made no attempt to assess the environmental, social, infrastructural, and economic consequences to communities of such rapid federally induced population growth.

A Cooling-Off Period

For twenty-eight years Billy Moy's One World Inn served Chinese food in a former train depot on an island in the Wisconsin River. Bridges connecting the western half of Wausau to its downtown, on the east side, route traffic past the depot. Before his retirement last year Billy Moy, who arrived in Wausau as a Chinese refugee, sat with me in a darkened back room and told the kind of colorful escape and success stories that traditionally have evoked warmhearted responses from Americans. As a teenager he fled the Chinese Communists in 1951 and arrived by train in Wausau in 1952. After years of hard work, perseverance, and saving, and six years in the U.S. Army reserves, Moy bought the island depot and turned it into his restaurant in 1965.

"I didn't know a word of English when I arrived," Moy told me. In that he was like many of the refugees arriving today. But his reception and his freedom to move into the economic mainstream were far different. Why? One explanation may be that Moy had more education than the Hmong, whose people didn't even have a written language until recent decades. More important, perhaps, he was a novelty in Wausau, rather than a member of a mass of newcomers which natives may find threatening. "I started with first-grade English and high school math," Moy said. "People were very nice, especially the teachers. Kids never harassed me. Never a bad word. I guess it was because I was the only one." Fred Prehn went to school with Moy's son during the 1960s and 1970s and recalls that the young Moy was the only minority student. That son now has an M.B.A. and is a business analyst in Milwaukee.

But today's economy has not offered as many opportunities to the large number of refugees of the eighties and nineties, Mary C. Roberts, of the Marathon County Development Corporation, told me. "The Southeast Asian unemployment rate is high," Roberts said. "I think it is kind of irresponsible for churches to bring more in without at least the equivalent of one job pledged per family. Churches look at this just from the humanitarian angles and not the practical."

Various Wausau residents told me they favor a "cooling-off period" before more refugees are resettled in their city. Few residents know it, but such a period played a major role in creating the homogeneous Wausau they now consider the norm. After the turn of the century, immigration caused a social upheaval in Wausau. Back then the Germans and the Yankees were distinct ethnic groups, neither of which found particular strength in diversity. From 1880 to the start of the First World War, Germans streamed into Wausau, eventually overwhelming its New England Yankee founders. Jim Lorence, a local historian, says that the Germans became the predominant ethnic group around 1910. By the end of the decade the immigrants had turned the once conservative Republican town into a Socialist powerhouse. After the November, 1918, elections nearly every county office and both of the county's seats in the state assembly were filled by German-elected Socialists, Lorence says. Amid the political turmoil, natives felt like foreigners in their own home town. Around the nation this period was a time of sweatshops, worsening inner-city squalor, and ethnic hatred that propelled the Ku Klux Klan to its greatest popularity ever. The KKK, however, never got a strong foothold in Wausau, Lorence says.

The federal government in 1924 responded to the problems in a way that had a profound effect on the future development of Wausau and the nation. Congress lowered immigrant admissions to a level more palatable to local labor markets, according to the labor economist Vernon Briggs, of Cornell University. In his recent book, *Mass Immigration and the National Interest*, he describes how the 1924 law gave the country a much-needed forty years to assimilate the new immigrants. The KKK's power receded nationally, and cultural wounds began to heal. Labor markets gradually tightened. That helped stimulate improvements in technology and productivity which supported the middle-class wage economy that Americans took for granted until the 1970s—when the labor supply ballooned owing to renewed mass immigration, the entry of the Baby Boomers into the job market, and a radical increase in the number of married women in the workplace. Since then wages have declined and disparities of wealth have widened.

After publishing his book, Briggs called for a moratorium on most immigration until the federal government figures out how once again to tie the immigration rate to the national interest. Among others independently urging a temporary halt to immigration (with varying exceptions) are the Federation for American Immigration Reform (FAIR); the National Hispanic Alliance; an Orange County, California, grand jury; the University of California ecology professor Garrett Hardin; Harold Gilliam, the environment columnist for the San Francisco Chronicle; and the environmental group Population-Environment Balance. A 1992 Roper poll commissioned by FAIR found that a majority of Americans support the idea of a moratorium. It and other polls have found that a majority of every substantial ethnic group in the United States desires reduced immigration.

Congress began to take part in the discussion about a cooling-off period late last year, when Senator Harry Reid and Representative James Bilbray, both Democrats from Nevada, introduced comprehensive immigration-reform bills that would cut the number of legal immigrants by roughly two thirds, to 300,000 and 350,000 a year. (The U.S. average from 1820 to 1965 was 297,000.) In February, Representative Bob Stump, an Arizona Republican, introduced a "moratorium" bill that would reduce immigration even further. The last time Congress cut the flow of immigrants, in the 1920s, Wausau began to experience social healing, Jim Lorence says. Though it took another thirty years for the major divisions between the German immigrants and the native Yankees to disappear, the disparate ethnic groups slowly began to achieve a unified and harmonious culture—the paradigm of a recoverable paradise.

 Article Review Form at end of book.

What is "balanced-budget conservatism," and how is it connected to rising anti-immigrant sentiment among California voters? Why does the author argue that California citizens are using their votes "symbolically"?

The New Politics of Immigration:

"Balanced-Budget Conservatism" and the Symbolism of Proposition 187

Kitty Calavita

University of California, Irvine

This paper focuses on the politics of the new immigration restrictionism as manifest in Proposition 187, passed by California voters in 1994. I first show that restrictionist sentiment and immigrant scapegoating have a long history in U.S. immigration politics, briefly reviewing three periods of early nativism: 1870s to the 1890s; 1900 to World War I; and World War I and its aftermath. I then make two principal arguments. First, I argue that the new nativism embodied in Proposition 187—which would bar undocumented immigrants in California from receiving social services, including public schooling—corresponds to specific features of the late twentieth-century political-economic landscape. In particular, I link the focus on the alleged tax burden of immigrants and their costly use of social services to ongoing economic transformations, the retrenchment of the welfare state, and what Plotkin and Scheuerman (1994) call "balanced-budget conservatism." Second, following Edelman (1977), I show that Proposition 187 is symbolic in that it derives from and evokes beliefs about immigrants' responsibility and blame for the current economic and fiscal crisis. In addition, I suggest that Proposition 187 may represent a new kind of symbolic politics in which alienated voters—those who bother to vote at all—use their ballot symbolically to express anger and "send a message."

Introduction

As the twentieth century comes to a close, developed countries around the world are increasing efforts to control immigration (see Cornelius, Martin, and Hollifield 1994). While international trade agreements undo barriers to the free movement of capital and goods in the name of unfettered economic exchange, immigration rhetoric is increasingly restrictionist. So pervasive is this new restrictionism that, in the United States at least, immigration is one of the few public policy issues in this contentious period on which most political leaders agree, with President Clinton and Newt Gingrich both calling for greater control of the borders (Bornemeier 1995; Lacey 1995; Shogren and Healy 1995).

The new restrictionism is manifest in California in a series of anti-immigrant policy proposals at the state level. One of the most extreme is Proposition 187, which was passed by a landslide in November 1994. Among its major provisions, Proposition 187 would bar undocumented immigrants from attending public schools and receiving non-emergency health care, and it would require school and health clinic personnel to report to the authorities those they suspect are undocumented.

In this paper I attempt to make sense of the new nativism as reflected in Proposition 187. But, my focus is not simply on the question, "Why has there been a

© 1996 by The Regents of the University of California. Reprinted from *Social Problems*, Vol. 43, No. 3, August 1996, pp. 285–305, by permission.

resurgence of nativism in the United States?" A long tradition of research has established that anti-immigrant sentiments often surface during economic downturns or social transformations such as the United States has been undergoing for the last two decades (Higham 1955; Cornelius 1982; Espenshade and Calhoun 1993). Instead, I explore two related, but somewhat more complex, questions. First, why is this latest round of nativism focused almost single-mindedly on immigrants as a tax burden, a focus that is unusual, if not unique in the history of U.S. nativism? In other words, it is the historically specific theme of the nativism underlying Proposition 187 that is of interest here.

I explain this immigrants-as-a-fiscal-burden focus by linking it to transformations in the late twentieth-century political economy. Specifically, I trace what has been called the "crisis of Fordism" that is reflected in workers' stagnant wages and increasing insecurity, and the dismantling of the welfare state (Piore and Sabel 1984; Lipietz 1985, 1987; Sayer and Walker 1992; Harrison and Bluestone 1982, 1988; Piven and Cloward 1993). I then argue that the targeting of immigrants and other marginalized groups as a fiscal drain is one symptom of the "balanced-budget conservatism" associated with this political-economic transformation (Plotkin and Scheuerman 1994).

Second, I explore how this balanced-budget conservatism and the socio-economic malaise in which it is grounded are embodied in Proposition 187. Here I argue that Proposition 187 is less a straightforward policy directive than it is a symbolic statement of fear, anger, and frustration emanating from the economic uncertainty that drives balanced-budget conservatism. One exit poll of California voters found that those who voted for Proposition 187 did

so above all to "send a message." Elaborating on Edelman (1964, 1977), I argue that Proposition 187 represents a new kind of symbolic politics in which voters use the ballot to "express discontents" (Edelman 1964:3), *fully cognizant of that purely symbolic function.*

The paper thus brings together two sets of literature to explain this latest instance of restrictionist lawmaking. First, I draw from the substantial body of literature documenting the "crisis of Fordism" in the late twentieth century, the decline in workers' standard of living, increases in job insecurity, and the retrenchment of the welfare state (Harvey 1982; Bowles, Gordon, and Weisskopf 1984; Lipietz 1987; Block 1987; Harrison and Bluestone 1988; Kolko 1988; Sayer and Walker 1992; Phillips 1993; Plotkin and Scheuerman 1994). These developments, and the balanced-budget conservatism to which they give rise, are critical to understanding Proposition 187 and the hostility to immigrants it represents.

In addition, however, I draw from the literature on symbolic politics (Gusfield 1963; Edelman 1964, 1977; Citrin, Reingold, and Green 1990; Calavita 1983, 1990; Engel 1987). In bringing together these two literatures, I argue that Proposition 187 is neither simply an instrumental response to economic conditions, nor a purely symbolic measure meant only to declare the cultural or political dominance of the majority. Rather, it can best be understood as a particular type of symbolic statement, the content of which and the motivation for which are grounded in prevailing economic conditions.

In a recent analysis of anti-immigrant sentiment in the United States, Espenshade and Calhoun (1993) contrast a "labor market competition" hypothesis and a "symbolic politics" hypothesis as if they were mutually exclusive explanations for hostility towards

immigrants: Immigrants are perceived as an economic threat; alternatively, the hostility towards immigrants is symbolic of a cultural identity crisis. Instead, this analysis of Proposition 187 suggests that to grasp the complexities of the new nativism we must integrate an understanding of underlying material conditions with an appreciation for the symbolic dimensions of political activity.

One more clarification is in order. While Proposition 187 is a California initiative, this is not a regional analysis of nativism, nor do I pretend to answer the question "Why specifically California?" Other states with a large influx of immigrants—such as Texas, Florida, and New York—have not (yet) undertaken similar initiatives; this probably has less to do with voters' potential receptivity to such a measure than to the idiosyncrasies of local politics and the related distinctive nature of immigration to those states (particularly Florida and New York, where settled immigrant communities have substantial political clout). As we will see, the systemic forces to which I link Proposition 187 and the new nativism are national and international in nature. Indeed, survey data and opinion polls that I will discuss suggest that there is widespread support for a federal law along the lines of Proposition 187, and several other states are now pursuing similar initiatives. While there are no doubt specific factors peculiar to California that contributed to the creation of this state initiative in 1994 (which I will mention briefly), the thrust of this paper is not on such micro-level regional analysis. Instead, I focus on the systemic factors that contribute to the initiative's widespread appeal, both in California and, according to surveys, across the country.

In the next section I provide a brief historical introduction to U.S. nativism. This selective review of three periods—the 1870s to the 1890s; 1900 to World War I; and World War I and its aftermath—suggests that while certain general themes (most notably, the implication of immigrant racial inferiority) recur throughout the history of nativism, the focal points shift with the political-economic landscape and corresponding ideological imperatives.

Nativism in Industrial America: A Thematic Review

Since at least the mid-1800s, each wave of new immigration to the United States has been accompanied by anti-immigrant backlashes and demands for restriction (See Calavita 1984; Higham 1955). The contemporary period is no different in this respect, although the illegal nature of much of the new immigration may add to the sense of powerlessness and lack of control that intensifies the new nativism.[1] What is unique about the contemporary backlash, however, is the almost single-minded focus on the fiscal burden of illegal immigration, with related policy efforts concentrated on barring immigrants from receiving social services.

It has often been observed that anti-immigrant backlashes intensify during economic downturns, perceived threats to national security, and social transformations (Higham 1955; Cornelius 1982; Espenshade and Calhoun 1993). However, far less attention has been paid to the fact that the content or central themes of nativism vary as well, corresponding to shifting ideological and political needs and their structural underpinnings. If immigrants serve as scapegoats for social crises, it stands to reason that the specific content of anti-immigrant nativism will shift to encompass the prevailing malaise. A few examples will illustrate such shifts his-torically and serve as a contrast for the "tax-burden" focus of contemporary nativism.

Immigrant As Strikebreaker, 1870–1890

Twenty-five million immigrants entered the United States in the last four decades of the nineteenth century, and the majority joined the industrial workforce. The advantages of this massive influx of immigrant workers, most of whom were from Europe, did not go unappreciated. Andrew Carnegie (1886:34–35) called immigration "a golden stream which flows into the country each year" and valued each adult immigrant at $1,500. A business journal echoed Carnegie's appreciation:

Men, like cows, are expensive to raise and a gift of either should be gladly received. And a man can be put to more valuable use than a cow (*New York Journal of Commerce* 1892:2).

The U.S. Industrial Commission (U.S. Congress, House Industrial Commission 1901:313–314) lauded the combined effect of mechanization and massive influxes of immigrant labor:

The fact that machinery and the division of labor opens a place for the unskilled immigrants makes it possible not only to get the advantages of machinery, but also to get the advantages of cheap labor.

When U.S. workers complained to Congress that employers were using the recent immigrants to break their fledgling strikes and reduce wages, Congressional debates focused on the inferiority of the "new immigrants" who, unlike earlier immigrants from northern Europe, were "slaves," "paupers," "serfs," and "lowest beings." It was thus the alleged inferiority of the new immigrants—not the new industrial order with its heightened levels of labor strife—that was the problem:

Large numbers of degraded, ignorant, brutal Italian and Hungarian laborers. . . . This is the class of persons, this is the species of immigration with which this [Congress] seeks to deal. . . (Congressional Record 1884:5349).

U.S. historian Frederick Jackson Turner similarly blamed the arrival of large numbers of inferior "new immigrants" from southern and eastern Europe for "counteracting the upward tendency of wages" and leading to "the sweatshop system" (quoted in Gossett 1973:292), as did many other leading historians, sociologists, and anthropologists of the day (see also Higham 1955). As Gossett (1973) points out, anti-immigrant sentiment developed along two main tracks—organized labor's concerns over wage reductions and job displacement, and "race-thinkers' " preoccupation with racial purity—often making for unusual political alliances between those who were diametrically opposed on other issues.

But, the issues of race and labor displacement were not mutually exclusive. As Gossett points out:

We find the racist argument in anti-immigrant agitation not merely among the defenders of the status quo, but also among men who were to become famous for their concern for the welfare of the masses (1973:292).

More important here, the alleged racial inferiority of immigrants became the *explanation* for depressed wages, labor strife, and the emerging "sweatshop system."

Immigrant As Socialist and Anarchist, 1900—World War I

By 1900 not only were new immigrants declared inferior by virtue of their "acceptance" of substandard wages, but they were now spotted for "un-American" militancy. As one social scientist had warned,

When [the immigrant] is out of work . . . he looks about and asks his fellow-citizens, sullenly, if not menacingly, what they are going to do about it. He has brought with him, too, what is called "the labor problem" probably the most un-American of all problems (Godkin 1887:173).

A leading business journal (quoted in *Public Opinion* 1886:355) even proclaimed that immigrants' propensity to radicalism was biological: "Anarchism is a blood disease."

Industrialists in this Progressive period relied on notions of immigrant inferiority to explain away class conflict in what they had declared a classless society. The rise of the Industrial Workers of the World (IWW) was attributed to a "foreign invasion of the anarchists and socialists, criminals and outcasts from other nations" (Bulletin of the National Association of Wool Manufacturers 1912:142). Miners' strikes in 1902 were the product of

[t]ens of thousands of the anthracite miners [who] are Poles, Hungarians, Slavs, and other foreigners, who cannot spell a word of English (quoted in Wiebe 1962:191).

The massive Lawrence Textile Strike in 1912 was similarly dismissed: All the troublemakers were "Italians and other foreign-born operatives" (Wiebe 1962:191). By 1911, the Dillingham Immigration Commission called for "selective" immigration measures that would weed out the defective immigrants (U.S. Congress, Senate Immigration Commission 1911).

World War I and "Hyphenated-Americans"

During World War I, English classes for immigrants were jointly sponsored by government and industry and focused on the development of patriotism and political conservatism. Henry Ford's English School was widely recognized as a pioneer in these "Americanization" efforts. The first words taught in Ford's school were "I am a good American."[2] By 1917, thirty-two government agencies and dozens of leading industrialists were involved in Americanization work. In the cli-

mate of fear in the immediate postwar period, some states enacted laws making attendance at Americanization classes compulsory for recent immigrants. The National Americanization Committee defined its goals:

The combating of anti-American propaganda . . . and the stamping out of sedition . . . . The elimination of causes of disorder, unrest, and disloyalty which make fruitful soil for un-American propagandists and disloyal agitators. . . . The creation of an understanding and love for America (quoted in Hill 1919:630).

Americanization was an attempt to reform the allegedly inferior southern and eastern European without restricting the supply of labor, but as race theories became more explicit, such efforts were increasingly regarded as irrelevant. The depiction of the immigrant as a radical and genetically inferior that had been used during the early 1900s to explain away industrial unrest was now the focus of arguments favoring immigration restriction. Pointing to the potential for disloyalty among genetically inferior "hyphenated-Americans," the *Saturday Evening Post* urged restrictions, asking, "Why . . . try to make Americans out of those who will always be Americanski?" (paraphrased in Higham 1955:262). The Russian Revolution of 1917 was regularly referred to by members of Congress who warned, "Practically all the IWW and Bolsheviki [in America] are foreigners" (U.S. Congress, House Committee on Immigration and Naturalization 1919:270). And,

We should formulate and . . . enforce a genuine 100 percent American immigration law. . . . The incoming flood remains dangerously alien" (Congressional Record 1921:4550).

Lothrop Stoddard, author of *The Rising Tide of Color* and *Revolt Against Civilization: The Menace of Under-Man* (1922), and noted eugenicist Harry Laughlin, testified at

the House hearings on immigration restriction in 1920. The House immigration committee thereafter appointed Laughlin its "expert eugenics agent" (U.S. Congress, House Committee on Immigration and Naturalization 1920). John Trevor, self-appointed expert on the "biological propensity of Jews toward radicalism," testified to the Senate immigration committee the following year (U.S. Congress, Senate Committee on Immigration 1921:293–300). Subsequently, Trevor attended all hearings and informal meetings of the House committee, even helping draft reports. These Congressional discussions of immigration revealed strong racist overtones. In 1924, Laughlin presented a report to Congress in which he used Army IQ data to argue that southern and eastern Europeans were feeble-minded and of inferior racial stock. When the House committee reported their new quota bill that year, they attached a report by Trevor in which he argued that America's racial makeup must be preserved.

The racism and fear of socialism and anarchism that pervaded this debate were similar in many respects to that of the previous period. However, as World War I gave way to the post-war red scare, immigrants were feared above all as disloyal and "un-American." In 1921, Congress passed the Emergency Quota Law (which was extended in 1924) to limit the number of immigrants from southern and eastern Europe, with the explanation that they were "abnormally twisted," "unassimilable," and "filthy un-American" (U.S. Congress 1920:10).

The pattern is repeated throughout the history of U.S. immigration. At moments of social, political, or economic crisis, nativism tends to increase as recent immigrants are singled out as the cause of the crisis. More to the point here, as the crises shift over time, so too do the depictions of immigrants and the prevailing themes of nativism. Since the historical record suggests that during times of crisis recent immigrants are often blamed, it makes sense that as the nature of the crisis changes, so too does the specific content of nativism.

The Resurgence of U.S. Nativism and Proposition 187

The last three decades have witnessed rapid increases in legal immigration, illegal immigration, and refugee flows to the United States. By 1994, 8.7 percent of the U.S. population—or 22.6 million people—were foreign-born. While that percentage is smaller than earlier in the century, the absolute numbers are unprecedented. The Census Bureau now estimates that approximately 4 million of the foreign-born reside in the United States illegally (*Los Angeles Times* 1995:A20).

Illegal immigration to the United States gained momentum with the termination of the Bracero Program in 1964. For more than 20 years, the Bracero Program had brought Mexican farm workers to work the fields of the southwestern United States on close to 5 million Bracero contracts. By the time the Bracero Program ended, a relationship of symbiosis between Mexican immigrants and U.S. employers had become well-entrenched, facilitated and nurtured by more than 50 years of U.S. policymaking (see Calavita 1992).[3] With the end of the program, the employment of Mexican labor went underground as the guest workers of one era became the illegal immigrants of the next.

Apprehensions of illegal immigrants by the U.S. Immigration and Naturalization Service (INS) went from about 23,000 in 1960 to 345,000 in 1970, and by 1978, the number of annual apprehensions had risen to more than 1 million

(Congressional Research Service 1980; U.S. Immigration and Naturalization Service 1978:19). INS apprehensions are of course not a definitive measure of undocumented immigration. Not all undocumented border crossers are ascertained, some are apprehended more than once, some "undocumented" immigrants enter legally and over-stay their visas, and some variation in apprehension rates is the result of shifts in border patrol policies or INS resources. However, there is little disagreement among experts that the dramatic increases in apprehensions in this period reflect a substantial increase in the undocumented flow (Bean, Vernez, and Keely 1989; Cornelius, Martin, and Hollifield 1994; Fix 1991; Martin 1994).

The first signs of contemporary restrictionism can be traced to the early 1970s when Representative Peter Rodino held hearings around the country on the topic of illegal immigration. The result was a five-volume Congressional document outlining the dangers of uncontrolled immigration and the contribution of illegal aliens to unemployment and wage reductions (U.S. Congress, House Committee on the Judiciary 1971–1972). In 1979, President Carter appointed the Select Commission on Immigration and Refugee Policy (SCIRP) to make recommendations for reforms that would "regain control of the border." By the time SCIRP recommended employer sanctions that would make it illegal to knowingly employ unauthorized immigrants, the vast majority of the U.S. public favored such a restrictionist approach (Gallup 1980). After three attempts, the Immigration Reform and Control Act (IRCA) was passed in 1986, with employer sanctions as its political centerpiece.[4]

For a variety of reasons (see Calavita 1990, 1995), employer sanctions did not significantly reduce undocumented immigration (Bean, Edmonston, and Passel 1990;

Fix 1991; Crane et al. 1990; U.S. Department of Labor 1991), and restrictionist sentiment continued unabated.[5] A *New York Times* poll in 1986 showed that 50 percent of respondents in a nationwide survey wanted immigration (both legal and undocumented) reduced. In 1988, a *Los Angeles Times* national poll found that 64 percent of respondents were convinced that immigrants cost more in social services and unemployment insurance than they contribute in tax revenues (cited in Citrin, Reingold, and Green 1990:1136). A 1993 survey of 1,031 southern Californians found that 87 percent believed illegal immigration to be a very serious or somewhat serious problem; one of the most frequently cited concerns was that undocumented immigrants are a burden on taxpayers (Espenshade and Calhoun 1993).

Scholarly attention also turned to the costs and benefits of the continued flow of immigrants. Without exception, these studies have focused on the tax revenues contributed by immigrants versus the cost of the social services they consume. For example, Parker and Rea (1993) estimate that the annual net cost of federal and local public services for illegal immigrants in San Diego County is $244.3 million and extrapolate that the net cost for California is $5 billion. Stewart, Gascoigne, and Bannister (1992) put the net cost for Los Angeles County at $807.6 million. Huddle (1993) concludes that immigrants (both legal and undocumented immigrants) cost the federal government $42.5 billion more than they contribute in taxes annually, with the cost in California at $18 billion.

Other studies have found that the cost of immigration to California is far less than previously imagined, and that at the national level there is a net fiscal gain (Passel and Edmonston 1994; Clark and Passel 1993; Fix and Passel 1994; Bornemeier 1994; Eisenstadt and Thorup 1994). An Urban

Institute study (Clark and Passel 1993) reports that legal and undocumented immigrants in California contribute $12 billion a year *more* in taxes than they consume in services, with the national figure at $28.7 billion. The authors of this latter study argue that Huddle (1993) overestimated undocumented immigration, using a figure that is 50 percent higher than INS estimates, ignored immigrants' Social Security contributions, and exaggerated the participation rate of immigrants in costly social services (cited in McDonnell 1994). Further, as Clark and Passel (1993) point out, none of these studies includes in its calculations the indirect benefits of immigration, for example the economic contribution of cheap immigrant labor that subsidizes many important industries, such as California agribusiness (see, for example, Arax 1994).

The point here is not to make a case for or against the fiscal/economic contribution of immigrants—a task that is clearly beyond the scope of this paper. Rather, it is to point out 1) that the scholarly literature on the costs/benefits of immigration is now almost exclusively focused on *fiscal* impacts, and 2) that there is substantial disagreement among the experts on the nature and size of those impacts. A Rand report (Vernez and McCarthy 1995) has recently compared these studies, finds that their disparate results have to do with radically different assumptions, and concludes that the data—particularly relating to the numbers of undocumented immigrants—are inadequate to resolve the debate. What is important to this analysis is the substantial gap between the speculative and contradictory nature of these findings and the unwavering convictions of most Americans.

A majority of the U.S. public now supports the enactment of new restrictionist measures and favor politicians who use this issue as a calling card (Klein 1993;

Decker 1994; Gibbs 1994). By early 1993, more than 20 restrictionist bills had been placed before the California legislature, and several provisions, including one that bars the undocumented from receiving drivers' licenses, have been passed (Bailey and Morain 1993).

Proposition 187, known as the Save Our State (SOS) initiative, is among the most extreme of restrictionist measures to gain favor. The initiative, which went directly to California voters through a referendum in November 1994, would bar undocumented immigrant children from attending public schools (and require school administrators to request documentation from "suspect" children), and would withhold from the undocumented all non-emergency medical care including prenatal care and inoculations. Despite the apparent unconstitutionality of the former[6] and the potentially dangerous public health consequences of the latter, Proposition 187 won by a wide margin—59 percent to 41 percent (Decker 1994; Nalik and Feldman 1994; Gibbs 1994).

All of the major provisions of Proposition 187 have been put on hold by the courts while numerous constitutional challenges are resolved. Nonetheless, the measure has already had a significant impact, legitimating hostility and discrimination and causing widespread fear in the immigrant community. According to a report in *The Christian Science Monitor* (Munoz 1994:19),

[A]lready a fifth grade teacher in one California school district has assigned her students to report their own immigration status and that of their parents. And a school security guard in Atherton, California, the day after the election, told two American-born Latinas, "We don't have to let Mexicans in here anymore."

Other reports of discrimination include a McDonald's worker who insisted on seeing immigration documents before serving a

customer; a pharmacist who refused to fill a prescription for someone they "suspected" was undocumented; a customer at a restaurant who asked the cook for his green card, adding "It's a citizen's duty to kick out illegals"; and a hotel owner who called the police when a U.S. citizen would not show immigration documents when registering for a room (Munoz 1994:19). Pregnant women are reportedly afraid to seek prenatal care for fear of deportation. In at least one case, the death of a child has been linked to such fear, when the parents of a severely ill eight-year-old postponed seeing a doctor (Romney and Marquis 1994; Romney and Brazil 1994; Martinez 1994).

Despite such damaging consequences even in the absence of enforcement, and despite the substantial legal challenges already posed, there is some impetus to seek a federal version of Proposition 187. Immediately after the election, California Governor Wilson called on Congress to pass a federal variant of the proposition (Brownstein 1994). The U.S. Commission on Immigration Reform—a bipartisan federal commission established by Congress in 1990—has proposed substantial cuts in the benefits received by the undocumented but stopped short of recommending their exclusion from public schools. While undocumented immigrants are already ineligible for most forms of public assistance, the commission recommended withholding all remaining assistance except emergency medical care, echoing one of the major provisions of Proposition 187.[7] A *Time Magazine* poll of 800 adult Americans in September 1994 reveals that 55 percent favor "a proposal to stop providing government health benefits and public education to illegal immigrants and their children" (Gibbs 1994:47). A sponsor of Proposition 187 reports that "[o]rganizers in Florida,

Washington, New York, and Texas are already calling us" asking advice on how to get similar measures passed in their states (Wood 1994:2).

In an effort to explain these developments, the next section traces the contours of the economic transformation under way in the United States, with a focus on the increased economic insecurity of American workers. Given the long-standing tendency to scapegoat immigrants in times of economic hardship or anxiety, the recent upsurge in nativism is perhaps not surprising. What is unusual is the focus of this round of nativism on immigrants' consumption of social services and the perceived burden on taxpayers.[8] There had been periodic concerns in the late nineteenth century over the immigration of "paupers" and immigrants who became "public charges" (Calavita 1984:68–95). In the depression of the 1930s, Mexicans in the United States were subjected to a racist campaign focusing in part on their burden on relief agencies, which resulted in several hundred thousand Mexican immigrants being "repatriated" (Gamio 1971; Hoffman 1974; Lopez 1981; Reisler 1976; Cockcroft 1986). But, the perception that immigrants in general are a drain on taxpayers and must be excluded from basic social services has never before been the dominant theme of nativist sentiment. In the following section, I argue that this theme derives from a particular set of material conditions and related ideological developments, in particular the rise of "balanced-budget conservatism" (Plotkin and Scheuerman 1994).

Economic Transformation and Balanced-Budget Conservatism

The U.S. economy—and that of many other advanced capitalist nations—has undergone a radical and rapid transformation in the last

20 years. By the early 1980s, a substantial literature began pointing to the decline in profitability of U.S. corporations and the "deindustrialization" of America following the economic boom of the post-war decades. Some (Harrison and Bluestone 1982, 1988; Piven and Cloward 1993; Plotkin and Scheuerman 1994) highlight the role of foreign competition in this profit squeeze on U.S. corporations that had enjoyed a virtual global monopoly after the destruction of World War II. Others (Harvey 1982; Lipietz 1985, 1987; Piore and Sabel 1984; Sayer and Walker 1992) place a greater emphasis on a broad "crisis of Fordism" that affects many advanced capitalist economies. These latter scholars point out that from World War II to the mid-1970s, most advanced capitalist countries operated on the "Fordist" principles of mass production of standardized products for mass consumption, with internal job ladders and vertically integrated sectors, supplemented by a government system of income maintenance and social security. As Lipietz (1985) explains, Fordism was predicated on a connection between profit rates, wages, and social security. By the 1970s, according to this interpretation, line-balancing problems (resulting in shortages and gluts in production inputs), labor resistance, corporate taxation policies, and a generally rigid structure of production, jeopardized profitability and the system began to unravel.[9] Whatever its precise causes, the average rate of profit of non-financial U.S. corporations plummeted from 10 percent in 1965 to little more than 5 percent by the late 1970s (Harrison and Bluestone 1988).

One response to this profitability crisis was to cut labor costs. The corporate strategy almost across the board was to reduce production costs and boost profitability by eliminating jobs, exporting many of them to developing countries, thereby reaping the

rewards not only of reduced labor costs offshore but also of an insecure domestic workforce wary of unions and afraid to make demands. According to a Brookings Institution researcher, 4 million manufacturing jobs were lost between 1978 and 1982 alone (Harris 1984). By 1986, industrial employment had fallen 17 percent in textiles, 30 percent in primary metals, and 40 percent in steel (Plotkin and Scheuerman 1994). By 1987, there were actually fewer workers in manufacturing in the United States than there had been in 1966 (Bluestone and Bluestone 1992). In the 1990s, the process continues as General Motors plans to do away with 70,000 more jobs and close 12 plants (Plotkin and Scheuerman 1994). Unemployment statistics reveal the overall trend. The official average U.S. unemployment rate for 1950–1959 was 4.5 percent; in 1960–1969, it was 4.8 percent; in 1970–1979; it rose to 6.2 percent; and, in 1980–1988, the average unemployment rate was almost double the 1950s figure, at 8.4 percent (Plotkin and Scheuerman 1994).

The effect on wages is clearcut. Between 1946 and 1973, real wages averaged a yearly increase of 1.84 percent in constant dollars, such that by the 1960s millions of U.S. blue-collar workers could purchase a home, buy a car, and send their children to a public university. Beginning in 1973, real average annual wages began to drop for the first time since the 1930s, and by 1990 they had fallen 19 percent. A study prepared for the Congressional Joint Economic Committee estimated that close to 60 percent of the workers added to the U.S. labor force between 1979 and 1984 earned less than $7,000 per year (cited in *Los Angeles Times* 1987:IV–3). A Commerce Department study reveals that in 1992, 18 percent of full-time workers in the United States earned $13,000 or less (the comparable figure for 1979 was 12 percent) (Rosenblatt 1994). In the early 1990s, fourteen million full-time workers—comprising one-fifth of the workforce—did not earn enough to keep above the official poverty level (Plotkin and Scheuerman 1994; Kolko 1988).

A central cost-cutting measure in this period of restructuring is to employ workers for specific tasks or periods of demand, letting them go when the demand has subsided. Approximately 30 percent of the U.S. workforce is now comprised of such "contingent" workers doing part-time work or on short-term contracts, who thereby accrue no seniority and enjoy few benefits (Ingwerson 1993). In 1982, approximately 25 percent of new jobs were for part-time or temporary work; a decade later, fully half of all new jobs were for such contingent work (Kilborn 1993). In dramatic contrast to the internal labor markets of the Fordist period, more and more work is subcontracted out or performed by "temps" employed for the duration of specific tasks. Between 1970 and 1984, the number of people working for agencies that provide temporary help increased at double the rate of the GNP (Harrison and Bluestone 1988). Elsewhere I have argued that this increase in contingent work and the downward pressure on wages is consistent with continued high levels of undocumented immigration. A large supply of "contingent"—that is, illegal—immigrant workers may be well-suited to the restructured economy of the late twentieth century with its proliferation of low wage, contingent work. As a former Secretary of Labor once said, undocumented immigrants "work scared and hard" (Marshall 1978:169).

In addition to these direct cuts in labor costs, the profitability crisis elicited a reduced commitment to entitlement programs and a gradual dismantling of the welfare state. As Lipietz (1985:109) puts it, "[B]etween 1974 and 1983 . . . all the major capitalist countries . . . adopted 'austerity' policies designed to make the workers pay for the crisis." Piven and Cloward argue that employers and the state see income-maintenance programs in this new economic climate as detrimental to labor discipline. Thus, certain protections of the welfare state have been eliminated "to compel workers generally to sell labor on whatever terms the market offers" (Piven and Cloward 1993:345).

The retrenchment of the welfare state of course saves money at a time of fiscal crisis. Feldstein (1985) estimates that social programs by the mid-1980s cost $300 billion a year compared to $19 billion two decades earlier, and now comprise one-half of all non-defense federal spending. But, this money-saving measure is, according to Piven and Cloward (1993:348), integrally related to the new economic austerity and efforts to increase profitability through cutting labor costs:

[T]he peaking of the welfare explosion in the early 1970s coincided with a growing crisis in the economy, and with the mounting of a campaign by business to solve its problems of profitability by forcing workers to take less.

I will show that the dismantling of entitlement and social service programs has been facilitated by the ideology of balanced-budget conservatism that itself is at least partly the product of widespread economic insecurity and frustration.

The "financialization" of the economy (Phillips 1994) is another response to the profitability crisis, compounding the effects of deindustrialization and the falling standard of living for U.S. workers. When manufacturing experienced a profit squeeze, U.S. corporations and other investors sought more lucrative opportunities for profit in financial transactions, draining investment from the already faltering industrial sector. This financialization of the economy, in which speculators and investors call the shots, has led to a disconnection between economic growth and worker well-being (Business Week 1985; Harrison and Bluestone 1988).

The takeoff in mergers, acquisitions, and hostile takeovers in the 1980s was part of this financialization of the economy and provided an important link to increased economic uncertainty for workers. With the economy increasingly driven by the logic of stockholder gains, corporations were gobbled up at an unprecedented rate. In 1984, these mergers, acquisitions, and buyouts consumed more than $140 billion. Not only did this siphon capital from investment in productive activity, but it meant that labor costs had to be cut further to pay for the massive corporate debts incurred, amounting to $1.8 trillion by 1988 (Business Week 1988).

As Phillips (1994) explains,

For the first time in modern U.S. history, stock prices decoupled from the real economy, enabling the Dow-Jones industrial average to keep setting records even as employees' real wages kept declining.

In 1993, the U.S. economy grew 3 percent, while household median income declined 1 percent. This disconnection helps explain the current "jobless economic recovery," and is one reason for the increasing polarization of wealth in the United States.

These economic transformations and dislocations are no secret, receiving mention both in President Clinton's first economic speech to Congress and in the mainstream media. The widely read book by political analyst and columnist Kevin Phillips, titled Boiling Point (1993), brought to centerstage these economic dislocations and the anger of the declining middle class. But, as Plotkin and Scheuerman (1994) explain it, public outrage is concentrated on the ballooning federal deficit and rising taxes.

Tracing the roots of this "deficit-mania," Plotkin and Scheuerman note that since the New Deal, Washington has stimulated the economy with government funds. They point out that President Reagan was particularly adept at spending beyond his means, despite his rhetoric of fiscal conservatism:

By piling huge tax cuts on top of even larger military spending increases, and continuing to apply such increases even after the economy entered recovery, Washington self-consciously and drastically built up the deficit to mountainous heights. . . . In this climate of growing budget and financial uncertainty, the more tangible problems of stagnant wages, job insecurity, and rising personal debt had a massive new symbolic target: the dizzying federal debt. . . . Here was a uniquely understandable, singular motive force behind the nation's economic troubles. . . . U.S. politicians have talked about little else since at least the mid-1980s (Plotkin and Scheuerman 1994:16).

But, political expedience and sound economics have prevented Congress from abruptly removing hundreds of billions of dollars in government spending from the economy to reduce the deficit. The result is simultaneously an ideological assault on the public sector ("The deficit has become the central ideological prop in the long-term conservative attack on the public sector" [Plotkin and Scheuerman 1994:20]), and frustration among taxpayers whose attention is focused on the inability of government to balance the budget. This "deficit-mania" and disdain for a government that is unable to balance its books, are the source of what Plotkin and Scheuerman call "balanced-budget conservatism." Among its symptoms are an entrenched anti-government ideology, suspicion of government spending, resistance to taxes, and a subtle semantic shift from "citizen" to "taxpayer" as the central unit of civic life.

This balanced-budget conservatism serves as a target for the frustration and anger of those facing economic uncertainty, deflects responsibility from the private sector's cost-cutting, and facilitates the austerity measures of the government as it dismantles the safety net. Lee Atwater, at the time the chief of Republican strategizing, implies that this balanced-budget conservatism was deliberately constructed, or at least self-consciously exploited:

In the 1980 campaign, we were able to make the establishment, insofar as it is bad, the government. In other words, big government was the enemy, not big business. If people think the problem is that taxes are too high, and government interferes too much, then we are doing our job (quoted in Plotkin and Scheuerman 1994:32).

Block (1987) argues that federal budget accounting is archaic, collapsing as it does capital expenditures and current spending (something that, he points out, private households and corporations do not do in their own accounting). The result is a far higher budget "deficit" than would be the case if capital expenditures were calculated separately and federal assets were factored in. But, Block argues, the "balanced-budget ideology" resulting from an inflated deficit is useful to those who would reduce government spending on social programs. Block (1987:137) paraphrases David Stockman, Ronald Reagan's budget director:

As David Stockman has acknowledged, the original Reagan tax cuts were a Trojan horse designated to facilitate the cutting of civilian programs by creating a huge shortfall of revenues.

The disdain for the public sector that is a hallmark of balanced-budget conservatism not only tempers opposition to the cutbacks, but celebrates them.

Balanced-budget conservatism is thus an ideological response to certain underlying material conditions and the ability of those who would limit social welfare spending to capitalize on those conditions. Whether or not the federal deficit is out of control (some, like Block, argue it is not), is not the key issue here. The perception that it is drives anti-government sentiment, contempt for the public sector, and hostility towards the poor. Neither does a balanced state budget seem to temper this "deficit-mania." Thirty-seven states including California now require a "balanced" budget (the definition of which turns out to be quite malleable),[10] but there is no indication that states with such requirements experience reduced levels of balanced-budget conservatism.

It was in this political-economic context that Proposition 187 was fashioned, and enjoyed almost instant popularity with California voters. No doubt, there are specific reasons why the initiative was developed in California and enjoyed such popular support there, even beyond the fact that California receives a disproportionate number of legal and illegal immigrants. For one thing, Californians have confronted a strong and lingering recession and defense cutbacks that enhance the effects of the more general economic restructuring, as well as high-visibility social crises such as the 1992 Los Angeles riot. Secondly, ballot-box initiatives are an important ingredient of the policymaking process in California, often leading to stunning victories of policies that might not otherwise make it through the legislature. The landslide victory of Prop. 13 in 1978, which froze property taxes and might be seen as a first sign of the preoccupation with reduced government spending and lower taxes, is exemplary. Finally, Governor Pete Wilson put all of his political weight behind this initiative—some have argued as a way to revive his lagging popularity in California and launch his bid for the White House (Brownstein 1994; Ostrow and Fulwood 1994; Scheer 1994). Whatever Wilson's motives, his aggressive campaigning for

Proposition 187 no doubt contributed to its high profile.[11] But, the easy receptivity of voters to such nativist rhetoric is by no means idiosyncratic to California, as indicated by several national surveys and polls, as well as a flurry of proposals to replicate Proposition 187 at the federal and state levels.

With the deficit seemingly out of control, increased economic uncertainty for all but the most affluent, and the safety net shrinking, frustrated and anxious voters are predisposed to place the blame on excessive government spending and the poor who are seen as the major cause of such spending. Immigrants are one among several targets consistent with this balanced-budget ideology and the scapegoating of the marginalized "other" that it spawns. The backlash against affirmative action, a growing rejection of "multi-culturalism," and the political appeal of welfare reform and its targeting of teenage mothers, probably share the same ideological space.[12] Plotkin and Scheuerman (1994:32) describe such marginalization and scapegoating:

[B]alanced-budget conservatism elevates protecting taxpayer interests to the highest priority of government, [and] stigmatizes poorer, property-less people as somehow less than fully citizens.

Those who are not even citizens—indeed, are not legal residents—are the ideal target of blame, more undeserving even than the traditional "undeserving poor." At a time when the welfare state is being dismantled in the name of cutting government spending, and economic uncertainty is on the rise even for the previously secure middle class, this scapegoating of immigrants as the cause of the crisis found a ready audience among the white middle-class who disproportionately make up the electorate. Indeed, previously unpopular Peter Wilson increased his ratings many times over with his vocal support of Proposition 187, and was swept into office for a second term.

It might be argued, of course, that the reason for the historically specific theme of this balanced-budget nativism is straightfoward: Since the vast social expenditures of the welfare state are a relatively new phenomenon, the expense of providing benefits associated with the welfare state could not have been a prevailing concern earlier in the century. There is something to this straightfoward explanation for the fiscal theme of the current nativism, and to the extent that it highlights the shifts in nativism as underlying social conditions change, it underscores my point. However, several issues should be kept in mind. First, much of the discussion in California and across the country centers on outlays for public education—a social expenditure predating the modern welfare state by half a century. Second, there *were* periodic concerns for the fiscal impact of immigrants in the last century, but they never dominated the discourse on immigration. Finally, it should not be forgotten that as recently as 1986 when IRCA was passed, the primary issue regarding illegal immigration was its alleged effect on depressing wages and displacing U.S. workers (hence, the employer sanctions centerpiece of that reform). Immigrants' consumption of costly social services was rarely mentioned in the SCIRP report of 1980, nor in the several years of debates leading up to IRCA in 1986.

The vast expenditures of the welfare state alone cannot explain the current fiscal nativism. This fiscal theme, as expressed in Proposition 187, is rooted not just in the reality of social welfare expenditures; more important, it is grounded in underlying material conditions (increased economic insecurity and the *dismantling* of the welfare state) and related ideological accounts of those conditions (balanced-budget conservatism).

Proposition 187 As Symbolic Law

While Proposition 187 is thus an expression of nativism in response to increased economic insecurity and the balanced-budget conservatism onto which that insecurity is deflected, its relationship to those economic and ideological conditions is not straightfoward. I argue that Proposition 187 was not simply a *policy* statement designed to limit undocumented immigration or reduce state spending; instead, it was a *political* statement, supported primarily to send a symbolic message. The content of that message is closely related to the balanced-budget ideology, with its dual hostilities towards immigrants and government.

An important research tradition has documented the symbolic dimension of political action. Gusfield's (1963) groundbreaking work examines the U.S. temperance movement as a symbol of Anglo-Saxon, Protestant cultural dominance at a time of industrialization, urbanization, and immigration. Citrin, Reingold, and Green (1990) similarly consider the symbolic politics of those who oppose voting rights for non-English speakers, bilingual education, and affirmative action, as a reinforcement of their own identity. In 1986, California voters passed by a 2–1 margin a ballot initiative (Proposition 63) that added an amendment to the state constitution declaring English the official language of the state; since then, Arizona, Colorado, and Florida have passed similar initiatives, as have numerous municipalities (Gurwitt 1988; Citrin, Reingold, and Green 1990). Citrin, Reingold, and Green (1990:1149) discuss the symbolic dimensions of these efforts, focusing on language as "a powerful symbol of national identity." Similarly, Engel (1984:580) discusses the rising opposition to "litigiousness" by those who suffer personal injury in a rural county in Illinois in the 1970s as a "ceremony of regret," or "one aspect of a symbolic effort by members of the community to preserve a sense of meaning and coherence in the face of social changes. . ."

The following analysis shares more with Edelman's (1964, 1977) work on symbolic action. Unlike Gusfield (1963), Citrin, Reingold, and Green (1990), and Engel (1987), who focus primarily on law or legal movements as symbolic statements of cultural dominance, identity, or meaning, Edelman points to the symbolic role of political action in the assignment of blame or responsibility for a variety of social problems.

According to Edelman (1977), all political language and public policies have a symbolic component in the sense that they derive from and evoke a set of political beliefs about responsibility and blame. For example,

A reference in an authoritative public statement or in a social security law to "training programs" for the unemployed is a metonymic evocation of a larger structure of beliefs that . . . workers are unemployed because they lack necessary skills, that jobs are available for those trained to take them (Edelman 1977:16).

Clearly, Proposition 187 was symbolic in this way. It reconfirmed to a predisposed electorate that illegal immigrants over-burden government services and contribute to the fiscal crisis. Thus, as the welfare state is dismantled, the cutbacks are blamed on illegal immigrants who have stretched the system beyond capacity. As one letter-writer to the San Diego Union-Tribune (1995:B9) put it, pointing out that "[o]ur national debt is approaching $5 trillion" and urging implementation of Proposition 187:

[T]here is a plan to cut projected Medicaid spending by $182 billion during the next seven years. In other words, we should provide free medical care and education to illegal immigrants while the government curtails medical aid for our own citizens?

This symbolic component of Proposition 187 both derives from the balanced-budget ideology and buttresses it, with disdain for the public sector increasing as its major clients are targeted as undeserving.[13]

Edelman has used the concept of symbolic politics in another way as well, to refer to political action that has little impact on objective conditions, but serves the purpose of placating the public. For example,

If the regulatory process is examined in terms of a divergence between political and legal promises on one hand and resource allocations on the other, the largely symbolic character of the entire process becomes apparent (Edelman 1964:23).

According to Edelman (1964:3), the electoral process itself acts as a "condensation symbol" in that elections "give people a chance to express discontents and enthusiasms, to enjoy a sense of involvement" even though this participation is largely ritualistic, as most decisions of significance are made elsewhere.

According to evidence provided by exit surveys and opinion polls, Proposition 187 did indeed allow people to "express [their] discontents." In fact, this seems to have been its primary appeal. According to a Los Angeles Times exit poll (Los Angeles Times 1994a:A22), 78 percent of those who voted for the measure did so because "it sends a message that needs to be sent." The responses, "it will force the federal government to face the issue" (51 percent) and "it will stop immigrants from using state services" (34 percent) placed a distant second and third respectively, as reasons for affirmative votes (only 2 percent voted for the initiative to "throw kids out of school").

Another poll, taken less than a month before the election, found that those committed to voting for Proposition 187 (59 percent) would vote for it regardless of any potentially negative impacts. When asked, "Do the following arguments make you more or less likely to vote for Proposition 187?" the modal response to arguments against the measure was "no effect." Presented with the argument that "denying illegal immigrants prenatal care and immunization against communicable diseases could create a public health hazard," 42 percent responded that this would have no effect on their vote, compared to only 33 percent who said it would make them less likely to vote for the measure (Feldman 1994:A22).

Voters had been encouraged by initiative sponsors to treat it as a symbolic statement. In the final weeks before the election, media coverage of the proposition was intense, and much of the coverage—addressing the potential negative public health consequences, for example, and revealing dissent from a number of national Republican leaders—was potentially damaging to the campaign. Proposition sponsors responded by characterizing the initiative as purely symbolic, as a "way to send a message" and register one's anger over uncontrolled illegal immigration. Governor Wilson repeatedly urged voters to support Proposition 187 to send a message of anger and frustration to Washington over its inability to control immigration—a federal responsibility—and to demand that the state be compensated financially for Washington's failures.

Hesitant voters were told not to worry about any potential negative consequences of the initiative, because it was not likely to be enforced. Initiative co-author, Harold Ezell (former Western Regional Commissioner of the Immigration and Naturalization Service) even declared that it was "ridiculous" to imagine that Proposition 187 would actually remove 300,000 children from school as opponents charged, since its constitutionality would be immediately challenged (National Public Radio, October 19, 1994). Instead, he said, the measure was meant to

send a message that even the White House will understand. . . . Proposition 187 is not enough, but it tells the federal government that California has had enough and we're not going to take it anymore (Ezell 1994:M5).

Much as Edelman might have predicted, then, Proposition 187 was symbolic in that it allowed people to "express discontents." But, the enactment of Proposition 187 introduces a political phenomenon not addressed by Edelman, and perhaps signals a new development in symbolic politics. Edelman (1964) had argued that the symbolic function of elections works only so long as the electorate *believes* it is doing something instrumental—in other words, only so long as they do not recognize the purely symbolic function. In order for elections to serve their symbolic function of appeasement, Edelman reasoned, voters must harbor the illusion that their actions will have consequences. But, in the case of Proposition 187, California voters enacted a measure they knew to be purely symbolic; indeed its symbolic dimension was extolled by voters and sponsors alike as its primary virtue. Without imagining that their votes would actually have consequences, and feeling disenfranchised and angry, approximately half of the eligible population did not vote at all; a substantial majority of the other half opted to send a message that they intended primarily as a way to express their anger.

As we have seen, the content of that message both draws from pervasive myths of responsibility and blame, and reinforces them. Thus, not only is the immigrant scapegoating implicit in Proposition 187 a symptom of balanced-budget conservatism as outlined above, but the message it sends legitimates the backlash. Whether or not Proposition 187 is ever officially implemented, its symbolic impact has already been substantial.

Conclusion

The passage of Proposition 187 signals a renewed nativism, the intensity of which has not been seen since the beginning of the century. Given the historical pattern, it is not surprising perhaps that nativism is on the rise in this period of wrenching economic change, capital flight, declining wages, and heightened insecurity. Less predictable is the relentless focus on the burden of immigrants on taxpayers and their consumption of costly social services.

In attempting to explain this fiscal focus of contemporary nativism, I draw from the literature on the crisis of Fordism (Sayer and Walker 1992; Lipietz 1985, 1987; Piore and Sabel 1984), deindustrialization and its effects on workers (Harrison and Bluestone 1982, 1988; Block 1987), and the dismantling of the welfare state (Piven and Cloward 1993). Most important, I borrow the concept of "balanced-budget conservatism" from Plotkin and Scheuerman (1994) to describe the deflection of attention away from these economic transformations and its concentration instead on government spending and the budget deficit as the source of economic and social malaise. The symptoms of this balanced-budget conservatism are an ideological attack on the public sector, disdain for government spending, taxpayer revolts, and hostility both toward the poor who are perceived to be undeserving parasites on hard-working taxpayers, and toward the government, which is seen as fiscally irresponsible. In this ideological and fiscal context, profligate government spending and the "undeserving poor" on whom tax dollars are spent—not economic transformations and corporate decision making—are the primary targets of responsibility for Americans' declining standard of living.

Proposition 187 fits well into this scenario. As the fiscal crisis and balanced-budget conservatism advance, hostility is directed at illegal immigrants—the most undeserving of the poor—who are spotted as the cause of runaway government spending and insatiable social service needs. Thus, not only is the recent rise of nativism in the United States linked to prevailing economic transformations and rising insecurities, but the fiscal theme of that nativism can be explained as a symptom of the balanced-budget conservatism that is the dominant ideological account of the economic and social crisis.

In addition to explaining this immigrants-as-fiscal-burden focus, I have argued that Proposition 187 is primarily symbolic, in at least two senses. First, following Edelman (1977), I demonstrate that the initiative evokes a belief system in which illegal immigrants are the scourge of efforts to control spending—and in this climate of balanced-budget conservatism—thus responsible for all that ails us. As economic insecurity and anger intensify with the continued globalization of the economy and the displacement of domestic labor, Proposition 187 simultaneously channels that anger into anti-immigrant nativism and legitimates the backlash. Whether or not any of its provisions are ever implemented, this symbolic aspect of Proposition 187 has already had, and will continue to have, serious consequences for the immigrant community (and for those "suspected" of being immigrant).

Proposition 187 was symbolic in another way as well. If we are to take California voters at their word, their support for Proposition 187 represented primarily a registration of anger rather than a reasoned effort at instrumental policymaking. As Edelman (1964:3) has put it, the election thus served symbolically as a way to "express discontents." But, in contrast to the electorate of 30 years ago described by Edelman, these voters were fully aware of the purely symbolic nature of the initiative, and indeed self-consciously used the ballot as a way to send a message. With regard to Proposition 187, these voters will probably prove right about their political impotence and symbolic power: Most of the major provisions of the initiative are likely to remain inoperative, at least for the immediate future, blocked by the courts as unconstitutional and/or in violation of federal law, but the symbolic impact of the proposition remains intact.

While immigration is an increasingly visible political issue, and the resurgence of nativism is an important component of this new politics of immigration, relatively few studies have explored these developments (For exceptions, see Cornelius, Martin, and Hollifield 1994; Citrin, Reingold, and Green 1990; Espenshade and Calhoun 1993). While some of this work has examined the connections between the rising restrictionist sentiment and ongoing economic transformations (e.g., Cornelius, Martin, and Hollifield 1994), none has discussed the unique fiscal emphasis of this new nativism. Nor have any studies explored the ways in which material conditions, ideological developments, and symbolic politics interact to produce specific expres-

sions of this nativism. The present study begins to fill this gap. It is hoped that future research will continue this endeavor, perhaps focusing on more regional analyses of the new politics of immigration, or exploring the interconnections between this aspect of the prevailing balanced-budget ideology and other political developments—such as the backlash against affirmative action and the popularity of "welfare reform"—that may share the same ideological space.

Notes

1. Much nineteenth-century immigration was by definition "undocumented" (but not illegal) since before 1875 there were no federal restrictions on immigration and no official system of documentation and control.

2. Ford's classes were technically voluntary and by invitation. The "invitation" read: "You are expected to attend the Ford English School. You must learn to read, write, and speak English. This school was established for your benefit, and you should be glad of this opportunity. . . . There is no excuse for your remaining away from school. Come to the 3rd floor on the Woodward Avenue side, after you ring out. COME TODAY" (quoted in Hill 1919:638; emphasis in original).

3. In the early years of the program, the Immigration and Naturalization Service often favored undocumented Mexican farm workers already in the United States over imported workers for Bracero status, encouraging the flow of illegal immigrants. Furthermore, substantial numbers of Braceros "skipped," leaving their employers before their contracts were up, seeking better wages and working conditions as undocumented "free agents." Finally, with the large influx of Braceros often came friends or family members who added to the illegal immigrant population. In 1954, Immigration Commissioner Joseph Swing launched "Operation Wetback," deporting thousands of undocumented Mexican workers and their families, and promising growers an abundant supply of

Braceros if they refused to hire the undocumented. For the duration of the Bracero Program, illegal immigration never reached its pre-Operation Wetback levels (see Calavita 1992; Craig 1971).

4. IRCA's Special Agricultural Worker program, and its amnesty provision, enabled the law to clear the hurdle of special interests and advocacy groups—most notably western agriculture and immigrant advocates, respectively. However, it was growing restrictionist sentiment that provided the original political impetus for the reform, which was first designed as an employer sanctions law, and popular support for employer sanctions continued to be the primary political motor driving IRCA (Montwieler 1987; Calavita 1989, 1990). Ironically, it was the legalization provisions that had the most significant impact.

5. While there were decreases in border apprehensions for two years after IRCA was passed, subsequent research indicates this was primarily due to the effect of legalizing close to three million previously undocumented immigrants through IRCA's two legalization provisions (Crane et al. 1990; Bean, Vernez, and Keely 1989; Fix 1991).

6. In *Plyler vs. Doe* (1982), the U.S. Supreme Court declared that the Texas policy of allowing school districts to bar undocumented children from public schools violated the equal protection clause of the Fourteenth Amendment.

7. One GOP welfare reform package being considered by Congress would deny legally resident immigrants AFDC payments, Supplemental Security Income, Medicaid, aid for the elderly and disabled, and food stamps (Owen 1995).

8. There are obviously a wide range of issues involved in the immigration debate. As the Executive Summary of the U.S. Commission on Immigration Reform (1994) makes clear, U.S. citizens are concerned, for example, about competition with immigrants for housing and jobs, as well as being ambivalent about a host of "multicultural" issues. I do not intend here to over-simplify this multifaceted debate, but rather to examine the dominant theme of contemporary U.S. nativism as expressed in Proposition 187.

9. Block (1987) argues against both the foreign competition thesis and the broader crisis of Fordism interpretation of declining profits, arguing instead that the declines are the essentially self-inflicted result of U.S. capitalists' failure to concentrate on the production of high value-added goods and to make the investments in human capital—such as education and training—necessary to this more complex production process.

10. Although California is required by its Constitution to balance its budget every year, according to the nonpartisan Citizens Budget Commission: California now holds the dubious distinction of having the highest proportion of short-term borrowing activity relative to its budget of any state in the nation (quoted in Skelton 1955:A3). In 1994, California borrowed $7 billion to help cover expenses for two years, but its books are "balanced" by creative accounting schemes.

11. One reviewer has suggested that the regional nature of Republican politics may have something to do with the absence of such initiatives in New York. For example, a number of prominent Republican institutions located on the East Coast are favorable toward immigration (most notably, the *Wall Street Journal* which is consistently pro-immigration). As this reviewer points out, "There are some intervening political variables between the growth of an immigrant population, cuts in social welfare expenditures, and the political outcome . . . in California." One of these variables no doubt was Governor Wilson's unflagging focus on this issue and his highly visible support for the initiative.

12. From this perspective, it may not be coincidental that Governor Wilson chose to focus on five key issues in his ill-fated presidential campaign: illegal immigration, affirmative action, government spending, welfare, and crime (Lesher 1995).

13. A *Los Angeles Times* exit poll is consistent with this interpretation of the political symbolism of Proposition 187 and the widespread appeal of the balanced-budget ideology it expresses. According to this poll (*Los Angeles Times* 1994b), a majority of respondents voted for Proposition 187 regardless of gender, household income, level of education, or "immigration status" (number of generations in the U.S.). Political ideology (liberal, moderate, conservative) was the most important factor distinguishing the electorate on this issue—with only 26 percent of self-identified "liberals" voting for the initiative and 78 percent of "conservatives" favoring it. Ethnicity/race was also a distinguishing factor, with 63 percent of whites, 47 percent of Blacks, 23 percent of Latinos, and 47 percent of Asians favoring the measure. Given the targeting of racial minorities implicit in much balanced-budget conservatism, and the racial undertones of the Proposition 187 campaign, it should not be surprising that the measure won a majority only among white voters (whites comprised 81 percent of all voters). What is perhaps more surprising is the significant numbers of ethnic minorities (including Latinos) who favored the initiative.

References

Arax, Mark. 1994. "Raisin farmers hit by shortage of workers." *Los Angeles Times*, September 27:A3.

Bailey, Eric, and Dan Morain. 1993. "Anti-immigration bills flood legislature." *Los Angeles Times*, May 3:A3.

Bean, Frank D., Barry Edmonston, and Jeffrey S. Passel. 1990. *Undocumented Migration to the United States: IRCA and the Experience of the 1980s.* Santa Monica, Calif.: The Rand Corporation.

Bean, Frank D., Georges Vernez, and Charles B. Keely. 1989. *Opening and Closing the Doors: Evaluating Immigration Reform and Control.* Santa Monica, Calif.: Rand Corporation.

Block, Fred. 1987. *Revising State Theory: Essays in Politics and Postindustrialism.* Philadelphia: Temple University Press.

Bluestone, Barry, and Irving Bluestone. 1992. *Negotiating the Future: A Labor Perspective on American Business.* New York: Basic Books.

Bornemeier, James. 1994. "U.S. study fuels debate on illegal immigrants' impact." *Los Angeles Times*, September 15:A1, A26.

————1995 "Clinton moves to curb illegal immigration." *Los Angeles Times*, February 8:A3.

Bowles, Samuel, David M. Gordon, and Thomas E. Weisskopf. 1984. *Beyond the Wasteland.* New York: Anchor Books.

Brownstein, Ronald. 1994. "Wilson proposes U.S. version of Prop. 187." *Los Angeles Times,* November 19:A1.

Bulletin of the National Association of Wool Manufacturers. 1912. No title.

Business Week. 1985. "The casino society." September 16:78–90.

————1988. "Learning to live with leverage." November 7:138.

Calavita, Kitty. 1983. "The demise of the Occupational Safety and Health Administration: A case study in symbolic action." *Social Problems* 30:437–448.

————1984. *U.S. Immigration Law and the Control of Labor, 1820–1924.* London: Academic Press.

————1989. "The contradictions of immigration lawmaking: The Immigration Reform and Control Act of 1986." *Law and Policy* 11:17–47.

————1990. "Employer sanctions violations: Toward a dialectical model of white-collar crime." *Law and Society Review* 24:1041–1069.

————1992. *Inside the State: The Bracero Program, Immigration and the INS.* New York: Routledge, Chapman and Hall, Inc.

Carnegie, Andrew. 1886. *Triumphant Democracy, or Fifty Years' March of the Republic.* New York: Charles Scribner's Sons.

Citrin, Jack, Beth Reingold, and Donald P. Green. 1990. "American identity and the politics of ethnic change." *The Journal of Politics* 52:1124–1154.

Clark, Rebecca L., and Jeffrey S. Passel. 1993. "How much do immigrants pay in taxes?" Program for Research on Immigration Policy Paper PRIP–UI–26. Washington, D.C.: The Urban Institute.

Cockcroft, James D. 1986. *Outlaws in the Promised Land: Mexican Immigrant Workers and America's Future.* New York: Grove Press.

Congressional Record. 1884. 48th Congress, 1st Session.

————1921. 66th Congress, 3rd Session.

Congressional Research Service. 1980. "History of the Immigration and Naturalization Service. A report prepared for the use of The Select Commission on Immigration and Refugee Policy." Washington, D.C.: U.S. Government Printing Office.

Cornelius, Wayne A. 1982. "America in the era of limits: Nativist reactions to the 'New' Immigration." Research Report Series 3. La Jolla: Center for U.S.-Mexican Studies, University of California, San Diego.

Cornelius, Wayne A., Philip L. Martin, and James F. Hollifield (eds.). 1994. *Controlling Immigration: A Global Perspective*. Stanford, Calif.: Stanford University Press.

Craig, Richard B. 1971. *The Bracero Program: Interest Groups and Foreign Policy*. Austin: University of Texas Press.

Crane, Keith, Beth Asch, Joanna Zorn Heilbrunn, and Danielle C. Cullinane. 1990. *The Effect of Employer Sanctions on the Flow of Undocumented Immigrants to the United States*. Lanham, MD: University Press of America.

Decker, Cathleen. 1994. "Voters back service cuts for illegal immigrants." *Los Angeles Times*, May 29:A1.

Edelman, Murray. 1964. *The Symbolic Uses of Politics*. Chicago: University of Illinois Press.

———1977. *Political Language: Words That Succeed and Policies That Fail*. New York: Academic Press.

Eisenstadt, Todd A., and Cathryn L. Thorup. 1994. "Caring capacity versus carrying capacity: Community responses to Mexican immigration in San Diego's North County." *Monograph Series* 39. Center for U.S.-Mexican Studies, University of California, San Diego.

Engel, David M. 1984. "The oven bird's song: Insiders, outsiders, and personal injuries in an American community." *Law and Society Review* 18:551–582.

Espenshade, Thomas J., and Charles A. Calhoun. 1993. "An analysis of public opinion toward undocumented immigration." *Population Research and Policy Review* 12:189–224.

Ezell, Harold W. 1994. "Enough is more than enough." *Los Angeles Times*, October 23:M5.

Feldman, Paul. 1994. "Anti-illegal immigration Prop. 187 keeps 2-to-1 edge." *Los Angeles Times*, October 15:A1.

Feldstein, Martin. 1985. "The Social Security explosion." *Public Interest* 81:94–106.

Fix, Michael. 1991. *The Paper Curtain: Employer Sanctions' Implementation, Impact, and Reform*. Washington, D.C.: The Urban Institute Press.

Fix, Michael, and Jeffrey S. Passel. 1994. "Who's on the dole? It's not illegal immigrants." *Los Angeles Times*, August 3:B7.

Gallup, George. 1980. "Most U.S. citizens favor a hard line toward illegal aliens." San Diego Union, November 30:A22.

Gamio, Manuel. 1971. *Mexican Immigration to the United States*. New York: Dover Publications.

Gibbs, Nancy. 1994. "Keep out, you tired, you poor . . . " *Time*, October 3:46–47.

Godkin, E.L. 1887. "Some political and social aspects of the tariff." *New Princeton Review* 3:173.

Gossett, Thomas F. 1973. *Race: The History of an Idea in America*. New York: Schocken Books

Gurwitt, Robert. 1988. "English-only campaign is spreading." *Governing* 1:67–68.

Gusfield, Joseph R. 1963. *Symbolic Crusader: Status Politics and the American Temperance Movement*. Urbana: University of Illinois Press.

Harris, Candee S. 1984. "The magnitude of job loss from plant closings and the generation of replacement jobs: Some recent evidence." *Annals of the American Academy of Political and Social Science* Vol. 475.

Harrison, Bennett, and Barry Bluestone. 1982. *The Deindustrialization of America*. New York: Basic Books.

———1988. *The Great U-Turn: Corporate Restructuring and the Polarizing of America*. New York: Basic Books.

Harvey, David. 1982. *The Limits to Capital*. Oxford: Basil Blackwell.

Higham, John. 1955. *Strangers in the Land: Patterns of American Nativism, 1860–1925*. New Brunswick, N.J.: Rutgers University Press.

Hill, Herbert C. 1919. "The Americanization movement." *American Journal of Sociology* 24:609–642.

Hoffman, Abraham. 1974. *Unwanted Mexican Americans in the Great Depression: Repatriation Pressures, 1929–1939*. Tucson: University of Arizona Press.

Huddle, Donald. 1993. *The Costs of Immigration*. Washington. D.C.: Carrying Capacity Network.

Ingwerson, Marshall. 1993. "Workers brave new job frontiers." *The Christian Science Monitor*, March 24:9, 12.

Kilborn, Peter T. 1993. "New jobs lack the old security in time of 'disposable workers'." *The New York Times*, March 15: A1, A6.

Kolko, Joyce. 1988. *Restructuring the World Economy*. New York: Pantheon.

Lacey, Marc. 1995. "New task force targets illegal immigration." *Los Angeles Times*, March 16:A3.

Lesher, Dave. 1995. "Wilson kicks off presidential campaign." *Los Angeles Times*, August 29:A1, A18–19.

Lipietz, Alain. 1985. *The Enchanted World: Inflation, Credit and the World Crisis*. London: Verso.

———1987. *Mirages and Miracles: The Global Crisis of Fordism*. London: Verso.

Lopez, Gerald P. 1981. "Undocumented Mexican immigration: In search of a just immigration law and policy." *UCLA Law Review* 28:615–714.

Los Angeles Times. 1987. "Minimum wage hike's real payoff." May 12, Part IV:3.

———1994a. "The Times Poll: Why They Voted." November 9:A22.

1994b. "Times Poll: A look at the electorate." November 11:A5.

———1995. "In U.S., 1 in 11 foreign-born, census finds." August 29:A20.

Marshall, Ray. 1978. "Economic factors influencing the international migration of workers." In *Views Across the Border*, ed. Stanley Ross, 163–180. Albuquerque, N.M.: University of New Mexico Press.

Martin, Philip L. 1994. "The United States: Benign neglect toward immigration." In *Controlling Immigration: A Global Perspective*, eds. Wayne Cornelius et al., 83–99. Stanford, Calif.: Stanford University Press.

Martinez, Ruben. 1994. "Perspective on Prop. 187: The nightmare is coming true." *Los Angeles Times*, November 28:B7.

McDonnell, Patrick J. 1994. "Immigrant study cites fiscal gain." *Los Angeles Times*, February 23:B4.

Montwieler, Nancy Humel. 1987. *The Immigration Reform Law of 1986*. Washington, D.C.: Bureau of National Affairs.

Munoz, Cecilia. 1994. "Harassment in the wake of Proposition 187." *The Christian Science Monitor*, December 27:19.

Nalik, John, and Paul Feldman. 1994. "Santa Ana schools condemn immigration measure." *Los Angeles Times*, September 24:A21.

New York Journal of Commerce. 1892. No title. December 13:2.

Ostrow, Ronald J., and Fulwood, Sam. 1994. "Wilson helped foster illegal influx, Reno says." *Los Angeles Times*, September 30:A3, A32.

Owen, Kelly. 1995. "Immigrants and welfare." *Los Angeles Times*, March 22:A5.

Parker, Richard A., and Louis M. Rea. 1993. "Illegal immigration in San Diego County: An analysis of the costs and revenues." A report to the California Senate. San Diego: State of California Senate, Special Committee on Border Issues.

Passel, Jeffrey S., and Barry Edmonston. 1994. "Immigration and race: Recent trends in immigration to the United States." In *Immigration and Ethnicity: The Integration of America's Newest Arrivals,* eds. Barry Edmonston and Jeffrey S. Passel, Chapter 2. Washington, D.C.: The Urban Institute Press.

Phillips, Kevin. 1993. *Boiling Point: Democrats, Republicans, and the Decline of Middle-Class Prosperity.* New York: Harper Perennial.

———1994. *Arrogant Capital: Washington, Wall Street, and the Frustration of American Politics.* Boston: Little, Brown.

Piore, Michael, and Charles Sabel. 1984. *The Second Industrial Divide.* New York: Basic Books.

Piven, Frances Fox, and Richard A. Cloward. 1993. *Regulating the Poor: The Functions of Public Welfare.* New York: Vintage Books.

Plotkin, Sidney, and William E. Scheuerman. 1994. *Private Interest, Public Spending: Balanced-Budget Conservatism and the Fiscal Crisis.* Boston, Mass.: South End Press.

Public Opinion. 1886. No title. Volume I:355.

Reisler, Mark. 1976. *By the Sweat of their Brow: Mexican Immigrant Labor in the United States, 1900–1940.* Westport, Conn.: Greenwood Press.

Romney, Lee, and Jeff Brazil. 1994. "Boy whose parents feared deportation had leukemia." *Los Angeles Times,* November 24:A3.

Romney, Lee, and Julie Marquis. 1994. "Youth dies as medical treatment is delayed." *Los Angeles Times,* November 23:A3.

Rosenblatt, Robert A. 1994. "Survey finds sharp rise in working poor." *Los Angeles Times,* March 31:D1.

San Diego Union-Tribune. 1995. "Many illegals would not enter U.S. if all aid was denied." Letter to the Editor, September 1:B9.

Sayer, Andrew, and Richard Walker. 1992. *The New Social Economy: Reworking the Division of Labor.* Cambridge, Mass.: Blackwell.

Scheer, Robert. 1994. "Prop. 187: Stick it to the kids." *Los Angeles Times,* October 13:B7.

Shogren, Elizabeth, and Melissa Healy. 1995. "Gingrich backs Wilson on illegal immigrant costs." *Los Angeles Times,* February 9:A1.

Skelton, George. 1995. "A matter of dollars and sense." *Los Angeles Times,* August 14:A3.

Stewart, William F., Mark Gascoigne, and R. Wayne Bannister. 1992. "Impact of undocumented persons and other immigrants on costs, revenues and services in Los Angeles County." A report prepared for Los Angeles County Board of Supervisors. November 6.

U.S. Commission on Immigration Reform. 1994. U.S. Immigration Policy. Restoring Credibility. A Report to Congress, Executive Summary. Washington, D.C.

U.S. Congress. 1901. House Industrial Commission. Reports of the Industrial Commission. House Document #184, Volumes 14, 15.

———1911. Senate Immigration Commission. Immigration Commission Report. Senate Document No. 747.

———1919. House Committee on Immigration and Naturalization. "Prohibition of immigration and the problem of immigration." Hearing before the Committee on Immigration and Naturalization.

———1920. House Report #1109.

———1971. "Illegal aliens." House Committee on the Judiciary. Hearings before the Subcommittee on Immigration, Refugees, and International Law of the House Committee on the Judiciary.

———1971-. "Illegal aliens." House Committee on the Judiciary. Subcommittee on Immigration,

———1972. Citizenship, and International Law. Hearings before the Subcommittee. Parts 1–5.

U.S. Congress. 1921. "Emergency immigration legislation." Senate Subcommittee on Immigration. Hearing before the Committee on Immigration.

U.S. Department of Labor. 1991. "Employer sanctions and U.S. labor markets: Second report." Bureau of International Labor Affairs. Washington, D.C.: U.S. Government Printing Office.

Vernez, Georges, and Kevin McCarthy. 1995. "The fiscal costs of immigration: Analytical and policy issues." Center for Research on Immigration Policy. Report DRU–958–1–IF.

Wiebe, Robert H. 1962. *Businessmen and Reform: A Study of the Progressive Movement.* Cambridge, Mass.: Harvard University Press.

Wood, Daniel B. 1994. "California's immigration revolt." *The Christian Science Monitor,* November 10:1–2.

 Article Review Form at end of book.

- Technological and cultural changes make the current wave of immigrants different in some important ways from earlier generations of newcomers.

- U.S. citizens increasingly express hostility toward immigrants that may be misplaced frustration with the domestic economy. European-American voters in California and community members in Wisconsin provide evidence of this analysis.

R.E.A.L. Sites

This list provides a print preview of typical **Coursewise** R.E.A.L. sites. (There are over 100 such sites at the **Courselinks**™ site.) The danger in printing URLs is that web sites can change overnight. As we went to press, these sites were functional using the URLs provided. If you come across one that isn't, please let us know via email to: webmaster@coursewise.com. Use your Passport to access the most current list of R.E.A.L. sites at the **Courselinks** site.

Site name: United States Immigration and Naturalization Service

URL: http://www.ins.usdoj.gov/index.html

Why is it R.E.A.L.? The INS is the governmental body charged with overseeing immigration to and naturalization in the United States. This site includes directions for people seeking naturalization, as well as information about "careers in the Border Patrol." As such, this site definitely takes us into the realm of "the real."

Key topic: immigration

Try this: Familiarize yourself with the resources of the site; then check out under "Reports" the government's statement about "Mail-order Brides." How do global and national racial politics serve as the background for this phenomenon? Who does the government seem to hold accountable? What would be done about this practice? Why? Write down your ideas and bring them to class for discussion.

Site name: Immigration in the 21st Century—Whom Do We Let In?

URL: http://www.libertynet.org/balch/html/body_immigration_in_21st_century.html

Why is it R.E.A.L.? This site reconstructs a public symposium on U.S. immigration policy in the next century. The featured speaker was Susan Forbes Martin, Executive Director of the U.S. Commission on Immigration Reform.

Key topics: immigration, policy debates

Try this: Read the dialogue between Susan Forbes Martin and her interlocutor, attorney Tsiwen Law. Analyze the assumptions and values each of them brings to the conversation and the understandings about race and stratification embedded in their conversation.

section 4

Racial and Ethnic Identities

Key Points

- By 2050, people of mixed racial ancestry will constitute 21 percent of the U.S. population, and corporate marketers are cashing in on that eventuality now.

- Gender identity is linked to ethnicity, and both change as a function of cultural, political, and historical events.

- Sexuality and romance in the United States are infused with power and politics that reflect racial and ethnic stratification. Sexual identity, like gender identity, must be understood in the context of ethnicity.

- European-Americans are increasingly identifying with Native American Indian culture and spirituality, while Indian peoples assert that their cultures are "not for sale."

WiseGuide Intro

We are not born with identities. Indeed, our identities—our senses of ourselves in relation to our society—change throughout life as we acquire new experiences, roles, and statuses. Early in life, we develop both gender identity—our sense of ourselves as male or female—and racial identity—our sense of ourselves as belonging to one or more racialized social groups. Like gender identity, racial identity seems to be part of children's senses of self by the time they are three or four years old. How do we learn our racial identities? Is the process of learning to be white the same as learning to be Black, or Latino, or Asian? Are the differences simply a matter of learning culture, or are they also a matter of learning about the relative positions of power occupied by various racialized groups?

We learn our racial identities through interactions with others, who give us messages about how they perceive us and what those perceptions mean. In the United States, race serves as a *master status*, a feature of an individual that takes on special social significance and strongly influences that person's experiences in society. "Whiteness" constitutes what sociologists sometimes call an "unmarked category." Whiteness is understood as the absence of having "a race" and is equated with "being human." North Americans learn that to be categorized as white is to be accepted as normal and that to be categorized as nonwhite means being seen as different, deviant, and inferior. Likewise, "American" has come to be equated with whiteness, and people who are not considered white are relegated to the "hyphenated American" categories: African-American, Asian-American, and Native-American. As a result, whites learn that the "problem of race" in the United States is not theirs. At the same time, people of color learn that the dominant society sees them first and foremost as members of particular racialized groups and only secondarily as individuals with particular talents, skills, interests, and strengths.

Of course, most of the ancestors of white people in the United States arrived here with a strong sense of racial and ethnic identity. Interestingly, a number of groups today seen as "white" were previously seen as "Black," including even the light-skinned Irish. Through various cultural, social, and legal processes, most people of European descent have come to be defined as white—and have come to constitute a statistical majority—while people of Latin American, Asian, and African descent have been defined in racialized ways. It is very important to note again that racialization and deracialization are social processes. Think, for example, of the historical "one-drop rule" applied as a legal standard in the United States to determine whether a person was white or Black: if the person had one great-grandparent of African descent and seven of European descent, he or she was considered Black: However, in many other countries—and in the United States today—the same person would be considered white, revealing again how race is socially constructed. While the "one-drop rule" no longer serves as part of a legal standard in the United States, this line of thinking clearly remains part of the culture. People of mixed racial ancestry are usually relegated to the category with lower social status. For example, despite his mixed racial heritage, American golfer Tiger Woods is usually seen as Black.

At the level of identity, how might we disrupt racism? Is the solution to ameliorate the cultural differences between groups and to create a culturally homogeneous society? To what extent is having a sense of racial or ethnic heritage meaningful to individuals and groups? What might be the consequences of living without racial identities? How might American racism be related to whites' distance from their own racial identities? These are some of the questions we must ask as we begin to think about the racialization of identities and its significance in people's lives.

The readings in this section address issues of racial identity in a variety of ways that demonstrate how racial identities are situated within broader social and historical patterns, as well as how they are linked to other master statuses, such as gender. Writer Rochelle Stanfield explores the reciprocal relationships between changes in public policies, the formation of "mixed" families, and racial identity construction in her article "Blending of America." In "The Meanings of Macho: Changing Mexican Male Identities," anthropologist Matthew C. Gutmann traces the social history of changes in "macho" identity, an identity located at the nexus of ethnicity and masculinity. Education professor Carla Trujillo examines how the politics of identity affect romantic and domestic intimacy in her first-person account, "Confessions of a Chicana Ph.D." Finally, anthropologist Diane Bell offers a critical report on the apparent upsurge in white Americans' identification with Indian and Aboriginal spiritualities, ethnicities, and identities in "Desperately Seeking Redemption: Rise of Native American Neo-shamanic Books and Workshops." As you read these articles, pay special attention to how demographics, politics, economics, and power shape the formation of racialized identities, as well as how identities are consequential for demographics, politics, economics, and power.

Which groups are more likely to inter-marry? Which groups are least likely to marry across racial lines? How can these patterns be explained?

Blending of America

Rochelle L. Stanfield

A dramatic upsurge in intermarriage has serious scholars once again talking about the notion of a "melting pot." But the government has lacked hard data on the extent of this quiet demographic counter-revolution.

As assistant chief of the Census Bureau's Population Division, Jorge DelPinal is supposed to fit people into neat, distinct racial and ethnic boxes; white, black, Hispanic, Asian or American Indian. As the son of an Anglo mother and a Hispanic father, however, he knows that's not always possible.

"My identity has evolved as being Hispanic, although I'm only half-and-half," he said recently. Not surprisingly, DelPinal understands the frustration of interracial couples who are expected to assign just one race to their children when they fill out government forms. "They're saying, 'Why should we have to choose between the parents?'" the Census Bureau official said.

Meanwhile, demographer Barry Edmonston used sophisticated mathematical modeling techniques to calculate how intermarriage is changing the face of America as part of an immigration study he directed for the National Research Council of the American Academy of Sciences, summarized in a report called "The New Americans: Economic, Demographic and Fiscal Effects of Immigration." But as the Canadian-born, white husband of sociologist Sharon Lee, a Chinese-American, Edmonston needed no computer to understand the transformation under way in this society. He and his family are living, breathing participants. (See NJ, 7/5/97, p. 1366.)

The face of America is changing—literally. As President Clinton has said in recent speeches: "Within 30 or 40 years . . . there will be no single race in the majority of America. . . . We had best be ready for it." Clinton is preparing for that time by talking about racial tolerance and the virtues of multiculturalism. Others are debating immigration policy. Almost all discussion focuses on the potential divisiveness inherent in an America that is no longer a predominantly white country with a mostly European ancestry.

But afoot behind the scenes is another trend that, if handled carefully, could bring the country closer together rather than drive it apart. This quiet demographic counter-revolution is a dramatic upsurge in intermarriage.

"Demography is a very intimate deal," said Ben J. Wattenberg, a senior fellow at the American Enterprise Institute for Public Policy Research (AEI) in Washington. "It's not about what activists say; it's about what young men and women do. And what they're doing is marrying each other and having children."

Edmonston's study projected that by 2050, 21 per cent of the U.S. population will be of mixed racial or ethnic ancestry, up from an estimate of 7 per cent today. Among third-generation Hispanic- and Asian-Americans, exogamy—"outmarriage" to the rest of us—is at least 50 per cent, he and others estimate. Exogamy remains much less prevalent among African-Americans, but it has increased enormously, from about 1.5 per cent in the 1960s to 8–10 per cent today.

Such a profound demographic shift could take place while no one was looking because, officially, no one has been looking. Federal agencies traditionally collect racial data using a formula—one person, one race—that's similar to the time-honored voting principle. Thus, the Census Bureau could estimate that at most, only 2 per cent of the population would claim to be multiracial on census forms. In the absence of a more straightforward count, no one knows for sure what the demographics are.

That's about to change. The Office of Management and Budget, which oversees federal statistical practices, is close to approving a directive that will allow people to check as many racial boxes as they believe apply to them. The change, which will be in place for the 2000 census, doesn't satisfy the demand of a handful of interest groups that insist on being able to check a "multiracial box." But it will permit the government to track the growth of "blended" Americans and still keep tabs on the original racial and ethnic categories, while complying with the law and with the demand of major civil rights and race-based groups.

Meanwhile, in the absence of official numbers, with the heightened tension surrounding racial issues, and with the mutual suspicion that exists among competing racial and ethnic interest groups, there's little agreement on what intermarriage will mean for American society in the future.

Some sociologists call Asian-white and Hispanic-Anglo intermarriage simply the latest addition to the melting pot that, since the start of this century, has fused so many Irish, Italian, German and other families of European origin. But despite the rise in black-white marriage, many doubt that African-Americans will be included in this mix.

"I think the almost ineradicable line in America is between blacks and all others," said Roger Wilkins, a history professor at George Mason University in Northern Virginia and longtime civil rights figure. "Blacks have always been the undigestible mass. Having said that, however, there's no doubt that something is happening," he continued. "Just look at the ads on television (with) beautiful models, male and female, who are not quite white. Are they a mixture of black and white, black and Asian, Hispanic and white? You just can't tell."

Others anticipate that the bedroom will accomplish what other catalysts could not. Douglas J. Besharov, an AEI resident scholar, for example, said in a 1996 article in The New Democrat that the growing numbers of mixed-race youth represent "the best hope for the future of American race relations."

Ramona Douglass, president of the Association of MultiEthnic Americans, enthused, "We're living proof that people with two different races or ethnic backgrounds can live together in harmony, that (interracial) families actually do function." Douglass's mother is Italian-American, and her father is a multiracial blend of African-American and American Indian.

Of course, many portray intermarriage as gradual genocide that will culminate in the disappearance of their particular group. That was the traditional view of the Jewish community, which throughout history closely guarded its small numbers from loss through assimilation. But the very high rate of Jewish out-marriage since World War II has caused an official rethinking among the progressive elements of American Judaism. Instead of shunning those who marry non-Jews, these groups are now courting them.

"The Jewish community, at least its liberal branches, moved from a posture of outrage to a posture of outreach," explained Egon Mayer, who is a sociology professor at Brooklyn College and co-director of the North American Jewish Data Bank at the City University of New York (CUNY). "There's been a tremendous upsurge in efforts to reach out to these families, to invite them in and, in a way, to have a multicultural cake and eat it, too."

Although sociologists are quick to point out the differences between Jews and other minority groups, they nonetheless acknowledge that the evolution of the Jewish approach to intermarriage

may provide a model for the nation as a whole as it discovers, and then confronts, the racial and ethnic blending of America.

Melting Pot

To see the new face of America, go to a grocery store and look at a box of Betty Crocker-brand mashed-potato mix. Betty's portrait is now in its eighth incarnation since the first composite painting debuted in 1936 with pale skin and blue eyes. Her new look is brown-eyed and dark-haired. She has a duskier complexion than her seven predecessors, with features representing an amalgam of white, Hispanic, Indian, African and Asian ancestry.

A computer created this new Betty more than a year ago by blending photos of 75 diverse women. That process was relatively quick, General Mills Inc., spokesmen explain, while acknowledging it is taking quite a while to spread the new image to more-familiar Betty Crocker products such as cake mix.

The slowness of that process itself could be a metaphor for gradual racial and ethnic intermixing in this country. Indeed, it's taking a long time for the new blended American to surface in society's consciousness. Tiger Woods, the young golf great, publicized the trend by identifying himself as Cablinasian, a mixture of caucasian, black, American Indian and Asian.

For the most part, the marketplace—not government—is leading the way in this evolution. Mixed-race models, particularly men, are in great demand, according to fashion industry experts. And multiracial child actors are now more likely to be tapped for television advertisements.

The ad agencies that hire those models and actors "are not idealistic people," Wilkins said. "They are out to sell stuff and they study trends very carefully. So, what they see is a big market out there that is reached by beautiful people who are not exactly white, or who are yearning for a melting-pot America."

That serious scholars should be talking about a melting pot is itself a reversal. As a metaphor for American diversity, the melting pot was first discredited after World War I, when the European immigrants streaming into American cities formed distinct ethnic and national enclaves that didn't melt together.

The timing was off, it turned out, and the metaphorical pot was in the wrong place. Interracial and multiethnic fusion started after World War II and happened in the suburbs. City folk moved from their Italian, Irish, Polish or Jewish urban neighborhoods into diffuse suburban settings, then sent their kids to large public universities, throwing them together with youngsters from other ethnic backgrounds who, nonetheless, came from families with similar lifestyles.

"Most people meet their potential partners either at college or when they start working," said sociologist Lee, a University of Richmond professor who is spending some time as a visiting scholar at Portland (Ore.) State University. "When you have a college education, you're likely to be in a milieu where there will be people of all kinds of ethnic backgrounds, and that increases the chances of marrying someone that's different from your own ethnic background." Lee is a case in point, having met her husband, Edmonston (recently appointed director of Portland State's Center for Population Research), when they were students.

David Tseng, a special assistant in the Labor Department's Pension and Welfare Benefits Administration, tells a similar story. His mother came from Ecuador; his father was the son of a Chinese diplomat in Washington. Their marriage in the late 1950s was unusual for the time, "but I think it helped that the people with whom they were friendly and socialized were educated and intelligent and comfortable with people from other lands and cultures," Tseng said.

That dynamic is now routinely seen among native-born Asian-Americans and Hispanic-Americans. "We're seeing very high rates of intermarriage for Hispanics and Asians who are living in fairly integrated areas outside their traditional areas (of concentration) in the Southwest and West," Edmonston said. He cited a study that showed an 80 per cent exogamy rate for young, native-born Asians in New England, for example.

Ironically, the rise in immigration and the trend toward multiculturalism that so many analysts view as major factors leading to divisiveness actually contribute to this blending of races and ethnic groups. "Once you fragment . . . the society into so many different ethnic origins, you make it mathematically less and less likely to meet somebody of your own ethnicity," Wattenberg said. "That's what happened, basically, to the Jewish population."

Whether blacks will follow other minorities into the melting pot remains a subject of debate. Skeptics point to the much smaller proportion of black-white marriages and say it won't happen soon. Others respond that the statistical base is very small because, until 1967, such marriages were illegal in 19 states.

Countervailing Forces

While many forces are at work to facilitate intermarriage, others mitigate against it. This is particularly the case for African-Americans.

The growing segment of the black community that is going to college, entering the middle class and moving out to the suburbs is also following the general trend toward intermarriage. This tendency is particularly noticeable in California and in cities such as Dallas, Las Vegas and Phoenix, where residential segregation has been less pronounced than in the older northeastern and midwestern cities, said Reynolds Farley, who until recently studied African-American residential patterns as a professor at the University of Michigan. In California, for example, among 25-to-34-year-old African-Americans, 14 per cent of the married black women and 32 per cent of the married black men had spouses of a different race, according to demographer Edmonston.

But in the isolated urban neighborhoods of the Northeast and Midwest, the old pattern remains. "There is a considerable fraction of the black population that still lives in inner-city areas— in Detroit, Chicago, New York City—that have not been caught up in dynamic economic growth," said Farley, now a vice president at the Russell Sage Foundation in New York City. "They've been left behind, and they are quite far out of it."

Another countervailing force is immigration. Immigrants generally don't marry outside their racial or ethnic group. Their children do to some extent, but out-marriage really is most prevalent in the third generation. The most recent large-scale wave of immigration has produced only first- or second-generation Americans.

Regardless of the real degree of racial and ethnic intermixing that goes on, the test of a blended society will be the proportion of people who identify as multiracial or multiethnic. Until now, that percentage has been small. That's partly because people tend to assume the racial or ethnic identity of one parent—often the minority parent, in the case of blacks and Hispanics. But to a large extent, that identity has been imposed by society. "I have a Spanish name and I speak Spanish, so people see me as being of Spanish origin," DelPinal, the Census Bureau official, said.

Racial identification can stem from other reasons, such as heightened ethnic pride or the opportunity to benefit from affirmative action and other programs. Over the last few decades, having American Indian ancestry has apparently become popular. Between 1970 and 1980, the number of people who checked off "American Indian" on their census forms grew from 800,000 to 1.4 million, a much faster increase than could be accounted for by births minus deaths. "People decided they wanted to identify as American Indians, to some extent because of rising ethnic consciousness," recalled Jeffrey S. Passel, director of the Immigration Policy Program at the Urban Institute and a former director of the Census Bureau's Population Division.

It is this positive approach to racial or ethnic identification on which liberal elements of the Jewish community are trying to capitalize. For two millennia, exogamy was a major transgression for Jews. (In many communities, prayers for the dead were recited for a Jew who married a non-Jew.) As a result, outmarriage was rare. Before World War II, it amounted to less than 7 per cent of Jewish marriages, according to Mayer of CUNY. But in 1970, a National Jewish Population Survey discovered that in the previous five years, 30 per cent of new Jewish marriages were to non-Jews. By 1990, that figure was more than 50 per cent.

After many meetings, much soul-searching and a lot of acrimonious debate, various non-Orthodox synagogue groups and Jewish civic organizations decided to reverse their approach and make the new interfaith families feel welcome.

Rabbi Daniel G. Zemel of Temple Micah in Washington was one of those who switched positions. In 1979, when he was ordained a rabbi, Zemel recalled recently, "I felt those rabbis who officiated at intermarriages should be excommunicated from the rabbinical associations. Since that time, my thinking has changed enormously. I think if you can find ways to conceive of a diverse, heterogeneous Jewish community, then that's what we'll be looking at in the future," he continued. But that, he acknowledged, will require a revolution in outlook for a community that has been tied together more by European ethnic roots than by its religious practices.

The sea change contemplated by Zemel is in some ways analogous to the shift required by America as it transforms itself from a mostly white nation to a multiracial, blended society. The first step down that path is probably figuring out just who we are. And that requires an accurate count of all colors and the various shades in between.

 **Article Review Form at end of book.**

What are the historical forces that led to shifts in Mexican men's conceptualizations of appropriate masculinity?

The Meanings of Macho:

Changing Mexican Male Identities

Matthew C. Gutmann

University of California at Berkeley

By 1992, most of the five-year-old boys in the San Bernabé Nursery School in Col. Santo Domingo cheerfully participated in the game called *"el baño de la muñeca,"* "the doll bath." Aurora Muñoz, the director of the Nursery, noted that the boys also now swept up, watered the plants, and collected the trash. When she began working at San Bernabé in 1982, however, many of the boys would protest: "Only *viejas* do that!" (similar to "That's girls' work!"). Aurora Muñoz attributed the changes to the fact that, as the boys themselves reported, their older brothers and fathers often did these things now, so why shouldn't they?[1] In the *colonia popular* neighborhood of Santo Domingo on the southside of Mexico City, where I began conducting ethnographic fieldwork on male identities in 1992, grandfathers sometimes remark on the changes in men and women in their lifetimes. When they were young, for instance, only girls were sent shopping for food, while today being allowed for the first time to go buy fresh tortillas marks a rite of passage for boys as well as girls.

In social science as well as popular literature the Mexican male, especially if he is from the lower classes, is often portrayed as the archetype of "machismo," which however defined invariably conjures up the image of virulent sexism (see Gilmore, 1990; Mernissi, 1975/1987; Paz, 1950/1992; Ramos, 1934/1992; Stevens 1973). On the face of it, the classifications "Mexican men" or "Spanish-speaking men" are anachronisms. Such general categories negate important differences which exist within regions, classes, age cohorts, and ethnic groups in Mexico and throughout Latin America and Spain. Yet Brandes is still one of the few scholars to point to this variety: "Over the years, I acquired an image of Tzintzuntzan, and the Lake Patzcuaro region as a whole, as deviating from the usual social-science portrait of Mexican machismo" (1988:30).

As this paper will show, the diversity of male identities in the neighborhood of Col. Santo Domingo alone is enormous. Nonetheless, despite this diversity of male identities, at the same time certain important similarities exist among men who share particular sociocultural and historical experiences. Here, in order to examine

Mexican male identities and to determine whether and how they may be transforming, I will explore intergenerational differences in what *ser hombre,* to be a man, means today in a lower class area of Mexico's capital city.

The history of Col. Santo Domingo makes it a good place to examine what, if any, are some of the changes in gender relations occurring today in Mexican society, and specifically, how male gender attitudes and behavior may be experienced and perceived differently today by both women and men. Before 1971, Santo Domingo was a wasteland of volcanic rocks, caves, shrubs, snakes, and scorpions. With migration from the impoverished countryside and other parts of the capital exacerbating the housing shortage in the cities, in one 24-hour period in early September 1971, nearly 5000 families "parachuted" into the inhospitable yet uninhabited lava fields of Santo Domingo. It still stands as the largest single land invasion in Latin American history.

In the period since the invasion, as in many other urban and rural areas of Latin America, popular movements for social services (water, electricity, schools, sewage, and so on) have been a major

Matthew C. Gutmann, "The Meanings of Macho: Changing Mexican Male Identities," *Masculinities* 2 (1), 1994, pp. 21–33. Reprinted by permission.

political force in the area. In these popular struggles, the women of Col. Santo Domingo have generally been among the most active participants and sometimes the leaders, including in opposition to continued government attempts to stop or coopt the independent organization of the residents of Col. Santo Domingo.

Change "By Necessity"

To a great extent this activity on the part of women has reflected the fact that most men can find jobs only outside the *colonia,* and that in many families it has been at least implicitly understood that women more than men had the job of trying to resolve day-to-day deprivations in the neighborhood. In addition, while Col. Santo Domingo was struggling into existence during the 1970s and 1980s, another change was occurring in the broader Mexican society that greatly affected men's relations with women, and therefore men's own identities: women in unprecedented numbers began to work outside the home.

The most common explanation offered by men and women of varying ages in Col. Santo Domingo as to why so many men are now taking greater responsibility for various household duties that previously were the rather exclusive duties of women is *"por necesidad,"* by necessity, because they have to. What they usually mean is that in many families, especially since the economic crisis of 1982, it has become economically necessary for both husband and wife to have paid work, and that this has often required the husband to do some of the household tasks that previously may have been done by the wife alone. What few men state, but what many women discuss with a certain relish, is that *por necesidad* can refer also to men being forced by the women with

| Table 1 | Women's and Men's Participation in the Economically Active Population (As Percentage of Total Population Over 12-Years-Old) for Mexico City and Mexico in 1990 |

	Mexico City (%)	Mexico (%)
Women	30.66	19.58
Men	66.81	68.01
Total	47.63	43.04

Source: *Estados Unidos Mexicanos, Resumen General, XI Censo General de Población y Vivienda, 1990.* Cuadro 27, p. 316. Mexico City: Instituto Nacional de Estadística, Geografía e Informática.

| Table 2 | Women's and Men's Participation in the Economically Active Population, by Selected Age Groups (As Percentage of Total Population Over 12-Years-Old) for Mexico City and Mexico in 1990 |

	Women	Men	Total
Mexico City			
20–24 years	40.14	69.61	54.28
25–29 years	44.85	88.97	65.96
30–34 years	43.94	94.48	67.75
35–39 years	43.22	95.42	67.71
40–44 years	41.06	94.93	66.37
Mexico			
20–24 years	29.10	77.10	52.02
25–29 years	28.42	89.32	57.43
30–34 years	26.87	92.11	58.10
35–39 years	24.85	92.18	57.35
40–44 years	22.56	91.17	56.00

Source: *Estados Unidos Mexicanos, Resumen General, XI Censo General de Población y Vivienda, 1990.* Cuadro 27, p. 316. Mexico City: Instituto Nacional de Estadística, Geografía e Informática.

whom they live to take on some of these responsibilities. That is, in terms of changes in cultural attitudes regarding housework, quite regularly it is women who change first and then make—or at least try to make—their men change.

Women's participation in remunerated employment is significantly higher in Mexico City than in any other part of the country; thus one important result of migration from the rural *campo* to this sprawling metropolis of 20,000,000 inhabitants is a change in many women's occupational patterns (see Table 1).[2]

While in Mexico City in 1990, around 30% of women worked for money, this figure was slightly less than 20% for the country overall. Statistics by age groups reveal an even starker contrast between Mexico City and the country as a whole: over 40% of women between the ages of 40 and 44 in the Federal District were still "economically active" in 1990. Only 22 percent of women in Mexico in the same age category were registered as having remunerated employment (see Table 2).

While I sat one day on a stool in his kitchen admiring the masonry work in his brick walls, Marcos washed the morning dishes. I asked Marcos if he had always done this chore. He paused for a moment, thinking, and then turning around to face me, shrugged and said: "I began doing it regularly four years, two months ago." Skeptical by nature and more than mildly surprised by the precision of his response, I inquired how he could so clearly remember his initiation into this task. "Quite simple, really," he replied with a grin—he knew exactly what I was driving at with my questions about men doing housework—"that's when my *vieja* began working full time. Before that she was around the house a lot more."

Gilberto Echeverría, a sixty-eight-year-old grandfather, offered his own experience. "Things used to be much more simple. For 40 years, I earned the family money as an *albañil* [laborer in construction], and my wife, before she died, she was responsible for everything in the home. "Now," he mused in a meditative tone, "now it's a wonder you can tell who's who. My daughter is also making money and my son-in-law helps [*ayuda*] her all the time in the house." Doña Berta says that her husband, who is still working on the line in the same factory after 20 years, used to get ridiculed by his brother when their five children were young, because Don Antonio would hold the children, change their diapers, and in general help a lot in raising them. Her brother-in-law's attitude was fairly typical of his generation. Now, she reports with a certain satisfied look, the tables have turned a lot and "the father who doesn't do these things is more likely to be the one being ridiculed."

It is not uncommon for husbands and fathers in their 20s and 30s in Col. Santo Domingo to wash dishes, sweep, change diapers, and go shopping on a regular basis. They will tell you about it if you ask, as will some of their wives, mothers, and sisters, and you will see them in their homes, in front of their houses, and in the neighborhood markets. One friend boasted to me one day: "Why sometimes I'm the one buying my daughters their sanitary pads. And, I'll tell you, I've got no problem with this as some guys still do. Well, so long as they tell me what brand to buy. After all, I'm not going to stand there like an asshole just gaping at all the feminine hygiene products!" It is certainly more common now than at any time in the past for men in Col. Santo Domingo to participate in most chores involved in running the household.

One exception to this is cooking, which among older and younger men—and not a few women—in various classes in Mexico City is still commonly seen as the consummately female task. Therefore rare is the man who prepares his or others' meals on a regular basis. Many men do cook when their wives or other women are not around, though this generally takes the form of reheating food which the women have left for them. And a lot of men like to cook for fiestas and on festive occasions, often having a special, signature meat dish (like calf brain tacos or a spicy goat stew). When asked about their not cooking more, some men explain that their wives will not let them enter the kitchen area much less cook. Some of these same wives clarified for me that the real issue was that their husbands are far better at giving excuses than working.

The partial and relatively recent changes within the division of labor in some households in the colonia are a reflection not simply of economic transformations, for example, women working outside the home, but also relate to cultural changes in what it means to be a man today in at least some working class neighborhoods of Mexico City. It is a further indication of the actual duties performed and of the cultural values still placed on these household tasks, by women as well as by men, that the expression used by nearly all to describe men's activities in the home is *ayudar a la esposa*, helping the wife. Men generally do not equally share in these responsibilities, in word or deed, and the cultural division of labor between women is still regarded as important and therefore enforced by many. The female *doble jornada*, second shift (literally double day), is an ongoing and significant feature of life for many households in Santo Domingo. In addition, and related to their often privileged position in Mexican society, men in particular sometimes admit to trying to take advantage of the situation, by attributing greater natural energy to women and greater natural *flojera* (laziness) to men.

Fathers and Sons

Even more than housework, cooking, and shopping, parenting is considered by some scholars as a habitually and often exclusively feminine domain, and the extent of shared parenting between women and men is deemed a key test of the degree of gender equality in societies (see, for example, Chodorow, 1978; Ruddick, 1989). At the same time, Margaret Mead once defined the distinctively human aspect as lying "in the nurturing behavior of the male, who among human beings everywhere helps provide food for women and children" (1949/1975, p. 188). If not nearly measuring up to Mead's idyllic classification, in various *colonias populares* in Mexico City, as in other parts of Mexico today and historically, there exists a tremendous variety in patterns of parenting, specifically with reference to the roles played by men in raising children, which may challenge findings based more exclusively on certain U.S. middle class settings.

True enough, in Col. Santo Domingo it is certainly the case that women usually spend more time with the children than men do, and in the minds of a lot of women and men there, children, especially young children, belong with their mother or other women. And it is still the case that a majority of women in *clases populares* list as their work *hogar* and *ama de casa*, housework and housewife; clearly they are still in most households the adults most responsible for parenting day in and day out. Yet historically, in certain rural regions of Mexico, for instance, men have often played a special role in raising boys, particularly after they have reached an age when they are finally deemed mature enough to help with, or at least not get in the way of, their fathers' work in the fields (see Lewis, 1951; Romney & Romney 1963).

In the cities today, some men speak with great pleasure about having jobs that allow them to spend time with their children while they are working, like those furniture repairmen or cobblers who have little workshops in their houses, or others like car mechanics who work in the street in front of their homes. In addition, while family sizes are growing smaller, in households with older children it is common to find older girls, and increasingly older brothers and male cousins, caring for younger siblings, for example after school when parents and other adults may still be working.

Some men in their seventies today who took part in the invasion of Santo Domingo 20 years ago, after their children were already grown, talk about having had a lot of responsibility for raising their boys in particular. In formal interviews conducted with men and women in Col. Santo Domingo, a common theme among older men is that their parenting role with their boys included two particular dimensions. One, frequently these men relate that they usually took the boys with them when they went out on errands or to visit friends during their "free time," especially on weekends. Two, they were responsible more than the boys' mothers for teaching the boys technical skills (a trade) that would be necessary in fulfilling their later, adult masculine responsibilities as economic providers. Significantly, older women and men both report having shared in providing moral instruction and discipline for the boys. At least with the older generation, girls were more exclusively raised by women.

Alejandra Sánchez, a mother of two teenage girls, is convinced that the main reason her husband has never taken much responsibility for the children is because they have no sons. She laments that had there been two boys instead, he would have had "to buck up," and life for her would have been very different. Her situation is felt by neighbors to be rather typical of old-fashioned relations between mothers and fathers, and in this sense more exceptional in a community that has undergone innumerable changes in cultural relations, including those between men and women. Whether she is right is impossible to say, but her perception that with boys her irresponsible husband would have been at least culturally pressured if not obligated to take on certain accepted male parenting duties is sure.

A division of labor, fathers—sons and mothers—daughters, still pertains in some younger families in Col. Santo Domingo, but many men with small children today like to claim as a point of pride that they treat their boys and girls the same. If they spend more time with the boys outside the home, they sometimes explain, it is because it simply works out that way, it is more convenient for both the father and mother, or it is because the boys want to spend time with them more than the girls do. To this must be added the fact that mothers—more than fathers—are often reticent to have their girls go out with the men. Despite the fact that men carry and walk their daughters, it remains the case that from very early on boys are shepherded off with their fathers by their mothers in a way that girls seldom are.

Changing economic conditions in Mexico, especially since 1982, have impelled further changes among broad sectors of the male population. Some older men in Col. Santo Domingo are being laid off from jobs they have held for decades, and thus find themselves unemployed (and semiemployable at best) at the age of 60. They frequently report having more daily contact with their grandchildren than they ever had with their own children, a situation only some find agreeable. Among intellectuals in the middle classes, tougher economic times have sometimes necessitated doing without the live-in maid/nanny who was ubiquitous only a short time ago. Therefore men in these strata find themselves caring for their children far more than ever in the past, and the expression "*Estoy de Kramer*," "I'm Kramering," has come into vogue, meaning "I've got the kids," recalling the U.S. movie "Kramer vs. Kramer," and pointing to certain U.S. cultural influences regarding modern family values and practices.

All in all, it is difficult in the case of Col. Santo Domingo to argue that in terms of attitudes and behavior parenting is identified exclusively with women. To some extent historically and without question today, for a variety of reasons, active, consistent, and long-term parenting is a central ingredient there for numerous, though obviously not all, men and women in what it means to be a man.

Machos Are Not What They Used to Be

It is common to hear women and men in Col. Santo Domingo say that while there used to be a lot of macho men, they are not as prevalent today. Some people who make this comment are too young to know anything first hand about the old days, but regardless, they are sure there was more machismo before. If some oldtimers like to divide the world of men into machos and *mandilones* (meaning female-dominated men), it is far more common for younger men in Col. Santo Domingo to define themselves as belonging to a third category, the "nonmacho" group, *"ni macho, ni mandilón,"* "neither macho nor mandilón,"[3] Though others may define a friend or relative as "your typical Mexican macho," the same man will not infrequently reject the label for himself, describing all the things he does to help his wife around the home, pointing out that he does not beat his wife (one of the few generally agreed on attributes of machos), and so on. What is most significant is not simply how the terms macho and machismo are variously defined— there is little consensus on their meanings—but more, that today the terms are so routinely regarded by men in the working class in Col. Santo Domingo, Mexico City as pejorative and not worthy of emulation.[4] Further, while many men in Col. Santo Domingo have (re)considered the relative merits of being macho, fewer have changed the way they refer to a group of men that, for them, is beyond the pale, that is, the *maricones,* queers, homosexuals, who thus constitute an especially marginalized fourth category of Mexican masculinities.

Table 3 Birthrates in Mexico from 1900 to 1988

Year	Average Number of Children Per Woman Over 12-Years-Old (at Any Given Time)
1900	5.0
1940	4.6
1960	4.5
1970	4.5
1977	3.8
1981	3.4
1983	3.1
1985	2.8
1988	2.5

Source: Adapted from Zavala de Cosfo, 1992:26,222,282.

Sociocultural changes directly involving women have propelled new ways of thinking and acting among men with regard to machismo. Such changes among women have required reevaluations and changes among men, for if womanhood no longer is so closely tied to motherhood, manhood too must be at least partially recast. As a single (and still childless!) young man of 27 explained, "For me, having a lot of kids to prove you're really macho is a bunch of bullshit. That stuff went out four decades ago." Not all would agree with his periodization, but the sentiment is more widespread than the conventional wisdom—that Mexican males need confirmation of their virility through procreation—would allow.

In 1970, the average number of children per woman (out of the female population over 12-years-old) in Mexico as a whole was 4.5 and for Mexico City 2.6. In 1990, the figure for Mexico City was 2.0, while for the country two years earlier it had dropped to 2.5 (see Table 3).[5] The drop in birthrates in the last 20 years in Mexico as a whole, and its urban centers in particular, has been dramatic. This decline has not necessarily led to direct changes in parenting atti-tudes and behavior on the part of men, but it certainly reflects changes in cultural practices by women regarding an area long closely identified with their gender identities.

Another sign of changes in gender identities in Col. Santo Domingo, especially in the last decade, has to do with women's alcohol consumption and adultery. While no precise figures are available, male and female residents of the neighborhood uniformly agree that women are drinking alcohol and *"saliendo,"* "going out" (in the sense of cheating on their spouses), in far higher numbers than ever before. There is disagreement as to whether men are drinking and cheating more. People are also divided, and of significance not neatly along gender lines, as to whether these developments among women are good or bad in the long run. Regardless of different individuals' opinions about how women today are "altering the rules," the changes have contributed, among other things, to the initiation of numerous discussions within families and among friends about the meaning of terms like equality when applied to gender relations.

Women Are "Natural Leaders" in Col. Santo Domingo

Aurora Muñoz of the San Bernabé Nursery School says that women "tend to be natural leaders in Santo Domingo because of the needs of the *colonia*." From the beginning of the neighborhood in 1971, women led in the fights to acquire water for all residents. Then for electricity and schools. Only recently, in 1992, were streets being torn up to lay sewage pipes for the over 150,000 residents of Col. Santo Domingo.

Older women and men seem to have an easier time responding to questions about what difference it might make to grow up in an area in which women are community organizers and leaders, as opposed to one in which even if women work outside the home they certainly do not play an integral role in the political campaigns and protests of the neighborhood. For those who have grown up in Col. Santo Domingo, or in other areas of Mexico City where "popular urban movements" have taken place in the past 15 years, it is far more difficult to even imagine a situation in which women are not community activists.

Few questions are received by younger adults in the *colonia* as being so absurd (to the point of provoking chuckles) as those which inquire about the *mujer sumisa* or *mujer abnegada,* the submissive or self-sacrificing woman. It is not that people do not recognize her to exist; everyone can point to a neighbor or aunt whom they will characterize in this way. And it is true that the disdainful laugh of some men at the question about submissive women barely conceals a defensiveness regarding their own behavior toward women. Yet even when people identify *la mujer sumisa* as a relic from the provinces, that is, a migrant from another part of the country, people commonly point out to the inquiring ethnographer that this really is not an accurate description of women in many of the villages of Mexico either.

"Sure," Manuel Ramos points out to me, "these women exist and have always existed, but with all the moving around people have done in the last 30 years do you think this has left everything the way it was once between women and men? Impossible."[6]

Further, as Fidel Aguirre, a technician working in a laboratory outside the *colonia* took pains to explain, "with women working outside the home it's not just a question of them having their own money now, as important as this has been. What's also involved is that women have met all sorts of different people which has changed them forever. And this has meant that the men have changed, for if they don't, more and more they're getting left behind by women. Let me tell you, this is what's happening."

In addition to these changes in the sociocultural landscape several others have of course greatly contributed to the questioning and challenging of gender relations among people in Col. Santo Domingo. Chief among these must be listed the fact that through at least the early years of college, the numbers of females and males are today roughly equivalent, and thus expectations of women themselves (and frequently, of parents for their daughters, husbands for their wives, and so on) are quite different from what they were with earlier generations. Television, and within this the cultural reach of the U.S., has had a profound impact. Some government family centers and some churches have developed forums in which such information has been disseminated as well. A grandfather of eight grinned when he said that while he had never changed the diapers on his own children he had since learned how to do it for the next generation. Where did he learn this? From a program in his church.

Finally, the women's movement and the struggles for homosexual rights have had important, if more indirect influences in Col. Santo Domingo on the self-conceptions that women of all ages, and to a lesser extent men of especially the younger generations, have concerning being women and men. This influence is realized in a number of ways, from women's health care workers who have been active in the community for over 10 years, to feminist magazines which at times have reached a mass circulation in some of the *colonias populares.*

Changing Men

In Mexico in the last 20 years, precisely the period in which Col. Santo Domingo has come into being, the entire society has witnessed rapid and widespread upheavals involving the economy, gender roles, struggles over ethnic identity, regional development and stagnation, ecological catastrophes, international migration, political insurgency and repression. For most of this century there was a sense among even the poor that times would get better. Now, for many, the mood is more akin to the postmodernist malaise that has struck indeterminate others around the globe.[7]

Each of these sociocultural factors has its own particular timetable and trajectory, and it is far from clear, in the case of gender relations for example, where things are truly heading. But while we must therefore be particularly cautious in our attempt to analyze changes in these phenomena, we must also guard against a perhaps even more debilitating contemporary notion that nothing ever does change, especially when it comes to life between women and men.

The changes in attitudes and behavior on the part of men and women in Col. Santo Domingo are deeply felt, and evidently part of a developing process of transforming gender relations throughout Mexico. They are not, however uniformly experienced or acknowledged. The ethnographic research reported in this paper has been conducted primarily in a lower class urban milieu, and secondarily among middle class merchants and professionals in Mexico City.

Lomnitz and Pérez-Lizaur (1987) conducted an ethnographic study of an elite Mexican family for 7 years. As the focus of their investigation concerned kinship networks their findings are quite pertinent here. They write that among the elites studied, the father's "participation in raising children is indirect; he may occasionally play with his small children or, when they grow up, gradually introduce his son to certain aspects of a man's world. Child rearing is the direct and formal responsibility of the mother" (p. 210).

For at least many fathers in Col. Santo Domingo, this is hardly the situation. Simply to note the greater responsibilities that women in both elite and popular classes have in parenting misses the enormous differences in the content of fathering in each context. Fathers in Col. Santo Domingo to a far greater extent appear to be integral in all stages of their children's lives, though to be sure in practice they are present more in the evenings and on weekends, commonly more with their boys than with their girls, and more with children over 3- or 4-year-olds. But beyond a merely quantitative, time-allocation difference in fathers' attention to their children, men in at least certain *colonias populares* define their own and others' masculinity in part in terms of their active role in parenting.[8]

Of course, as important as fathering may be to numerous men in Col. Santo Domingo, it is not all there is to being a man. In a conversation with an older couple on what had changed between women and men in their lifetimes, the woman (whom neighbors like to describe as a classic *mujer abnegada*) offered, "Why, the liberation of the woman!" She did not care to expand on this opinion except to add that it had been women who had changed the most since her youth, implying that the men were lagging behind. Her husband, a straight-talking character, dismissed his wife's comment with a wave of his hand and countered that what was different was that: "Today there're a lot of queers who've stopped being men." Clearly the directions in which changes have occurred are not uniform, either between women and men or between generations.

As a sign of continuing subordination of women to men, and despite the greater financial liberty brought to women by earning their own salaries, far more women are still economically dependent on men than men on women in Col. Santo Domingo. Talking with women who have endured years of battering from their husbands with no end yet in sight, this point is made repeatedly.

Birthrates have dropped, and contraceptives are used more than ever before, yet it is still most common to find women being held mainly responsible for birth control: a woman from Col. Santo Domingo went to get condoms at a state health service and was told by a male government doctor that prophylactics were only for promiscuous women, and that since they are not comfortable for men anyway, she should give her husband a break and use an I.U.D.

And while the boys in the San Bernabé Nursery School today play "girl's games" and, with the girls,

help to clean up more than they used to, most of the girls, when they remember, are still careful to not get their clothes dirty, and most of the boys are still embarrassed when they cry, because their mothers and fathers are still teaching them that girls don't play like that and boys don't cry.

The developments and transformations in Col. Santo Domingo do not indicate full equality, cooperation, and mutual respect suddenly blossoming in gender relations there. Nonetheless, as part of the broader society and because of certain specific conditions pertaining in this largely self-built community, the "Mexican macho" stereotypes so common in the social sciences are today inappropriate and misleading in understanding large sections of men in this area, how they see themselves and how the women with whom they share their lives see them, their history, and their future.

Notes

1. I am not proposing that getting boys to play with dolls in any manner resolves the issue of male dominance, as may be inferred from some socialization theories in psychology. Rather, boys playing with dolls is used here as an indication of changing sociocultural attitudes and practices.

2. See also earlier figures and discussion in García, Muñoz, and de Oliveira, 1982, pp. 34ff. Both tables 1 and 2 are based on 1990 census data which unquestionably underestimate many forms of paid employment, semi-employment, illegal employment, "informal" employment, etc. Nonetheless, for purposes of comparison (e.g., Were more women employed in Mexico City or in the *campo*?), we may reasonably draw limited conclusions from these figures.

3. *Mandilón* comes from *mandil* (apron) and translates literally as "apron-er."

4. See de Barbieri's (1990) provocative paper on "possible erosions in Mexican machismo."

5. The 1970 figure for Mexico City comes from the *IX Censo General de Población*. Cuadro 30, p. 513 (Secretaria de Industria y Comercio, Dirección General de Estadística). For 1990, the figure is from the *XI Censo General*, Cuadro 24, p. 273 (Instituto Nacional de Estadística, Geografía e Informática). Since women who will go on to have other children are averaged into these totals, these figures do not represent the fertility rates for these areas.

6. Though a friend still describes the division of labor between men and women in his Zapotec village in the sierra Oaxaca as *"mucho, mucho más tajante"* ("much, much sharper").

7. See Bartra (1987).

8. See also Arizpe (1989) on the relation between class, gender, and household roles.

References

Arizpe, L. (1989). *Culturay desarrollo: Una etnografía de las creencias de una comunidad mexicana.* Mexico City: Porrua/Universidad Nacional Autónoma de México.

Bartra, R. (1987). *La jaula de la melancolia: Identidad y metamorfosis del mexicano.* Mexico City: Grijalbo. (In English: *The Cage of Melancholy: Identity and Metamorphosis of the Mexican.* Christopher J. Hall, trans. New Brunswick: Rutgers University Press, 1992.)

Brandes, S. (1988). *Power and persuasion: Fiestas and social control in rural Mexico.* Philadelphia: University of Pennsylvania Press.

Chodorow, N. (1978). *The reproduction of mothering: Psychoanalysis and the sociology of gender.* Berkeley: University of California Press.

de Barbieri, T. (1990). Sobre géneros, prácticas y valores: notas acerca de posibles erosiones del machismo en México. In J. M. Ramírez Sáiz (Ed.), *Normas y prácticas: morales y cívicas en la vida cotidiana* (pp. 83–106). Mexico City: Universidad Nacional Autónoma de México.

García, B., Muñoz, H., and de Oliveira, O. (1982). *Hogares y trabajadores en la Ciudad de México.* Mexico City: El Colegio de México/Universidad Nacional Autónoma de México.

Gilmore, D. (1990). *Manhood in the making: Cultural concepts of masculinity.* New Haven: Yale University Press.

Lewis, O. (1951/1963) *Life in a Mexican village: Tepoztlán restudied.* Urbana: University of Illinois Press.

Lomnitz, L., and Pérez-Lizaur, M. (1987). *A Mexican elite family: 1820–1980.* Princeton: Princeton University Press.

Mead, M. (1949/1975). *Male and female: A study of the sexes in a changing world.* New York: Wm. Morrow.

Mernissi, F. (1975/1987). *Beyond the veil: Male-female dynamics in modern Muslim society.* Bloomington: University of Indiana Press.

Paz, O. (1950). *El laberinto de la soledad.* Mexico City: Fondo de Cultura Económica. (In English: *The Labyrinth of Solitude: Life and Thought in Mexico.* Lysander Kemp, trans. New York: Grove, 1961.)

Ramos, S. (1934). *El perfil del hombre y la cultural en México.* Mexico City: Espasa-Calpe Mexicana. (In English: *Profile of man and culture in Mexico.* Peter G. Earle, trans. Austin: University of Texas Press, 1962.)

Romney, K., and Romney, R. (1963). The Mixtecans of Juxtlahuaca, Mexico. In B. Whiting (Ed.), *Six cultures: Studies in child rearing* (pp. 541–691). New York: John Wiley.

Ruddick, S. (1989). *Maternal thinking: Toward a politics of peace.* Boston: Beacon.

Stevens, E. (1973). *Marianismo:* The Other Face of *Machismo* in Latin America. In A. Pescatello (Ed.), *Male and Female in Latin America* (pp. 90–101). Pittsburgh: University of Pittsburgh Press.

Zavala de Cosío, M. E. (1992). *Cambios de fecundidad en México y políticas de poblacíon.* Mexico City: El Colegio de México.

Article Review Form at end of book.

What are the implications of the "eroticization of difference"?

Confessions of a Chicana Ph.D.

Carla Trujillo

The question began the first day of class. Fourth grade. Five Black girls cornered me in a hallway and demanded to know "what" I was. I didn't know "what" I was. I never had to think about it before, but immediately realized that whatever I was mattered. Remembering that my family ate a lot of beans and tortillas (we were poor) and that my parents spoke fluent Spanish, I blurted out, "Mexican . . . or something like that." "Well," they replied, "you better find out quick." I did. At home that evening, at my instigation, my father lectured me on the historical roots of the family. We were Mexican Americans, a people mixed with Spanish and Indian. "We are poor," he said, "but we work hard and we are proud. Always be proud of who you are, *mijíta*. Never let anyone think they're better than you because you're Mexican." To my ten-year-old mind it made me secure to have my identity confirmed.

My parents never denied their ethnicity or allowed us to forget our past. While Mexican *corridos* rang through the house, cooking, politics, and religion were discussed. This free exchange made

learning profound and rapid. Consequently I soon figured out the family's (at least my mother's) view of interracial relationships. Women in the family often commented on male cousins who had married white women. Disapproval ran rampant, focusing on "those gringas" not being up to par particularly in the domestic arena as dutiful wives, good house-keepers, or even makers of tortillas. And although I participated in the anger my mother and aunts directed towards these white women, they actually seemed to be more upset with the men (but they never said as much). It was as if they implicitly understood that these men valued white women for reasons beyond domestic abilities and duties. If the marriage ended in divorce, which often happened, there was always a defiant, "I told you so!"

This early inculcation stayed with me as I grew up. Before I "came out," whenever I dated white or Chicano men, I always considered the implications of doing so, and so did my parents. Parental approval or disapproval depended on my date's class as well as his skin color. The number of acceptable men was narrowly defined and strictly enforced,

encompassing only Mexican Americans or lighter skin and "class" (later I discovered this to be a relative term), or white men of any class. Eventually, however, my father would have accepted anyone from the male species.

I've been out as a lesbian for thirteen years and the issues around interracial relationships haven't become any less complicated. If anything, they've gotten more tangled. Contradictions abound, particularly in the lesbian community, which supposedly espouses beliefs in racial validation, recognition, and self-education for those who haven't yet "dealt with" their racism. Contrary to Jackie Goldsby's observation that gay men eroticize differences while lesbians generally politicize them (OUT/LOOK #9), I contend that lesbians not only politicize our differences, but eroticize them as well. We just don't talk about it.

Early on I also learned from my father that our society is an unjust one. At work he had been bypassed for a training stewardship as a welder for a white man with less seniority. Immediately he had the San Francisco office of the U.S. Commission on Civil Rights sending in an investigative committee from D.C. He also hired a labor

Carla Trujillo, "Confessions of a Chicana Ph.D.," *Out/Look* 4 (3) (Winter), 1992, pp. 23–27.

lawyer to file suit against the employer. The company backed down and reinstated my father. Of course we couldn't afford the lawyer, but at age thirteen I was beginning to understand that sacrifices were sometimes necessary and that fighting for your rights is always a just cause. This was a lesson for me in entitlement to rights as a human being regardless of race or class.

Later, in college, I was active in various feminist groups and worked on issues concerning Chicanos and women of color. At the time I was one of the very few lesbians of color, much less Chicana lesbians. My lack of access to other Chicana lesbians in this isolating world limited me to white or Jewish women as lovers. And while this was acceptable considering my options, I couldn't shake the views and opinions of mixed-race relationships learned as a child. Something was amiss. I mistrusted my white lovers' motivations and attractions to me. I mistrusted myself. Was lack of access to a diversity of women the only issue involved? If not, what else was at work here? Many Chicanos never graduate from high school, and fewer still go on to college. Despite my background I was able to go to college and I had to make very quick adjustments in order to survive that middle-class world. And while I never considered myself "better" than anyone who hadn't gone to college, grudgingly I had to admit higher education had changed me. While my identity remained firmly rooted in a world without advantage, I now had access to it. My acquisition of privilege, however, gave way to what felt like a fracturedness in my ethnic identity, upbringing, and general trust of the world—especially the lesbian world. The more I thought about my place of privilege, the more I thought about others without it. The more I thought about who I was attracted to, the

more I questioned my underlying motivations.

Because of the egalitarian lessons learned from my father, I had to believe that any woman, regardless of class, race, or education, could be a potential lover. Politically it was wrong to feel any other way. But could I believe it in my heart? I continued on to graduate school in the Midwest, where I had a brief relationship with a poor white woman. No one in her family had gone to college. She was in the Army reserves when I met her, and there was hesitancy between us even though our attraction was readily apparent. We continually misunderstood each other, making assumptions about the other's exposure to and experience in the world. She admitted feeling inadequate around me, never comfortable with what she thought were my expectations. In a supermarket I once asked her to pick out an avocado. When I realized she didn't know what an avocado was I was shocked. I simply assumed that everybody knew what they were. Confused about her lack of exposure to what I thought were everyday (read: white) things, I was naïve enough to think "white" could compensate for anything, even lack of money. Our efforts at communication were futile and ironic. I was a Chicana working on a Ph.D.; she was white and in the military reserves.

All of my father's speeches, rhetoric from the lesbian community, and Marxian and post-feminist analysis did nothing to provide the "how-do's" in linking theory with actual practice. My comfortable, though ignorant, self-concept had been shattered. I was stunned, realizing that class differences, not racial differences, were at the core of the problem. In my isolation there was no one who understood my confusion. Those I told were often silent, disapproval in their eyes, disappointment in the little

that they did say because I questioned doctrinaire, politically "correct" positions on love and life. Had college done this to me? Using my academic situation as therapy, I began to research Chicano performance in higher education. I armed myself with the efforts of others to better understand myself. This was difficult, for I found practically nothing in the academic literature on working-class Chicanas pursuing doctorates.

Eventually I began to pursue feelings for other Chicana lesbians. Was there some other reason why I hadn't been partners with other Chicanas? Thinking I had been tolerant of difference and experience, I had to acknowledge that this was not always so. I wanted a Chicana lover, but I was also afraid. In college I never took the time to question why I was never, conveniently, "compatible" with Chicanas that I did encounter. Now I was asking myself if I had dealt with my own self-hatred enough to love another Chicana completely. I wasn't sure I had. I had to admit, however, that my attraction was colored. I was looking for a certain Chicana, one who understood me and accepted my future lifestyle. Having fought so hard to get this far, and meeting so many middle- and upper-class white people who didn't understand me, I was desperate for someone who could take me into her heart and accept where I was going. At one time I thought she could be any Chicana I was attracted to, but now I realize it wasn't such an easy goal: class had intersected with race and my options had been narrowed even more.

Over time, I dated several Latinas and remained in a relationship with a Chicana for several years. She fulfilled me, and for once I felt I had finally come home. Her strong identification as a *Mexicana* meant that there was no need for me to explain, translate, or pray for understanding. Many things went unsaid because they were understood: language, the love of food, our customs, the importance of family, music, the color of her skin, her eyes, her hair. Coming home. Needless to say, she also had a college education. And even though the relationship eventually ended, I was touched deeply, a desire lingering for others like her long after the breakup. This hasn't changed.

The rhetoric of Chicano nationalism tells me that those of us who have white lovers dislike something about the Mexican in themselves. True nationalism exalts the efforts to uplift the race at all costs. You become politically "suspect" if your intimate partner is not of the same race. Why we tend to equate one's political philosophies with sleeping partners I'm not sure. Perhaps it's an overall suspicion of anything white, dominant, or privileged. Guilt by association always prevails. Though I see Latina lesbians together, I see much more variation. I notice that many lovers of very political lesbians of color are white. I see ethnic studies faculty with white lovers. I know that many famous Latino artists, writers, and musicians are with white women. So what gives? How is it one's political philosophies can differ so much from personal attraction?

I ask a good friend of mine, who identifies herself as a Chicana nationalist, a theoretical question: If she met two women, one white and the other Chicana, both with equal characteristics, which would she choose? "The white one," she says without hesitation. "I do this work all day and at night I don't want to come home and continue to process. It takes a lot more work to be with another Chicana. I can't process all the time. I need a break, something different to come home to." When I push her on how others might perceive this relationship, she replies sharply, "I don't let people judge me in my personal

life." This is not to say her white lover of six years is naïvely out of touch with my friend's activism and beliefs.

Another strongly identified Chicana friend indicated she could be with no one else except another Latina. "After all," she said, "I wouldn't be able to be myself. I'd always have to be on my guard. Watch what I say. I've been with white women before, but it's a lot more work. I don't think we should be in "mixed-up" relationships. That's what we called them in the seventies; that's what they are."

Recently I was drawn to a white woman who expressed her attraction for me but confessed she had a "problem" with Mexicans. "I don't know where these views come from," she acknowledged, "the media, whatever . . . I feel uncomfortable telling you, of all people, that I have these problems." I admire her vulnerability, yet I raged at the words and challenged her, "What, then, do you call me?" "Well, you're different." She continued, "Besides, you should be glad that I admitted my racism to you." Rather than sustain my anger, I am, finally, disappointed. My accessibility to others who choose to eliminate me on the basis of group membership is something I encounter every day. This is just one more pitfall in the paradox of being Chicana with some of the privileges and trappings of dominant white society. The thought of fighting this woman's racism and the possibility of a resurgence of my own self-hatred are too much to bear. I can't possibly think of working so hard to love someone.

As a Chicana I have to deal simultaneously with dual identities. Michael Omi and Howard Winant's theorizing on race relations in America locates these racial identities at the "micro" level, your personal identity based upon daily interaction with others; and the "macro" level, where

dominant society impinges its categorization upon you. Since people of color are so dually affected, we must be dually conscious of how these identities are played out in a racist society. Gloria Anzaldúa says that we are all either racist, have internalized racism, and/or possess cross-racial hostility. Two people of different races who fall in love are not absolved from any of these conditions. If I'm attracted to a white woman, does her whiteness have something to do with it? How much advantage do I gain access to if I'm with a white woman? If a white woman is attracted to me, how do skin color, culture, and my luscious Latina lips play a role in her attraction? Is guilt waiting in ambush somewhere in the bedroom?

Finally, about this thing called attraction. I would like to believe that a woman's race has nothing to do with my attraction to her, but that would be a lie. Sure, it's hard to shake early patterns, but I've worked very hard to accept and love all aspects of myself as a Chicana. On the other hand, I have Chicano/a friends who are only attracted to blonde, blue-eyed people. They may own up to self-hatred, shrug and say, "Yeah, I know it's bad, but hey, it's what makes me wet." We've heard it all before, but there's something wrong with a society that teaches us to value only certain "standardized" aspects of beauty. I can't lie and tell you that I'm not attracted to white women. It's just more difficult to consider a white woman a serious contender for my heart. To dismiss a white woman as a potential partner simply because of race is as dehumanizing as those white women who have nothing to do with me because I'm Mexican. For me to love a white woman means I must know that she's taken a step past herself. She must learn where her prejudices and stereotypes originate and then find out who Latinas really are.

I realize that I'm more accessible to white middle-class women. I've learned a white science, language, procedure. I have learned, out of necessity, to arm myself by acquiring "their" language and fighting my battles more effectively using "their" tools. Though I have run the risk of becoming fractured, fearing the potential loss of self, I realize I haven't lost myself at all. Education and upward mobility have indeed affected my lifestyle. I can never, however, deny or negate the part of myself most integral to my identity, that is, being Chicana and having been poor. My life is one of paradox, and whether my sense of isolation is self-imposed or not, I know that my options leave nothing more than honesty to get me through each day. I expect this from my partner. To do or believe otherwise and compromise this honesty is something I simply couldn't live with.

 Article Review Form at end of book.

What might explain white people's romanticization of Native American spirituality? Why is the author suspicious of this trend?

Desperately Seeking Redemption:

Rise of Native American Neo-shamanic Books and Workshops

Diane Bell

Writing for the Lakota Times *in 1991, Avis Little Eagle summed up the growing anger of many indigenous peoples concerning the practices of self-styled New Age shamans. Throughout the 1980s, the American Indian Movement had protested, picketed, and passed resolutions condemning those individuals and institutions that packaged Indian sweat lodges, vision quests, shamanic healing, and sun dances for the spiritually hungry. Two years later, at the Parliament of the World's Religions in Chicago, the Dakota, Lakota, and Nakota Nations issued a Declaration of War Against Exploiters of Lakota Spirituality.*

This theme has been developed by a number of Native American writers and activists. Ward Churchill, in *Fantasies of the Master Race* (1992), calls the exploiters "plastic medicine men" and cites them as evidence of the continuing genocidal colonization of Native Americans. Poet-anthropologist Wendy Rose writes of "white shamanism" as a form of cultural imperialism, and feminist Andrea Smith, in her article "For All Those Who Were Indian in a Former Life," calls these "wannabes" to account. Echoing the defiant stand taken in the nineteenth century by the Lakota and Cheyenne over the Black Hills, these activists insist that their "spirituality is not for sale."

Lynn V. Andrews, the Los Angeles-based author of the highly successful Medicine Woman trilogy says, "I write of my own experience. I am not an anthropologist." The books, workshops, and promotional tours of this self-proclaimed shaman, however, have been cited as a prime example of the appropriation and commercialization of indigenous peoples' spirituality. According to Andrews, the teachings of her Canadian spiritual guide, a "Native American medicine woman" named Agnes Whistling Elk, include Lakota, Cree, and Hopi terms and concepts. Such eclecticism deeply troubles many Native Americans, who see the mixing and matching of different traditions from different tribes as an assault on the integrity of the extremely personal and specific ties of kin and country that underpin their beliefs and practices. In addition, Andrews writes of being introduced into the Sisterhood of the Shields, a secret organization of forty-four women from different Native American tribes. Andrews's loyal readers, however, are not deterred. Over and over, as I research the appeal of these texts, I hear, "I don't care if it's not true; it speaks to me."

In *Mutant Message Down Under*, Marlo Morgan—a self-described alternative health care provider from Kansas City—describes her 2,000-mile trek across the burning deserts of Australia with a hitherto unknown tribe of Aborigines she calls the Real People. She claims she must keep the location of their "opal cave" secret for fear that the government might imprison them or blow up their sacred site. Australian Aborigines have protested that her book is, at best, nonsense and, at worst, a violation of their law. Harper-Collins lists her book as fiction, but Morgan continues to lecture on the Real People as though they were real. Although exposes have appeared in the American and Australian media, this best-seller has reached millions of readers, many of whom report, "It changed my life."

In both Morgan's book and Andrews's *Crystal Woman*, Aboriginal life is simple. Neither author (unlike ethnographers whose careful work rarely reaches a general audience) finds the need to grapple with the intricacies of kinship and land-based relations among Aboriginal groups. Both authors avoid the complexities of local languages, and the books' spiritual folks frequently communicate by telepathy or by giggling and winking their way through the stories. Andrews's meeting with the Sisterhood of the Shields takes place in a native "village" near a brook in the middle of the arid Australian desert. At this unlikely site, she meets with her Native American Sisters, as well as with female Aborigines. In reality, no group of people could travel for a thousand miles through Australia without having to negotiate access through the territories of many other groups. (But how convenient for government authorities if this were true! Relocation policies would be perfectly acceptable because one piece of land would be as good as the next to the Aborigines.)

Enraged that a gullible public was consuming these misrepresentations—and that yet again exotic stereotypes of Aborigines were obscuring the gritty realities of the lives of many of these peoples—Robert Eggington, coordinator of the Dumbartung Aboriginal Corporation (Western Australia), led a group of Aboriginal elders to Los Angeles in January 1996 to protest Morgan's book and a planned film. Morgan responded to the protest in a radio interview reported in the *Weekend Australian.* "I'm terribly sorry," she said, "and my sincere apologies to any Australian Aboriginal person if I have offended them in any way . . . please read this book . . . with an open mind and see if there is anything, anything at all that is derogatory."

Morgan's and Andrews's readers often tell me that these books offer a vision of a world in which all life forms coexist in physical and spiritual harmony; where one person's journey can undo centuries of abuse; where women are wise; where, despite differences in language, history, geography, economic status, and personal skills, we are all one. Here is community, meaning, belonging—all the, connectedness for which the self-absorbed, postindustrial, fragmented individual yearns. I certainly agree that we should be open to wisdom from a range of sources, but must we suspend all critical faculties in the process? It matters that the beliefs and practices of Native Americans and Australian Aborigines have been put through a cultural blender. It matters that the stories of those engaged in ongoing struggles for their very lives are marginalized, and that these representations of indigenous peoples are romantic and ahistorical. Morgan and Andrews shroud their "native teachers" in mystery while telling us that they hold the keys to true and authentic ways of knowing.

Marketers of neo-shamanic books and workshops claim that indigenous wisdom is part of our common human heritage. By sharing such knowledge, the argument goes, together we can save the planet. But is this sharing or a further appropriation? There is a bitter irony in turning to indigenous peoples to solve problems of affluent urbanites. In the midst of the wealth of first-world nations, most native peoples endure appalling health problems, underemployment, and grinding poverty. A philosophy of reverence for the earth rings hollow in the reality of toxic waste dumps and nuclear testing on native lands. As Ines Talamantez, of the University of California, Santa Barbara, says: "If the impulse is for respect and sharing, then come stand with us in our struggles for religious freedoms and the return of skeletal remains and against hydroelectric dams and logging roads."

We anthropologists, too, have been part of the problem. Too often our power to define "the other" has displaced and silenced indigenous voices. Here, I am not speaking for indigenous peoples; rather I am turning the anthropological gaze on Western cultures so that we may understand why so many individuals seek healing, meaning, and spiritual answers in the lives of peoples whose lands and lives have been so devastated by Western colonialism.

 **Article Review Form at end of book.**

WiseGuide Wrap-Up

- The ways in which we conceive of ourselves as members of racial or ethnic groups reflect the broader systems of categorization supplied to us by science. As ethnic boundaries break down, government is considering the implications for describing our national demographic profile. Our conceptions of our own identities and of our national ethnic/racial characteristics are likely to change as a result.

- Historical forces, such as emigration, political upheaval, and social movements, influence our racial and gendered identities—which, as in the case of "machismo," are often intimately intertwined.

- Racial and ethnic identities are consequential not only for gender but also for sexuality; in racially stratified societies, power differences between groups affect sexual attraction, as well as partnership choices.

R.E.A.L. Sites

This list provides a print preview of typical **Coursewise** R.E.A.L. sites. (There are over 100 such sites at the **Courselinks**™ site.) The danger in printing URLs is that web sites can change overnight. As we went to press, these sites were functional using the URLs provided. If you come across one that isn't, please let us know via e-mail to: webmaster@coursewise.com. Use your Passport to access the most current list of R.E.A.L. sites at the **Courselinks** site.

Site name: Lesbians of Color Site

URL: http//www-lib.usc.edu/~retter/loc.html

Why is it R.E.A.L.? Lesbians of color are said to be "triply burdened"—as women, as people of color, and as members of a sexual minority group. This site provides a look at these issues.

Key topics: race, ethnicity, sexuality, lesbian history

Try this: Review this site and, analyzing the topics presented, write a brief paper about issues of concern to lesbians of color. How might these issues differ from those of heterosexual women of color? from white lesbians? How do these categories overlap? What are the implications for organizing to challenge racism, sexism, and homophobia?

Site name: United States Census Bureau News

URL: http://www.census.gov/pubinfo/www/news.html

Why is it R.E.A.L.? The Census Bureau is charged with maintaining an accurate demographic profile of the people in the United States. This profile is consequential for public policy, voter districting, and our perception of ourselves as a nation. This site introduces you to the Census Bureau, current issues related to the census, and census data.

Key topics: census, public policy, demography

Try this: Explore the links on this site. Write down what you discover about the demographic profile of the country along the lines of race and ethnicity. Remembering what you learned about systems of racial categorization in Section 1, make some notes about the advantages and disadvantages of the racial and ethnic categorization system used in the 1990 and 2000 censuses. Is the system for the 2000 Census an improvement? What would be your recommendations about the racial categorization used in future census efforts?

section 5

Key Points

- There is a difference between racial reconciliation and racial justice.

- The racism of the white supremacy movement is intimately linked to homophobia, anti-Semitism, and sexism.

- In order to challenge the practice of lynching, Southern women had to simultaneously challenge "chivalry."

- Ideas about masculinity and femininity vary with the power distributed across racialized groups, as demonstrated by a study of fraternity men and "little sisters."

Race and Gender

 Race and gender constitute intersecting systems of social organization. According to sociologist Patricia Hill-Collins, they form interlocking lines on our cultural "matrix of domination." For individuals, gender, like race, is an important master status—a feature of identity that defines who we are and shapes how we are seen by others. For our society, gender, like race, is structural; it is the basis of one of the most pervasive and stable social patterns that organize our society. Our society assigns traits, values, roles, jobs, responsibilities, and possibilities to us according to our sex. Like race, these assignments are based not on our aptitudes for them but on the social significance this society attaches to biological differences between men and women. Gender, then, is the social significance assigned to biological sex, and, like race, it structures the social world around us and deeply influences the trajectories of our lives.

While it is possible analytically to segregate gender and race as features of individuals and as systems in society, scholars increasingly recognize that gender and race cannot be separated in people's everyday lives. Many of the selections in this reader demonstrate the understanding that we cannot talk meaningfully about the lives of people of a racialized group without taking into account how the experiences of men and women in that group differ. Likewise, simple generalizations about differences between men and women do not take into account how the lives of men of color and white men or European-American women and women of color differ. Such analyses give us too little insight into the social world. Gender and race are intersecting, interlocking systems, and the experiences of people in this society reflect their social locations within these systems.

Too often, movements for social justice in this country have suffered from conflicts created by the structural organization of gender and race: movements for sexual equality, such as the Women's Suffrage Movement, have been divided by racism; movements for racial equality, such as the Civil Rights Movement, have been marred by sexism. Such conflicts have benefited only those most privileged by racial and gendered social hierarchies and have reduced the possibilities of organizing across the lines of race and gender. By understanding how race and gender interact to maintain an unjust social system, we can imagine ways of ending racism that do not depend on sexism, as well as ways of ending sexism that do not depend on racism.

In Section 4, we examined racial identity. In this section, we become more sophisticated in our thinking by adding gender to our analysis of race. Does being white and male differ from being Black and male? Does being a Black man differ from being a Black woman? How are masculinity and femininity shaped by our racial locations in society? What do we learn from our particular locations? What have we not learned because of them? How are we, as men and women, complicit in keeping the racial structure of our society in place? What are our interests, as men and women, in maintaining racial differences?

This section highlights how sexism—the privileging of one sex over the other—and racism—the privileging of some races over others—work together. Social beliefs about race and rape come to mind as a good example of this interaction. Many whites are taught that the person most likely to rape a white woman is a Black man. As you will learn, this belief has a long history in the United States and serves many social functions: it encourages white women to maintain their dependence on white men and makes them vulnerable to assault by them; it serves as a cover for white men, who actually are most likely to rape white women; it encourages Black men to avoid interactions with whites in order to avoid the consequences of rape allegations; and it teaches white women to avoid anyone who is not white, from a sense of fear based more in cultural beliefs than in empirical reality. In this way, beliefs about rape are not simply beliefs about gender but also beliefs about race; these beliefs maintain existing social stratification along the lines of gender and race.

The readings in this section examine a variety of circumstances in which the structures of race and the structures of gender reinforce each other in this society. Sociologist Michael Kimmel analyzes how the "racial reconciliation" rhetoric of Christian Promise Keepers men's groups does not actually promote racial justice. Another sociologist, Suzanne Harper, examines the interactions of sexism, homophobia, racism, and anti-Semitism in the documents of the male-dominated white supremacy movement. Writer Jacquelyn Dowd Hall explores the connections between racism and sexism in myths about rape and demonstrates how women of various backgrounds worked to end lynching, which Southern whites often rationalized as a reasonable response to alleged interracial sexual assaults. Finally, sociologists Mindy Stombler and Irene Padavic describe how the broader structures of race influence differences in gender hierarchies in campus organizations.

Questions

Reading 14. How does the Promise Keepers' position on race relations fall short of promoting racial equality? How is the form of masculinity promoted by the Promise Keepers dependent on sexism?

Reading 15. Why and how does white supremacist discourse promote not only racism but also sexism, homophobia, and anti-Semitism?

Reading 16. How did male chauvinism and white racism work together to justify the lynching of Black men by whites? How might strategies for combating lynching be modified to combat other forms of racially motivated violence today?

Reading 17. What are the differences in norms for masculinity and femininity these authors see in Black and white fraternity Little Sister organizations? How can these differences be explained?

How does the Promise Keepers' position on race relations fall short of promoting racial equality? How is the form of masculinity promoted by the Promise Keepers dependent on sexism?

Promise Keepers:

Patriarchy's Second Coming As Masculine Renewal

Michael S. Kimmel

Michael S. Kimmel's most recent book is Manhood in America: A Cultural History *(Free Press, 1996). He teaches sociology at SUNY at Stony Brook.*

It was Shea Stadium in late September, after all, so a crowd of 35,000 men chanting, whooping, hollering, and high-fiving each other wasn't all that unusual. But the Mets attract barely half that number late in their woeful season. And there are no women in the stands. That is unusual. And besides, the Mets are on the road.

On this day Shea is the setting for the latest rally by Promise Keepers, a Christian organization that seeks to revitalize men through a mass-based evangelical ministry. The dramatic growth and continuing appeal of Promise Keepers indicate that the movement of masculine fundamentalism has struck a nerve among American men with its messages of personal responsibility and racial reconciliation: Promise Keepers is arguably the largest "men's movement" in the nation. Its calls to men to be more domestically responsible, socially conscious and responsive friends, fathers, and husbands

make Promise Keepers seem innocuous at worst, and potentially a force for masculine reform. But its ominous ties with fanatic right-wing organizations and their views on women, homosexuals, and non-Christians, however, suggest that the rest of us had better start paying attention.

Who Are Promise Keepers?

Promise Keepers hasn't been around very long to have caused such a monumental stir. The group was founded in 1990 by former University of Colorado football coach Bill McCartney who had brought a national title to his school that year. A devout Catholic, McCartney had become, he admits, a workaholic absentee husband who demanded that family life be subordinated to his professional ambitions. In 1989, his unwed teenage daughter Kristyn had given birth to a child fathered by one of McCartney's players. The following summer, after a religious epiphany, he left the Catholic church for the more evangelical Protestant Vineyard Christian Fellowship and heeded the call to

expand his mission from athletes to men in general.

The move wasn't that uncharacteristic. McCartney had always been pulled towards the charismatic and evangelical. While an assistant coach at Michigan in 1970s, he had become involved with the right-wing Catholic "Word of God" movement, with its emphasis on Biblical literalism. The Vineyard Fellowship's cultish theology uses faith healing, miracles, and other "signs and wonders." With a diagnosis of the nation's moral and spiritual crisis gleaned partly from his family's sexual scandals and partly from the Vineyard Fellowship's ultra-right political agenda, McCartney put out a call to men to come to a rally for masculine Christian renewal. Just over 4000 men turned up in July, 1991, at the Colorado basketball arena.

From that modest beginning, the organization's growth has been almost exponential. Twenty-two thousand men half-filled the Colorado football stadium in 1992, and 50,000 filled it the next year. In 1994, 278,600 men attended several stadium events, 700,000 came in 1995, and an estimated 1.2 million met this year at 22 sites. Now, the

Reprinted from TIKKUN MAGAZINE, A BI-MONTHLY JEWISH CRITIQUE OF POLITICS, CULTURE, AND SOCIETY. Information and subscriptions are available from TIKKUN, 26 Fell Street, San Francisco, CA 94102.

organization is promising their own two-million man march in Washington for 1997. (One assumes they'll keep their promise.)

The organizational infrastructure has kept pace, growing from 22 full-time staff with a budget of $4 million in 1993 to more than 400 full-time employees, and a budget of more than $100 million today. They publish a slick magazine, New Man, which places devotional stories and prayers alongside political debates on questions like home schooling (they're for it), more practical tips like "how to save bucks on your home mortgage" (standard fare like comparing rates, paying more than the monthly premium, and refinancing the home), and advertisements for various Christian consumables. McCartney himself now works for the organization full-time, having resigned from his more secular coaching duties followers still call him "coach"—in 1994, after Kristyn had given birth to yet another illegitimate child fathered by another of his players, and his wife had threatened to divorce him if he did not pay more attention to his home life.

Although data on the rank-and-file Promise Keepers is scarce, the National Center for Fathering in Shawnee, Kansas found that, as of 1995, 88% of rally attendees were married, 21% had been divorced, and about 20% had parents who were divorced. Median age was 38, and 84% were white. Over one-fourth reported becoming Christian after age 24, and one-third had attended Baptist or Southern Baptist churches. Half reported that their own fathers were absent while they were growing up.

Unlike the Fellowship for Christian Athletes, which organizes prayer meetings among athletes in virtually every sport, including those little devotional moments at midfield for religious gridders from both teams, Promise

Keepers wants more than just jocks. They want all men.

Sports seem to be the way they intend to get them, at least metamorphically. At their stadium rallies, the parade of speakers, dressed in vertically striped polo shirts, khakis and sneakers, look more like a lineup of sales clerks at Foot Locker than of evangelical stump preachers. Coach McCartney, and the other speakers—who include Ed Cole, organizer of the Christian Men's Network, who had the guys high-fiving for Jesus, and Charles Colson, convicted Watergate conspirator who found God in prison and now runs the Prison Fellowship Ministries—exhort their "worshipping warriors" with manly homilies like "go the distance," snatched from that masculine weepy, Field of Dreams, and "break down the walls," the rally's theme, which sounds like a cross between Home Improvement and a karate exhibition. The massive tent set up in the parking lot is a virtual messianic mini-mall, hawking books, T-shirts, and souvenirs; but the best-selling items by far are the ubiquitous baseball caps.

Non-Muscular Christianity?

Such a move to bring men back into the church by muscling up is not new in American history. And, after all, athletes are used by advertisers to sell everything from shoes to cologne and flashlight batteries, so why not God? At the turn of the century, the fleet-footed former Chicago Cub right fielder Billy Sunday quit professional baseball and remorphed into a Bible-Belt evangelist, preaching "Muscular Christianity" to throngs of men, and bringing, in the words of one journalist, "bleacher-crazed, frenzied aggression to religion." To Sunday, Protestantism had turned Christ into a henpecked wimp,

whose angelic countenance smiled down even on his enemies from the national pulpit. Inveighing against this "dainty, sissified, lily-livered piety" to massive men-only crowds in tents throughout the Midwest and the South—the same states where Promise Keepers today find the majority of their audience—Sunday offered his minions a "hard muscled, pick-axed religion, a religion from the gut, tough and resilient." Jesus, himself was no "dough-faced lick-spittle proposition," he roared, but "the greatest scrapper who ever lived." Some Promise Keepers echo Sunday's critique of feminized masculinity. "The demise of our community and culture is the fault of sissified men who have been overly influenced by women," writes Tony Evans, a black Dallas-based evangelist, who is among the Promise Keepers' most popular rally speakers. Men, he admonishes, must "reclaim" their manhood, saying, "I want to be a man again." But in the bright September sun at Shea Stadium one would search in vain for such hypermasculine bravado. Gone also are the virulent misogyny, the homophobia, and the spectre of theocracy that has brought most of the criticism of the organization. Instead, one is struck by the immense sincerity of the guys in attendance, the earnestness of their searching, the heartful expressions of remorse. Were it not for the exclusion of women and the endless, tacky sports stuff, this could have been any Billy Graham Crusade. And were it not for the Christian fundamentalism, this might have been a mythopoetic men's meeting with Robert Bly and Sam Keen.

While Muscular Christians railed against a feminized Christianity grown soft and indolent, drawing on inspiring oratory about religious combat and righteous rage, most Promise Keepers are virtual SNAGs, "sensitive new age guys" celebrating Christian sweetness and kindness. They are less Christian soldiers "marching as to war," and more friends, confidants, therapists and partners, promising to listen carefully to their wives and children, sharing with their friends, healing their wounds and their worlds.

A Kinder, Gentler Patriarchy

The message has certainly resonated for large numbers of American men, who feel their lives are less deeply fulfilling, less meaningful, less animated by higher purpose than the one to which they believed they were entitled. Without community, a sense of purpose and connection, masculinity can feel hollow; we become ectomorphs—hard-shelled workaholics who are afraid there is nothing of any substance inside, and who deny that fear with drugs, alcohol, or strings of meaningless affairs. The marketplace is a perilous place to seek to prove one's manhood, what with plant closings, corporate layoffs, and downward mobility. Better to seek affirmation of manhood someplace safe, like as a father, husband, and an ethical man among men.

Promise Keepers ministers brilliantly to men's anxieties and needs, while promoting that masculine sense of entitlement that we believe is our birthright. The key words in their message are relationships and reconciliation. The organization's founding document proclaims the group's dedication "to uniting men through vital relationships to become godly influences in their world." Men have abdicated responsibility; at home, husbands are "not giving their wives the support they need," and are absent in the lives of their children or their friends. Among the "Seven Promises of a Promise Keeper" (also the title of their chief

doctrinal book) are building strong marriages, families, and friendships, and working in the church.

Promise Keepers promotes a kind of soft patriarchy, male domination as obligation, surrender and service—sort of "Every Man's Burden." There's lots of rhetoric about men becoming servants of Christ at home, administering to their families as he did to his church. "A real man is one who accepts responsibilities and doesn't run away from them. He raises his family and takes a leadership role," says one rally-goer. Men are entitled to lead; expected to do it, soberly and responsibly. Masculine malaise, the search for meaning and community, is resolved by the reassertion of a kinder, gentler patriarchal control.

At one rally, Bill Bright, head of the Campus Crusade for Christ, opined that while men should respect women, the man "is the head of the household and women are responders." At Shea, Rev. Ed Cole reminded the audience that "God's revelation comes through man," not woman, and so the two genders can never be equal, and self-anointed "Bishop" Wellington Boone noted that "how you handle your wife" would reveal how you "handle the world." Boone relies on Biblical inversion of biology—"woman came from man, not man from woman" and describes his own conversion from absentee landlord to dutiful dad and husband. It's a form of competition, "spiritual warfare," a test of masculine strength, to do more at home than his wife does. "I'm never gonna let no woman outserve me," he shouts to thunderous applause. In his essay in Seven Promises of a Promise Keeper, the organization's best-selling text, Tony Brown advises men to "sit down with your wife and say: 'Honey I've made a terrible mistake. I've given you my role. I gave up leading this family, and I forced you to take my place. Now I must

reclaim that role. Don't misunderstand what I am saying here. I'm not suggesting that you ask for your role back, I'm urging you to take it back . . . [T]here can be no compromise here. If you're going to lead, you must lead.' " (For their part, women are urged to give it back, "[f]or the sake of your family and the survival of our culture.")

To some women, this traditional patriarchal bargain sounds a whole lot better than the deals they'd already cut. After all, the organization lists among its primary goals, deepening "the commitment of men to respect and honor women." In return for submission, or being "responders," women are promised the respect and honor that went with the traditional patriarchal pedestal—and they get in return husbands and fathers who forswear drinking, drugs, smoking, and gambling, who lovingly support their families by steady work, and who even choose to go shopping with them as a form of Christian service. Not bad, perhaps—even if it does require that women remain absolutely obedient and subordinate to men. It's unclear to me whether having a job or even going to college fits into that picture. Some members want their wives home at all times; others say they still need the money. Perhaps we'll know soon enough: Promise Keepers has announced a women's organization, "Suitable Helpers," sort of its Ladies' Auxiliary, where, according to the Christian Coalition, women can "learn what it means to be a godly support and partner to man." In addition, an organization called Women of Faith is drawing thousands of women to its "Joyful Journey" rallies that will happen in more than one dozen cities this year, using what seems to be a Promise Keeper model.

To some listeners, though, this message sounds like male supremacy with a beatific smile. "Promise Keepers are about the return of patriarchy in its Sunday best: spiffed up, polite, and earnest but always, and ultimately, in charge," noted Unitarian minister Rev. David Blanchard of Syracuse. The resolution of the crisis of masculinity cannot come at the expense of women. Though the Promise Keepers hear men's anguish, they offer a traditional patriarchal salve on a wound that can only be closed by gender equality.

The Racism of Racial Reconciliation

Promise Keepers message of racial reconciliation is as compelling as it is troubling. On the one hand, reconciliation means that white people must take responsibility for racism and take the initiative in seeking fellowship with men of color. Noting that eleven o'clock on Sunday morning is the most racially divided hour of the week, Promise Keepers seeks to heal racial divisiveness by bringing black and white men together under the canopy of patriarchy. At Shea Stadium, it falls to McCartney—grandfather to two interracial children (both of Kirstyn's lovers were men of color)—to sound the call for racial reconciliation. Racism is a white problem, he argues. A "spirit of white racial superiority" maintains "an insensitivity to the pain of people of color." Like harmony between women and men, which can be won only when men return to the home, racial harmony relies on white people's initiative. It is the privileged who must act.

Racial reconciliation is the organization's boldest move into the political arena, and it makes Promise Keepers one of the few virtually all-white groups in the nation willing to confront white racism. At Shea Stadium, that message energized the mostly white (I estimated about 80%) crowd. Rich, who is 39 and white, is a single parent from New Jersey, who brought his two sons. He feels that the racial component is important. "In Christ we're all the same," he says. Daniel, a white 27 year-old, from a working-class neighborhood in Queens came with another man from his Baptist Church, Joseph, a 35 year-old black man originally from Ghana. "As a white person, you kind of take race for granted, you don't see it," Daniel says. "I'm not the one being hurt, but my people have done some terrible things to blacks. As a white person, it's important to take responsibility."

So, what's wrong with this picture of white people taking responsibility for racism, of men becoming more loving, devoted and caring fathers, friends, and husbands? It's a nagging question that emerges once you begin to examine what lies outside the framing of each carefully orchestrated PK photo-op. For one thing, there's the message of reconciliation itself. Theirs is not a call to support those programs that would uplift the race and set the nation on a course toward racial equality. This is not about anti-discrimination legislation or affirmative action—heck, it's not even about integration. It's about being kinder and more civil. It's about hearing their pain, not supporting its alleviation. It's choosing to be nicer, but not about policies that force us to be fairer. In the PK world view, racial reconciliation is an individual posture, but not a collective struggle. Being less racist in one's personal life may be laudatory, but without a program of institutional remedies, it leaves untouched the chief forces that keep that inequality in place. Which is why it doesn't seem so strange to see who else is eagerly lining up to slap some high-fives on the Promise Keeper rank and file. Although McCartney and the Promise Keepers elite maintain a publicly apolitical position, there are increasingly ominous signs of connections between Promise Keepers and far right religious organizations like Focus on the Family, Christian Coalition and the Campus Crusade for Christ. James Dobson, founder of Focus on the Family, appears regularly at Promise Keeper functions, as does Bill Bright, whose Campus Crusade lent 85 full-time staffers to the Promise Keeper headquarters, and whose most recent book (sold at all Promise Keepers rallies) raves against the "homosexual explosion," the teaching of evolution, and abortion, as well as the laws against school prayer.

In addition to McCartney's well-publicized right-wing ties, other Promise Keepers maintain a "warm fellowship" with the far right. Mark DeMoss, the organization's national spokesman, worked for Jerry Falwell before serving on the advisory committee for Pat Buchanan's presidential campaign. In a sense DeMoss neatly encapsulates the three successive waves of the religious right in America—from Falwell's Moral Majority to Reed's Christian Coalition, to a sanitized theocracy designed to appeal to Generation X. Promise Keepers is only the most recent example of a well-established and well-financed theocratic movement.

This movement promises that "America will be a Christian nation by the year 2000"—not a cheery prospect for Jews, Moslems, atheists, agnostics, and others. Urging his followers to "take this nation for Jesus," McCartney has made clear the political agenda: What you are about to hear is God's word to the men of this nation. We are going to war as of tonight. We have divine power; that is our weapon. We will not compromise. Wherever truth is at risk, in the schools or legislature, we are going to contend for it. We will win.

So much for the avowed apolitical stance of the organization. Theocracies are not known for their tolerance of difference, and their use of these earnest young minions is reminiscent of some New Left organizations, which were propelled from below by youthful idealism but steered from above by hacks who were not especially taken with the idea of participatory democracy. But the radical religious right is currently jumping on the racial reconciliation bandwagon, in part because it allows them to sound supportive of people of color, without actually having to support any of the political and social policies that would benefit people of color. Even Ralph Reed, Promise Keeper supporter and head of the Christian Coalition, protested the burning of black churches this past summer, only to be more than a little embarrassed when his organization floated overtly racist mock-election guides to potential voters.

Such racial tokenism extends also to the black clergy who are part of the Promise Keepers team. Wellington Boone and other black speakers like E. V. Hill, from Los Angeles, and Pittsburgh's Joseph Garlington are also on the Steering Committee of the Coalition on Revival (COR) an extreme right-wing religious group that espouses Biblical literalism and promotes "Christian reconstructionism." Boone himself was a consultant to Pat Robertson's presidential bid.

Though the Shea Stadium rally was endorsed by several prominent local black clergy, other prominent religious leaders, like Rev. Calvin Butts of the Abysynnian Baptist Church in Harlem or the ubiquitous Rev. Al Sharpton, were conspicuously absent from the mutual love fest. Nationally, too, some black clergy are skeptical, to say the least. "It doesn't translate into how you bring black and white together," noted the Rev. Christopher Hamlin, pastor of the 16th Street Baptist Church in Birmingham, Alabama.

"The barriers that are broken down in the stadiums are still there when people come home to their communities. I think most black pastors see it as being rhetoric, which is something most of the black community has heard for a long time."

Eventually, those black pastors who have innocently supported Promise Keepers' masculinist ministry will have to face the seamier political underside of their messages of hope. Though Promise Keepers were among the only white organizations to raise money for burned black churches this past summer (they raised over $1 million), the traditional liberalism of the black religious constituency, which favors welfare, civil rights, and women's right to choose will sit uneasily with a right-wing theocratic evangelism. Though both sides agree that racism is a white problem, about the only policy issue they agree on is home schooling.

What is more, the infusion of men of color comes at an exorbitant multicultural price—lopping off several bands of the rainbow through continued exclusion. Gays and lesbians, for example, don't even get near the pearly gates. Echoing familiar "love the sinner, hate the sin" rhetoric, McCartney and Dr. Raleigh Washington sidestep the question at the rally's press conference. "It's like lying," says Washington. "God doesn't like lying but he loves liars." Perhaps, but would God support a Constitutional amendment banning marriages between liars? Would God sanction discrimination against confessed liars? Though rallygoers barely heard a word about it, homosexuality is a hot topic among both rank and file, and PK leaders. It's the hottest topic on Promise Keepers' web site. Since the Bible never uses the term, or clearly defines homosexuality, these Biblical literalists are forced to struggle with interpretations.

The leaders see no ambiguity nor any need for equivocation. When he pronounced homosexuality "an abomination against Almighty God," McCartney was a board member of Colorado for Family Values, the statewide coalition of right-wing religious groups that sponsored Amendment 2, the unconstitutional Colorado initiative that would have permitted discrimination against gays and lesbians. Later, McCartney called homosexuals "a group of people who don't reproduce yet want to be compared to people who do." (One pities Bob and Elizabeth Dole and the Buchanans, as well as other non-breeders.) He's also addressed Operation Rescue rallies, calling abortion "a second Civil War." Given such obviously political positions, it would appear that Promise Keepers' notion of gender reconciliation is also an individual outpouring of concern, however heartfelt, for individual women, while ignoring collective efforts at building a new society together. Good, kind, decent men (and white people) can indeed develop better, more emotionally resonant and caring relationships with women and people of color, and then support precisely those policies that perpetuate their pain.

Male Supremacy As Racial Healing

Perhaps what we are witnessing in this strange alliance of right-wing evangelists and liberal black clergy is that the reassertion of male supremacy can serve as the foundation for both to sit down at the table of brotherhood. "What happened here is that the boys' club has expanded to include people of color," writes Chip Berlet, who is researching right-wing populism in America. "When push comes to shove, what's more important, race or gender?" Here, then, is a concept that both black and white clergy can unite behind. The resurrection of responsible manhood is really the Second Coming of patriarchy. Gender and racial healing is a more unified masculine entitlement. Such allies could even reach out to Louis Farrakhan, the Black Muslim leader of his Million Men, and invite him to the party, since he also excludes women and gay men and lesbians from the table of humanity.

Of course, like the Million Man March, the earnestness and sincerity of the movement adherents—and a genuine alliance with a wide range of black clergy—might in time outstrip Promise Keepers' right wing political agenda. More likely, and more ominous, however, is the possibility that the repressive and censorious voices of theocratic authoritarianism will continue to whisper in the ears of the movement leaders, long after the shouts of the men themselves have died down.

 **Article Review Form at end of book.**

Why and how does white supremacist discourse promote not only racism but also sexism, homophobia, and anti-Semitism?

Subordinating Masculinities/ Racializing Masculinities:

Writing White Supremacist Discourse on Men's Bodies

Suzanne Harper

Florida Atlantic University

Race and gender oppression may both revolve around the same axis of disdain for the body; both portray the sexuality of subordinate groups as animalistic and therefore deviant. (Collins, 1990, p. 171)

Perhaps sexuality is a dynamic in racism and ethnic prejudice as well as in gender bias. (MacKinnon, 1993, p. 63)

White fear of black sexuality is a basic ingredient of white racism. (West, 1993, pp. 124–1255).

A white man stands erect in front of bridges, planes, and skyscrapers; the caption around this image reads "White Men *Built* this Nation—White Men are This Nation!" A black man slouches grasping his crotch; the caption here reads "Today's Young Coon." A Jewish man appears small, effeminate, yet menacing; the heading here, "The Evil Jew." An emaciated gay man walks with a cane and spits invectives; a caption tells the reader that this is "Another AIDS-Infected Faggot." Yet another

white man places his foot on the neck of a black man while he sodomizes him with a Confederate flagpole. These are the disturbing images that appear in the pages of contemporary white supremacist organization publications. The body and sexuality are central to white supremacist discourse, and these particular images share an emphasis on men's bodies: white men's, black men's bodies, Jewish men's bodies, gay men's bodies. The comments of Collins, MacKinnon, and West all point to the centrality of the body and sexuality in understanding the connections between systems of gender oppression and those of racial oppression, that is, the body and sexuality. Indeed West, in addressing the "taboo" of black sexuality in white supremacist ideology, asserts that, "white supremacist ideology is based first and foremost on the degradation of black bodies in order to control them" (1993, p. 122). The aim of this paper is to develop these insights about the

centrality of the body in racial and gender oppression by exploring the connections between racism and notions of gender and sexuality in the publications of six white supremacist organizations, with a particular focus here on representations of men and masculinities.

While some may argue that the discourse of white supremacist publications is so repulsive and degrading we should ignore it, I contend that we must try to put to one side our disgust and anger so that we can map and explore the intricate connections of race, class, gender and sexuality which are the central nexus of white supremacy, both in extremist publications and as it is institutionalized within the broader cultural context. In this paper I argue that the discourse in white supremacist publications is forged as a response to the perceived erosion of white male dominance and is an attempt to recreate what, for white heterosexual men, is a lost world of unchallenged privilege.

Recent research in the study of gender has expanded to include the, by now, obvious point that the analysis of men and masculinities is crucial to our understanding of gender stratification. One of the key insights of this research has been that rather than a consolidated, unified, male "sex role" or "masculinity" there are multiple masculinities (Brod, 1987; Connell, 1987; Franklin, 1984; Kimmel, 1987; Kimmel & Messner, 1989; Segal 1990). Further, some forms of masculinity are hegemonic while other forms are subordinated (Connell, 1987; 1992). The particular forms of masculinities which are hegemonic or subordinated are not static but are forged within an on-going, historical, political and cultural struggle.

Some of this research focuses on the way masculinities are subordinated along racial lines (Brod, 1988; Franklin, 1984; 1988). Black men and Jewish men find themselves in very different social locations when it comes to issues surrounding masculinity. For Jewish men, prevailing images construct them as the essence of softness, "feminine," even castrated, while almost as if in a reverse photographic image, black men carry the "shadow of instinct, of unconscious urge, of the body itself—and hence of the penis-as-animal" (Bordo, 1993, pp. 701–702).

Of course, recognition of the link between race and "sex" is not new. As early as the turn of the century, writers such as Ida B. Wells-Barnett and Jane Addams (1901/1977) and Jessie Daniel Ames (e.g., Hall, 1979) pointed out the stark reality of racial and sexual oppression which lay behind the mask of white chivalry used to justify lynching. And, throughout this century others have continued to point to the link between racial and sexual oppression as crucial (Dollard, 1937; Hernton, 1965; Hoch, 1979; Smith, 1949; Stember,

1976). Still, some of these fail to incorporate a critique of masculinity (equality being simply and merely reduced to black men having equal access to white women) and certainly none question heterosexuality. The writer who provides one of the earliest critiques of white masculinity and heterosexuality, perhaps not surprisingly given his status as a man proud to be both black and gay, is James Baldwin. Baldwin writes that the "white man's unadmitted—and apparently, to him, unspeakable—private fears and longings are projected onto the Negro," (1963, p. 35). All these however, share an exclusive focus on "race" as constructed along a black-white dichotomy and tend to ignore class. Still, these early writings are significant for their emphasis on the interconnectedness of race, gender and sexuality.

Other research specifically examines the connections between white supremacy and masculinities (Theweleit, 1987). Klaus Theweleit's compendious book, *Male Fantasies,* explores the development of fascism in the precursors to the Nazis, the German *Freikorps.* Theweleit asserts that central to the appeal of fascism was a style of masculine identity based upon a dread of women, sex, and the body. He attributes the appeal of this style of masculinity to psychodynamic causes, specifically a failed relationship with mother in childhood.[1] While this is important for understanding the appeal for those who join organizations such as the *Freikorps,* the focus in this study is on the ways white supremacist discourse is written on men's bodies.

My intention here is to build on this research by exploring the ways in which the process of racializing and subordinating masculinities is central to white supremacist discourse. The purpose of this paper is to examine the construction of hegemonic and subordinated mas-

culinities within the discourse of white supremacist organizational publications with a particular focus on the way these masculinities are shaped along lines of race, class, gender and sexuality.

Method

This study includes publications produced by six different contemporary white supremacist organizations. The publications, from the Klanwatch[2] collection, span the years from 1976 through 1991, and include *The Klansman,* edited by J. W. Farrands; *Newspaper of the NAAWP* published by David Duke's National Association for the Advancement of White People (NAAWP); *Truth at Last* (previously *The Thunderbolt*) the publication of the National States' Rights Party (NSRP) headed for many years by J. B. Stoner, and currently by Ed Fields; *Racial Loyalty,* the publication of the Church of the Creator (C.O.T.C.—followers refer to themselves as "creators"), Ben Klassen founder and publisher; *The Torch,* published by Thom Robb, a minister within the Christian Identity branch of the movement; and *WAR* (White Aryan Resistance) published by the father-son team of Tom and John Metzger. Each publication represents a different white supremacist organization and these six are a roughly accurate representation of the range of groups recognized by adherents and outsiders alike as the white supremacist movement in the U.S. today.[3] Although there are differences between the various factions (mainly along lines of God[4] and nation[5]) these differences are eclipsed by what their ideologies share (foremost, an abiding faith in the superiority of the white race and an astonishingly similar view of the gender/sexual order). Hence, for the purposes of this analysis I have used the publications as relatively interchangeable representatives of white supremacist ideologies. Where there are differences I deem significant, I have noted these in the text.

In selecting publications to include, I considered those that had been published over the longest period of time.[6] In this way, I used "length of publication" as a reasonable proxy for the size of the readership, the relative effectiveness of these periodicals, and their "success" at constructing racist ideologies. The sample includes a total of 369 publications.

This study utilizes discourse analysis to examine these publications. The goal of this method is to provide a deep examination of text, both words and images, paying particular attention to their juxtaposition. Further, discourse analysis should provide an understanding of the text as a site of ideological struggle, located within a given social context, so that "text," or "discourse," do not become disembodied entities removed from any grounding in historical, material or cultural conditions (Wetherell & Potter, 1992). Thus, for the purposes of this paper it is imperative to keep in mind that the texts and images analyzed here, as crude and horrifying as they are, exist within a historical, material and cultural context which systematically affirms white supremacy in a myriad of ways most of which are less crude, but perhaps only slightly less horrifying.

Racializing Masculinities

The construction of masculinities within the discourse of white supremacist publications is explicitly shaped along racial lines. Although we might expect to find that "race" in such a context is a taken-for-granted conceptualization, in fact, what it means to be "white," "black," or "Jewish," and perhaps more importantly, precisely who "qualifies" as belonging in each racial categorization, are subjects of much debate in white supremacist rhetoric.

In an era in which "scientific" racism is widely believed to be at an end[7], the racial categorizations within white supremacist discourse are quite explicitly embedded in biological notions of "race." In this discourse, it is evident that the process of racialization, of marking people as belonging to specific racial categorizations, is situated in the body. Racial oppression is premised on the disdain for particular bodies and the valorization of other bodies. This process of racialization does not, however, exist apart from gender and sexuality.

While women are by no means completely obscured in white supremacist publications, indeed, women—white, black, and Jewish—are essential foils against which masculinities are constructed, it is men who are the central figures (Harper, 1994). Specifically, it is white, heterosexual men who are the primary agents and actors in the texts. White men, and white masculinity, exist only in contrast to other men and other, racialized, masculinities. In each of the following illustrations, we see evidence of this process of racializing masculinities.

It is critical within a white supremacist lexicon to know who "qualifies" as white; for, when one is classified as white, the designation connotes all manner of privileges, meanings, and responsibilities, especially if one is white, male and heterosexual. Biological characteristics, such as white skin, blond hair, and blue eyes, are represented as paradigmatic of "whiteness;" although, some white supremacists argue that this is too narrow a definition, and that "white" should be broadened to include those with hair and eyes that are other than blond and blue, but not those with "less than white" skin.[8] Along with features of skin tone, hair and eye color, "whiteness" also includes a host of more ephemeral characteristics like "purity," "honor," and "superiority." What all of these attributes share, from blond hair, blue eyes, and white skin, to "purity," "honor" and "superiority," according to white supremacist discourse, is that they are genetically encoded markers of "race."

Racial categorizations are simultaneously masculinized within white supremacist discourse, because what it means to be "white" is paradigmatically what it means to be a white man (See Figure 1*). In this illustration (regularly featured in a number of white supremacist publications), a white man stands in the foreground, with airplanes and bridges in the background. The accompanying text reads, "White Men *Built* This Nation, White Men *Are* This Nation!" [emphasis in the original]. This one illustration conveys several messages. First, it signals a link between race, "whiteness," and masculinity, specifically "white men," such that white men are the central, indeed, the *only* actors visible. Even though the appeal in the illustration is one intended for all whites, both men and women, it is men who occupy the privileged position here. White women's contributions, either independently from white men or in concert with them, are effaced.

Further, the image points to a connection between white masculinity and class position. The white men to which the illustration presumably refers are those materially involved in "building" an infrastructure, those who literally "build" the bridges, airplanes and skyscrapers featured in the background while it simultaneously obliterates the labor of racial and ethnic minorities, both men and women, whose labor did, in fact, build this country. The working-

*Figure is not included in this publication.

class position of the man in the drawing is further signified by his attire: he is dressed in what appears to be a work shirt, vest, and hard hat, all signifiers of a working-class position. The illustration can also be read as referring to middle-class white men; those white men who researched, engineered, and developed the bridges, airplanes and skyscrapers. Again, such a reading eliminates from view the contributions of people of color and white women to such technology. Further, it completely elides the material advantages of white men which have allowed them to produce such technology; advantages gained at the expense of white women, whose domestic and emotional labor as wives is appropriated, and people of color (both men and women), who are effectively eliminated from competition with white men by a system of de facto segregation which ensures their exclusion from schools, universities, and the labor force, and whose labor is also exploited as laborers, domestics, launderers, and fast food workers.

The white man in this illustration stands tall, his posture indicating that his body is as erect and impenetrable as the buildings in the background. Thus, this one white man comes to represent all white (heterosexual) men, who are—within the context of white supremacist discourse—the embodiment of the phallic will and conscious control, and hence, deserving of respect or even worship (Bordo, 1993, pp. 701–702).

Whiteness, as it is embodied in the man in this drawing, is a clearly marked and delineated space. Within that space exists all manner of privilege; here, the twin privileges of agency and creation—available only to white men—are featured. The fact that whiteness is so conspicuously evident is a decided contrast to the culturally unmarked and unnamed quality of whiteness described by Frankenberg in her study of white women (1994). The distinction is an important one, but no less important are the similarities to Frankenberg's analysis of whiteness. Frankenberg characterizes whiteness as an implicit, and often unrecognized, standard against which all else is measured. In white supremacist discourse, whiteness is also the standard against which all else is measured; yet, it is explicitly recognized and actively constructed by framers of the discourse. This suggests a connection, that "whiteness" as is it constructed in white supremacist discourse shares some characteristics with more mainstream aspects of "whiteness," not the least of which is the racializing of masculinity. Another connection suggested by Frankenberg's work is that "whiteness"—whether in white supremacist publications or in more mainstream contexts—is constructed as an oppositional category in reference to some Otherness, most often "blackness."

"Blackness," within white supremacist discourse, is perhaps most importantly defined as that which is "not white." Blacks are depicted as the antithesis of whites in every way; the dichotomy between "blackness" and "whiteness" is unmistakable and inescapable. Juxtaposed to the inherent "purity" and "goodness" that is "Whiteness," "blackness" is an essence associated with "everything bad, muddy, ugly, evil and diseased." The basis of this essential difference is argued to be biological. Most prominent within the discourse as biological markers are skin color, the shape of nose and lips, and hair texture. All the illustrations in the publications which feature blacks emphasize exaggerated versions of these physical characteristics. Blacks are uniformly pictured with very dark skin, broad noses, enormous lips, and "kinky" hair. "Blackness," and its alleged biological inferiority, is viewed as determinative of low intelligence. For all the biological markers of "blackness," it is not always clear precisely who belongs in the category. Distinctions between the essence of "blackness" and "whiteness" are crystallized in discourse involving "mulattos," (the term used for those of a "mixed" racial heritage) so that all "good" characteristics are attributable to white ancestors while any "bad" can be blamed on black heritage.

"Blackness," within white supremacist discourse, is most often situated in the body of a black man (See Figure 2*). In this caricature of a black man, he is shown beneath the caption, "Today's Young Coon," indicating that he is typical of all young black men. He stands near a jam box, holding a smoking gun in his right hand, and grabbing his sizable crotch with his left hand. He appears disheveled and unclean, as flies circle his head. Making the explicit message of the drawing still more overt, the text in the side-bar accompanying the drawing (not included here) describes the man as:

crude, smelly, loud, uneducated, inarticulate and preoccupied with the most base and petty endeavors . . . He's very committed to his music . . . which shamelessly promotes violent revolution, irresponsible sexuality and the mindless worship of trinkets and trends. (*WAR*, Vol. 8(2), 1989, p. 11)

The text and the drawing create an image of black men as beasts, a bestiality located in the body. That the man here stands slouched, grabbing his crotch, indicates that he is centrally concerned with the body, and most importantly his penis. Indeed, as Fanon noted in his analysis of white psychiatric patients, "One is no longer aware of the Negro, but only of a penis: the Negro is eclipsed. He is turned into a penis. He *is* the penis" (1970, p. 120). Here, the black man who is "preoccupied with the most base

*Figure is not included in this publication.

and petty endeavors" and listens to music which promotes "irresponsible sexuality" is eclipsed, he *is* the penis.

The threat of political power implicit in this imagery cannot be overlooked. In his other hand, the black man holds a gun that appears to have been recently fired (at whites?). The text refers to the music which "shamelessly promotes violent revolution." The association of the phallic gun and the reference to "violent revolution" points to the real fear that underlies much of white supremacist discourse. While large segments of the black population continue to be politically and economically disenfranchised, and among the least powerful members of our society, it is precisely these people that white supremacists fear. The thought that blacks, especially young black men, could arm themselves and foment a "violent revolution" is a fear that is deeply ingrained in white supremacist ideology and in more mainstream reports of "fear of crime." Both are linked in the white imagination to images like this one of black man-as-penis, black man-as-animal. The fear is that black men will shift the focus of their rage away from each other and toward whites. The irony of this type of projection, of course, is that it is white supremacists who are advocating a violent revolution. In addition, the implication of the drawing elides the fact that young black men are statistically much more likely to harm each other than whites. And, projecting the possibility of "violence" against whites on to young black men distorts the reality that for centuries violence by whites against black men (and women) has been institutionalized whether historically in slavery, sharecropping peonage, Jim Crow segregation, lynching, or currently in de facto segregation coupled with economic and political disenfranchisement.

This drawing further illustrates the centrality of the body to the construction of racist discourse. Indeed, in this instance the body of a black man furnishes the "metaphorical medium for distinguishing the pure from the impure, the diseased from the clean and acceptable, the included from the excluded" (Goldberg, 1990, p. 305). This black man's body signifies all that is impure, diseased and excluded in white supremacist discourse. The juxtaposition of the white man in the previous illustration, and the black man in this drawing, highlights the contrasting images of white and black masculinities and the centrality of the body to each. Both white and black masculinities are set against yet another, Jewish masculinity.

The third leg of the tripod of white supremacist racial classification is "Jewishness," which constitutes a racial identity apart from "whiteness" within white supremacist discourse. The importance of being Jewish, rather than "white," is a critical distinction. The application for membership into the Invisible Empire, Knights of the Ku Klux Klan, for example, requires potential new members to check a box stating "I am not a Jew;" there is no corollary box to be checked stating "I am not black" or "I am not Gay."

The designation of "white skin," so meaningful in the construction of whiteness, becomes much more confounding when the discussion turns to Jews. "White skin," it turns out, is merely an essential, but by no means sufficient, prerequisite for being deemed "white" rather than "Jewish." Indeed, white supremacists recognize that Jews—along with half a dozen other racial categorizations of people—have "white skin." In order to distinguish Jews from whites then, white supremacists must turn to other measures. White supremacists distinguish Jews from

"whites" on a number of criteria, including religious identity, biology, and character. While white supremacists acknowledge that some Jews may "pass" as whites in terms of religious preference and physical appearance, they contend that it is ultimately impossible for them to remain hidden because their true Jewish [read: sinister] character will eventually be revealed.

"Jewishness," like "blackness," is most often incarnated as a man. In the illustration "The Evil Jew," it is a caricature of a Jewish man that symbolizes the archetypal white supremacist image of Jews (See Figure 3*). This drawing depicts a much different kind of racialized masculinity inscribed on an invisible body and suggests an ambiguous sexuality. The Jewish man who personifies "The Evil Jew" is only a head, indeed the body is barely visible in the illustration. Although historically anti-Semitic images of Jewish men have featured them as rapists (Mosse, 1978), this seems to no longer be the predominant portrait drawn of Jewish men in white supremacist literature.[9] Instead, Jewish men are most frequently featured as in control of an elaborate conspiracy which operates the key governmental and economic institutions, often referred to as "ZOG," an acronym for Zionist Occupational Government. In this capacity, Jewish men are cast as the primary, if not exclusive, owners, holders, hoarders, and manipulators of money. This construction of Jewish masculinity is not only economic, it is sexualized as well. For, as Dworkin suggests, ". . . when people say that Jews control the money, they are talking about a kind of male sexual power" (Dworkin, 1988). Within the context of white supremacist discourse, however, Jewish men's sexual power is complex and contradictory.

*Figure is not included in this publication.

In contrast to the images of the phallic white man and the black man-as-penis, the Jewish man is represented as both emasculated and powerful. He is "feminine," and carries with him the "taint" of a feminizing influence. The supposed feminizing influence of Jewish men on white men—and, by extension, the U.S.—are evident in the following excerpt from an article entitled, "North America's No. 1 Enemy," in which the author points out the dangers of Jewish control:

One of the characteristics of nations which are controlled by the Jews *is the gradual eradication of masculine influence and power and the transfer of influence into feminine forms* [emphasis mine] (WAR, Vol. 8(2), 1989, p. 14).

It is clear from this quote that Jewish men pose a threat to the masculinity of white men, and the decline of all "masculine influence and power." What, exactly, it means to have power transferred "into feminine forms" is not clear from the article, but the implications of such a process for the U.S. are unmistakable. Elsewhere in the same article it is noted that Jews have "spawned a wave of homosexuality and degeneracy in America . . . " (WAR, Vol. 8(2), 1989, p. 14). Hence, the threat to white masculinity posed by Jewish men leads directly and inexorably along one course, that is toward homosexuality and "degeneracy."

The implications in terms of class politics suggested by these constructions of masculinities, white, black and Jewish, should not be overlooked. While it is white men who are positioned as the rightful holders of working-class or middle-class status, black men and Jewish men are constructed as threats to that status but from different directions. Black men are constructed as threats from "below," that is, from class positions below those of white working- or middle-class white men. The

reference to the possibility that young, black men might incite a "violent revolution" demonstrates a perception that they are below white men in class position. Jewish men, on the other hand, pose a much different threat, a threat from "above." As the supposed leaders of the international economic cabal, Jewish men are constructed as threats to white men's class position from a superior economic position. Thus, white men in white supremacist discourse see their class position as precarious, to say the very least, under attack from every direction by men racialized as Others (see Figure 4*).

Racializing masculinities is fundamentally about sexualizing them as well. White masculinity, as it is constructed here, is phallic, erect, impenetrable, imbued with creative powers. Black masculinity is animalistic, bestial, debased. Jewish masculinity is feminized, emasculated, degenerate. This process of simultaneously racializing and sexualizing masculinities suggests that the hegemony of white (straight) men is reliant on the dual aspects of this process. In white supremacist publications men—here, black men and Jewish men—are constructed as racialized/sexualized Others for the consumption of (predominantly) white men. The net result is (straight) white men who are valorized and given agency while simultaneously their hegemony confirmed, the dominance of the subaltern is affirmed, and resistance rendered inconceivable.

There is some evidence to suggest that the class, race, and gender politics of white supremacist literature resonates for more than just those who count themselves members of these organizations. In 1993, *Newsweek* magazine featured a cover story entitled, "White Male Paranoia—Are They

*Figure is not included in this publication.

the Newest Victims or Just Bad Sports?" (Gates, 1993). The article reported on the growing sentiment among white males that they are under attack, bearing the brunt of social and cultural change in the U.S. In a Gallup poll conducted especially for the issue, 56% of white males (compared to 38% of all others) surveyed agreed with the statement that white men are "losing an advantage in terms of jobs and income." Clearly, white men beyond the parameters of white supremacist organizations view themselves as threatened explicitly in terms of race, gender and class.

Further evidence is suggested by a film released the same year, "Falling Down," which features Michael Douglas as a white, middle-class, heterosexual Everyman who pleads for "everything to be just like it was before," as he unleashes his rage—and unloads his automatic weapon—on racial and ethnic minorities. Douglas' character in the film is an archetype of a particular form of white masculinity, the ordinary-man-turned-warrior, emblematic of post-Vietnam era U.S. popular culture (Gibson, 1994; Jeffords, 1989).

In addition to public opinion polls and popular films, presidential politics also offer some suggestive evidence that these themes reverberate beyond white supremacist publications. In 1988, George Bush was elected president of the U.S. in no small measure because Lee Atwater, his campaign manager, decided to make "Willie Horton Dukakis' running mate." William Horton is a black man and a convicted felon who assaulted a white woman and her fiance while on a furlough from prison. The images of Horton used for the campaign drew on the basest images of the black-man-as-dangerous-beast, black-man-as-penis. Worse still, repressive crime control policies, with the foreseeable [and intentional?] disproportionate impact on black men, have been at the forefront of both Republican and Democratic national agendas for at least the last two decades. One scholar has astutely observed of these policies that "The text may be crime. The subtext is race" (Tonry, 1995, p. 6). And, I would add the subtext is also about class, gender and sexuality.

Subordinating Masculinities

In white supremacist discourse, it is the body which is central, for it is on the body that race, class, gender and sexuality are inscribed. Concurrent with the process of racializing masculinities, they are subordinated. Racializing masculinities is not simply a process of placing bodies within different racial categorizations, but more importantly, about situating those bodies within a hierarchy which subjugates particular masculinities (black and Jewish) while valorizing others (white). The implication is unequivocally one that white masculinity is superior to either black or Jewish masculinities. Thus, masculinities are simultaneously racialized and subordinated.

Subordinating masculinities occurs at many sites in the ideological terrain of white supremacist discourse. The process of subordinating masculinities is premised on notions of dominance: one form of masculinity is hegemonic while others are subaltern. Struggles for dominance, whether based on class or sexuality, are at the heart of white supremacy.

White supremacist masculinity is characterized by conflict for dominance with other men. White men are featured in the discourse as struggling against other groups of men and other definitions of masculinity for dominance in a number of realms. Germane to the discussion here is white men's struggle for sexual dominance.

Sexual Dominance and Racialized/Subordinated Masculinities

White men, as the central actors in and framers of white supremacist discourse, cast themselves as engaged in conflict with Others for dominance, frequently of a distinctly sexual nature. This conflict is taken to an extreme in the illustration featured here (See Figure 5*). In the drawing, a white man holds down a black man with one foot, while at the same time sodomizing him with a flagpole. At the other end of the flagpole is a Confederate flag.[10] Next to this image is a long scroll (not included here) which mentions the controversy over the Confederate flag and suggests that as whites in the past have fought and died for this symbol, they might be so inspired again. After asserting that blacks cannot possibly "grasp the noble concept of preserving family heritage," the text goes on to conclude:

Consequently, it's safe to say that they feel little allegiance to their own past family and have absolutely *no* regard, respect or understanding for ours . . . But I can tell you one thing these ignorant coon bastards *will* feel if they persist with their campaign to ban the FLAG OF DIXIE! [all emphasis in the original] (*WAR*, Vol. 8(3), 1989, p. 3).

The debate over the Confederate flag is here framed as a conflict between white and black masculinity. Even if black men are legally successful in banning the flag, a symbol of white "family heritage" and masculinity, the unambiguous threat in this illustration is that white men will ultimately triumph in a most masculinized manner, through an act of penetration. Not coincidentally, the white man in this illustration is inflicting this violence in defense of "family heritage," emblem of white heterosexuality. The white man in the illustration can sodomize a black man yet without challenging his

*Figure is not included in this publication.

heterosexual credentials. Indeed, it is precisely through this act of penetrating another man that he is defending (white) heterosexuality as an institution, much as supposedly straight, gay-bashing young men report sodomizing gay men because "homosexuality is wrong" (Comstock, 1991).

The subordination of the black man and by extension, black masculinity, in this drawing is located in the body and is accomplished through penetration. The subordinated other, a black man, is penetrated by a white man, the agent of penetration. The body of the Other is racialized and sexualized for the purpose of penetration. In a stunning reversal of the image favored by white supremacists of the black-man-as-rapist, here a white man symbolically and literally rapes a black man. Amending the centuries-old imagery of black-men-as-rapists of white women, white supremacist publications are rife with stories of white men who are raped in prisons by black men. This image, viewed in the context of these stories, can be considered an amazing instance of projection: taking white men's fear of being raped, either literally or symbolically, by a black man and inflicting this back on him.

Simultaneously, and perhaps not surprisingly, white men see themselves as in conflict with another group of men: gay men of all races. White men who engage in "homosexualism" voluntarily and openly by proclaiming a gay identity appear to be the only white men who are excluded from white male privilege in the discourse. While race and ethnicity are not highlighted in discussions of homosexuality, neither are they completely effaced. As the HIV-AIDS pandemic devastated the gay male community in 1980s and 1990s, the image of gay men within the publications became one conflated with sickness and disease. The HIV-AIDS epidemic increased the already existent hostility toward gay men and simultaneously provided a provocative symbol for what some, including many beyond members in white supremacist organizations saw as the natural link between homosexuality and disease.

The drawing featured here illuminates this link between the threat of illness and the sense of conflict between white heterosexual men and gay men of all races (See Figure 6*). In this illustration an emaciated gay man walks with a cane, while other (presumably heterosexual) figures flee in the background. Even though this man is gaunt and his clothes appear to be loose-fitting in general, the detail of his pants shows a clear indentation, representative of penetration. The caption above the drawing reads, "The Last Pitiful Squeak from Any AIDS Ravaged Fag." In a break with the conventions of distance between illustrator and illustrated, the gay man in the drawing, between gasps, makes an accusation of homophobia toward the illustrator, and, by extension, to the reader. The illustrator, in conjunction with and giving voice to the reader, responds to this accusation in a long and vitriolic diatribe, concluding with:

So SHUT UP and take your F * N' medicine, you plague ridden pansies . . . Be a F * N' man just once in your loathsome life, will ya?!! [all emphasis original] (WAR, Vol. 8(3), 1989, p. 3).

In this statement about being a "man" the illustrator unequivocally demarcates masculinity, in this instance white supremacist masculinity, as that which is *not* homosexual, with that which penetrates, rather than that which is penetrated. Central to this definition of masculinity, and its concomitant view of homosexuality, is not the contour of relationships between men, but rather the body, and more precisely the penetration of the body. In what can only be called a

*Figure is not included in this publication.

stunning juxtaposition, this drawing (Figure 6) and the previous illustration (Figure 5) appear on the same page of WAR. In the former, a white (supposedly heterosexual) man is triumphant in his masculinity through the act of penetrating a black man; in the latter, a gay, white man is stripped of his masculinity precisely *because* he is penetrated. The site of the body, and its penetration, is foremost among markers of dominance. Sexual dominance is central here and is a key element of hegemonic white supremacist masculinity.

This juxtaposition of images also highlights the contradictory nature of masculinity, or as Segal puts it, the more masculinity "asserts itself, the more it calls itself into question" (Segal, 1990, p. 123).

Conclusion

We can expand our understanding of racialized masculinities and of white supremacist discourse if we can set aside our revulsion for a moment at these images and begin to take the messages they offer seriously. In white supremacist discourse, race, class, gender and sexuality are inscribed on bodies that are racialized/sexualized as Others for the purpose of creating objects of penetration, the ultimate act of domination. The bodies in white supremacist discourse are stand-ins for larger racialized categories—whites, blacks, Jews,—and their place in the white supremacist imagination. Not coincidentally, these categories most often take on corporeality in the racialized and sexualized bodies of men.

The various racialized masculinities of white supremacist discourse—white, black, and Jewish—are constructed on the site of men's bodies within the texts. White supremacist ideology is, as Cornel West (1993) has noted, first and foremost about the degradation of black bodies in order to con-

trol them (1993); it is also about the degradation of Jewish bodies and gay bodies. And, frequently (though by no means exclusively), it is specifically about the degradation of certain men's bodies through the dominance of other men's bodies.

Sexual dominance is a key feature of white supremacist ideology. Here, I have explored the ways sexual dominance gets produced on men's bodies and this is through the act of penetration, constructed in these publications as the essence of domination itself. The racialized/sexualized bodies of men are penetrated as markers of domination, and the men who penetrate are affirmed in their dominance.

The domination portrayed here is not disconnected from broader society. White supremacist discourse utilizes extreme images that both create racism and reflect core, mainstream values of the U.S. Surely part of the explanation for why white supremacist ideologies remain intractable features of the political landscape in the U.S. (Bell, 1992; Goldberg, 1993) lies in the way white supremacy relies on class antagonism as well as notions of gender and sexuality for its justification. The challenges of the 1960s and 1970s from a variety of political movements effectively called into question not only "whiteness" (Omi & Winant, 1986), but also "white masculinity" and the normative constraints implicit in a white male heterosexual center. While such challenges have succeeded in making explicitly racist claims socially unacceptable, this change may signify that such sentiments have merely been subordinated, rather than eliminated, and given voice only in a cultural and ideological space designated as "extremist."

I am not arguing that white supremacist discourse is not extreme, it most certainly is. Rather, I contend that the widespread appearance of many white supremacist motifs in popular culture, with many of the connections between race, class, gender and sexuality laid out here still intact, suggests that such themes resonate effectively beyond the audience of avowed white supremacists. Indeed, to recall just one example, the use of the Willie Horton advertisement in the 1988 Bush campaign (or any random sample of network news broadcasts on the topic of "crime") attests, the black-man-as-beast imagery of the white supremacist drawing, "Today's Young Coon," is not far removed from mainstream politics. Just as the degrading images of women in some heterosexual pornography are rejected for pushing the bounds of excess, strikingly similar images of women are embraced when they appear in mainstream advertisements for perfume, underwear, or bathing-suit editions of men's magazines.[11] The point remains however that despite the extreme, often crude, nature of white supremacist rhetoric, this work demonstrates that, if taken seriously, the discourse can provide us with important insights into the elaborate nexus of race, class, gender and sexuality.

Finally, white supremacist discourse is classified as speech, or to use MacKinnon's phrase, "only words," and is therefore protected under the First Amendment. The repercussions of this protection are worthy of reflection. First of all, though there is much debate about precisely how this relationship works, the fact is consumers of these images *do act* on their messages with deadly consequences for their victims (Dees & Fiffer, 1993). Further, if we are to truly listen to the victims of racist hate speech, concern about who will or will not act on these images is compounded by the assaultive quality of the words themselves (Feagan & Sikes, 1994; Matsuda et al., 1993). Indeed,

the assaultive nature of the language is given still more power in a society which implicitly condones such sentiments and institutionalizes white supremacy by labeling this kind of symbolic violence "protected speech." If, as I suggest, white supremacist discourse is forged as a response to the perceived erosion of white male dominance and is an attempt to recreate what white heterosexual men imagine to be a lost world of unchallenged white supremacy, the question before us is a difficult one. And it is this: what kind of society can we imagine, and more importantly create, for ourselves, one based on exclusion and domination —such as that in white supremacist discourse—or one, perhaps only recently glimpsed, based on equality, diversity and inclusion?

Notes

1. Reich (1970), among others, have contributed to an analysis of fascism that draws on psychodynamic causes.
2. Klanwatch is a division of the Southern Poverty Law Center located in Montgomery, Alabama which monitors white supremacist groups throughout the country and maintains an extensive collection of thousands of white supremacist publications.
3. Two of the publications, *WAR* and *Racial Loyalty*, claim to have an international readership.
4. Protestant Christianity no longer serves as a unifying theme for white supremacists. Although *The Klansman, Truth at Last* (aka *Thunderbolt*), and *The Torch* all utilize Christian symbols such as the cross in their rhetoric, others, such as *NAAWP* take a decidedly secular approach (despite Duke's brief claim to born-again status) to white supremacy, while *WAR* advocates a return to pagan, Anglo-Saxon rituals for white supremacist spirituality. A truly new development in recent white supremacist organizations is Ben Klassen's C.O.T.C., which is as violently anti-Christian (*Racial Loyalty* frequently features articles on what they refer to as "BOOB's" or "Born-again Boobs") as it is anti-Semitic.

5. White supremacist organizations do not embrace identical forms of nationalism. *The Klansman, NAAWP,* and *The Torch* share a nativist, and in some sense fairly traditional, view of the U.S. and advocate strategies which operate within existing political systems (as indicated by Duke's run for public office and Robb's school for training what he hopes to be "a hundred Dukes") to advance the cause of white supremacy. Yet both *The Torch* and *NAAWP* have published calls for a division of the territory of the U.S. into racially distinct and separate nation-states. Both *WAR* and *The Thunderbolt* reflect a deep mistrust of the U.S. government, typically referred to as ZOG (Zionist Occupation Government), while *Racial Loyalty* conceives national boundaries as diversions from their global vision of a "white planet."
6. Issues of readership (how many people actually read these publications?), relative "effectiveness" (are some periodicals more "effective" in terms of recruiting or persuading readers to embrace white supremacy?), and the appropriation of white supremacist ideologies (how, precisely, are readers appropriating, or resisting, the messages contained in these texts?), are beyond the scope of this study. However, these were concerns of mine as I selected the specific publications to include in the study.
7. Of course, it is not, as many have pointed out, especially: Martin Barker, "Biology and the New Racism," pp. 18–37 in *Anatomy of Racism,* Minneapolis: University of Minnesota Press, 1988; Sander L. Gilman, *Difference and Pathology,* Ithaca, NY: Cornell University Press, 1985; and, R. C. Lewontin, Steven Rose, and Leon J. Kamin, *Not in Our Genes: Biology, Ideology, and Human Nature,* New York: Pantheon Books, 1984.
8. However, even those making such a claim do not deny the superior value of blond hair and blue eyes. They only argue that such superiority should be minimized for strategic reasons; the intention, of course, is to broaden the appeal of the white supremacist movement by broadening the definition of "white."
9. This does emerge occasionally within white supremacist literature, as in the case of Leo Frank, a Jewish man who allegedly raped and

murdered Mary Phagan, a white girl. Frank was lynched, and his guilt or innocence has been the subject of much debate. Articles featuring this story appear in *The Thunderbolt* periodically, but overall the image of Jewish men as rapists is relatively rare in contemporary white supremacist discourse.

10. The drawing is a response to the controversy in several southern states over the use of the stars and bars in state flags. Many Blacks have protested the use of the symbol as a vestige of a racist past, while many whites contend that the flag represents a proud heritage.

11. Indeed, the connection between white supremacist discourse—with its images of racialized and sexualized Others constructed primarily for white, male, heterosexual consumption—and pornography—with its images of racialized and sexualized Others constructed primarily for white, male, heterosexual consumption—is an intriguing one that should be investigated further.

References

Addams, J., & Wells-Barnett, I. B. (1901/1977). In B. Aptheker (Ed.), *Lynching and rape: An exchange of views*. (Occasional Papers Series Number Twenty-Five). San Jose, CA: American Institute for Marxist Studies.

Baldwin, J. (1963). *The fire next time*. London: Michael Joseph.

Barker, M. (1990). Biology and the new racism. In D. T. Goldberg (Ed.), *Anatomy of racism* (pp. 18–37). Minneapolis, MN: University of Minnesota Press.

Bell, D. (1992). *Faces at the bottom of the well: The permanence of racism*. New York: Basic Books.

Bordo, S. (1993). Reading the male body. *Michigan Quarterly Review*, 696–737.

Brod, H. (Ed.). (1987). *The making of masculinities: The new men's studies*. Boston: Allen and Unwin.

Brod, H. (Ed.). (1988). *A mensch among men*. Freedom, CA: The Crossing Press.

Collins, P. H. (1990). *Black feminist thought: Knowledge, consciousness, and the politics of empowerment*. Boston: Unwin Hyman.

Comstock, G. D. (1991). *Violence against lesbians and gay men*. New York: Columbia University Press.

Connell, R. W. (1987). *Gender and power: Society, the person and sexual politics*.

Palo Alto, CA: Stanford University Press.

Connell, R. W. (1992). A very straight gay: Masculinity, homosexual experience, and the dynamics of gender. *American Sociological Review*, 57(December), 735–751.

Dees, M., & Fiffer, S. (1993). *Hate on trial: The case against America's most dangerous neo-nazi*. New York: Scribner.

Dollard, J. (1937). *Caste and class in a Southern town*. New York: Doubleday.

Dworkin, A. (1988). The sexual mythology of anti-semitism. In H. Brod (Ed.), *A mensch among men* (pp. 118–123). Freedom, CA: The Crossing Press.

Dworkin, A. (1981). *Pornography: Men possessing women*. New York: Perigee.

Fanon, F. (1970). *Black skin, white masks*. London: Paladin.

Feagin, J. R., & Sikes, M. (1994). *Living With Racism*. New York: Beacon Press.

Frankenberg, R. (1994). *White women, race matters: The social construction of whiteness*. Minneapolis: University of Minnesota.

Franklin, C. W., II. (1984). *The changing definition of masculinity*. New York: Plenum.

Franklin, C. W., II. (1988). *Men and society*. Chicago: Nelson-Hall.

Gates, D. (1993). White male paranoia: Are they the newest victims or just bad sports? *Newsweek*, March 29, 48–54.

Gibson, W. J. (1994). *Warrior dreams: Paramilitary culture in post-Vietnam America*. New York: Hill and Wang.

Gilman, S. L. (1985). *Difference and pathology: Stereotypes of sexuality, race, and madness*. Ithaca, NY: Cornell University Press.

Goldberg, D. T. (1990). *Anatomy of racism*. Minneapolis: University of Minnesota.

Goldberg, D. T. (1993). *Racist culture: Philosophy and the politics of meaning*. Oxford: Blackwell.

Hall, J. D. (1979). *Revolt against chivalry: Jessie Daniel Ames and the women's campaign against lynching*. New York: Columbia University Press.

Harper, S. (1994). "Welfare Queens" and Vanessa Williams: The construction of black women in white supremacist publications. Submitted for publication.

Hernton, C. (1965). *Sex and racism in America*. New York: Doubleday.

Hoch, P. (1979). *White hero, black beast*. London: Pluto Press.

Jeffords, S. (1989). *The remasculinization of America: Gender and the Vietnam*

War. Bloomington: University of Indiana Press.

Kimmel, M. S. (Ed.). (1987). *Changing men: New directions in research on men and masculinity*. Newbury Park, CA: Sage.

Kimmel, M. S. (Ed.). (1991). *Men confront pornography*. New York: Meridian.

Kimmel, M. S., & Messner, M. A. (Eds.). (1989). *Men's lives*. New York: Macmillan.

Lawrence, C. R., III. (1993). If he hollers let him go: Regulating racist speech on campus. In M. J. Matsuda et al. (Ed.), *Words that wound* (pp. 53–88). Boulder: Westview Press.

Lewontin, R. C., Rose, S., & Kamin, L. J. (1984). *Not in our genes: Biology, ideology, and human nature*. New York: Pantheon Books.

MacKinnon, C. A. (1993). *Only words*. Cambridge Harvard University Press.

Matsuda, M. J., Lawrence, C. R. III, Delgado, R., & Crenshaw, K. W. (1993). *Words that wound: Critical race theory, assaultive speech, and the first amendment*. Boulder: Westview Press.

Mosse, G. L. (1978). *Toward the final solution: A history of European racism*. New York: Harper & Row.

Omi, M., & Winant, H. (1986). *Racial formation in the United States: From the 1960s to the 1980s*. New York: Routledge & Kegan Paul.

Reich, W. (1970). *The mass psychology of fascism*. New York: Farrar, Straus, and Giroux.

Segal, L. (1990). *Slow motion: Changing masculinities, changing men*. London: Virago.

Smith, L. (1949). *Killers of the dream*. New York: W. W. Norton & Co.

Stember, C. H. (1976). *Sexual racism: The emotional barrier to an integrated society*. New York: Elsevier.

Theweleit, K. (1987). *Male fantasies: Women, floods, bodies, history* (S. Conway, trans.). Minneapolis: University of Minnesota Press.

Tonry, M. (1995). *Malign neglect: Race, crime and punishment in America*. New York: Oxford University Press.

WAR. (1989). Vol. 8(2).

WAR. (1989). Vol. 8(3).

West, C. (1993). *Race matters*. Boston: Beacon Press.

Wetherell, M., & Potter, J. (1992). *Mapping the language of racism: Discourse and the legitimation of exploitation*. New York: Columbia University Press.

Article Review Form at end of book.

How did male chauvinism and white racism work together to justify the lynching of Black men by whites? How might strategies for combating lynching be modified to combat other forms of racially motivated violence today?

The Mind That Burns in Each Body:

Women, Rape, and Racial Violence

Jacquelyn Dowd Hall

I. Hostility Focused on Human Flesh

Florida to Burn Negro at Stake: Sex Criminal Seized from Jail, Will Be Mutilated, Set Afire in Extra-Legal Vengeance for Deed
> —Dothan [*Alabama*] Eagle,
> *October 26, 1934*

After taking the nigger to the woods . . . they cut off his penis. He was made to eat it. Then they cut off his testicles and made him eat them and say he liked it.

> —*Member of a lynch mob, 1934*

Lynching, like rape, has not yet been given its history. Perhaps it has been too easily relegated to the shadows where "poor white" stereotypes dwell. Perhaps the image of absolute victimization it creates has been too difficult to reconcile with what we know about black resilience and resistance. Yet the impact of lynching, both as practice and as symbol, can hardly be underestimated. Between 1882 and 1946 almost 5,000 people died by lynching. The lynching of Emmett Till in 1955 for whistling at a white woman, the killing of three

civil rights workers in Mississippi in the 1960s, and the hanging of a black youth in Alabama in 1981 all illustrate the persistence of ritual violence in the service of racial control, a tradition intimately bound up with the politics of sexuality.

Vigilantism originated on the eighteenth-century frontier, where it filled a vacuum in law enforcement. Rather than passing with the frontier, however, lynching was incorporated in the distinctive legal system of Southern slave society.[2] In the nineteenth century, the industrializing North moved toward a modern criminal justice system in which police, courts, and prisons administered an impersonal, bureaucratic rule of law designed to uphold property rights and discipline urban workers. The South, in contrast, maintained order through a system of deference and customary authority in which all whites had police power over all blacks, slave owners meted out plantation justice undisturbed by any generalized rule of law, and the state encouraged vigilantism as part of its overall reluctance to maintain a system of formal authority that would have undermined the mas-

ter's prerogatives. The purpose of one system was class control; of the other, control over a slave population. And each tradition continued into the period after the Civil War. In the North, factory-like penitentiaries warehoused displaced members of the industrial proletariat. The South maintained higher rates of personal violence than any other region in the country and lynching crossed over the line from informal law enforcement into outright political terrorism.

White supremacy, of course, did not rest on force alone. Routine institutional arrangements denied to the freedmen and women the opportunity to own land, the right to vote, access to education, and participation in the administration of the law. Lynching reached its height during the battles of Reconstruction and the Populist revolt; once a new system of disenfranchisement, debt peonage, and segregation was firmly in place, mob violence gradually declined. Yet until World War I, the average number of lynchings never fell below two or three a week. Through the 1920s and '30s, mob

Jacquelyn Dowd Hall, "The Mind That Burns in Each Body: Women, Rape, and Racial Violence," *Southern Exposure*, 1985, pp. 61–71 in *Powers of Desire: The Politics of Sexuality*, eds. Ann Snitow, Christine Stansell, Sharon Thompson, Monthly Review Press, 1983. Reprinted by permission.

violence reinforced white dominance by providing planters with a quasi-official way of enforcing labor contracts and crop lien laws, and local officials with a means of extracting deference, regardless of the letter of the law. Individuals may have lynched for their own twisted reasons, but the practice continued only with tacit official consent.[3]

Most important, lynching served as a tool of psychological intimidation aimed at blacks as a group. Unlike official authority, the lynch mob was unlimited in its capriciousness. With care and vigilance, an individual might avoid situations that landed him in the hands of the law. But a lynch mob could strike anywhere, any time. Once the brush fire of rumor was ignited, a manhunt organized, and the local paper began printing special editions announcing a lynching in progress, there could be few effective reprieves. If the intended victim could not be found, an innocent bystander might serve as well. It was not simply the threat of death that gave lynching its repressive power. Even as outbreaks of mob violence declined in frequency, they were increasingly accompanied by torture and sexual mutilation.

At the same time, the expansion of communications and the development of photography in the late nineteenth and early twentieth centuries gave reporting a vividness it had never had before. The lurid evocation of human suffering implicated white readers in each act of aggression and drove home to blacks the consequences of powerlessness. Like whipping under slavery, lynching was an instrument of coercion intended to impress not only the immediate victim but all who saw or heard about the event. And the mass media spread the imagery of rope and faggot far beyond the community in which each lynching took place.

Writing about his youth in the rural South in the 1920s, Richard Wright describes the terrible climate of fear: "The things that influenced my conduct as a Negro did not have to happen to me directly; I needed but to hear of them to feel their full effects in the deepest layers of my consciousness. Indeed, the white brutality that I had not seen was a more effective control of my behavior than that which I knew. The actual experience would have let me see the realistic outlines of what was really happening, but as long as it remained something terrible and yet remote, something whose horror and blood might descend upon me at any moment, I was compelled to give my entire imagination over to it."[4]

A penis cut off and stuffed in a victim's mouth. A crowd of thousands watching a black man scream in pain. Such incidents did not have to occur very often, or be witnessed directly, to be burned indelibly into the mind.

II. Never Against Her Will

White men have said over and over— and we have believed it because it was repeated so often—that not only was there no such thing as a chaste Negro woman—but that a Negro woman could not be assaulted, that it was never against her will.

—*Jessie Daniel Ames (1936)*

Schooled in the struggle against sexual rather than racial violence, contemporary feminists may nevertheless find familiar this account of lynching's political function, for analogies between rape and lynching have often surfaced in the literature of the anti-rape movement. To carry such analogies too far would be to fall into the error of radical feminist writing that misconstrues the realities of racism in the effort to illuminate sexual subordination.[5]

It is the suggestion of this essay, however, that there is a significant resonance between these two forms of violence. We are only beginning to understand the web of connections among racism, attitudes toward women, and sexual ideologies. The purpose of looking more closely at the dynamics of repressive violence is not to reduce sexual assault and mob murder to static equivalents but to illuminate some of the strands of that tangled web.

The association between lynching and rape emerges most clearly in their parallel use in racial subordination. As Diane K. Lewis has pointed out, in a patriarchal society, black men constituted a potential challenge to the established order.[6] Laws were formulated primarily to exclude black men from exercising adult male prerogatives in the public sphere, and lynching meshed with these legal mechanisms of exclusion.

Black women represented a more ambiguous threat. They too were denied access to the politico-jural domain, but since they shared this exclusion with women in general, its maintenance engendered less anxiety and required less force. Lynching served primarily to dramatize hierarchies among men. In contrast, the violence directed at black women illustrates the double jeopardy of race and sex. The records of the Freedmen's Bureau and the oral histories collected by the Federal Writers' Project testify to the sexual atrocities endured by black women as whites sought to reassert their command over the newly freed slaves. Black women were sometimes executed by lynch mobs, but more routinely they served as targets of sexual assault.

Like vigilantism, the sexual exploitation of black women had been institutionalized under slavery. Whether seized through outright force or granted within the master-slave relation, the sexual access of white men to black women was a cornerstone of patriarchal power in the South. It was used as a punishment or demanded in exchange for leniency. Like other forms of deference and conspicuous consumption, it buttressed planter hegemony. And it served the practical economic purpose of replenishing the slave labor supply.

After the Civil War, the informal sexual arrangements of slavery shaded into the use of rape as a political weapon, and the special vulnerability of black women helped shape the ex-slaves' struggle for the prerequisites of freedom. Strong family bonds had survived the adversities of slavery; after freedom, the black family served as a bulwark against a racist society. Indeed, the sharecropping system that replaced slavery as the South's chief mode of production grew in part from the desire of blacks to withdraw from gang labor and gain control over their own work, family lives, and bodily integrity. The sharecropping family enabled women to escape white male supervision, devote their productive and reproductive powers to their own families, and protect themselves from sexual assault.[7]

Most studies of racial violence have paid little attention to the particular suffering of women.[8] Even rape has been seen less as an aspect of sexual oppression than as a transaction between white and black men. Certainly Claude Levi-Strauss's insight that men use women as verbs with which to communicate with one another (rape being a means of communicating defeat to the men of a conquered tribe) helps explain the extreme viciousness of sexual violence in the post-emancipation era.[9] Rape *was* in part a reaction to the effort of the freedman to assume the role of patriarch, able to provide for and protect his family. Nevertheless, as writers like Susan Griffin, Susan Brownmiller, and others have made clear, rape is first and foremost a crime against women.[10] Rape sent a message to black men, but more centrally it expressed male sexual attitudes in a culture both racist and patriarchal.

Recent historians of Victorian sexuality have traced the process by which a belief in female "passionlessness" replaced an older notion of women's dangerous sexual power.[11] Even at the height of the "cult of true womanhood" in the nineteenth century, however, views of women's sexuality remained ambivalent and double-edged. The association between women and nature, the dread of women's treacherous carnality persisted, rooted, as Dorothy Dinnerstein persuasively argues, in the earliest experiences of infancy.

In the United States, the fear and fascination of female sexuality was projected onto black women; the passionless lady arose in symbiosis with the primitively sexual slave. House slaves often served as substitute mothers; at a black woman's breast white male babies experienced absolute dependence on a being who was both a source of wish-fulfilling joy and of grief-producing disappointment. In adulthood, such men could find in this black woman a ready object for the mixture of rage and desire that so often underlies male heterosexuality. The black woman, already in chains, was sexually available, unable to make claims for support or concern; by dominating her, men could replay the infant's dream of unlimited access to the mother.[12]

The economic and political challenge posed by the black patriarch might be met with death by lynching, but when the black woman seized the opportunity to turn her maternal and sexual resources to the benefit of her own family, sexual violence met her assertion of will. Thus rape reasserted white dominance and control in the private arena as lynching reasserted hierarchical arrangements in the public transactions of men.

III. Lynching's Double Message

The crowds from here that went over to see [Lola Cannidy, the alleged rape victim in the Claude Neal lynching of 1934] said he was so large he could not assault her until he took his knife and cut her, and also had either cut or bit one of her breast [sic] off.

—Letter to Mrs. W. P. Cornell, October 29, 1934, Association of Southern Women for the Prevention of Lynching Papers

. . . more than rape itself, the fear of rape permeates our lives . . . and the best defense against this is not to be, to deny being in the body, as a self, to . . . avert your gaze, make yourself, as a presence in the world, less felt.

—Susan Griffin, Rape: The Power of Consciousness (1979)

In the 1920s and 1930s, the industrial revolution spread through the South, bringing a demand for more orderly forms of law enforcement. Men in authority, anxious to create a favorable business climate, began to withdraw their tacit approval of extralegal violence. Yet lynching continued, particularly in rural areas, and even as white moderates criticized lynching in the abstract they continued to justify outbreaks of mob violence for the one special crime of sexual assault.

For most white Americans, the association between lynching and rape called to mind not twin forms of white violence against black men and women, but a very different image: the black rapist, "a monstrous beast, crazed with lust";[13] the white victim—young, blond, virginal; her manly Anglo-Saxon avengers. Despite the pull of modernity, the emotional logic of lynching remained: only swift, sure violence, unhampered by legalities, could protect white women from sexual assault.

The "protection of white womanhood" was a pervasive fixture of racist ideology. In 1889 a well-known historian offered this commonly accepted rationale for lynching: black men find "something strangely alluring and seductive . . . in the appearance of the white woman; they are aroused and stimulated by its foreignness to their experience of sexual pleasures, and it moves them to gratify their lust at any cost and in spite of every obstacle."

In 1937, echoing an attitude that characterized most local newspapers, the *Daily News* in Jackson, Mississippi, published what it felt was the *coup de grace* to anti-lynching critics: "What would you do if your wife, daughter, or one of your loved ones was ravished? You'd probably be right there with the mob." Two years later, 65 percent of the white respondents in an anthropological survey believed that lynching was justified in cases of sexual assault.[14] Despite its tenacity, however, the myth of the black rapist was never founded on objective reality. Less than a quarter of lynch victims were even accused of rape or attempted rape. Down to the present, almost every study has underlined the fact that rape is overwhelmingly an intraracial crime, and the victims are more often black than white.[15]

A major strategy of anti-lynching reformers, beginning with Ida B. Wells-Barnett in the 1880s and continuing with Walter White of the NAACP and Jessie Daniel Ames of the Association of Southern Women for the Prevention of Lynching, was to use such facts to undermine the rationalizations for mob violence. But the emotional circuit between interracial rape and lynching lay beyond the reach of factual refutation. A black man did not literally have to attempt sexual assault for whites to perceive some transgression of caste mores as a sexual threat. White women were the forbidden fruit, the untouchable property, the ultimate symbol of white male power. To break the racial rules was to conjure up an image of black over white, of a world turned upside down.

Again, women were a means of communication, and the rhetoric of protection—like the rape of black women—reflected a power struggle among men. But impulses toward women as well as toward blacks were played out in the drama of racial violence. The fear of rape was more than a hypocritical excuse for lynching; rather, the two phenomena were intimately intertwined. The "Southern rape complex" functioned as a means of both sexual and racial suppression.[16]

For whites, the archetypal lynching for rape can be seen as a dramatization of cultural themes, a story of the social arrangements and psychological strivings that lay beneath the surface of everyday life. The story such rituals told about the place of white women in Southern society was subtle, contradictory, and demeaning. The frail victim, leaning on the arms of her male relatives, might be brought to the scene of the crime, there to identify her assailant and witness his execution. This was a moment of humiliation. A woman who had just been raped, or who had been apprehended in a clandestine interracial affair, or whose male relatives were pretending that she had been raped, stood on display before the whole community. Here was the quintessential Woman as Victim: polluted, "ruined for life," the object of fantasy and secret contempt. Humiliation, however, mingled with heightened worth as she played for a moment the role of the Fair Maiden violated and avenged.

Only a small percentage of lynchings revolved around charges of sexual assault, but those that did received by far the most attention and publicity—indeed, they gripped the white imagination far out of proportion to their statistical significance. Rape and rumors of rape became the folk pornography of the Bible Belt. As stories spread the rapist became not just a black man but a ravenous brute, the victim a beautiful young virgin. The experience of the woman was described in minute and progressively embellished detail, a public fantasy that implied a group participation in the rape as cathartic as the subsequent lynching. White men might see in "lynch law" their ideal selves: patriarchs, avengers, righteous protectors. But, being men themselves, and sometimes even rapists, they must also have seen themselves in the lynch mob's prey.

The lynch mob in pursuit of the black rapist represented the trade-off implicit in the code of chivalry: for the right of the Southern lady to protection presupposed her obligation to obey. The connotations of wealth and family background attached to the position of the lady in the antebellum South faded in the twentieth century, but the power of "ladyhood" as a value construct remained. The term denoted chastity, frailty, graciousness.

"A lady," noted one social psychologist, "is always in a state of becoming: one acts like a lady, one attempts to be a lady, but one never *is* a lady." Internalized by the individual, this ideal regulated behavior and restricted interaction with the world.[17] If a woman passed the tests of ladyhood, she could tap into the reservoir of protectiveness and shelter known as Southern chivalry. Women who abandoned secure, if circumscribed, social roles forfeited the claim to personal security. Together the practice of ladyhood and the etiquette of chivalry controlled white women's behavior even as they guarded caste lines.

Pro-slavery theorist Thomas R. Dew spelled out this dialectic. The "essence of manhood," he wrote, is "predation." The essence of womanhood is "allure." Only the rise of gallantry and the patriarchal family offered a haven from male aggression. Stripped to its bare essentials, the difference between the sexes was the opposition between the potential rapist and the potential victim of sexual assault, and the family metaphor that justified slavery offered the exchange of dependence for protection to the mistress as well as to the slaves. Dew's notion of female sexuality, however, did not deny a woman passions of her own. On the contrary, because her role was not to seek, "but to be sought . . . not to woo, but to be wooed," she was forced to suppress her "most violent feelings . . . her most ardent desires."[18] In general, the law of rape expressed profound distrust of women, demanding evidence of "utmost resistance," corroboration by other witnesses in addition to the victim's word, and proof of the victim's chastity—all contrary to the rules of evidence in other forms of violent crime.

In sharp contrast, however, when a black man and a white woman were concerned, intercourse was prima facie evidence of rape. The presiding judge in the 1931 Scottsboro trial, in which nine black youths were accused of rape, had this to say: "Where the woman charged to have been raped, as in this case is a white woman, there is a very strong presumption under the law that she would not and did not yield voluntarily to intercourse with the defendant, a Negro; and this is true, whatever the station in life the prosecutrix may occupy, whether she be the most despised, ignorant and abandoned woman of the community, or the spotless virgin and daughter of a prominent home of luxury and learning."[19]

Lynching, then, like laws against intermarriage, masked uneasiness over the nature of white women's desires. It aimed not only to engender fear of sexual assault but also to prevent voluntary unions. It upheld the comforting fiction that at least in relation to

black men, white women were always objects and never agents of sexual desire.

Although the nineteenth-century women's movement for the most part advocated higher moral standards for men, not sexual liberation for women, opponents insisted that it threatened the family and painted feminists as spinsters or libertines, sexual deviants in either case. It may be no accident, then, that the vision of the black man as a threatening beast flourished during the first phase of the Southern women's rights movement, a fantasy of aggression against boundary-transgressing women as well as a weapon of terror against blacks.[20]

When women in the 1920s and 1930s did begin to assert their right to sexual expression and to challenge the double standard Thomas Dew's injunctions implied, inheritors of the plantation legend responded with explicit attacks that revealed the sanctions at the heart of the chivalric ideal. William Faulkner's *Sanctuary*, published in 1931, typified a common literary reaction to the fall of the lady. The corncob rape of Temple Drake—a "new woman" of the 1920s—was the ultimate revenge against the abdicating white virgin. Her fate represented the "desecration of a cult object," the implicit counterpoint to the idealization of women in a patriarchal society.[21]

IV. Lady Insurrectionists

The lady insurrectionists gathered together in one of our southern cities. . . . They said calmly that they were not afraid of being raped; as for their sacredness, they would take care of it themselves; they did not need the chivalry of lynching to protect them and did not want it.

—*Lillian Smith,* Killers of the Dream *(1949)*

On November 1, 1930, 26 white women from six Southern states

met in Atlanta to form the Association of Southern Women for the Prevention of Lynching. Organized by Texas suffragist Jessie Daniel Ames, the association had a central, ideological goal: to break the circuit between the tradition of chivalry and the practice of mob murder. The association was part of a broader interracial movement; its contribution to the decline of lynching must be put in the perspective of the leadership role played by blacks in the national anti-lynching campaign. But it would be a mistake to view the association simply as a white women's auxiliary to black-led struggles. Rather, it represented an acceptance of accountability for a racist mythology that white women had not created but that they nevertheless served, a point hammered home by black women's admonitions that "when Southern white women get ready to stop lynching, it will be stopped and not before."[22]

Jessie Ames stood on the brink between two worlds. Born in 1883 in a small town in East Texas, a regional hotbed of mob violence, she directed the anti-lynching campaign from Atlanta, capital of the New South. She drew eclectically on the nineteenth-century female reform tradition and advocated an implicitly feminist anti-racism that looked backward to the abolitionist movement as well as forward to feminists of our own times.

Ames had come to maturity in a transitional phase of the women's movement, when female reformers used the group consciousness and Victorian sense of themselves as especially moral beings to justify a great wave of female institution building. When Jessie Ames turned from suffrage to the reform of race relations, she looked naturally to this heritage for her constituency and tactics.

The association drew its members from among small-town church women who had been schooled for decades in running their own affairs within YWCAs, women's clubs, and missionary societies. These women were sensitized by the temperance and suffrage movements to a politics that simultaneously stressed domestic order and women's rights.[23] Ames's strategy for change called for enfranchised women to exercise moral influence over the would-be lynchers in their own homes, political influence over the public officials who collaborated with them, and cultural influence over the editors and politicians who created an atmosphere where mob violence flourished. Like Frances Willard in the temperance campaign, she sought to extend women's moral guardianship into quintessentially masculine affairs.

Ames's tenacity and the emotional energy of her campaign derived from her perception that lynching was a women's issue: not only an obstacle to regional development and an injustice to blacks, but also an insult to white women. Like black women leaders before her, who had perceived that the same sexual stereotyping that allowed black women to be exploited caused black men to be feared, she challenged both racist and patriarchal ideas.[24] Disputing the notion that blacks provoked mob action by raping white women, association members traced lynching to its roots in white supremacy.[25]

More central to their campaign was an effort to dissociate the image of the lady from its connotations of sexual vulnerability and retaliatory violence. If lynching held a covert message for white women as well as an overt one for blacks, then the anti-lynching association represented a woman-centered reply. Lynching, it proclaimed, far from offering a shield against sexual assault, served as a weapon of both racial and sexual terror, planting fear in women's minds and dependency in their

hearts. It thrust them into the role of personal property or sexual objects, ever threatened by black men's lust, ever in need of white men's protection. By asserting their identity as autonomous citizens, requiring not the paternalism of chivalry but the equal protection of the law, association members resisted the part assigned to them.

If, as Susan Brownmiller proclaims, the larger anti-lynching movement paid little attention to lynching's counterpart, the rape of black women, the women's association could not ignore the issue. In 1920 Carrie Parks Johnson, a white interracialist and women's rights leader who had come to her understanding of racial issues through pioneering meetings with black women, warned a white male audience: "The race problem can never be solved as long as the white man goes unpunished [for interracial sex], while the Negro is burned at the stake. I shall say no more, for I am sure you need not have anything more said. When the white men of the South have come to that position, a single standard for both men and women, then you will accomplish something in this great problem."[26]

In the winter of 1931, Jessie Daniel Ames called a meeting of black and white women for an explicit discussion of the split female image and the sexual double standard. The women, she thought, should gather in closed session with no men present "because there are some vices of Southern life which contribute subtly to [lynching] that we want to face by ourselves." The black leader Nannie Burroughs agreed: "All meetings with white and colored women on this question should be held behind closed doors and men should not be admitted."

The group explored the myths of black women's promiscuity and white women's purity, and noted how this split image created a soci-

ety that "considers an assault by a white man as a moral lapse upon his part, better ignored and forgotten, while an assault by a Negro against a white woman is a hideous crime punishable with death by law or lynching." Relationships among women interracialists were far from egalitarian, nor could they always overcome the impediments to what Ames called "free and frank" discussion.[27] Yet on occasions like this one the shared experience of gender opened the way for consciousness-raising communication across the color line.

If such discussions of male behavior had to be held behind closed doors, even more treacherous was the question of sex between black men and white women. In 1892 Memphis anti-lynching reformer and black women's club leader Ida B. Wells-Barnett was threatened with death and run out of town for proclaiming that behind many lynchings lay consensual interracial affairs. More than 60 years later, in the wake of the famous Scottsboro case, Jessie Daniel Ames began delving beneath the surface of lynchings in which white women were involved. Like Wells-Barnett, she found that black men were sometimes executed not for rape, but for interracial sex. And she used that information to disabuse association members of one of the white South's central fictions: that, as a Mississippi editor put it, there had never been a Southern white woman so depraved as to "bestow her favors on a black man."[28]

But what of lynching cases in which rape actually had occurred? Here association leaders could only fall back on a call for law and order, for they knew from their own experience that the fear engendered in their constituency by what some could bring themselves to call only "the unspeakable crime" was all too real. "Whether their own minds perceive danger where none exists, or whether the fears have been put in their minds by men's fears," Ames commented, women could not but see themselves as potential victims of black assault.[29] It would be left to a future generation to point out that the chief danger to white women came from white men and to see rape in general as a feminist concern. Association leaders could only exorcise their own fears of male aggression by transferring the means of violence from mobs to the state and debunking the myth of the black rapist.

In the civil rights movement of the 1960s, white women would confront the sexual dimension of racism and racial violence by asserting their right to sexual relationships with black men. Antilynching reformers of the 1930s obviously took a very different approach. They abhorred male violence and lynching's eroticism of death, and asserted against them a feminine standard of personal and public morality. They portrayed themselves as moral beings and independent citizens rather than as vulnerable sexual objects, and the core of their message lay more in what they were than in what they said: Southern ladies who needed only their own rectitude to protect them from interracial sex and only the law to guard them from sexual assault. When Jessie Ames referred to "the crown of chivalry that has been pressed like a crown of thorns on our heads," she issued a cry of protest that belongs to the struggle for both racial and sexual emancipation.[30]

V. The Decline of Chivalry

As male supremacy becomes ideologically untenable, incapable of justifying itself as protection, men assert their domination more directly, in fantasies and occasionally in acts of raw violence.

—*Christopher Lasch*, Marxist Perspectives (1978)

In the 1970s, for the second time in the nation's history, rape again attracted widespread public attention. The obsession with interracial rape, which peaked at the turn of the nineteenth century but lingered from the close of the Civil War into the 1930s, became a magnet for racial and sexual oppression during that period. Today the issue of rape has crystallized important feminist concerns.

Rape emerged as a feminist issue as women developed an independent politics that made sexuality and personal life a central arena of struggle. First in consciousness-raising groups where autobiography became a politicizing technique, then in public "speakouts," women broke what in retrospect seems a remarkable silence about a pervasive aspect of female experience. From that beginning flowed both an analysis that held rape to be a political act by which men affirm their power over women, and strategies for change that ranged from the feminist self-help methods of rape crisis centers to institutional reform of the criminal justice system and medical care systems. After 1976 the movement broadened to include wife-battering, sexual harassment, and, following the lead of Robin Morgan's claim that "pornography is the theory, rape the practice," media images of women.[31]

By the time Susan Brownmiller's *Against Our Will: Men, Women and Rape* gained national attention in 1975, she could speak to and for a feminist constituency already sensitized to the issue by years of practical, action-oriented work. Her book can be faulted for supporting a notion of universal patriarchy and timeless sexual victimization; it leaves no room for understanding the reasons for women's collaboration, their own sources of power (both self-generated and derived), the class and racial differences in their experience of discrimination and sexual danger. But it was an important milestone, pointing the way for re-

search into a subject that has consistently been trivialized and ignored. Many grassroots activists would demur from Brownmiller's assertion that all men are potential rapists, but they share her understanding of the continuum between sexism and sexual assault.[32]

The demand for control over one's own body—control over whether, when, and with whom one has children, control over how one's sexuality is expressed—is central to the feminist project because, as Rosalind Petchesky persuasively argues, it is essential to "a sense of being a person, with personal and bodily integrity," able to engage in conscious activity and to participate in social life.[33]

It is this right to bodily integrity and self-determination that rape, and the fear of rape, so thoroughly undermine. Rape's devastating effect on individuals derives not so much from the sexual nature of the crime (and anti-rape activists have been concerned to revise the idea that rape is a "fate worse than death" whose victims, if no longer "ruined for life," are at least so traumatized that they must rely for recovery on therapeutic help rather than on their own resources) as from the experience of helplessness and loss of control, the sense of one's self as an object of rage. And women who may never be raped share, by chronic attrition, in the same helplessness, "otherness," lack of control. The struggle against rape, like the anti-lynching movement, addresses not only external dangers but also internal consequences: the bodily muting, the self-censorship that limits one's capacity to "walk freely in the world."[34]

The focus on rape emerged from the internal dynamics of feminist thought and practice. But it was also a response to an objective increase in the crime. From 1969 to 1974 the number of rapes rose 49 percent, a greater increase than for any other violent crime.

Undoubtedly rape statistics reflect general demographic and criminal trends, as well as a greater willingness of victims to report sexual attacks (although observers agree that rape is still the most underreported of crimes).[35] But there can be no doubt that rape is a serious threat and that it plays a prominent role in women's subordination. Using recent high-quality survey data, Allan Griswold Johnson has estimated that, at a minimum, 20 to 30 percent of girls now 12 years old will suffer a violent sexual attack sometime in their lives. A woman is as likely to be raped as she is to experience a divorce or to be diagnosed as having cancer.[36]

In a recent anthology on women and pornography, Tracey A. Gardner has drawn a parallel between the wave of lynching that followed Reconstruction and the increase in rapes in an era of antifeminist backlash.[37] Certainly, as women enter the work force, postpone marriage, live alone or as single heads of households, they become easier targets for sexual assault. But observations like Gardner's go further, linking the intensification of sexual violence directly to the feminist challenge. Such arguments come dangerously close to blaming the victim for the crime. But they may also contain a core of truth. Sociological research on rape has only recently begun, and we do not have studies explaining the function and frequency of the crime under various historical conditions; until that work is done we cannot with certainty assess the current situation. Yet it seems clear that just as lynching ebbed and flowed with new modes of racial control, rape—both as act and idea—cannot be divorced from changes in the sexual terrain.

In 1940 Jessie Ames released to the press a statement that, for the first time in her career, the South could claim a "lynchless year," and in 1942, convinced that lynching was no longer widely condoned in the name of white womanhood, she allowed the Association of Southern Women for the Prevention of Lynching to pass quietly from the scene. The women's efforts, the larger, black-led anti-lynching campaign, black migration from the rural South, the spread of industry—these and other developments contributed to the decline of vigilante justice. Blacks continued to be victimized by covert violence and routinized court procedures that amounted to "legal lynchings." But after World War II, public lynchings—announced in the papers, openly accomplished, and tacitly condoned—no longer haunted the land, and the black rapist ceased to be a fixture of political campaigns and newspaper prose.

This change in the rhetoric and form of racial violence reflected new attitudes toward women as well as toward blacks. By the 1940s few Southern leaders were willing, as Jessie Ames put it, to "lay themselves open to ridicule" by defending lynching on the grounds of gallantry, in part because gallantry itself had lost conviction.[38] The same process of economic development and national integration that encouraged the South to adopt Northern norms of authority and control undermined the chivalric ideal. Industrial capitalism on the one hand and women's assertion of independence on the other weakened paternalism and with it the conventions of protective deference.[39]

This is not to say that the link between racism and sexism was broken; relations between white women and black men continued to be severely penalized, and black men, to the present, have drawn disproportionate punishment for sexual assault. The figures speak for themselves: of the 455 men executed for rape since 1930, 405 were black and almost all the complainants were white.[40] Nevertheless, "the protection of white womanhood" rang more hollow in the postwar New South and the fear of interracial rape became a subdued theme in the nation at large rather than an openly articulated regional obsession.

The social feminist mainstream, of which Jessie Ames and the anti-lynching association were a part, thus chipped away at a politics of gallantry that locked white ladies in the home under the guise of protecting them from the world. But because such reformers held to the genteel trapping of their role even as they asserted their autonomous citizenship, they offered reassurance that women's influence could be expanded without mortal danger to male prerogatives and power.

Contemporary feminists have eschewed some of the comforting assumptions of their nineteenth-century predecessors: women's passionlessness, their limitation to social housekeeping, their exclusive responsibility for childrearing and housekeeping. They have couched their revolt in explicit ideology and unladylike behavior. Meanwhile, as Barbara Ehrenreich has argued, Madison Avenue has perverted the feminist message into the threatening image of the sexually and economically liberated woman. The result is a shift toward the rapaciousness that has always mixed unstably with sentimental exaltation and concern. Rape has emerged more clearly into the sexual domain, a crime against women most often committed by men of their own race rather than a right of the powerful over women of a subordinate group or a blow by black men against white women's possessors.[41]

It should be emphasized, however, that the connection between feminism and the upsurge of rape lies not so much in women's gains but in their assertion of rights within a context of economic vulnerability and relative powerlessness. In a perceptive article published in 1901, Jane Addams traced lynching in part to "the feeling of the former slave owner to his former slave, whom he is now bidden to regard as his fellow citizen."[42] Blacks in the post-Reconstruction era were able to express will and individuality, to wrest from their former masters certain concessions and build for themselves supporting institutions. Yet they lacked the resources to protect themselves from economic exploitation and mob violence.

Similarly, contemporary feminist efforts have not yet succeeded in overcoming women's isolation, their economic and emotional dependence on men, their cultural training toward submission. There are few restraints against sexual aggression, since up to 90 percent of rapes go unreported, 50 percent of assailants who are reported are never caught, and seven out of 10 prosecutions end in acquittal.[43] Provoked by the commercialization of sex, cut loose from traditional community restraints, and "bidden to regard as his fellow citizen" a female being whose subordination has deep roots in the psyches of both sexes, men turn with impunity to the use of sexuality as a means of asserting dominance and control. Such fear and rage are condoned when channeled into right-wing attacks on women's claim to a share in public power and control over the bodies. Inevitably they also find expression in less acceptable behavior. Rape, like lynching, flourishes in an atmosphere in which official policies toward members of a subordinate group give individuals tacit permission to hurt and maim.

In 1972 Anne Braden, a Southern white woman and long-time activist in civil rights struggles, expressed her fear that the new anti-rape movement might find itself "objectively on the side of the most reactionary social forces" unless it heeded a lesson from history. In a pamphlet entitled *Open Letter to Southern White Women*—much circulated in regional women's liberation circles at the time—she urged anti-rape activists to remember the long pattern of racist manipulation of rape fears. She called on white women, "for their own liberation, to refuse any longer to be used, to act in the tradition of Jessie Daniel Ames and the white women who fought in an earlier period to end lynching," and she went on to discuss her own politicization through left-led protests against the prosecution of black men on false rape charges. Four years later, she joined the chorus of black feminist criticism of *Against Our Will*, seeing Brownmiller's book as a realization of her worst fears.[44]

In the midst of this confrontation between the Old Left and the New, between a white woman who placed herself in a Southern tradition of feminist anti-racism and a radical feminist from the North, a black women's movement has also brought its own perspectives to bear. White activists at the earliest "speakouts" had acknowledged "the racist image of black men as rapists," pointed out the large number of black women among assault victims, and debated the contradictions involved in looking for solutions to a race- and class-biased court system. But not until black women had developed their own autonomous organizations and strategies were true alliances possible across racial lines.

A striking example of this development is the Washington, DC, Rape Crisis Center. One of the first and largest such groups in the country, the center has evolved from a primarily white self-help project to an aggressive interracial organization with a multifaceted program of support services, advocacy, and community education. In a city with an 80 percent black population and more than four times as many women as men, the center has recruited black leadership by channeling its resources into staff salaries and steering clear of the pitfalls of middle-class voluntarism on the one hand and professionalism on the other. It has challenged the perception of the anti-rape movement as a "white women's thing" by stressing not only rape's devastating effect on women but also its impact on social relations in the black community. Just as racism undermined working-class unity and lynching sometimes pitted poor whites against blacks, sexual aggression now divides the black community against itself. In a society that defines manhood in terms of power and possessions, black men are denied the resources to fulfill their expected roles. Inevitably, they turn to domination of women, the one means of asserting traditional manhood within their control. Through consciousness-raising groups for convicted rapists and an intensive educational campaign funded by the city's public school system, and aimed at both boys and girls from elementary through high school, the center has tried to alter the cultural plan for both sexes that makes men potential rapists and women potential victims.[45]

As the anti-rape movement broadens to include Third World women, analogies between lynching and rape and the models of women like Ida B. Wells-Barnett and Jessie Daniel Ames may become increasingly useful. Neither lynching nor rape is the "aberrant behavior of a lunatic fringe."[46] Rather, both grow out of everyday modes of interaction. The view of women as objects to be possessed, conquered, or defiled fueled racial hostility; conversely, racism has continued to distort and confuse the struggle against sexual violence. Black men receive harsher punishment for raping white women, black rape victims are especially demeaned and ignored, and until recently, the different historical experiences of black and white women have hindered them from making common cause. Taking a cue from the women's anti-lynching campaign of the 1930s as well as from the innovative tactics of black feminists, the anti-rape movement must not limit itself to training women to avoid rape or depending on imprisonment as a deterrent, but must aim its attention at changing the behavior and attitudes of men. Mindful of the historical connection between rape and lynching, it must make clear its stand against *all* uses of violence in oppression.

Notes

1. Quoted in Howard Kester, *The Lynching of Claude Neal* (New York, 1934).
2. Michael Stephen Hindus, *Prison and Plantation: Crime, Justice, and Authority in Massachusetts and South Carolina, 1767–1878* (Chapel Hill, 1980), pp. xix, 31, 124, 253.
3. For recent overviews of lynching, see Robert L. Zangrando, *The NAACP Crusade Against Lynching, 1909–1950* (Philadelphia, 1980); James R. McGovern, *Anatomy of a Lynching* (Baton Rouge, LA, 1982); and Jacquelyn Dowd Hall, *Revolt Against Chivalry: Jessie Daniel Ames and the Women's Campaign Against Lynching* (New York, 1979).
4. Quoted in William H. Chafe, *Women and Equality: Changing Patterns in American Culture* (New York, 1977), p. 60.
5. Margaret A. Simons, "Racism and Feminism: A Schism in the Sisterhood," *Feminist Studies* 5 (Summer 1979): 384–401.
6. Diane K. Lewis, "A Response to Inequality: Black Women, Racism, and Sexism," *Signs* 3 (Winter 1977): 341–42.
7. Jacqueline Jones, *Freed Women?: Black Women, Work, and the Family During the Civil War and Reconstruction,* Working paper No. 61, Wellesley College, 1980; Roger L.

Ransom and Richard Sutch, *One Kind of Freedom: The Economic Consequences of Emancipation* (New York, 1977), pp. 87–103.
8. Gerda Lerner, *Black Women in White America: A Documentary History* (New York, 1972), is an early and important exception.
9. Robin Morgan, "Theory and Practice: Pornography and Rape" in Laura Lederer, ed., *Take Back the Night: Women on Pornography* (New York, 1980), p. 140.
10. Susan Griffin, "Rape: The All-American Crime," *Ramparts* (September 1971): 26–35; Susan Brownmiller, *Against Our Will: Men, Women, and Rape* (New York, 1975). See also Kate Millet, *Sexual Politics* (Garden City, N.Y., 1970).
11. Nancy F. Cott, "Passionlessness: An Interpretation of Victorian Sexual Ideology, 1790–1850," *Signs* 4 (Winter 1978): 219–36.
12. Dorothy Dinnerstein, *The Mermaid and the Minotaur: Sexual Arrangements and Human Malaise* (New York, 1977). See also Phyllis Marynick Palmer, "White Women/Black Women: The Dualism of Female Identity and Experience," unpublished paper presented at the American Studies Association, September 1979, pp. 15–17. Similarly, British Victorian eroticism was structured by class relations in which upper-class men were nursed by lower-class country women. See Ellen Ross and Rayna Rapp, "Sex and Society: A Research Note from Social History and Anthropology" in Ann Snitow, Christine Stansell, and Sharon Thompson, eds., *Powers of Desire: The Politics of Sexuality* (New York, 1983).
13. A statement made in 1901 by George T. Winston, president of the University of North Carolina, typifies these persistent images: "The southern woman with her helpless little children in a solitary farm house no longer sleeps secure. . . . The black brute is lurking in the dark, a monstrous beast, crazed with lust. His ferocity is almost demoniacal. A mad bull or a tiger could scarcely be more brutal" (quoted in Charles Herbert Stember, *Sexual Racism: The Emotional Barrier to an Integrated Society* [New York, 1976], p. 23.)
14. Philip Alexander Bruce, *The Plantation Negro as a Freeman* (New York, 1889), pp. 83–84; *Jackson Daily News*, May 27, 1937; Hortense

Powdermaker, *After Freedom: A Cultural Study in the Deep South* (1939; New York, 1969), pp. 54–55, 389.
15. For a contradictory view, see, for example, S. Nelson and M. Amir, "The Hitchhike Victim of Rape: A Research Report," in M. Agopian, *et al.*, eds., *Victimology: A New Focus: Vol. 5: Exploiters and Exploited* (1975), p. 47; and "Black Offender and White Victim: A Study of Forcible Rape in Oakland, California" in *Forcible Rape: The Crime, The Victim, and the Offender* (New York, 1977).
16. Winthrop Jordan, *White over Black: American Attitudes Toward the Negro, 1550–1812* (Baltimore, 1969); W. J. Cash, *The Mind of the South* (New York, 1941), p. 117.
17. This reading of lynching as a "cultural text" is modeled on Clifford Geertz, "Deep Play: Notes on the Balinese Cockfight," in *The Interpretation of Cultures: Selected Essays by Clifford Geertz* (New York, 1973), pp. 412–53. For "ladyhood," see Greer Litton Fox, " 'Nice Girl': Social Control of Women Through a Value Construct," *Signs* 2 (Summer 1977): 805–17.
18. Quoted in William R. Taylor, *Cavalier and Yankee: The Old South and American National Character* (Garden City, N.Y., 1963), pp. 148–51.
19. Dan T. Carter, *Scottsboro: An American Tragedy* (Baton Rouge, 1969), p. 36.
20. Belle Kearney, *A Slaveholder's Daughter* (New York, 1900), p. 96; Myrta Lockett Avary, *Dixie After the War* (1906; New York, 1969), pp. 377–90. See also John E. Talmadge, *Rebecca Latimer Felton: Nine Stormy Decades* (Athens, Ga., 1960), pp. 98–124.
21. Leslie Fiedler, *Love and Death in the American Novel* (New York, 1966), pp. 320–24.
22. Adrienne Rich, "Disloyal to Civilization: Feminism, Racism, Gynephobia," in her *On Lies, Secrets and Silence: Selected Prose, 1966–1978* (New York, 1979); Jessie Daniel Ames to Mary McLeod Bethune, March 9, 1938. Association of Southern Women for the Prevention of Lynching Papers, Atlanta University (henceforth cited as ASWPL Papers). For black women's prior activities, see Ida B. Wells, *Crusade for Justice: The Autobiography of Ida B. Wells* (Chicago, 1970); Lerner, *Black Women*, pp. 194–215; Bettina Aptheker, Lynching and

Rape: An Exchange of Views, Occasional Paper No. 25, American Institute of Marxist Studies (1977); and Angela Y. Davis, *Women, Race, and Class* (New York, 1982), pp. 169–98.

23. For this reform tradition, see Estelle Freedman, "Separatism as Strategy: Female Institution Building and American Feminism, 1870–1930," *Feminist Studies* 5 (Fall 1979): 512–29; Mari Jo Buhle, *Women and American Socialism, 1780–1920* (Urbana, Ill., 1981); and Barbara Leslie Epstein, *The Politics of Domesticity: Women, Evangelism, and Temperance in Nineteenth-Century America* (Middletown, Conn., 1981).

24. Deb Friedman, "Rape, Racism—and Reality," *Aegis* (July/August, 1978): 17–26.

25. Jessie Daniel Ames to Miss Doris Loraine, March 5, 1935, ASWPL Papers.

26. Carrie Parks Johnson Address, Commission on Interracial Cooperation, CIC Papers, Atlanta University.

27. Jessie Daniel Ames to Nannie Burroughs, October 24, 1931; Burroughs to Ames, October 30, 1931, ASWPL Papers; "Appendix F. Digest of Discussion," n.d. [November 20, 1931], Jessie Daniel Ames Papers, University of North Carolina at Chapel Hill.

28. *Jackson (Mississippi) Daily News*, February 1931, ASWPL Papers.

29. Jessie Daniel Ames, "Lynchers' View on Lynching," ASWPL Papers.

30. Quoted in Wilma Dykeman and James Stokely, *Seeds of Southern Change: The Life of Will Alexander* (Chicago, 1962), p. 143.

31. Noreen Connell and Cassandra Wilsen, eds., *Rape: The First Sourcebook for Women* (New York, 1974); Morgan, "Theory and Practice."

32. Interview with Janet Colm, director of the Chapel Hill-Carrboro (North Carolina) Rape Crisis Center, April 1981. Two of the best recent analyses of rape are Ann Wolbert Burgess and Lynda Lyle Holmstrom, *Rape: Crisis and Recovery* (Bowie, Md., 1979) and Lorenne M. G. Clark and Debra J. Lewis, *Rape: The Price of Coercive Sexuality* (Toronto, 1977).

33. Rosalind Pollack Petchesky, "Reproductive Freedom: Beyond 'A Woman's Right to Choose,' " *Signs* 5 (Summer 1980): 661–85.

34. Adrienne Rich, "Taking Women Students Seriously" in *Lies, Secrets and Silence*, p. 242.

35. Vivian Berger, "Man's Trial, Women's Tribulation: Rape Cases in the Courtroom," *Columbia Law Review* 1 (1977): 3–12. Thanks to Walter Dellinger for this reference.

36. Allan Griswold Johnson, "On the Prevalence of Rape in the United States," *Signs* 6 (Fall 1980): 136–46.

37. Tracey A. Gardner, "Racism in Pornography and the Women's Movement" in *Take Back the Night*, p. 111.

38. Jessie Daniel Ames, "Editorial Treatment of Lynching," *Public Opinion Quarterly* 2 (January 1938): 77–84.

39. For a statement of this theme, see Christopher Lasch, "The Flight from Feeling: Sociopsychology of Sexual Conflict," *Marxist Perspectives* 1 (Spring 1978): 74–95.

40. Berger, "Man's Trial, Woman's Tribulation," p. 4. For a recent study indicating that the harsher treatment accorded black men convicted of raping white women is not limited to the South and has persisted to the present, see Gary D. LaFree, "The Effect of Sexual Stratification by Race on Official Reactions to Rape," *American Sociological Review* 45 (October 1980): 842–54. Thanks to Darnell Hawkins for this reference.

41. Barbara Ehrenreich, "The Women's Movement: Feminist and Antifeminist," *Radical America* 15 (Spring 1981): 93–101; Lasch, "Flight from Feeling." Because violence against women is so inadequately documented, it is impossible to make accurate racial comparisons in the incidence of the crime. Studies conducted by Menachen Amir in the late 1950s indicated that rape was primarily intraracial, with 77 percent of rapes involving black victims and black defendants and 18 percent involving whites. More recent investigations claim a somewhat higher percentage of interracial assaults. Statistics on reported rapes show that black women are more vulnerable to assault than white women. However, since black women are more likely to report assaults, and since acquaintance rape, most likely to involve higher status white men, is the most underreported of crimes, the vulnerability of white women is undoubtedly much greater than statistics indicate (Berger, "Man's Trial, Women's Tribulation," p. 3, n. 16; LaFree, "Effect of Sexual Stratification," p. 845, n. 3; Johnson, "On the Prevalence of Rape," p. 145).

42. Quoted in Aptheker, *Lynching and Rape*, pp. 10–11.

43. Berger, "Woman's Trial, Man's Tribulation," p. 6; Johnson, "On the Prevalence of Rape," p. 138.

44. Anne Braden, "A Second Open Letter to Southern White Women," *Generations: Women in the South*, a special issue of *Southern Exposure* 4 (Winter 1977), edited by Susan Angell, Jacquelyn Dowd Hall, and Candace Waid.

45. Interview with Loretta Ross and Nkenge Toure, Washington, DC, May 12, 1981. See also Rape Crisis Center of Washington, DC, *How to Start a Rape Crisis Center* (1972, 1977).

46. Johnson, "On the Prevalence of Rape," p. 137.

 Article Review Form at end of book.

What are the differences in norms for masculinity and femininity these authors see in Black and white fraternity Little Sister organizations? How can these differences be explained?

Sister Acts:

Resisting Men's Domination in Black and White Fraternity Little Sister Programs

Mindy Stombler

Texas Tech University

Irene Padavic

Florida State University

Fraternity little sister programs on college campuses both produce and resist gender inequality. This study draws on data from 40 in-depth interviews and participant observation on college campuses in the Southeast to examine race differences in types of resistance. Black little sisters used collective forms of resistance, which had greater success than white little sisters' individual forms of resistance. Structural and ideological differences in little sister organizations account for these different responses, which we trace to different cultural prescriptions for women's reliance on men and different knowledge about individual and collective resistance.

Much research examines institutional school practices, such as sexist texts and a lack of women mentors, that help create and maintain gender inequality (Gabriel and Smithson 1990; Sadker and Sadker

1994), and many feminists fight to remove institutional barriers and curb sexist practices in schools. Others examine the informal peer interactions that help reproduce gender relations, a line of inquiry we pursue in this paper. Thorne (1993), for example, found that elementary school students, far more than adults, eagerly demarcated boys' from girls' territory in lunchrooms and playgrounds and exacted stiff penalties on the few deviants who ventured onto the opposite sex's turf. Most high school peer groups pressure girls to conform to a narrow stereotyped version of femininity (Coqwie and Lees 1981; Lees 1993; McRobbie 1978; Wilson 1978). College level peer groups also reproduce gender inequality; college students report out-of-classroom experiences as their "most important reason for coming to college in the first place, their central pleasure while in it, and what they often remembered most fondly about college after they graduated" (Moffatt 1989:29; see also Becker 1972). The college peer group experience need not

perpetuate gender inequality, of course. College offers most late adolescents their first extended contact with extra-familial life and the opportunity to develop alternative conceptions of gender and sexuality (Sanday 1990).

The Greek system often quashes these alternatives and reasserts male privilege, though its success is not uniform. This paper examines how female members of one kind of peer group—little sisters—both uphold and challenge, accommodate and resist men's domination on college campuses. Little sister programs are organizations of women who serve fraternity men in the supportive capacity of hostesses or boosters. These groups exist on both predominantly-black (where they sometimes are called "sweethearts") and predominantly-white college campuses, although programs differ in important ways. In all cases, little sisters are affiliates of the fraternity, but receive few privileges and rights associated with full membership (Martin and Stombler 1993).[1]

Researchers (Stombler and Martin 1994) and the press (Lifetime Television 1993; *New York Times* 1989a, 1989b) paint a bleak picture of male dominance and female subordination in little sister programs. Institutional oversight of these programs is minimal: university officials, national fraternities, local alumni and advisors, and women students have little supervisory authority.[2] Fraternity men can thus exploit little sisters for their physical labor (e.g., cleaning up after parties or fulfilling brothers' community service obligations), for their emotional labor (e.g., using little sisters as confidantes or intramural sports cheerleaders), and for their sexuality (e.g., having little sisters model in bikinis for full-color fraternity-rush advertisements).

Resistance

Oppressive social institutions are not definitive, but have internal contradictions that offer opportunities for human agency; oppositional elements always exist to some degree that can subvert the given order (Giddens 1984). This opposition does not have to be formal, public, or organized to qualify as resistance (Scott 1985, 1990; Willis 1977; Fisher and Davies 1993):

Where everyday resistance most strikingly departs from other forms of resistance is in its implicit disavowal of public and symbolic goals. . . . [E]veryday resistance is informal, often covert, and concerned largely with immediate, *de facto* gains. (Scott 1985:33)

"Everyday" resistance can be most useful for oppressed groups, particularly women, who find it "tactically convenient as well as necessary" to avoid openly challenging the dominant ideology. " 'Real' gains are possible, in other words, so long as the larger symbolic order is not questioned" (1985:33). Thus, acts requiring "lit-

tle or no coordination," such as "individual acts of foot dragging and evasion," are often the only recourse open to oppressed people.

"Everyday" resistance is only one formulation of the concept of resistance. The critical education tradition holds that while educational institutions reproduce class relations (or gender relations, in some versions), this process is not an "iron law of transmission." The reproduction of inequality is subject to contestation, as students resist, either overtly or subtly. Two dimensions are commonly used to determine whether an act qualifies as resistance: the outcome of the act and the actor's intention.

Some researchers (Carnoy 1989; Davies 1995; Fernandes 1988) suggest that whether an act qualifies as resistance depends on whether its chief outcome counters the dominant ideology or furthers it. In our assessment, however, using an "outcome" criterion that acknowledges only effective resistance conflates the act with its outcome, and thus strips all agency from actors. Outcomes cannot determine the existence of an act. For example, workers' petty pilfering channels their frustrations in a relatively harmless direction and thus reproduces the status quo, yet is resistance from the workers' point of view (Jermier 1988). Similarly, workers who unsuccessfully attempt to establish labor unions or initiate strikes nevertheless successfully identify their oppression to themselves and others. Even quitting a job can be a defiant act (Jermier 1988). Another problem with the "outcome" criterion is that it allows only two options: resisting or reproducing cultural inculcation. This dichotomy is problematic because cultural reproduction and social change are not mutually exclusive; cultural production can, at the same time, exhibit both reproductive and resistance aspects (Scott 1985; Fernandex 1988). For

these reasons, while we assess the effectiveness of different resistance strategies, we do not use outcomes to define resistance.

Some researchers argue that for an act to qualify as resistance, an actor must intend the act as a protest against an oppressive system, while others argue that this is not necessary (Davies 1995). Willis' (1977) classic text, *Learning to Labor*, illustrates the latter stance. His observations of working class boy's resistance to the processes of class reproduction inherent in British schooling led him to identify some resistance acts as "symbolic," meaning that the boys themselves did not recognize them as being in response to an oppressive system, while the researcher did. For example, the boys did not question the impetus behind their valorization of manual labor and reviling of "pen-pushing"; Willis attributed these attitudes and accompanying actions to resistance against the authority structure of the school. Davies' (1995:1471) critique of "symbolic" resistance notes that ethnographic research has "uncovered countless instances of 'submerged' opposition [or symbolic resistance] yet few inspiring tangible examples." We evaluate instances of resistance using the more rigorous definition of the intention criteria. Thus, we consider resistant only those acts that little sisters themselves explicitly identify as protest.

Scholars agree on the importance of moving beyond simple race-blind gender dominance explanations to examine how men's exploitation and women's responses are affected by race in different contexts (West and Fenstermaker 1995:9). Since women do not experience domination identically due to race and class differences (Collins 1990; hooks 1989), it is not surprising that little sisters' resistance differed for black and white women.

This research shows that black little sisters have been more successful than their white counterparts in resisting men's exploitation through collective resistance. Some white little sisters resisted, mostly as individuals, but they were more likely to be accommodating than the black little sisters. In order to understand why we found white little sisters more likely to engage in "foot dragging" methods while black little sisters engaged in more confrontational ones, we examine quotidian interactional events—the "micropractices of everyday life"[3] (Davis and Fisher 1993)—that can be "raced" as well as gendered (Morrison 1992). There are several reasons for these differences: black and white women had different goals, selection processes and expectations differed between the groups, and black women drew on an ideological script rooted in the historical legacy of an oppositional culture. By remaining open to racial differences in the ways that black and white little sisters "negotiate femininity" (Davis and Fisher 1993:7), we hope to add to the feminist project of understanding the oppressions women face—and their responses to it—without collapsing the differences among them into the "universal woman" (Kristeva 1981); in other words, we seek to turn "woman's standpoint" into "women's standpoints."[4]

Gender Inequality and Peer Group Interactions

Students' everyday peer relations create and maintain gender inequality. Heterosexual peer groups transmit traditional expectations about gender relations (Gwartney-Gibbs and Stockard 1989; Handler 1995; Holland and Eisenhart 1990); through peer associations, both black and white women learn that being attractive to men (as evidenced, for example, by having a "boyfriend") is essential to self-worth (Holland and Eisenhart 1990).

Examining gender relations on a predominantly black and a predominantly white campus in the United States, Holland and Eisenhart (1990) found that the differences between black and white women did not overshadow the importance of the gender barriers that all the women faced. Their primary finding was race neutral: black and white women both were "on a sexual auction block," consumed with romance or finding male companionship. Nevertheless, they found that black college women were less single-minded in their focus on men and were less likely to believe that men would support them economically in the future. Similarly, Fuller (1980), found that black girls in London high schools sought to obtain academic qualifications to assert their capability and intelligence—qualities that school authorities did not expect from them. Moreover, unlike white girls, they did not seek life answers in an ideology of domesticity:

I want a proper job first and some kind of skill so that if I do get married and have children I can go back to it; [I] don't want [to be] just relying on him for money, 'cause I've got to look after myself. (Fuller 1980:57)

Thus, limited research indicates that women of color share a focus on career goals that they prioritize over men's approval and support. Research on white students' peer cultures has not found a similar countervailing message to the dominant focus on heterosexual social life.

In particular, college fraternities socially construct and reaffirm traditional gender relations and thus actively create gender inequality (Sanday 1990; Martin and Hummer 1989). Only a few sociological studies have analyzed the structure and dynamics of white fraternity little sister programs (e.g., Stombler and Martin 1994). Whether black fraternity men also exploit fraternity little sisters, how this may differ from white fraternity men, and how black women respond are largely unexplored territories. Our examination of fraternity little sister programs allows us to explore how peer dynamics are structured, codified, accommodated, and resisted and how these dynamics differ for black and white women.

Methods and Data

In-depth interviews over a five-year period in the early 1990s on public university campuses in the Southeast provide most of the data for this study. The first author conducted interviews with 40 women (21 black, 19 white) of traditional college age who currently or recently participated in little sister organizations in eight different fraternity chapters. Most respondents were recommended by Interfraternity councils, individual fraternities, or fellow little sisters, although in some cases we asked for referrals to women whose experiences were different from those of the recommender. Interviews averaged an hour and a half and took place in settings chosen by the respondents, including restaurants, student apartments, empty classrooms, fraternity houses, and university offices. Seven interviewees participated in a focus group.

The interviewer was close in age to the women she interviewed. Because she is white, her race potentially could have made black women reluctant to speak openly, but we do not believe this was the case for two reasons. First, both groups of women frankly discussed both positive and negative (sometimes painful) experiences; we had not expected such candor in light of fraternity members' typical defensiveness about a system they perceive to be (and often is) under attack. Second, we had very few refusals: black women eagerly agreed to be interviewed, perhaps because we emphasized the need for documenting experiences that had long been ignored in popular press and scholarly accounts.

Interviews with several others gave us a broader view: an Interfraternity Council president who had led a campus drive to disband little sister organizations; two little sister program coordinators (fraternity men appointed by the fraternity to work closely with little sister programs); a fraternity president; the head of a Greek Affairs Task Force that had recommended disbanding little sister organizations; eight university officials; and a live-in adult supervisor at a fraternity. We changed the names of respondents, fraternities, and fraternity symbols.

The first author also conducted participant observation in one predominantly white fraternity: she attended little sister rush, several parties and social events, and an orientation meeting of newly chosen little sisters. Although the interview and participant observation data are from the Southeast, national data, including national fraternity and sorority newsletters, televised news reports, and talk show transcripts, support our findings. While geographically limited ethnographic research cannot offer definitive answers about fraternity little sister programs, it suggests how gender inequality is reproduced and resisted on campus.

Results

Black little sister programs offered more liberating structural and cultural elements than white organizations; this predisposed black women toward a more activist stance than their white counterparts. We discuss these differences and then turn to the types of resis-

tance strategies the two groups tended to use.

Structural and Cultural Factors Enabling Resistance

The concepts of structure and culture (like the concepts of race and gender) are inseparable in reality (Aronowitz and Giroux 1993). Disentangling "cultural" elements from "structural" ones necessarily ignores the many ways they are intertwined. For example, Bowles and Gintis (1976) and other "structuralists" incorporate agency, ideology, language, gender, and race into their analyses. Similarly, Bourdieu and Passeron (1977) and other "culturalists" recognize the importance of structural elements in understanding ideologies and meaning systems. In this section, we first enumerate structural and cultural components separately, and then discuss them together in analyzing the actual practices in little sister organizations.

At the structural level, several features distinguished black from white programs: black programs gave veteran little sisters a say in little sister selection; used a little sister pledge period to enhance women's bonding; created separate, semi-autonomous organizational forms for little sister programs; and, in most cases, sponsored question-and-answer interest meetings instead of more sexualized rush events. White little sister organizations, in contrast, had none of these structural features. They provided no official role for veteran little sisters. Their organizations had no autonomy. Their recruitment process involved rush-style events where women visited a fraternity party *en masse,* trying to impress as many men as possible to enhance their chances of being chosen as little sisters. Nor did white little sisters have a structured "bonding" mechanism—such as a serious pledge period—because it

was considered more important for white women to become acquainted with brothers than with other little sisters.

Cultural differences also help explain different resistance strategies. Little sisters of both races described an organizational culture where fraternity men viewed little sisters as partial and inferior members of the fraternity. (National and local fraternity officials described little sisters as "half-members" and "quasi-members.") Rarely did little sisters question their position. Little sisters outwardly accepted the fraternity as the men's property and domain; their purpose was to provide support for the brothers. However, ideological distinctions between the white and black groups fostered different propensities to critique the brothers' behavior. Below we discuss the differences in the ideologies that undergirded both women's motivations for joining and their orientations to sisterhood. We then show how, within the structure of female subordination, black women were able to draw on the empowering ideology of "getting ahead" to mobilize for opposition more effectively than white women, who relied on an ideology of "getting a man," leading to a more accommodationist stance. We now turn to specific discussions of the structural and ideological features that informed the selection process, women's motivations for joining little sister programs, and women's notions of sisterhood.

Differences in Little Sister Selection: Pretty Girls and Strong Women

White and black little sister organizations had very different notions of the characteristics desirable in little sisters. The recruiting and selection practices that they instituted to realize these preferences yielded little sisters with differing propensities to resist exploitation;

this partially explains the different types of resistance that the black and white women tended to adopt. At white fraternities, the main qualities that men sought in potential little sisters were beauty and sociability. In contrast, according to our respondents, men at black fraternities—along with veteran little sisters, who actively participated in recruitment in most fraternities—sought women who had strong characters and were willing to work for the fraternity.

Describing the qualities men looked for in recruits, a white little sister reported, "First of all they look at your face, then they look at your body, and then they say, 'Hi!' " Another said that requirements included:

Personality, maybe, [but] it's minuscule . . . [What matters are] your body and your whole outlook on the guys. . . . We didn't have to do anything but look good.

Another gave more credit to personality, which she believed gave her the edge over another would-be little sister:

I'm usually really upbeat and outgoing and really easygoing. I like to go up to a brother and just talk to him. [Women the brothers reject are] shy people when you first meet them.

Black little sisters rarely mentioned beauty or sociability as elements in selection. Instead, recruiters emphasized their desire for "strong" women, an attribute ferreted out with questions such as:

"I'm going to give you three categories: woman, XYZ sweetheart, and black woman. What order would you put them in and why?"

Or this one:

[They asked me,] "Who do you think is the epitome of the black woman and why?" I said that I felt like it was a close race between my mother and Oprah Winfrey. . . . You want to give the impression that you're sure of yourself.

According to our respondents, brothers and veteran little sisters looked for a woman who "remained collected" during her response; but poise and self-confidence were not the only selection criteria, as this veteran little sister pointed out:

We are looking for someone who is headstrong—who knows that there is a time to play and a time to work. We want people who are not selfish, because in order to do community service you can't be selfish. . . . We are really looking for strong black women, to tell you the truth, because a chain is only as strong as its weakest link and we don't want any weak links.

White little sisters, in contrast, were more likely to be punished than rewarded for being headstrong, as when a fraternity forced a group to close their little sister bank account because their president had been "too bossy."

The selection event was much more emotionally charged for white women than for black women, highlighting the importance of women's relationships with men. Black fraternities—who accepted the vast majority of rushees—simply notified the women by mailing letters of acceptance. The proportion of women accepted for membership in the white organizations was much smaller, fostering the women's sense of being among the chosen few. Moreover, white fraternity men publicly acknowledged a woman's selection by taking her for a limousine ride, serenading her in public, or regaling her with flowers. One woman described the process:

They come in and they sing and put you on their lap and lean on one knee. They sit you down, give you a rose and sing a [fraternity] love song.

Another:

It was seen as a big honor. It feels good that so many guys have picked you. When they came and got me, I was so light-headed that I almost fell over.

Thus, the symbolic importance of being chosen by men to be affiliated with a men's group, structured differently in black and white organizations, was far more integral to white women's experience than to black women's, perhaps helping them to identify more closely with the fraternity men's interests than with the interests of their little sister fraternity subgroup. More importantly, white organizations selected women for their beauty and sociability, hardly traits associated with opposition, while black organizations' choice of "headstrong" women promoted the opposite effect.

Motivations for Joining: Getting a Man Versus Getting Ahead

Black and white little sisters shared some motivations for joining: a desire to meet people, to have a social outlet, to be connected to Greek and campus life, and to be part of a "family" away from home. Interviews clarified, however, that white little sisters primarily joined to meet, befriend, and date men. The white women desired the privileged access to fraternity men that membership brought and saw this access as the main benefit of little sisterhood. For example, when asked why she joined, one little sister replied:

You get to meet the brothers. . . . They are always calling the little sisters and telling them to go places with them.

Another credited the program with finding her a boyfriend:

I date a boy . . . that I probably wouldn't be dating if I wasn't a little sister. You get to meet men.

Black little sisters' focus was quite different. They acknowledged men as potential dates and good friends or "real brothers" who could protect them or come to their aid if necessary, but many downplayed the importance of meeting men. A large majority claimed that their chief motivation for joining was to have an outlet for community service work, and their substantial time investments in this work corroborated the claim. One said:

When I first went to hear about sweethearts I wasn't interested at all until the brothers really stressed community service. Then I said I would do it.

Beyond the genuine desire to help the black community, many women used participation in community service activities instrumentally, to enhance their attractiveness to sororities:

Sororities want to know . . . what you have done in the community. So I thought that by being a sweetheart I could get my community service.

In a roundabout way, black women used little sisterhood as an opportunity to get ahead in their careers. The first step, according to many, was acceptance into a *sorority* (see also Berkowitz and Padavic 1997; Giddings 1988; Glover 1993). Beyond the high status that women achieve on campus through association with sororities, black women turned to sororities as networks for future professional achievement and community involvement. Black sororities facilitate career advancement, train black women leaders, and mobilize political and social practices that improve the black community (Giddings 1988; Glover 1993). In fact, members of black sororities tend to be more active after college graduation than before, quite unlike members of white sororities. Our black respondents clearly viewed sororities, not little sister programs, as organizations that would "help you get along in whatever you do." One explained:

I see sororities as a way to get ahead. Many women in national and state politics are XYZ [sorority]. It is a way to get ahead. That name can help you get connections in the job world. It could help you get hired.

Black little sisters said that little sisterhood could enhance their likelihood of sorority acceptance in three ways: it allowed them to accumulate the hours of community service that sororities consider crucial for admittance; it proved that they could forge bonds with other women; and it provided access to sorority members, who attended fraternity functions. Thus, for most, little sister status opened doors to their desired end—sorority membership—and was not an end in itself.

I kind of see it as them [the brothers] introducing us to the sororities. . . . I do remember a lot of sorority girls being there [at a fraternity ball] and they [the brothers] kind of showed us off. . . . The sororities look among the sweethearts for potential pledges.

Another described her little sisterhood as: "something I needed to learn to go on to better things, like a sorority."

Black little sisters' tendency to regard their affiliation with a men's group as a means to achieve a more important affiliation with a woman's group underscores their collective realization of the importance of connections with other women, in contrast to white little sisters' unadulterated focus on men. Black little sisters, situated in a context where men dominate women, worked the existing system on their own behalf. While it is ironic that black men had any connection at all to women's participation in sorority life, in a further twist of irony, the little sisters were essentially "using" fraternity men.

Sisterhood

The most marked difference between white and black little sister organizations involves their conceptions of sisterhood. White women reported few, if any, experiences of closeness to other women in the program: "You always knew the guys; the guys stood out. . . . I didn't like the lack of communication between all the girls." Many white women reported competing with one another to get men's attention, or, in one instance, to avoid it. In a striking display of unsisterly behavior, during a fraternity event that called for little sisters to dance provocatively, one woman corralled another sister:

This is so bad!. . . I got a girl I knew could dance [excitingly] . . . and got her to go up there with me so they wouldn't be watching me, they would be watching her!

In contrast, the black little sisters stressed the importance of the bonds between women in the little sister program. Many aspects of the pledging process structured such bonding. In sharp contrast to white women's experiences, at initial interest meetings at one black fraternity, veteran little sisters and brothers explained to rushees that they were pledging the little sister organization, not the fraternity, and instructed rushees to meet other little sisters so they could "begin to bond." One veteran little sister explained:

You would want to know the sweethearts on a personal level a little bit more than you would the brothers, because you're not trying to become a brother. . . . This is our organization and the girls want to come into our organization.

The institution of "line mothers" or "line mommies"—little sister presidents in charge of training the incoming pledge class or "line"—contributed to the black women's *esprit de corps*. One line mother, who described herself as a "mother hen," became upset when some of her pledges went to breakfast at four A.M. with men from a fraternity on another campus:

That upset me. They had never met these guys before. They didn't know these guys or their history or their attitudes. They could have been killed, raped, brutalized, or anything. [The men] could have drugged their drinks and we could have never seen them again. I was really angry because I was so scared.

In another example, one line mother described the little sisters' organizational response when a pledge asked for help:

I ran across campus to go and get her. I was there until 6:00 A.M. and I had an 8:00 A.M. class. The next day it [news about the situation] went around the [little sister] organization like wildfire. There were thirty sweethearts in her [dorm] room the next day. . . . If anyone came into that room we were going to kill 'em. We had a bond.

Fraternities even tested rushees on their ability to bond with other women:

We had to write papers on sisterhood. Now true sisterhood should tell you that we would turn in one paper, [not] twenty-nine. The fraternity brother said, "You guys are just not learning sisterhood. You all do it again." He'd say, "You all bring in food" and we'd bring in 29 items instead of one. See, if there was a true sisterhood, a true unit, we would have all gotten together!

Not surprisingly, given such training, feelings of sisterhood sometimes superseded loyalty to the brothers. One woman pointed out:

We had enough people [little sisters] to say [to the fraternity brothers], "You're not going to run over us." The women stuck up for one another.

In short, sisterhood was the *modus vivendi* for black little sisters but not for their white counterparts and it became a resource for them to draw on in altercations with fraternity men. Black women—and men—drew heavily on an ideology of "strong, black womanhood" to formulate their notions of sisterhood and the qualities desirable in a sister.

Why would men select women for these traits when they heighten women's ability to resist? We speculate that powerful women—and many little sisters were campus leaders—added to the fraternities' campus prestige, which the men appreciated, just as they would appreciate the prestige

attending to a male campus leader. It is also possible that black men are familiar with and accept strength in women because of the larger history and valorization of black women's labor force participation, family headship, and participation in the civil rights struggle—a movement in which many fraternity chapters were active. Or black fraternity men's encouragement of sisterhood ties may have resulted from earlier institutional battles between brothers and little sisters that were resolved in the women's favor and whose results are now a normalized part of the institution.

To return to the issue of black women's sisterhood, Lerner (1979) described turn-of-the-century women's clubs whose goal was to "uplift the race" and to dispel negative stereotypes about black women. Updating this mission, some little sister organizations defined their organizations as part of the movement to improve black women's social status. For example, one little sister president organized a seminar on black women:

I figured that while I'm in office I'm going to make sure that I'm going to do things that go down in history. We organized a seminar called "The Uplifting of the Black Woman" and we got a professor, a female black psychologist at the university, to speak. The whole fraternity [brothers and sisters] was there.

This type of activity—unheard of in white little sister programs—sends the message that strong women are desired in black little sister programs because they foster the ideology—begun 100 years ago—that black women are not merely victims of oppression but generators of their own successes.[5]

The structures and ideologies of black little sister programs that emphasized the bonds of sisterhood and mitigated invalidation by men sharply contrasted with the lack of these structures and em-

powering ideologies in white little sister programs. Structural elements, like having a voice in recruitment, a pledge period that facilitates bonding with women, and some degree of organizational autonomy, lay the necessary foundation for empowerment. Ideologies gave black little sisters a language of collective resistance with which to fight oppressive situations; these women drew on resources within little sister programs to make the organization less oppressive. As we show below, without these structures and ideologies to legitimate collective resistance, white women responded by accommodating or resisting as individuals.

Strategies of Resistance

Most conflicts between fraternity brothers and little sisters emerged over women's attempts at self-governance and men's resistance to it. Fraternity structure and culture rarely legitimated the *rights* of little sisters to speak up, object, express an opinion, or share in deciding how things were done, although in some cases fraternity men granted them permission. Most women found ways to accommodate their second-class citizenship. This white little sister, irate at the fraternity's practice of using little sisters as "bait"—expecting them to hostess at men's rush parties where they serve drinks, make name tags and show their "smiling faces"—spoke for many interviewees who felt disgruntled, but were unwilling to rock the boat:

Something that made me so mad was when they would tell us to go up to the would-be [male fraternity] pledge and make sure that he is having a good time. "Dance with him or give him a drink or something or walk outside with him." I wouldn't complain about this in front of everybody. I wouldn't stand up at a little sister meeting and say, "They're using us!" I didn't feel like I had the power to do that.

Most women complied with men's expectations and viewed whatever was asked of them as legitimate; they served the fraternity men in exchange for the men's approval and companionship. One white little sister echoed this acceptance of male dominance, claiming that little sisters "didn't deserve any rights whatsoever." Others resented the fraternities' demands and their lack of rights but felt powerless to oppose them. By participating in activities requiring subservience, little sister programs generally helped to structure and reproduce gender inequality on campus. Although some women did resist, white women tended to resist as individuals, while black women tended to resist collectively—with more successful results.

Individual Actions

Disaffected white women chose listless compliance and quitting as ways to act on their frustration. For example, at some white fraternities little sisters participated in an annual fundraiser called the "Slave Auction." Some women felt it was degrading because it called for dancing seductively on stage for the brothers and then being auctioned off to the highest bidder to perform a week of "slave" services (such as baking brownies, cleaning, or chauffeuring). Brothers at one fraternity bid more money and cheered louder for women who simulated sex on a pole erected in the middle of the stage.

Despite feeling intensely embarrassed or humiliated by this ritual, the little sisters never considered refusing to participate as a group. Instead, they adopted individual strategies of resistance. Several chose not to attend:

I didn't do it. That's one thing I don't approve of. I skipped town.

Another:

Some guys said you had to do it. I was like, 'I don't *have* to do anything!'

Another was willing to dance but only in a decidedly non-provocative way. By participating half-heartedly, she was still a good sport but had not soiled her reputation by responding to the brothers' chant, "Hump the pole!" After much agonizing and discussion with her biological brother, another adopted a similar strategy of "safe" rebellion:

I just got up there and stood there. I didn't move. . . . I wouldn't try to stop the whole thing . . . and I [wouldn't want to] make everybody mad. But, yeah, I personally wouldn't do it.

Quitting was the other option that individual resisters in predominantly-white fraternities employed. One white woman quit upon discovering the brothers' practice of "selecting" women: choosing a woman that several men decide to have sex with by a certain date. She confronted the fraternity president and asked him if what she had heard about a particular woman's "selection" was true. He replied, "Let's just put it this way: one, two and three are done [three brothers had had sex with the woman so far]." She admonished two more brothers for "taking advantage of drunk girls." They said, "What do you want us to do about it?" She replied, "Stop it!" They replied that what they chose to do sexually was their own business and it wasn't her place to lecture them about it. After warning the woman who had been selected, she quit. "After that situation, I came to a realization . . . that I didn't want to be involved with this. . . . I [even] started doing research on date rape."

Another little sister quit in anger when her fraternity "revamped" the program by discharging all the little sisters and inviting only the "pretty girls" to come back:

I'm disgusted with it. I think they are slime.

She was incensed that her close friend had not been asked back and described how:

The more my roommate and I talked about it, the madder we got. . . . We ended up talking to the little sister coordinator . . . and I was just bitching him out, totally. . . . He expected me to come back?! That's ridiculous!

Thus, in white fraternities, resistance involved individual acts of half-hearted participation or quitting, akin to Scott's (1985) subterfuge strategies. We found only one instance of a white little sister group that attempted a collective strategy to control the brothers' behavior, and their plan backfired. These little sisters devised "Snake, Slug, Goose" awards corresponding to individual brothers' exhibition of nice behavior (e.g., helping a little sister with a tax return), rude behavior (e.g., vomiting in a little sister's purse), or unbecoming behavior (e.g., standing up a little sister on a date). The brothers ridiculed those men who received the awards for niceness and celebrated those who received the dishonorable awards, undermining the white little sisters' attempts at solidarity.

Collective Actions

Black little sisters were much more likely to use collective, above ground strategies to resist fraternity men's exploitation. The most bitter collective protests centered on men's tight control of the organization. In one such protest:

The little sisters had a car wash and the brothers tried to control [the proceeds]. The little sisters got angry and broke away and had a big cookout with some of the money and split the rest of it. They got kicked out . . . but the brothers really learned their lesson after that and treated [the next group] well.

New little sisters were aware of their predecessors' mobilization and said that this realization tightened their sisterly bonds, making them feel like respected members of the fraternity. Thus, this act of resistance led to at least semi-permanent change: it emboldened incoming little sisters and improved the men's treatment of future little sisters. However, the brothers' final authority was another "lesson," whether or not the women attended to it: the militant sisters were, in fact, ousted.

Fraternities often discouraged women from acting collectively on their own behalf. When several black little sisters wanted to party on their own at a different hotel during a regional fraternity conference, the brothers attempted to escort the women back to the brothers' hotel. When the women protested, claiming they had the right to act as they chose, the men threatened them:

So we were upstairs at my friend's hotel and all of a sudden there was this knock at the door. Our chapter's brothers were outside and they asked me to come into the hall. They said, "Tell the rest of the sweethearts that they have to come back with us." I said, "Those are grown females in there; why don't *you* tell them to come." We stayed. The brothers started calling us trouble-makers. They told us that if we did anything else like it, that they would refund our activity fee and tell all the other chapters of our fraternity in the country that we couldn't be sweethearts. We were like, "We're not your children [but] that is how you talk to us! We're just as able to do what you can do."

She "understood" the terms of little sisterhood: "if it wasn't for the frat, sweethearts wouldn't exist," but felt that disobeying was necessary to prove the point that, "we are not beneath them . . . and we're not going to be subservient to anyone—you can forget that—it's not gonna happen."

If enough clashes occurred—if the woman could no longer accommodate the terms of the little sister bargain—it was not unusual for black little sister organizations, unlike white organizations, to create semi-autonomous little sister organizations. (Another reason for creating semi-autonomous organizations was some national fraternity organizations' unwillingness to allow officially affiliated women's groups.) These groups still operated within the fraternity but coined separate names, assumed more self-governance and autonomy, planned their own social events, and chose their own community service projects. Redefining their relationship to the men's group made the women feel empowered and enhanced their focus on women:

I felt closest to the women [rather than to the men]. We had our own meetings and our own projects and things that we were working on. So the women were the people that I had more constant contact with.

In no instance did reorganizing resolve the fundamental disagreement between the women and men over the fraternity authority structure, and clashes continually surfaced, particularly about choosing new little sisters.

[We] pledged our own girls. That was a problem because the guys were also allowed to participate . . . and were doing things like groping the pledges. They would blindfold them and grab on them and then say, "Oh, that was a mistake! I didn't mean to do that."

As this example illustrates, many brothers met little sisters' resistance with continued social control. In several fraternities where men tried to remove little sisters' say in selection and pledging, the women argued with them at chapter meetings. According to hooks (1989:8), "talking back" is an "act of resistance, a political gesture that challenges the politics of domination . . . a courageous act—as such, it represents a threat." Often the men did not accommodate such threats. For example:

We had chosen who we wanted on the line and then the brothers wanted to go back and re-choose the line. We had done all the work! . . . And yet the brothers wanted to come behind us and rechoose! That caused friction. . . . We got mad because they should have listened to us! We all protested to the brothers.

Black little sisters realized that the men were uncomfortable with even the relatively modest amount of power the women held:

All of the sweethearts stuck together. . . . The brothers stopped us from having meetings by ourselves because we were starting to get too much power [laughs proudly]. I know [another university] canceled their sweethearts right in the middle of the semester because their sweethearts started getting too much power.

She continued to reflect on little sisters' power:

We thought we were getting a lot of power, but in reality we weren't, because we could not do anything without going through them. They stopped us from having regular meetings. We still had meetings like once a week or once every two weeks [for a while] but they didn't seem worth the problems.

These little sisters' lack of true membership rights meant that brothers won most altercations. Even when black little sisters formed separate organizations, their impact was more cosmetic than fundamental. Fraternity men still controlled the little sisters' actions; the men retained the power to abolish these organizations when they saw fit. Clearly, little sisters did not undo the fraternity's overarching system of patriarchy, but in their own backyards, we found little sister resistance that challenged the organizations and actions of their fraternity brothers.

Despite the considerable constraints on their autonomy, little sisters of both races fought back, as either individuals or groups. White women were much more likely to use individual strategies, but on at least one occasion, they, too, tried collective action. We find it interesting that they felt the need to cast their critique in jocular terms (the "Snake, Slug, Goose" awards), probably because overt rebellion ran a higher risk of annihilation. Black little sisters were far more likely to use collective strategies to protest injustices and seemed less concerned with making the message palatable to the men. Not all of their protests were collective, of course; black women, too, objected as individuals. One, for example, stood up to a fraternity man who claimed he had slept with her: "I confronted him at a large gathering and I set the record straight loud enough so that those in the fraternity heard." So while individual strategies were not exclusively the province of white women nor collective ones the province of black women, clearly, the tendencies toward particular forms of resistance lay in those directions. Neither form sought to overthrow or even question the fraternity system, only to create more room for autonomous action or dignity.

Evaluating Resistance

Just as power sometimes subtly operates like a "capillary' circulating through the social body and exerting its authority through . . . micropractices . . ." so, too, can resistance. When power is dispersed in such a penetrating way, resistance to that power is unlikely to be "reduced to a single locus of rebellion or revolt" (Davis and Fisher 1993:8). Therefore, it becomes necessary to examine how resistance unfolds in everyday interactions to understand everyday exertions of power.

Yet, defining everyday acts as resistance can be difficult. Some criticize the concept of resistance as being so inclusive as to be meaningless. Davies' (1995:1468) critique of critical education theory, for example, claims that "almost anything short of joyful compliance has been infused with partisan meaning, [a trend that dilutes] the substance of resistance," and

Quadagno and Fobes (1995:184) warn that instances of resistance can be "highly colored by the researchers' interpretation."

We assess the evidence using the criterion of whether the actor intends the act to be one of protest or not. Recall that either the actor or the researcher can identify intentions to resist. In our study, we used the more rigorous former category: little sisters *themselves* identified these as moments when they refused to comply and resisted the demands of the fraternity system. Black little sisters clearly intended their collective acts—such as appropriating fundraising money for their own cookout, refusing to return to the conference hotel with the brothers, and creating autonomous organizations—as protests.

The intent to protest may appear less obvious in regard to white little sisters' individual acts, however. White little sisters considered their acts of quitting as protest, and thus these acts meet the "intention" criterion. Their statements make clear that they did not quietly drift away from the organization: they told the brothers *why* they quit. How effective was this resistance? Such acts may lead to positive change: quitting in protest effectively ended these women's participation in an oppressive system, and their "bitching out the brothers" —explaining their reasons for quitting—registered the protest. (Ironically, compared to black little sisters' collective resistance that allowed them to remain in the organization, white little sisters' acts of quitting removed them from an oppressive set of relationships.) Quitting did not bolster gender reproduction; furthermore, putting brothers on notice that some women found the slave auctioning and the practices of "selecting" women for sexual conquests "disgusting," could potentially lead to

their curtailment. (Compare such acts to accounts of resistance that *furthered* an oppressive system, such as Willis' lads whose defiant rule-breaking in school limited them to dead-end jobs, thus reproducing the class system.)

The case of the little sisters who participated in the slave auction by dancing halfheartedly is ambiguous and raises the question of how to assess defiant acts that both accommodate and resist oppression. Accounts of oppressed groups' ideologies and behaviors commonly include a mix of accommodation and resistance to subordination (Genovese 1972; Giroux 1983; Scott 1990). Writing about high school girls' negotiating cross-sex relationships, for example, Lees (1993:263) notes:

Girls may adopt different practices at different times. At one moment girls accept sexual abuse as natural and fail to contest the terms, at another, they contest the terms of abuse that macho boys adhere to.

For little sisters, acts of resistance can both controvert the gender oppression of the fraternity and go along with it, as in this case. On a social psychological level, these young women strove to find a balance between maintaining their personal dignity and upholding the organization's official commitment to participate. On one hand, their compromise solutions of lackluster participation and skipping the event failed to challenge the terms of the slave auction; on the other, they refused to submit to the brothers' demands to act like a sex object and to be shamed. Although these women experienced the resolution on a personal level, as subjectively transformative, such moments of defiance have implications for future defiant acts that may be *socially* transformative. Arguing for an intellectual bridge to connect social movements with individual experiences of shame and resistance,

Honneth (1995:138) notes: "[I]t is only by regaining the possibility of active conduct that individuals can dispel the state of emotional tension into which they are forced as a result of humiliation," possibly leading to political resistance. Even acts that make no apparent dent in the system, but transform the actor, have transformative potential. Be that as it may, their intent—to not play by the rules of the game laid out by the brothers—is clear. What is most important is not the success of little sisters' defiant acts, but that they were defiant at all within an oppressive system.

Discussion

Fraternity little sister organizations are features of campus culture that help reproduce men's dominance. Yet both black and white women continued to participate in them to further their goals. These goals differed, however, as did the strategies women used to obtain them. Our results show that white women's primary goal was to find a man, perhaps to make him a life partner. This goal and the structure and ideology of their little sister organizations—which provided no niche for veteran little sisters and no support for the concepts of sisterhold or womanly strength—inhibited their ability to mobilize for their rights. Nevertheless, they engaged in resistance, characterized by "noncompliance, subtle sabotage, evasion, and deception" (Scott 1985:31) instead of overt rebellion.

While meeting men was a benefit for black little sisters, performing community service and negotiating access to sororal life were more important. Because black little sister organizations offered them more room to maneuver than white little sisters—by giving them a say in recruitment and endorsing sisterhood—they created a space for actions on their own behalf. Their emphasis on sisterhood bonds and the desirability of strength in women allowed them to collectively protest injustices with some success.

We draw two larger conclusions from these themes. First, our data show that existing gender relations are not immutable; even in retrograde organizations, they are subject to the "countervailing processes of resistance, challenge, conflict, and change" (Thorne 1995:497). Because they could draw on liberating elements in the interstices of their organizations, black little sisters' acts of resistance had greater success than white women's, but even white women tried to change some aspects of their organizations to better serve their purposes.

Second, while black and white women both experienced a campus peer culture replete with gender inequities and exploitation, their reactions were remarkably different. We argue that both endogenous and exogenous factors account for their different resistance strategies. Regarding the former, we have shown that different resistance strategies are partly due to the more liberating ideologies of the black little sister organizations that endorsed sisterhood and the relative importance of relations with women over men. They are also undoubtedly partly due to the different levels of tenacity with which black and white brothers maintained their claims on little sisters. According to Scott (1985:299):

The parameters of resistance are also set, in part, by the institutions of repression. To the extent that such institutions do their work effectively, they may all but preclude any forms of resistance other than the individual, the informal, and the clandestine.

Yet this analysis begs the question of why black fraternity little sister programs were structured to allow greater female empowerment and why the goals and strategies of the two groups differed. To understand these factors, we must turn to exogenous explanations.

One such explanation draws on differences in the cultural prescriptions for women's survival. The economic oppression of black men forced a measure of economic independence on black women from the time of emancipation (Jones 1985; King 1988). Due in part to the scarcity of good jobs at good wages for men, black culture relied on women's labor force participation and on an extended family system in which women provided material help to one another (Cherlin 1992; Stack 1974). These emphases diminished the economic basis of the husband-wife bond that characterizes white culture (Cherlin 1992). As Collins (1991:42) discovered when asking young black women about lessons they learned from their mothers, most answers stressed self-reliance, e.g., "want more for yourself than just a man." Higginbotham and Weber (1992:429) drew a similar conclusion from their quantitative analysis of parents' instructions: "Unlike white women, Black women are typically socialized to view marriage separately from economic security, because it is not expected that marriage will ever remove them from the labor market." Culturally, then, these women's notions of "strong, black womanhood" and life success do not include future economic dependence on men. White little sisters can more straightforwardly follow the cultural prescription of "getting a man" as a route to success. This prescription is based on the nineteenth-century social construction of women's economic dependency on men (Cancian 1989:19), and encourages women to shape their lives on the basis of intimate relationships (Blumstein and Schwartz

1989:125). From their cultural "legacy," they extract "the culture of romance" on which to pin their hopes (Holland and Eisenhart 1990). Drawing from their culture, black women extricate notions of strength and sisterhood. Neither group is simply victimized by fraternity men; women draw on their cultural resources to further their goals as they see them in a fraternity structure designed to subordinate them.

A different exogenous explanation might be that black and white women enter these organizations with different bases of knowledge about individual and collective resistance. The Civil Rights Movement, for example, galvanized many black women into political action against injustice. Black women of all backgrounds, while rarely recognized as leaders, not only initiated and strategized protests, but also mobilized the resources to successfully complete these actions. This participation taught black women about the strategies for and effectiveness of collective action (Barnett 1993). Black little sisters' collective resistance is also reminiscent of church women in the Civil Rights Movement who vigorously fought the conservatism of the men who controlled the church hierarchies. Thus, while our evidence clearly shows that endogenous forces were at work, they may have combined with repertoires of resistance and orientations to men and women that were imported from other social venues, organizations, and past experiences.

More broadly, we argue, along with postmodern feminists, that knowledge about white women does not automatically translate into knowledge about black women: their experiences are often just too different. Nevertheless, we agree with standpoint feminists' claim that a political focus on local interest groups can

sidetrack a "collective feminist struggle against women's persistent location at the margins of power" (Davis and Fisher 1993:10). While the postmodern and standpoint perspectives might seem irreconcilable, through empirical exploration of the tensions between structured forms of constraint and women's agency, we may make some headway in understanding and perhaps improving women's lives. This paper has tried to bridge the gap between these orientations by pointing out both the constraints that fraternities place on women and the different factors that underlie women's resistance.

Notes

1. Some little sisters are also sorority members, although the relationship between sororities and little sister programs differs across campuses. Interviews with little sisters show that some join both organizations in order to increase the variety of connections they have with Greek men. Some join as a less expensive and less structured alternative to sororities that nevertheless facilitates participation in the Greek system.

2. Since the early 1990s, many national and local fraternity organizations and university administrators have disbanded little sister programs. National fraternity organizations cite increased insurance rates, possible loss of legal sex-segregated organizational status, diversion of resources away from chapter operations, disharmony among brothers, and the distraction of chapter members from the "performance of essential duties" as reasons to disband little sister programs. University officials cite sexism and rape prevention as reasons for abolishing the programs. While no national level data on the number of little sister programs exist, national fraternity and sorority organizations and college administrators recognize that, each semester, thousands of college women in all regions of the country continue to "rush" these organizations. Some fraternities ignore national resolutions and continue to sponsor little sister

programs, while others "work the system" by calling their little sisters by a new name. Still other fraternities have pushed their organizations underground (sources listed in Stombler 1994, Appendix).

3. Researchers in the critical education tradition documents such micropractices as they appear in students' repertoires of resistance. For example, McRobbie (1978:104) found that British schoolgirls would often, "jettison the official ideology . . . and replace it with a *more* feminine, even sexual one" and Thomas (1980) found sexually defiant behaviors among Australian schoolgirls.

4. Some feminist theorists argue that examining the "micropractices of everyday life" is a way to bridge the gap between "standpoint" feminist theory (which focuses on the structural impediments capitalism and patriarchy impose on women) and postmodern feminist theory (which denies the existence of a feminist "privileged knower" whose view of reality can speak for all women) (Barrett and Phillips 1992).

5. Black women assumed central leadership roles in the community and in liberation politics. As King (1988) noted, "We founded schools, operated social welfare services, sustained churches, organized collective work groups and unions, and even established bands and commercial enterprises. That is, we were the backbone of racial uplift. . . ." The same message of racial uplift, geared to masculine accomplishments, is a part of black fraternities' mission statements, and partly may account for the brothers' acceptance of little sisters' independent sisterhood.

References

Aronowitz, Stanley, and Henry A. Giroux. 1993. *Education Still Under Siege*. Westport, Conn.: Bergin & Garvey.

Barnett, Bernice McNair. 1993. "Invisible southern black women leaders in the civil rights movement: The triple constraints of gender, race, and class." *Gender & Society* 7(2):162–182.

Barrett, Michelle, and Anne Phillips. 1992. *Destabilizing Theory: Contemporary Feminist Debates*. Cambridge: Polity Press.

Becker, Howard S. 1972. "What do they really learn at college?" In *College and Student: Selected Readings in the Social Psychology of Higher Education*, Kenneth A. Feldman (ed.), 103–108. New York: Pergamon Press.

Berkowitz, Alexandra, and Irene Padavic. 1997. "Getting a man or getting ahead: A comparison of white and black sororities." Unpublished manuscript, Department of Sociology, Florida State University.

Blumstein, Philip, and Pepper Schwartz. 1989. "Intimate relationships and the creation of sexuality." In *Gender and Intimate Relations: A Microstructural Approach*, Barbara J. Risman and Pepper Schwartz (eds.), 120–129. Belmont, Calif.: Wadsworth.

Bourdieu, Pierre, and J. C. Passeron. 1977. *Reproduction in Education, Society, and Culture*. Translated by Richard Nice. London: Sage.

Bowles, Samuel, and Herbert Gintis. 1976. *Schooling in Capitalist America*. New York: Basic Books.

Cancian, Francesca M. 1989. "Love and the rise of capitalism." In *Gender and Intimate Relations: A Microstructural Approach*, Barbara J. Risman and Pepper Schwartz (eds.), 12–25. Belmont, Calif.: Wadsworth.

Carnoy, Martin. 1989. "Education, state, and culture in American society." In *Critical Pedagogy, the State, and Cultural Struggle*, Henry Giroux and Peter McLaren (eds.), 3–23. Albany: State University of New York Press.

Cherlin, Andrew. 1992. *Marriage, Divorce, and Remarriage*. Cambridge, Mass.: Harvard University Press.

Collins, Patricia Hill. 1990. *Black Feminist Thought: Knowledge, Consciousness, and the Politics of Empowerment*. Boston: Unwin Hyman. 1991. "The meaning of motherhood in black culture and black mother-daughter relationships." In *Double Stitch: Black Women Write About Mothers and Daughters*, Patricia Bell-Scott, Beverly Guy-Sheftall, Jacqueline Jones Royster, Janet Sims-Wood, Miriam DeCosta-Willis, and Lucille P. Fultz (eds.), 42–60. New York: Harper Perennial.

Cowie, C., and Sue Lees. 1981. "Slags or drags." *Feminist Review* 9:17–31.

Davies, Scott. 1995. "Leaps of faith: Shifting currents in critical sociology of education." *American Journal of Sociology* 100(6):1448–1478.

Davis, Kathy, and Sue Fisher. 1993. "Power and the female subject." In *Negotiating at the Margins: The Gendered Discourses of Power and Resistance*, Sue Fisher and Kathy Davis (eds.), 3–22. New Brunswick, N.J.: Rutgers University Press.

Fernandes, Joao Viegas. 1988. "From the theories of social and cultural reproduction to the theory of resistance." *British Journal of Sociology of Education* 9:169–180.

Fuller, Mary. 1980. "Black girls in a London comprehensive school." In *Schooling for Women's Work*, Rosemary Deem (ed.), 52–65. London: Routledge and Kegan Paul.

Gabriel, Susan L., and Isaiah Smithson. 1990. *Gender in the Classroom: Power and Pedagogy*. Urbana: University of Illinois Press.

Genovese, Eugene. 1972. *Roll, Jordan, Roll: The World Slaves Made*. New York: Vintage.

Giddens, Anthony. 1984. *The Constitution of Society: Outline of the Theory of Structuration*. Cambridge: Polity Press.

Giddings, Paula. 1988. *In Search of Sisterhood: The History of Delta Sigma Theta Sorority, Inc*. New York: Morrow.

Giroux, Henry A. 1983. "Theories of reproduction and resistance in the new sociology of education: A critical analysis." *Harvard Educational Review* 53(3):257–293.

Glover, Cynthia. 1993. "Sister Greeks: African-American sororities and the dynamics of institutionalized sisterhood at an ivy league university." Paper presented at the annual meetings of the Eastern Sociological Society, Boston, Mass.

Gwartney-Gibbs, Patricia, and Jean Stockard. 1989. "Courtship aggression and mixed-sex peer groups." In *Violence in Dating Relationships: Emerging Social Issues*, Maureen A. Pirog-Good and Jan E. Stets (eds.), 185–204. New York: Praeger.

Handler, Lisa. 1995. "In the fraternal sisterhood: Sororities as gender strategy." *Gender & Society* 9(2):236–255.

Higginbotham, Elizabeth, and Lynn Weber. 1992. "Moving up with kin and community: Upward social mobility for black and white women." *Gender & Society* 6:416–440.

Holland, Dorothy C., and Margaret Eisenhart. 1990. *Educated in Romance: Women, Achievement, and College Culture*. Chicago: University of Chicago Press.

Honneth, Axel. 1995. *The Struggle for Recognition: The Moral Grammar of Social Conflict*. Translated by Joel Anderson. Cambridge: Polity Press.

hooks, bell. 1989. *Talking Back: Thinking Feminist, Thinking Black*. Boston: South End Press.

Jermier, John M. 1988. "Sabotage at work: The rational view." Research in the *Social Organization at Work* 6:101–134.

Jones, Jacqueline. 1985. *Labor of Love, Labor of Sorrow: Black Women, Work, and the Family from Slavery to Present*. New York: Basic Books.

King, Deborah H. 1988. "Multiple jeopardy, multiple consciousness: The context of a black feminist ideology." *Signs* 19:42–72.

Kristeva, Julia. 1981. "Women's time." Translated by Alice Jardine and Harry Blake. *Signs* 7:13–35.

Lees, Sue. 1993. *Sugar and Spice. Sexuality and Adolescent Girls*. New York: Penguin Books.

Lerner, Gerda. 1979. *The Majority Finds its Past: Placing Women in History*. New York: Oxford. Lifetime Television.

1993. "Scary frat boys." Aired on The Jane Pratt Show, April 17.

Martin, Patricia Yancey, and Robert A. Hummer. 1989. "Fraternities and rape on campus." *Gender & Society* 3(4):457–473.

Martin, Patricia Yancey, and Mindy Stombler. 1993. "Gender politics in fraternity little sister groups: How men take power away from women." Unpublished manuscript, Department of Sociology, Florida State University.

McRobbie, Angela. 1978. "Working class girls take issue." In *Women Take Issue: Aspects of Women's Subordination*. Centre for Contemporary Cultural Studies Working Papers in Cultural Studies (ed.), 96–108. London: Hutchinson.

Moffatt, Michael. 1989. *Coming of Age in New Jersey: College and American Culture*. New Brunswick, N.J.: Rutgers University Press.

Morrison, Toni. 1992. *Race-ing Justice, En-gendering Power: Essays on Anita Hill, Clarence Thomas, and the Construction of Social Reality*. N.Y.: Pantheon Books.

New York Times. 1989a. Fraternities phase out "little sister groups." September 17:59. 1989b. "Little sisters' program stopped after assaults." October 22:43.

Quadagno, Jill, and Catherine Fobes. 1995. "The welfare state and the cultural reproduction of gender: Making good girls and boys in the job corps." *Social Problems* 42(2):171–190.

Riley, Kathryn. 1985. "Black girls speak for themselves." In *Just a Bunch of Girls: Feminist Approaches to Schooling,* Gary Weiner (ed.), 63–76. London: Open University Press.

Sadker, Myra, and David Sadker. 1994. *Failing at Fairness: How Schools Cheat Girls.* New York: Charles Schribner's Sons.

Sanday, Peggy Reeves. 1990. *Fraternity Gang Rape: Sex, Brotherhood, and Privilege on Campus.* New York: New York University Press.

Scott, James C. 1985. *Weapons of the Weak: Everyday Forms of Peasant Resistance.* New Haven: Yale University Press. 1990. *Domination and the Art of Resistance.* New Haven: Yale University Press.

Stack, Carol B. 1974. *All Our Kin: Strategies for Survival in a Black Community.* New York: Harper and Row.

Stombler Mindy. 1994. "Buddies' or 'slutties': The collective sexual reputation of fraternity little sisters." *Gender & Society* 8(3):297–323.

Stombler Mindy, and Patricia Yancey Martin. 1994. "Bringing women in, keeping women down: Fraternity 'little sister' organizations." *Journal of Contemporary Ethnography* 23(2):150–184.

Thomas, Claire. 1980. "Girls and counter-school culture." Melbourne Working Papers, Melbourne.

Thorne, Barrie. 1993. *Gender Play: Girls and Boys in School.* New Brunswick, N.J.: Rutgers University Press. 1995. "Symposium on West and Fenstermaker's 'Doing differences';" *Gender & Society* 9:497–499.

West, Candace and Sarah Fenstermaker. 1995. "Doing difference." *Gender & Society* 9:8–37.

Wilson, Dierdre. 1978. "Sexual codes and conduct: A study of teenage girls." In *Women, Sexuality, and Social Control.* C. Smart and B. Smart (eds.), 65–73. London: Routledge and Kegan Paul.

Willis, Paul. 1977. *Learning to Labor.* Westmead, England: Saxon House.

Article Review Form at end of book.

WiseGuide Wrap-Up

- Hegemonic white masculinity differentiates itself not only from women, but also from men who are stereotyped as effeminate—Jewish men, gay men, and Asian men—and men who are seen as uncivilized—Black men, American Indian men, and Latino men.

- Although Promise Keepers preaches racial reconciliation among men, it does not promote social justice for people of color and thereby keeps racial hierarchies among men in place.

- Women in the antilynching movement understood that white men used chauvinism as a legitimation for racism and that racial and gendered hierarchies are intricately interconnected.

- Gendered hierarchies are differently structured across racial and ethnic communities, in ways that reflect each group's history and its current location within the stratification system.

R.E.A.L. Sites

This list provides a print preview of typical **Coursewise** R.E.A.L. sites. (There are over 100 such sites at the **Courselinks**™ site.) The danger in printing URLs is that web sites can change overnight. As we went to press, these sites were functional using the URLs provided. If you come across one that isn't, please let us know via email to: webmaster@coursewise.com. Use your Passport to access the most current list of R.E.A.L. sites at the **Courselinks** site.

Site name: A Sense of Self

URL: http://www.libertynet.org/balch/html/body_a_sense_of_self.html#TheArtists

Why is it R.E.A.L.? This site provides links to a set of sites centered on issues of interest to women of color from various ethnic communities.

Key topics: women of color, women artists

Try this: Visit three or more of the links you find on this page. Do the concerns of women of color across racial and ethnic groups have similarities? What are they? What seem to be the important sources of difference? Make notes on your observations and compare them with those of a classmate who has visited three other sites.

Site name: The Convention on the Elimination of All Forms of Discrimination Against Women

URL: http://www.un.org/womenwatch/daw/cedaw/conven.htm

Why is it R.E.A.L.? More than 165 countries, including the United States, have signed The Convention on the Elimination of All Forms of Discrimination Against Women. This important document makes us aware that discrimination against women is a global problem and that antiwoman discrimination includes discrimination on the bases of race, ethnicity, nationality, religion, and class.

Key topics: women, international policy, United Nations

Try this: Read the documents on this site. Think about the intellectual and activist advantages of conceptualizing women as a worldwide group that suffers from gender, racial, sexual, and class oppression. What are the disadvantages of thinking so broadly? Finally, imagine how you might encourage the UN to hold accountable the countries that have signed this declaration.

section 6

Key Points

- Dating "outside the race" raises questions about power, loyalty, comfort, and commitments.

- Like the meaning of motherhood, the meaning of medical science varies for women along the lines of race, ethnicity, and class.

- Among Black women, the discovery that a teenage daughter is pregnant calls into question the mother's identity as well as the stability of their relationship with each other.

Family

 **WiseGuide Intro**

Most sociologists would agree that families are "primary groups" in our society. Although families take many forms—opposite-sex and same-sex couples with or without children, single parents and their children, and so on—they have some things in common. As people bound by ties of mutual affection and interdependence, families socialize their members: they create our senses of self, help determine our positions in the wider social world, and teach us about the values and norms of our society. It is in families that we learn about and pass on beliefs about our own racial identities and those of others and about the traditions, expectations, and values associated with our ethnic heritages. Many families understand themselves as racially and ethnically homogeneous and discourage their members from bringing into the family people from different ethnic, cultural, religious, or racial backgrounds. As a result, families often reproduce and maintain the racial boundaries of our society.

A number of factors have encouraged Americans to maintain racially homogeneous families. In addition to deeply held cultural traditions, various laws have forbidden marriage between particular racialized groups throughout U.S. history. While historians document much intermarriage between early European male explorers and settlers and both Native American Indian and African women, such relationships were outlawed with the institutionalization of slavery—and the arrival of more white women to the continent. The last state-level law banning marriage between whites and Blacks was overturned fewer than thirty-five years ago in a Supreme Court case called *Loving v. Virginia.* Many of the parents of the students using this reader were born into a world in which it was actually illegal in some states for African-Americans and European-Americans to marry one another.

Despite cultural, structural, and legal obstacles, some people have always found ways of creating interracial families. The decriminalization of interracial marriages has resulted in a marked increase in such families in recent decades. Today, a significant minority of families serve as sites of "cultural contact," places in which people from two or more cultures interact. Families raising children in multiethnic or multiracial households contribute to cultural change by promoting interracial understanding and by denaturalizing the presumedly natural segregation of racialized groups.

Clearly, our society's belief that race is rooted in biology, and its stratification around the social significance assigned to biology, promotes the belief that people should not "date outside their races," let alone marry, form partnerships, or have children with people from other racial groups. How does this belief help maintain racial stratification? How do the messages we receive about interracial relationships help maintain this broader pattern of segregation? How will an increased number of multiracial families change this landscape? While many would agree that segregation is not healthy for our society and would maintain that racial homogeneity increases both segregation and discrimination, it should also be noted that forming families across racial lines raises issues for members of both racial minority and racial majority groups; members of minority groups express concerns about losing their cultural uniqueness through assimilation into the dominant culture, while racially dominant groups worry about losing their place in the social hierarchy.

In the articles in this section, we explore how families are affected by racialization and how the meaning of children and family varies across the lines of race and culture. In the first article, four gay male writers from diverse racial and ethnic backgrounds hash over the politics, problems, and pleasures of relationships across the lines of racial and ethnic difference. Anthropologist Rayna Rapp moves us from dating to reproduction in her article on amniocentesis, which explores differences among women from three ethnic groups as they contemplate the meaning of information about fetal health in the early stages of their pregnancies. Finally, Elaine Bell Kaplan, a sociologist, studies the impact of teenage girls' pregnancies on their own mothers within the context of the African-American community. As you read these articles, keep in mind how the broader system of racial stratification in this society shapes the experiences of individuals as they struggle to create, define, and maintain the connections we think of as constituting "family."

Questions

Reading 18. What are the advantages and disadvantages of dating across racial lines? Are same-sex relationships different from cross-sex relationships when it comes to interracial dating?

Reading 19. How do white, Black, and Hispanic women differ in their reliance on high-tech medicine for assistance in deciding whether to continue or end pregnancies?

Reading 20. Why are Black women among the strongest critics of teenage pregnancy? How does a daughter's pregnancy change the mother-daughter relationship?

What are the advantages and disadvantages of dating across racial lines? Are same-sex relationships different from cross-sex relationships when it comes to interracial dating?

Sleeping with the Enemy?

Talking about Men, Race, and Relationships

Tomás Almaguer, Rüdiger Busto, Ken Dixon, and Ming-Yeung Lu

Editor's Introduction

One of the most frequently recurring, but private, topics of discussion among the men on Out/Look's *editorial board is interracial relationships. This issue invariably raises questions about the tension between one's individual sexual desires and the growing pressure to maintain primary relationships within one's own ethnic group. Rather than attempt a self-consciously theoretical analysis of these questions, we decided that the men of color on the board should try to tease out a few of the issues from a personal point of view. Admittedly, the men on the* Out/ Look *board do not speak definitively for all men of color on this issue. The fact that all four editors have graduate school educations, for example, means they speak for only a small segment of the "colored" population. On the other hand, having negotiated their way through the hallowed bastions of white institutions, they have learned to manipulate "the master's tools" in more ways than one!*

Both Latino editors, Tomás Almaguer and Rüdiger Busto, come from working-class barrios in the Southwest, have been active in Chicano politics for many years, and are now academics. Ming-Yeung Lu is an immigrant from Hong Kong active in several political organizations and is currently working on a Ph.D. in modern thought and literature. Ken Dixon is an actor, administrator, and long-time African American activist. The following candid conversation took place over coffee.

Why Have Interracial Relationships Become an Issue?

Tomás: It seems to me that one of the things happening in the cultural and political sphere is the tremendous emphasis given to dating people within one's own group. I think Marlon Riggs's film, *Tongues Untied*, crystallized some of that sentiment. The credo of the film—"Black men loving Black men is the revolutionary act"—set off a lot of discussion about interracial relationships.

Ming: That's an interesting entry point because Marlon is one of a few Black gay men creating images within the African American community. This discussion has relevance for other groups out there, like the one I'm a member of—Gay Asian Pacific Alliance (GAPA)—which to some degree suggests to the larger gay and lesbian community a controversial racial separatism. I have lots of gay Asian friends—some new immigrants from Chinatown, some just like me—who have never had problems dating other Asian men and their "objects of desire" are pretty much the "United Nations"—that is, of all races. What I'm trying to say is that the statement "Black men loving Black men is the revolutionary act" has to be understood in a certain socio-political context, in this instance a racist and homophobic society. For someone like myself, who has a colonial background, coming from Hong Kong, and has been taught to aspire to "white" culture as a model of success, dating other gay Asians was difficult for me for a long time. Loving another Asian becomes a deeply liberating and affirming "event" both personally and politically.

Ken: I went to graduate school in Boston and was one of fifteen

Tomás Almaguer, Rüdiger Busto, Ken Dixon, and Ming-Yeung Lu, "Sleeping with the Enemy? Talking about Men, Race, and Relationships," *Out/Look* 4 (3) (Winter), 1992, pp. 30–38.

graduate students in clinical psychology, two of whom were Black. All my educational experience, virtually all my work experience has been in the mainstream culture. However, I've had relationships pretty much equally with Blacks and whites.

Rudy: There's two things going on here. One of them is the "official" back-to-the-race, politically correct, going back and dating "one's self" like Marlon Rigg's film, but then when you look at his own relationship . . .

Ken: He has a white lover . . .

Rudy: Exactly. So there's something going on. An apparent rift between theory and practice?

Tomás: I think Marlon tried to clarify that point. Not by explaining it away, but saying that the message of Black men loving Black men was not to be taken solely in terms of relationships and sexuality, because people of color are getting in touch with themselves in a broader kind of way. Marlon was talking about us learning to love ourselves.

Rudy: But isn't that a cop out?

Ming: Within my community we're very invested in the affirmation of gay Asians loving each other, but some of us are very careful not to make it into a political dictum because we're not out there to legislate desire. The first time I had a passionate affair with another Asian gay man (but not the first time I had sex with one) was during a Gay Pride Week in the first months of my immersion in the GAPA community. I remember feeling that I'd finally come to a fulfillment of who I am. But that feeling wore off pretty quickly, because I had to deal with the tensions existing between two gay Asian men. When the romanticism wears off you are forced to see that affirmation in perspective. If you make it the primary condition of a fulfilling relationship, then I think it's not only naive, but can be oppressive itself.

Rudy: It has to do sometimes with cultures.

Ming: Or class.

Tomás: That's really weird for me. I understand people getting in touch with their own and all of the political sensibilities that go along with that. At a very fundamental level it often represents assimilated, middle-class gay men of color reconnecting with their ethnicity and undergoing a profound cultural catharsis. It represents a coming home for many people, an affirmation of sameness. But I didn't become gay just to go to one corner of the candy store. I want the whole thing!

Ming: Precisely. But the problem is that a lot of us gay Asians are stuck with sugar daddies—or white sugar—and do not realize that candies have always come in lots of varieties. For me, a community like GAPA not only provides a space where we can have the choice to be both gay and Asian, but also to say that we gay Asians are there for each other, to love and fuck. Personally, I used to go through the personal ads and skip the Asian ones—that, to me, means not having a choice.

Rudy: Wait a minute; so not considering the Asian personals was not a choice?

Ming: To go out with another Asian was not a choice for me because I repressed that desire. There was something in the back of my mind which excluded that possibility. I'd been acculturated to see white people, white men in particular, as more attractive. Even though I was brought up in a city which is 90% Chinese, or Asian, if a white person came into a room suddenly the atmosphere, the class atmosphere became elevated. For me, the gay Asian community now provides the means to have a choice. Now I can say I'm attracted to Asians as well as to white men.

Rudy: Well, I definitely have a "type": somebody approximately my age with dark hair, white, educated, and middle class; although now I'm living with a fair-haired man and we're very different kinds of people in temperament and tastes. As far as lust goes, I'd like to believe that I'm more open to the directions lust leads me. A friend of mine says that there are "types"—men who you fuck—and then there are "boyfriends." I know, for example, that I'm increasingly attracted to Latino men, but I've never had a relationship with one. This attraction is a recent development probably having to do with the large Latino population here in the Bay Area. When I went to college in the late 1970s, there were no gay student organizations on campus; there were no gay Latino or Asian men that I knew personally. Now campuses like Berkeley have a whole range of organizations and groups. I think it's very liberating for gay college students of color to have organizations. I wish I had had that advantage. Back then all of the gay men that I knew, every last one of them, were white.

Being Gay in Our Own Communities

Ken: I grew up in a Black community, in a Black neighborhood and to be gay was to be effeminate— basically a Black queen. The first man I fell in love with was Black. He was a football player, and he had been in the Marines. My experience with him was always one that didn't have really as much to do with race as it had to do with his difference from everything my father said gay men were. We were together from the time I was sixteen until I was twenty two. I didn't really start dating white men until I got to graduate school, so it wasn't so much me climbing to power.

Ming: What Ken says brings up the community issue again. For me there was no gay Asian community, and so there was a lot of alienation from my own community. When I came out, not knowing other gay Asians, I naturally dated from the majority of the "gay community" which was white. And until there was a gay Asian community, I didn't have choices. This is something new that I see happening to my friends and myself.

Rudy: That's true for me also, because I'm half Latino and half Asian, and that has meant living on the margins of both of those communities. Then you add on the dimension of sexual preference! Who were my role models going to be when both racial communities are essentially homophobic? The only gay people I had access to were, of course, white men.

Tomás: My earliest sexual experiences were exclusively with other Chicanos, from a very early age. I didn't become sexually involved with white men until I was in my mid-twenties. At that point, I was thoroughly colonized and had internalized the racist messages of white society. When I finally came out—and declared myself "gay" like all the other white boys—I wanted and went after the fantasy images that are fetishized in narcissistic gay culture. Sure, it has all the trappings of self-negation and pure fetishization of difference but it's still a major turn on. I don't think I want to be completely reprogrammed for the sake of anyone's identity politics of the moment.

Eroticizing Racial Differences

Rudy: I personally don't have that "candy store" experience because I've only been in relationships with white men. Not that many; I've tried to make them long term. For me the attraction had a lot to do

with coming from the barrio, from the poor side of town. My second lover was middle class, "white bread" all over, from Pasadena, and on his way up the socio-economic ladder. Being with him was my initiation into the process of climbing up that same ladder to privilege. My desire was not only to be middle class, but to be with an upwardly mobile, middle-class white man and participate in middle-class America that way. I'm not quite sure what to think about that now, but class definitely has something to do with it.

Tomás: It has to do with power and how we eroticize difference in a racist society. We are socialized into European standards of beauty, but our sexual attractions are mediated by being at the bottom of the racial hierarchy. At the center of power, at the very top, is mighty whitey: the white male! So, when it comes to experiencing homosexual desire, it's easy to understand how it is mediated by our structural position in society. I mean, after a while, who wants another fieldhand like themselves! I want the master! The master's piece, to be more specific. It's really a case of unadulterated colonial desire, but we live in a world full of contradictions. The point is, learn to work with them— and enjoy them.

Rudy: When I was in school in Boston, I discovered that being brown was actually a novelty. First of all, I wasn't Black, and historically the racial categories there have been Black and white. I was somewhere in between, and I was also educated. So I was this novelty walking into gay clubs there. I met a lot of white men because they were curious about "what" I was. People have crazy ideas of who I am, so it was actually quite enjoyable for me because at that point my desire for "types"—which were all white—was beginning, as Tomas said, to crystallize. And as

Ming pointed out, up to that point I had no community with which to explore same-race relationships.

Tomás: What do you think is going on for those white men in their attractions for you?

Rudy: It has to do with seeing men of color as libidinous. Seeing them as somehow more animalistic, more sensual, and at some level, more provocative and mysterious than white men. Of course, this is a type of racism that foregrounds stereotypes over individuality. The question is, then, should we exploit that fetishism as a kind of reverse power trip?

Ming: I've heard many stories about white American men who were supposedly heterosexual, went to Asia, and discovered their homosexual desire while they were there and having sex with Asian men. And they developed this particular taste for Asian men during that "coming-out" process. These stories of white-American-men-fucking-Asian-boys are interesting examples of how Americans are conditioned to see races— "white," "Black," "Oriental"—in terms of power differences. There are so many internalized issues here, really—homophobia, racism! It's as if these white American men can be "gay" with someone who is neither white nor American, so they don't have to deal with their own gayness. By highlighting certain racial and national differences, they can keep some of their most deeply held images of power intact.

Rudy: Yes, I agree there's a cultural conditioning in this country which feminizes the Asian male. Asian men are emasculated by white men as a response to their potential economic and numerical strength and then sexualized/exoticized along with Asian women. Think about it. There is a deep cultural inscription here in the West between white men and Asian women—Madame

Butterfly for example. And now there is the incredible statement by David Hwang's play M. Butterfly where "Cio-cio san" is, in reality, a man! For some white men then, Asian men may be the bridge between internalized homophobia and homoerotic desire.

Ming: When I think about my fear of other gay Asian men before I got used to interacting with them, I think it had something to do with my internalized stuff. I could deal with white men because they are not like me, at least racially. But when I would see someone who is like myself, I'd get uncomfortable, you know, because of something in me. . . .

Rudy: . . . a reflection of yourself? That reminds me of a brief fling I had once in D.C. with an incredible Cambodian man. It was wonderful because it was the first time I'd ever had sex with somebody who was of the same skin color as I; we had similar values in terms of how to treat each other. It was definitely some of the best sex I ever had. There was a familiarity and unstated trust in that brief relationship that I have yet to encounter again. There is something about finding out who you are inside with somebody of your own race.

Tomás: I want to get back to the attractions of white men towards Asian men. I've seen parallels in the way that white men get attracted to Chicano men, and it happens in one of two ways. We are either infantilized and feminized in such a way that puts them in charge—they want submissive "brown boys"—or they transform us into a potent, supermasculinized object choice. These men we affectionately refer to as "chorizo chasers" because they are symbolically negating their privilege by assuming the bottom role. There is an interesting sexual politic that underlies the way these desires get played out.

PC Sex

Ken: But I'm not sure if desire needs to be put in politically correct terms. You see someone that you're attracted to. Do you then want to know, is he the right class? Is he the right color? I mean, that's not what you're thinking about in that instant. For me I find that stuff comes up maybe after I'm in a relationship. I've been in long-term relationships with all types of men, except for someone Asian. I cannot remember saying to myself, "Oh, this is a nice Black man that I should be in a relationship with." It's more like, "This is the man I want to take to bed."

Tomás: I've just never been able to get beyond thinking about categories of people. I understand and appreciate what you are saying, but it doesn't compute for me. I'd like to be able to get into a more aggressive affirmative action program; it may be time to press for the Chicano agenda. It might be a nice change—white boys can get pretty boring after awhile.

Rudy: So, what about lust?

Ken: Maybe I'm apolitical in some ways, but for me there's a place in the world for lust. Lust is just that. If you go out to a club and you want to sleep with somebody, you don't run through a list of what you are looking for in a partner.

Tomás: We're so different. I'm just the other way. That list immediately comes up for me. The check list. Ok, what categories does this person embody? And I eroticize all of those categories: white, middle class, mid- to late twenties. I could go down the list. Or I could give you the catalogue, the J. Crew Catalogue! Or perhaps any one of the homoerotic Calvin Klein ads.

Ken: I'm curious, has that changed over time?

Tomás: No. I've been totally fixated with those categories. That doesn't mean that I like the same story-line or that the role I play is just as fixed. No, I love turning the tables on white boys. I become the producer and director of the sexual drama; I don't relinquish all the power but enjoy playing with it. It's like the sisters always say: "The personal is political."

Ming: What if you're interested in a guy who fits all of the categories on your check list, but he turns to you and says, "Well, you're not white. I don't want you for that reason."?

Tomás: That happens, but that's his problem—he's got provincial tastes. What is the real turn on and what makes things work is for the person to buy into the eroticization of someone being Latino. That's when the sparks fly. They also objectify the hell out of us and cast us into their own latently racist sexual dramas.

Interracial Relationships

Ming: Being in an interracial relationship is a complicated issue, and I'm not ready to theorize or make it black and white . . . or yellow! It's not so much having to do with what or whom I fantasize about when I masturbate. When I go to the gym, I may see this great all-American looking boy and start to imagine what it would be like to have sex with this guy, with this GQ image. That's fine, and I can do that, but I know that if I get into a relationship with him there will be a lot of complications with the social and political parts of it. I guess there's all these different levels of questioning.

Tomás: But that's the difference between sexual attractions and desires versus getting to know people and entering into a relationship.

Rudy: Ken, it's interesting that you don't really think about the class or the race of a person if you find him attractive. I want to push you on that. When you see someone who's attractive enough to want to go to bed with, your initial reaction is just pure lust. But isn't there a second order reflection where you think, "Well, but I couldn't have a relationship with him because he's "blank?"

Ken: Well, no, because it depends on the situation. If I'm out cruising to sleep with somebody, I'm not thinking about a relationship. I mean, it's going to be something that happens during the course of that encounter that's going to bring up the idea that maybe this is a person I'm interested in and want to see again. I met the man I'm living with now at a straight disco. What attracted me to him was his beard and the lust in his eye, to be perfectly honest. I was already in a relationship with someone and no one had looked at me like that in a long time! He wanted me to go home with him and I wouldn't. I said, "No, I'm in a relationship and I'm monogamous." But it never dawned on me—I didn't say, "Oh, he's got a cute beard and he's got lust in his eyes and he's white!"

Rudy: What about roles and power relations in your relationships? You can't deny that something goes through your mind about who is going to do what to whom as soon as you tear each other's clothes off!

Ken: When I've been involved with Black men there's a lot more power issues; who's going to be on top and who's going to be on the bottom. I think it has to do with growing up in a matriarchal society and Black men having less power in their own social structure. So when two Black men come together you just complicate that because they have both come out of a matriarchal society. Somebody's going to have to vie for position on top. But I haven't been that kind of person, so my relationships with Black men have

suffered in some ways because I don't play that power game.

Rudy: With a white man are the roles any less complicated?

Ken: I think that it is different. My experience with Black men is that I don't play out the role. I'm not a top and I'm not a bottom and I don't let any man, white or Black, or any other, put me in that kind of slot. With Black men it comes up more.

Ming: What about the problems within interracial relationships themselves?

Rudy: When I'm walking with my lover on Market or Castro street, I find myself singling out interracial couples and thinking, "Oh yeah, those two people are of different races and that's very interesting to see. I wonder how they met." This, of course, is completely apart from the fact that I am also on the street with a white man, never imagining that someone might be looking at us through some sociological or psychological lens.

Tomás: So what do you process when you see this? What occurs to you?

Rudy: Well, often, when I see a white man with an Asian man I get a little angry. I just assume, especially if the Asian man seems to be younger, that the Asian man is being fetishized by the white man. If I see a white man with a Chicano, you know what I think? I think that there's got to be a power struggle going on. That there's probably a lot of negotiating and working out of cultural conflicts, which recapitulates in microcosm the struggle historically between Spanish-speaking and English-speaking people. When I see a Black man and a white man together I don't think too much about it because I'm used to seeing that combination.

Ming: When I walk down Castro street holding hands with another Asian man, we get a lot of stares.

Ken: That also happens when two Black men walk down Castro holding hands.

Ming: If I were in a relationship with a white man, he would have to understand where I am coming from in terms of my politics, my socialization and so on. If he ran around flaunting his white privilege, it would be really hard for me to deal with that. It would bring up all of those questions about insecurities and power relations that I don't think I'm ready to deal with at this point in my life.

Tomás: It's almost like white men are in a different world. I mean the way they process things and the way they think about them. Even the little things immediately come to mind, especially cultural sensibilities. . . .

Rudy: . . . the food! For me it's also been the way arguments take place. It's a very reasoned, rational, let's-talk-it-out kind of thing. The way I grew up, boy, you screamed and yelled until you got it out, then it was over. But in my relationships with white men disagreements have had to take a certain "civilized" format, and to me that is always odd. But you know, I have to say that I'm also attracted to Jewish men. Not to generalize, of course, but many Jewish men that I have been attracted to seem to have a sense of "culture" in terms of tradition, roots, and family orientations. I find that enormously attractive . . .

Tomás: There is definitely a cultural bond between Chicanos and Jews and also Chicanos and Irish Catholics. Jews, for example, are as close to being truly ethnic or "colored" as white people get but I'm convinced that they share other European Americans' view of us as "domesticated savages." Our Europeanized culture and Judeo-Christian background makes us a safe "other"; we are not their complete antithesis, like the African American man.

Ming: I am also attracted to Jewish men. I had a boyfriend who was Jewish and I respected the culture in the sense of traditions. I wonder though, how are issues of anti-semitism and racism similar or different? One would expect some similarities in that Jews are also viewed as outsiders, but they are not quite the same.

Rudy: What happened to love? That's always the foil when talking about the politics or theories about interracial relationships. What do you do with love? Yes, our desires are conditioned by society, but you could fall in love with people you don't think you'd ever fall in love with! Again, the "types" versus the "boyfriend."

Tomás: Those things do seem to happen. I'd like to think that in spite of all the odds, love does seem to find a way.

 Article Review Form at end of book.

How do white, Black, and Hispanic women differ in their reliance on high-tech medicine for assistance in deciding whether to continue or end pregnancies?

Constructing Amniocentesis:

Maternal and Medical Discourses

Rayna Rapp

When we walked into the doctor's office, both my husband and I were crying. He looked up and said, "What's wrong? Why are you in tears?" "It's the baby, the baby is going to die," I said. "That isn't a baby," he said firmly. "It's a collection of cells that made a mistake."

—*Leah Rubinstein, white housewife, 39*

The language of biomedical science is powerful. Its neutralizing vocabulary, explanatory syntax, and distancing pragmatics provide universal descriptions of human bodies and their life processes that appear to be pre-cultural or non-cultural. But as the field of medical anthropology constantly reminds us, bodies are also and always culturally constituted, and their aches, activities, and accomplishments are continuously assigned meanings. While the discourse of biomedicine speaks of the inevitable march of scientific and clinical progress, its practices are constantly open to interpretation. Its hegemonic definitions routinely require acceptance, transformation, or contestation from the embodied "objects" whose subjectivity it so powerfully affects.

The necessary contest over the meaning assigned embodied experiences is particularly clear in the field of reproductive health care, where consumer movements, women's health activism, and feminist scholars have sharply criticized biomedical practices. Public accusations against the demeaning and controlling nature of gynecological and obstetrical health care have led to dramatic results. Over the last 20 years, such criticisms have influenced the reform of medical services, occasionally encouraged the development of alternative health practices, and often inspired women to advocate for themselves and others. Contests over the means and meanings of women's reproductive health services are, thus, an ongoing part of American social and institutional life. These conflicts reflect the complex hierarchies of power, along which both providers and consumers of health care organized. They cannot easily be resolved because the practices of biomedicine are at once emancipatory and socially controlling, essential for healthy survival yet essentializing of women's lives.

Reproductive medicine and its feminist critique thus share a central concern with the problem of female identity. In both discourses, as throughout much of American culture, motherhood stands as a condensed symbol of female identity. Changes in sexual practices, pregnancy, and birth are widely believed to be transforming the meaning of "womanhood" itself. This connection between women's reproductive patterns and a notion of female gender is longstanding: cries of alarm have been raised for over a century concerning the future of "the sex" as birth control practices spread, as abortion was criminalized and medicalized, as childbirth moved from the hands of female lay practitioners to male professionals, and as a discourse of explicitly female sexual pleasure became articulated. There is, of course, great diversity in women's experiences with medical care in general, and the medicalization of sexual activity and reproduction in particular. Yet, the image of "womanhood" as a central symbol in American culture has often been constructed as if motherhood were its stable, and uniform core, threatened by external changes in technology, education, labor force participation, medicine, and the like.

This shared and shifting object of embodied gender is revealed when we examine what have come to be called "the new reproductive technologies", dramatic and well-publicized interventions into fertility, conception, and pregnancy management and screening. Biomedical claims about the NRTs are usually framed in the available language of neutral management of female bodies to insure progress; feminist critiques are often enunciated as protection of women's core experiences against intrusion by "technodocs". Both discourses are fraught with old assumptions about the meaning of pregnancy, itself an archetypically liminal state. And both discourses are shot through with contradictions and possibilities for the health care providers, pregnant women, and feminist commentators who currently must make sense of the rapid routinization of new reproductive technologies.

This article presents an analysis of amniocentesis, one of the new reproductive technologies.[1] My examples are drawn from an ongoing field study of the social impact and cultural meaning of prenatal diagnosis in New York City, where I have observed more than 250 intake interviews, in which genetic counselors interact with pregnant patients; interviewed over 70 current users and refusers of amniocentesis; collected stories of 30 women who received what is so antiseptically referred to as a "positive diagnosis" (i.e., that something was wrong with their fetus), and participated and interviewed in a support group for parents of children with Down syndrome, the most commonly diagnosed chromosome abnormality, and the condition for which pregnant women are most likely to seek amniocentesis.[2]

In New York City, unlike many other parts of the United States, prenatal diagnosis is funded by both medicaid and the City's Health Department, so it is available to a population of women whose ethnic, class, racial and religious backgrounds are as diverse as the City itself. The City's cytogenetic laboratory through which I work reaches a population of pregnant women who are approximately one-third Hispanic, one-third African-American, and one-third white, according to the racial/ethnic categories provided by both the City and State Health Departments. But these categories undoubtedly conceal as much as they reveal. At the present time, "Hispanic" includes Puerto Ricans and Dominicans long familiar with City services and the "new migrants" of Central America, many of whom are drawn from rural backgrounds, are desperately poor, and often undocumented, as well as middle-class, highly educated Colombians and Ecuadorians who may be experiencing downward mobility through migration. African-Americans include fourth-generation New Yorkers, women whose children circle back and forth between the City and rural Alabama, and Haitians who have lived in Brooklyn only a few months. "White" encompasses Ashkenazi and Sephardic Jews, Irish, Italian and Slavic Catholics, Episcopalian and Evangelical Protestants, as if being neither Black nor Brown placed them in a homogenized racial category. The categories themselves thus freeze a "racial map," which ignores the historic complexity of identity endemic to New York, and many other urban areas in contemporary America. Despite any understanding of the historic processes by which such a map has been created and promulgated, it is nearly impossible to escape its sociological boundaries when conducting and describing fieldwork in New York City.

My interviews and observations are tuned to the tension between the universal abstract language of reproductive medicine, and the personal experiences pregnant women articulate in telling their amniocentesis stories. Differences among women are revealed in their reasons for accepting or refusing the test; their images of fetuses and of disabled children; and the meaning of abortion in their lives. My working assumption is that a conflict of discourses necessarily characterizes the arena of reproductive technology, where nothing is stable: scientific "information", popular struggles both feminist and anti-feminist, and the shifting meaning of maternity and womanhood for individuals and communities with diverse ethnic, racial, religious, sexual, and migration histories are all currently under negotiation.

As one of the new reproductive technologies, prenatal diagnosis makes powerful claims to reveal and characterize biological bodies. Bypassing women's direct experiences of pregnancy, prenatal diagnosis uses sonography, an amniotic tap, and laboratory karyotyping to describe fetal health and illness to the woman (and her support network) within whose body the fetus grows[3]. Prenatal diagnosis focuses on pregnancy, first decontextualizing it and then inscribing it in a universal chronology, location, and ontology. Maternal serum alphafetoprotein blood screens (MSAFP), for example, may suggest a neural tube defect if readings are too high for a given pregnancy's dates, or a fetus with Down syndrome if values are too low. But the calibration of values is tricky, and potentially abnormal results must be recalibrated against a sonogram, whose measurement of cranial circumference and femur length is commonly considered the most accurate indicator of pregnancy dates. There is thus ample room for negotiating interpretations within the biomedical model. Many women already hold firm opinions about the dating of their pregnancies before they become acquainted with this highly technical process. Any woman may insist that she knows exactly when she became pregnant, or date her own growing pregnancy by signs phenomenologically available only to herself, contesting the narrative strategy of MSAFP, LMP (last menstrual period) and sonodates. But when pregnancies are medically managed, most women learn to redescribe their bodily changes through the language of technology, rather than dating their pregnancies experientially. There is thus a continuous negotiation circling the description of any pregnancy in which a woman reveals and embeds herself and her perceptions of her fetus in a language shot through with medical, personal, and communal resources.

The Language of Testing

Women use very different language and reasons in describing their acceptance or refusal of the test. When I first began interviewing middle-class pregnant women about their amniocentesis decisions, it was hard for me to hear their cultural constructions, for, like my own, they mirrored the progressive message of science. Most (but not all) middle-class women, a disproportionately white group, accepted the test with some variant of this statement:

I always knew I'd have amnio. Science is there to make life better, so why not use its power? Bill and I really want a child, but we don't want a baby with Down's, if we can avoid it.
(Susan Klein, white accountant, 37)

But even white, middle-class women often express ambivalence and they do so in a language intricately intertwined with the language of medicine itself. Their fears and fantasies reflect thoughts that both question and sustain the dominant discourse itself, for example:

I cried for two days after I had the test. I guess I was identifying with universal motherhood, I felt like my image of my womb had been shattered. It still feels like it's in pieces, not like such a safe place as before. I guess technology gives us a certain kind of control, but we have to sacrifice something in return. I've lost my brash confidence that my body just produces healthy babies all by itself, naturally, and that if it doesn't, I can handle whatever comes along as a mother.
(Carola Mirsky, white school teacher, 39)

The low-income African-American women with whom I talked were far less likely to either accept, or be transformed by, the medical discourse of prenatal diagnosis. American black women who had grown up in the South, especially the rural South, often described alternate, non-medical agendas in their use of amniocentesis, invoking other systems for interpreting bodily states, including pregnancy. Dreams, visions, healing sessions, root work and herbal teas could be used to reveal the state of a specific pregnancy. One such woman, who at 27 became the mother of a Down syndrome baby, told me she had been refused amniocentesis in five city hospitals, always because of her young age. When I asked why she had wanted the test, she described a dream which recurred throughout the pregnancy:

So I am having this boy baby. It is definitely a boy baby. And something is wrong, I mean, it just is not right. Sometimes, he is missing an arm, and sometimes, it's a leg. Maybe it's a retarded baby. You can't really tell, it's all covered in hair. Once or twice, they give him to my husband and say, 'look at your son, take him the way he is.' As if the way he is isn't all right. I tried to get that test to make peace with that dream (Q: would you have had an abortion if you'd had the test?) Oh, no. The whole thing was going back to the dreams . . . just so's I could say, 'this baby is the baby in the dreams' and come to peace with it.
(May Norris, African-American hospital orderly, 27)

Another African-American woman, pregnant with a fourth, unexpected child at the age of 42, had this to say:

So I was three months pregnant before I knew I was pregnant, just figured it was change of life. The clinic kept saying no, and it's really the same signs, menopause and pregnancy, you just feel that lousy. So when they told me I was pregnant I thought about abortion, I mean, maybe I figured I was too old for this. But in my neighborhood a lot of Caribbean women have babies, a lot of them are late babies. So I got used to it. But the clinic doctor was freaked out. He sent me for genetic counseling. Counseling? I thought counseling meant giving reassurance, helping someone accept and find their way. Wisdom, help, guidance, you know what I mean. This lady was a smart lady, but right away she started pullin' out pictures of mongoloids. So I got huffy: 'I didn't come here to look at pictures of mongoloids', I says to her. So she got huffy and told me it was about mongoloids, this counseling. So we got more and more huffy between us, and finally, I left. Wasn't gonna sit and listen to that stuff. By the time I got myself to the appointment (for the test) I'd been to see my healing woman, a healer, who calmed me down, gave me the reassurance I needed. I knew everything was gonna be ok. Oh, I wouldn't have had an abortion that late in the game. I just got helped out by the healer woman, so I could wait out the results of that test without too much fussin.'
(Naiumah Foster, school teacher, 43)

And among women whose background includes no prior encounter with the scientific description of amniocentesis, the test may be accepted out of the desire to avoid the suffering of children; a respect for the authority of doctors (or the conflated image of genetic counselors in white coats); or simple curiosity. One recently arrived Salvadoran, now working as a domestic, told me, for example, that she wanted the test because science had such miraculous powers to show you what God had in store. This mixing of religious and secular discourses is no less awed (and awesome!) than that of the native-born professional woman who told me she wanted her test to be an advancement to science. She knew it was the only way geneticists could legally obtain amniotic fluid for their research, to which she ardently wished to make a contribution. Both women characterized amniocentesis as a path of enlightenment, but their motivations for its use differed sharply. The one characterized it in terms of God's grace; the other in light of scientific progress.

Even those rejecting the test often express amazement and interest in the powers of reproductive medicine. A Haitian Evangelist who said she would never accept amniocentesis wavered briefly when she learned it could tell her the sex of her baby: did such information cost more, she queried? (as the mother of four daughters, she had high hopes and great curiosity). Among those rejecting the test, reasons included anti-abortion attitudes often (but not always) articulated in religious terms[4]; fear of losing the baby after medical invasion[5]; anger and mistrust of the medical system; and fear of needles.

When I first began observing counseling sessions, it was easy for me to share the psychological lingo many counselors use privately, in evaluating patients' motives for accepting or rejecting the test. A discourse of fluent Freudian phrases is used by counselors trained in psychological-psychoanalytic thinking, as well as in human genetics. Women may easily be labelled "denying," "regressed," "passive," or "fatalistic" when their choices are seen as irrational to professionals trained to balance empathy against epidemiological statistics. Such labels, however, reduce social phenomena and cultural contexts to individual idiosyncrasies. I have often observed communication gaps, negotiated decisions, and situations of multiple meaning, which cannot be understood when reduced to a model of individual

decision-making. When a Puerto Rican garment worker, aged 39, who is a Charismatic Catholic, replied to the offer of "the needle test," "No, I take this baby as God's love, just the way it is, Hallelujah," one genetics counselor felt hard pressed to understand what was going on. It was easier to fall back upon individualizing psycho-speak than to acknowledge the complexity of the patient's cultural life, which profoundly influenced her choices. When a Hungarian-born artist, 38, refused amniocentesis because "it wouldn't be done in my country until 40, and besides, we are all very healthy," I observed a genetics counselor probe extensively into genealogy, and finally discover one possibly Ashkenazi Jewish grandparent. Because of this, the counselor was able to recommend Tay-Sachs screening. Visibly shaken, the pregnant woman agreed. In instances such as these, the hegemonic discourse of science encounters cultural differences of nationality, ethnicity, or religion and often chooses to reduce them to the level of individual defensiveness. Yet what is being negotiated (or not negotiated, in the first example) is the power of scientific technology to intersect and rewrite the languages previously used for the description of pregnancies, fetuses, and family problems.

What Is Seen

Whether they accepted or refused amniocentesis, virtually all the women with whom I spoke had undergone a sonogram by the mid-trimester of pregnancy. My data on images of fetuses have been collected in light of the powerful restructuring of experience and understanding this piece of obstetrical technology has already accomplished. Several native Spanish-speaking women (both poor and middle-class) described their fetuses in nontechnological

imagery: "it's a liquid baby, it won't become a solid baby until the seventh month"; "it's like a little lizard in there, I think it has a tail"; "it's a cauliflower, a bunch of lumps growing inside me". Their relative autonomy from technological imagery may be due as much to having recently emigrated from countries and regions where hospital-based prenatal care is both less common and less authoritative, as to anything inherently "Hispanic".

Most women were fascinated with the glimpses they received of the fetal beating heart; its imagery fits nicely into a range of Christian symbols. And several were also impressed by the fetal brain, which is measured during sonography. Heart and brain, feeling and intellect, are already subjects of prenatal speculation among women for whom fetal imaging has been objectified.

Most women born in the United States, whatever their ethnic and class background, invoked the visual language of sonography and its popular interpretations to answer my query, "Tell me what the pregnancy feels and looks like to you now?" For one it was "a little space creature, alone in space"[6], for another it was "a creature, a tiny formed baby creature, but because its eyes are closed, it is only a half baby". Another woman told me that as her pregnancy progressed, she felt the fetus' image becoming more finely tuned in, like a television picture coming into better focus. White middle-class women (especially those having a first baby) frequently spoke of following fetal development in books which included week-by-week sonograms. Thus, technological imagery is reproduced in text as well as image, available to be studied privately, at home, as well as in public, medical facilities. Learning about what the technology can do, and about what the baby appears to be, proceed simultaneously.

Poorer women were unlikely to have such primers, but they, too, had been bombarded by the visualization of fetuses (and amniocentesis, with its attendant moral dilemmas) in the popular media. When asked where they first learned about amniocentesis, many Hispanic and white working class women mentioned three episodes of "Dallas" in which prenatal diagnosis plays a large part, and one African-American woman said she knew about Down syndrome "because the Kennedys had one" in a story she'd read in the *National Enquirer*. In the weeks following a Phil Donahue show devoted to Down syndrome children and their families, clinic patients spoke with great interest about that condition. Increasingly, health care providers must confront the popularization of their technologies, with all its attendant benefits and distortions, in their interviews with patients.

The widespread deployment of sonographic imagery is hardly innocent. Whatever its medical benefits, the cultural contests it enables are by now well known: anti-abortion propaganda is shot through with sonographic images, to which those who would defend abortion rights have had to respond.[7] Some people use this technology for political advantage in medical settings, as well as in popular culture. Several genetic counselors offered stories about Right-to-Life sonographers who aggressively insisted on delivering detailed verbal descriptions of fetuses and handing fetal images to women who were planning to have abortions after positive diagnoses. While this punitive behavior may seem excessive, even the seemingly neutral language of reproductive medicine affects pregnant women, who sometimes describe themselves as "maternal environments" in interviews. Until well after World War II, there were no med-

ical technologies for the description of fetuses independent of the women in whose body a given pregnancy was growing. Now, sciences like "perinatology" focus on the fetus itself, by-passing the consciousness of the mother, and permitting her, as well as biomedical personnel, to image the fetus as a separate entity. I will return to the importance of this internal disconnection and reconnection to fetal imagery in the next section.

Because amniocentesis was explicitly developed to probe for chromosome-based disabilities and confront a woman with the choice to end or continue her pregnancy based on its diagnostic powers, my interview schedule includes questions about the images of disabled fetuses women carry and disabled children they might raise. Here, too, television and magazine representations of disability loom large. One Peruvian factory worker who had lived in New York for 14 years spoke of them as Jerry kids (a reference to Jerry Lewis' telethons—an image hotly contested by the disability rights movement). A white working-class woman who had adopted two disabled children told this story about arriving at her maternal choices watching the telethons:

Ever since I was a little girl, I always watched those telethons, I always knew it was a shame, a crying shame that no one loved those kids enough. So when I was a teenager, I got to be a candy-striper, and I worked with kids in wheelchairs, and I always knew I'd adopt them before I'd have them for myself. I'm not afraid of problems. I've got a daughter with spina bifida, and they said she'd be a vegetable. Fat chance! My other one's gonna be mentally retarded. I can handle it. I learned these kids need love on the telethon.
(Lisa Feldman, white home maker, 26)

Most women in my sample could recall someone in their own childhood or community who had a

child with Down's syndrome. Their memories invoke mothers intensely involved and devoted. Many described positive relationships that women had with their mentally retarded children. And some even talked about the hidden benefits of having a "permanent child" as the mother herself grew older, and became widowed. Most middle-class women, however, drew a contrast between themselves and those Down syndrome mothers they had encountered:

It's too much work. There's a certain kind of relationship I want to have with my child, and it isn't like that one, that's so dependent, forever. I wouldn't be any good at it, I'd resent my child.
(Ilene Cooper, white college professor, 40)

Oh, I know I'd work really hard at it, I'd throw myself into it, but I'm afraid I'd lose myself in the process. I wouldn't be like her, she was a really great mother, so self-sacrificing.
(Laura Forman, white theatre producer, 35)

My aunt was terrific. But she stayed home. I know I'm going back to work after this baby is born, and I can't imagine what it would take to do it her way.
(Susan Klein, white accountant, 37)

What accompanied these she/me distinctions in the discourse of white, middle-class women was a running battle over the question of selfishness and self-actualization, a problem linked to the central importance of "choice" as a cultural value and strategy. This is a subject to which I will return below.

Working class and low-income African-American women were no less concerned about the possible diagnosis of Down syndrome, but they often saw their decision-making as taking place within networks of support. One low-income African-American single mother expressed strong anti-abortion sentiments, but requested the test. Had the results been positive, she intended to move home to Georgia, where her mother would help her to raise a baby with health problems. A black secretary married to a black plumber chose to end her third pregnancy after a prenatal diagnosis of Down Syndrome. When I asked her how she'd made the decision, and who had given her advice, support or criticism, she described the active involvement of clergy and community members in the church to which she belonged.

Among many Hispanic women, mostly working-class and low-income (both those choosing and refusing amniocentesis), the image of mothering a disabled child conjured less ambivalence than among white, middle-class women. Friends and relations with sickly children were recalled, and testimonies about the sacrificial qualities of maternity were offered. There was often a conflation of maternal and child suffering, including this madonna-like image:

When they told me what the baby would suffer, I decided to abort. But it was Easter, so I couldn't do it, I just couldn't do it until His suffering was ended. Then my child could cease to suffer as well.
(Lourdes Ramirez, Dominican house cleaner, 41)

The Meaning of Abortion

The meaning of abortion loomed large in the consciousness of pregnant women discussing amniocentesis. All women could articulate reasons for and against late abortion after a prenatal diagnosis of a serious condition. These included the evaluation of the child's suffering; the imagined effects of a disabled baby on other siblings and on the parents themselves; the sense of responsibility for having brought a baby into the world who might never grow to "independence"; and, sometimes, the "selfishness" of wanting one's own life to be free

of the burdens a disabled child is thought to impose. For Hispanic women, fear of the child's suffering was most salient, followed closely by the effects its birth would have on other children. They were, in principle, more accepting of the sacrifices they imagined disabled children to call forth from their mothers. It is hard to disentangle ethnicity, language, class and religion in these responses. As one Honduran domestic worker awaiting amniocentesis results told me:

Could I abort if the baby was going to have that problem? God would forgive me, surely, yes, I could abort. Latin Catholics, we are raised to fear God, and to believe in His love and forgiveness. Now, if I were Evangelical, that's another story. It's too much work, being Evangelical. My sisters are both Evangelicals, they go to Church all the time. There's no time for abortion for them.
(Maria Acosta, 41)

Many Hispanic women reported having had early, multiple abortions and did not discuss the procedure as morally problematic. Yet many also identified *late* abortion as a sin, because quickening has occurred. In this case, a set of subtle and differential female experiences is being developed as popular theology.

Low-income African-American women weighed nonmedical agendas in deciding to accept amniocentesis and possibly consider abortion: confirmation of dreams, prior omens and use of healers all figured in the stories they told about why the test might be of use to them. Many low-income Hispanic women appear wrapped up in intertwined images of maternal and child suffering. White middle-class women seem most vulnerable to the abortion controversy currently raging in our national, political culture. Virtually all of the women I interviewed from this group, whether Catholic, Jewish, or Protestant, provided critical exegeses on the tension

between "selfishness" and "self-actualization". Again and again, in assessing the possibility or the reality of aborting a disabled fetus, women questioned whether that decision would be selfish. Their concerns revealed something of the limits of self-sacrifice that mothers are alleged to embody.

I share a lot of the feelings of the Right-to-Life Movement, I've always been shocked by the number of abortion clinics, the number of abortions, in this city. But when it was *my* turn, I was grateful to find the right doctor. He helped me to protect my own life, and that's a life, too.
(Mary Fruticci, white home maker, 44)

This reflection over selfishness and self-actualization is mirrored in two counter-discourses, one particularly "male", one more classically "female". Several middle-class, white husbands went to some length to point out that a decision to bring a disabled child into the world knowingly was, in their view, "selfish":

If you have a child that has severe defects, the natural thing I think that would happen would be that it would die at a very early age and what you're doing is you're prolonging, artificially, the child. And I think that most of the people that do that, do it for themselves, they don't really do it for the child, and it tends to be a very selfish thing for people to do.
(Jim Norton, white lawyer, 42)

Their inversion of selfishness neatly reverses the vector of blame, which Right-to-Life imagery would pin on their wives.

Several white, middle-class women articulated a different discourse, one which confronted selfishness with an implicit critique of medical technology, and nostalgia for a lost and imagined maternity:

The whole time they were doing more sonograms, checking the chromosomes, confirming their diagnosis, that whole time I kept thinking, "I'll keep the baby, I'll go to the hospital, I'll nurse right there. Who knows, in a year, two years,

this baby might get better". I just kept romancing that, wanting to believe that I could be that kind of mother.
(Jamie Steiner, white health educator, 33)

If only I could have become supermom, given that baby everything she needed. But I can't even bake an apple pie, so how could I do it all? Meanwhile, I kept going for more tests, more consultations. (Q: why did you take a month to make the decision to abort?) The technology was so interesting. And you know what, I became an interesting case. I know this sounds sick, but I've got to be honest and tell you that this technology replaced the baby in what was making me special.
(Sybil Wootenberg, white artist, 41)

For some, the critique of technological reasoning is more explicit:

You know, I kept thinking after the genetic counseling, the amniocentesis, they just keep upping the ante on you, they really do. Now, I'm not even allowed to pet my cat, or have a glass of wine after a hard day's work. I'm supposed to think that three cigarettes a day is what caused my first miscarriage. They can see a lot of patterns, but they sure can't explain them. But they talk as if they could explain them. I mean, they want you to have a baby by the statistics, not from your own lifestyle.
(Laura Forman, white theatre producer, 35)

I was hoping I'd never have to make this choice, to become responsible for choosing the kind of baby I'd get, the kind of baby we'd accept. But everyone, my doctor, my parents, my friends, everyone urged me to come for genetic counseling and have amniocentesis. Now, I guess I'm having a modern baby. And they all told me I'd feel more in control. But I guess I feel less in control. It's still my baby, but only if it's good enough to be our baby, if you see what I mean.
(Nancy Smithers, white lawyer, 36)

Why are white middle-class women so self-critical and ambivalently technological? Three themes contextualize their concerns.

The first is that the material conditions of motherhood really are changing, dramatically so, within these women's lifetimes. White women who "have careers"

and postpone babies are directing their lives differently than the women in the communities from whom they learned to mother. Unlike African-American women, for whom working mothers are longstanding community figures, and motherhood is a culturally public role, and unlike many Hispanic respondents, who painted images of sacrificial motherhood, for white middle-class women, individual self-development looms large as a cultural goal.

While *all* Americans prize "choice" as a political and cultural value, large scale changes in education, labor-force participation, postponed marriage and childbirth have enabled many white middle-class women to maintain at least an illusion of control over their lives to a degree unprecedented for other groups. Their relative freedom from unwanted pregnancies and child illness and death is easily ascribed to advances in medical science. Medical technology transforms their "choices" on an individual level, allowing them, like their male partners, to imagine voluntary limits to their commitments to children.

But it does not transform the world of work, social services, media, and the like on which a different sense of maternity and the "private" sphere would depend. Moreover, that "private" sphere and its commitment to child bearing is now being enlarged to include men. Fathers, too, can now be socially created during the pregnancy, through birth-coaching, and early bonding. These new fathers may also claim the right to comment on women's motives for pregnancy and abortion in powerful ways.

Individually, white middle-class women may be "becoming more like men", freer than ever before to enter hegemonic realms of the culture from which they were formerly barred, but at the price of

questioning and altering their traditional gender identity.[8] Modern, high-technological maternity is part of the gender relations now under negotiation, and may belong to new, emergent traditions. But it presently lies in an ambivalent terrain, a kind of "no man's land" between the technological claims to liberation through science, and the feminist recovery and romance with nurturance as a valuable activity.

A second reason for white middle-class women's ambivalence about prenatal diagnosis and abortion may well be, paradoxically, their close connection with the benefits and burdens of the increasing medicalization of pregnancy. While "everybody" now undergoes pregnancy sonograms, not everybody is as committed as this group to the medical discourse, and its images in pregnancy primers. For them, a paradoxical separation and reconnection to fetuses appears to be underway. On the one hand, they can "see" their fetuses in pictures and on medical screens. This allows for the "early bonding" which runs rampant through the parenting and obstetrical literature. But a seen fetus is also a separate fetus, one to whom one connects as a "maternal environment", in obstetrical language, and as a "sanctuary" in the words of The Silent Scream.[9] Paradoxically, white middle-class women are both better served by reproductive medicine, and also more controlled by it, than women of less privileged groups. They are likely to be educated in the same institutions in which doctors are produced, and their own language closely mirrors medical speech and its critique in both the Right-to-Life's discourse of "selfishness" and mainstream feminism's "self-actualization".

A third reason for complex and contradictory feelings about abortion is not confined to white middle-class women, although the cultural and medical importance of individualism may make them particularly vulnerable to its effects. This reason concerns the shifting historical ground on which abortion practices rest. That point was dramatically made to me in one amniocentesis story:

For three weeks, we tried to develop further information on oomphaloceles and satellites on the chromosomes, and the whole time, my mother kept saying, "why are you torturing yourselves, why don't you just end it now, why do you need to know more"? She'd had an abortion between her two pregnancies. And my mother-in-law had even had a late abortion when she first got to this country, and she kept saying the same thing: "I put away one, just do it, and get it over with". And I was so conflicted, and also so angry. So finally I turned on my mother and asked her, "How can you be so insensitive, it's such a hard decision for us, you can't just dismiss this". And as we talked, I realized how different their abortions were from mine. They were illegal. You've got to remember that, they were illegal. They were done when you worried about the stigma of getting caught, and maybe, getting sick. But you didn't think about the fetus, you thought about saving your own life. (Jamie Steiner, white health educator, 33)

Illegal abortions were dangerous and expensive. They were performed under the shadow of death—maternal, not fetal. Morbidity and mortality from the complications of abortion dropped sharply after 1973, in the wake of Roe V. Wade. Indeed, "Abortion related deaths have decreased by 73 percent" within a decade of abortion decriminalization.[10] Criminal prosecution, morbidity and mortality, were the fears attached to illegal abortions but not "selfishness." A variety of social forces, including medical reform and feminist political organization, led to abortion law reform. On the heels of its success, the Right-to-Life movement was quickly organized. We cannot really understand the talk of "selfishness" articulated by middle-class women, and used against all

women, until we locate the meaning of abortion at the intersection of culture, politics, technology, and social change.[11]

Science speaks a universal language of progress. But women express their diverse consciousness and practices in polyglot, multicultural languages. When women speak about the medicalization of reproduction, what they tell us must be placed in its historical, social context. Amniocentesis and other new reproductive technologies open a Pandora's box of powerful knowledge, constructed through scientific and medical practices. But messages sent are not necessarily messages received. New technologies fall onto older cultural terrains, where women interpret their options in light of prior and contradictory meanings of pregnancy and childbearing. Any serious understanding of how "motherhood" is changing under the influence of the New Reproductive Technologies depends on realizing women's stratified diversity. Otherwise, it will reproduce the vexing problem of the false universalization of gender which feminism itself initially promised to transcend.

Notes

Earlier drafts of this article were read by Faye Ginsburg, Evelyn Fox Keller, Shirley Lindenbaum, and Anna Tsing. I thank them for their criticisms and suggestions. Faye Ginsburg deserves my greatest gratitude: without her support and direction, this paper would never have been completed.

1. Support for the field research on which this article is based was provided by the National Science Foundation, the National Endowment for the Humanities, the Rockefeller Foundation's "Program in Changing Gender Roles", and the Institute for Advanced Study. I thank them all. I am especially grateful to the many health care providers who shared their experiences with me, and allowed me to observe them at work, and to the hundreds of pregnant women and their supporters who shared their amniocentesis stories with me. Where individual illustrations are provided in the text, all names have been changed to protect confidentiality.

2. Additional reports on the fieldwork from which this article is drawn can be found in "Moral Pioneers: Women, Men and Fetuses on a Frontier of Reproductive Technology," *Women & Health* 13 (1987): 101–116; "The Powers of Positive Diagnosis: Medical and Maternal Discourses on Amniocentesis," in Karen Michaelson, ed. *Childbirth in America: Anthropological Perspectives* (South Hadley, Mass.: Bergin & Garvey, 1988); "Chromosomes and Communication: The Discourse of Genetic Counseling," *Medical Anthropology Quarterly* 2 (1988): 121–142; and "Accounting for Amniocentesis," in Shirley Lindenbaum and Margaret Lock, eds., *Analysis in Medical Anthropology* (New York: Cambridge University Press, forthcoming).

3. See Ann Oakley, *The Captured Womb* (Oxford, England: Blackwell, 1984), ch. 7, for an interesting discussion of how medical technology bypasses and reconstructs knowledge of fetuses, which excludes the perceptions of pregnant women.

4. Religiously framed anti-abortion sentiments were expressed more often among Evangelicals than Catholics, at least among Hispanics and Caribbean Blacks. At the same time, many Hispanic Pentecostals and Charismatic Catholics, and Black Seventh Day Adventists accept amniocentesis in City clinics. It is important to distinguish official Church theology from local practices, including the discursive resources, social networks, and strategies particular church membership may provide.

5. Amniocentesis adds an increase of one-third of one percent to the miscarriage rate. This is considered statistically insignificant, but as genetic counselors are quick to point out, no risk is insignificant when assessing a given pregnancy, rather than simply constructing statistics. And prior reproductive history powerfully shapes how this statistic is interpreted.

6. Barbara Katz Rothman, *The Tentative Pregnancy* (New York: Viking Penguin, 1986), 114, provides an excellent discussion of the implications of sonography for maternal/fetal separation. Rosalind Petchesky has written a powerful critique of the history and hegemony of fetal images in "Fetal Images: the Power of Visual Culture in the Politics of Reproduction", *Feminist Studies* 13 (1987): 263–292. See Oakley, *The Captured Womb*, for a history of sonography.

7. My understanding of the importance of fetal imagery in political struggles is deeply indebted to Rosalind Petchesky, "Fetal Images . . ." Most activists have viewed "The Silent Scream" and Planned Parenthood's video "Response to the Silent Scream" and clips from both were widely available on television in 1984 and 1985, the years of their release.

8. Faye Ginsburg, "Dissonance and Harmony: The Symbolic Function of Abortion in Activists' Life Stories," in The Personal Narratives Group, ed., *Interpreting Women's Lives* (Bloomington, Ind.: Indiana University Press, 1989).

9. Again, see Rosalind Petchesky, "Fetal Images . . ."

10. Rosalind Petchesky, *Abortion and Woman's Choice* (Boston: Northeastern University Press, 1984), 157.

11. See Faye Ginsburg, *Contested Lives: The Abortion Debate in an American Community* (Berkeley & Los Angeles, Calif: University of California Press, 1989) for an excellent analysis of these historical intersections.

 Article Review Form at end of book.

Why are Black women among the strongest critics of teenage pregnancy? How does a daughter's pregnancy change the mother-daughter relationship?

Black Teenage Mothers and Their Mothers:

The Impact of Adolescent Childbearing on Daughters' Relations with Mothers

Elaine Bell Kaplan

University of Southern California

The popular view assumes that Black families condone teenage motherhood. This study argues that this assumption is incorrect, finding instead that teenage motherhood can produce long-term conflict both in family relations and structure. The 22 teenage mothers interviewed for this qualitative study believed that their mothers did not support them emotionally. Interviews with nine adult mothers* of the teenagers

*The mothers of teen mothers (including those who were themselves teenage mothers) will be referred to as adult mothers.

A version of this paper was presented at the 1994 annual meeting of the American Psychological Association. A special thanks to Gwyneth Kerr Erwin, Eun Mee Kim, Mike Messner, Pierrette Hondagneu-Sotelo, Barrie Thorne, and the anonymous reviewers for *Social Problems* for their comments on an earlier draft. The material in this study was taken from a larger study. "Not Our Kind of Girl' Black Teenage Motherhood: Realities Hiding Behind the Myths" (forthcoming). Correspondence: Elaine Bell Kaplan, University of Southern California, Los Angeles, CA 90089-2539.

substantiated this belief: Their daughters' early motherhood threatened their deeply held moral values as well as their reputations in the community. This study concludes that sociologists need to address these relational problems through linking these mothers' socioeconomic conditions with gender, class, and race inequalities.

Well, my momma said to me, "You shouldn't have gotten pregnant. You ain't married. You don't have no job. You ain't this and you ain't that" (16-year-old Susan).

Susan should give the baby up to foster care, to someone who can take care of it (37-year-old Janet).

As these quotes suggest, relations between teenage mothers and their mothers can be complex and disturbing: Teenage motherhood serves as a source of conflict for everyone involved. Social scientists who study teenage motherhood have engaged in an on-going theoretical and, many times, politicized debate about these mother-daughter relationships. Embedded in some theoretical posi-

tions is a culture-of-poverty notion that Black, female-headed families produce more of their kind: that is, teenage girls with few values—a slap in the face of the central ideas of America's "family values" (Moynihan 1965). In this theory it is the rule of the father (and not the mother) that establishes the family's mainstream values and behavior.

Wilson (1987) responds to this position by arguing that economic restructuring during the 1960s created havoc for Black families—high unemployment rates for Black men, which in turn led to high divorce rates or fewer marriages. These changes produced a population of Black mothers who live in depleted and hostile inner-city neighborhoods. In such neighborhoods, Black mothers watch their sons seek shelter in gang involvement while their daughters seek significance in motherhood. While Wilson (1987) shows how family life is changed by economic conditions and how people's sense of their lives is mitigated by their structural conditions, his theory does not pay sufficient attention to the way gender ideology contributes to family dynamics, nor does he directly tackle the thorny question: Do teenage mothers and their mothers share values that are antithetical to mainstream values?

I argue that these political debates have limited our view of Black teenage mothers. Rather, they have produced stereotypical portrayals of Black teenage mothers and their mothers, obscuring both the way in which Black women's norms and values are actually shaped by mainstream ideology and the complex nature of their obligations as mothers, especially when their adolescent daughters become young mothers.

So far, the research focusing specifically on relations between mothers and daughters suggests that it is common for mothers and daughters to struggle over issues of independence and identity during the daughters' adolescent years (Rich 1990; Fischer 1986; Gilligan 1990). However, most of these studies primarily focus on white middle-class daughter-mother relationships; therefore they limit the ability to theorize about how Black teenage mothers and their mothers might respond to a crisis such as teenage motherhood.

There are studies that focus on the relationships of Black daughters and mothers (George and Dickerson 1995; Mayfield 1994; Rogers and Lee 1992; Apfel and Steiz 1991; Collins 1987; Burton and Bengston 1985; Ladner and Gourdine 1984; Furstenberg 1980). But these studies do not sufficiently discuss the conflict between teenage mothers and their mothers. Some find that "baby getting" and "baby keeping" are cultural survival strategies (Stack 1974) that do not have a long-term negative effect on the mother (Geronimus

1990). Ladner and Gourdine (1984) studied Black mothers and daughters' relationships to find that adult mothers do not condone their daughters' pregnancies. While this study shows that adult mothers feel themselves swept up in a "tide of circumstances with few options available to them" (p. 23), it does not sufficiently articulate the underlying mothering obligation, nor its subsequent conflicts. These studies do not link gender, race, and class in their analyses.

Collins (1990), who explores the institution of motherhood from the standpoint of Black mothers, argues that Black motherhood as an institution is both dynamic and dialectical. Collins argues that an ongoing tension exists between the dominant society's efforts to mold the institution of Black motherhood to benefit systems of race, gender, and class oppression and efforts by Black women to define and value their motherhood experiences (also see Brewer 1995).

My study explores gender, racial, and economic oppressions by examining how Black teenage mothers and their daughters cope with teenage motherhood. Gender ideology in U.S. society has been crucial to the notion that motherhood is the primary task for women of all racial and class backgrounds. In the literature on women's obligations as mothers, Russo (1976) argues that, in U.S. society's view, it is the women, but not the men, who are charged with caring for others. Further, being a good mother carries the responsibility of providing moral training to their children, supporting their children regardless of one's own needs, and spending all one's time and energy on children, even getting them out of difficult life experiences (Russo 1976). Russo's (1976) theory of motherhood directly connects the family structure to patriarchy—fathers provide the

economic leadership and authority, while mothers are responsible for the reproduction of children's mainstream values and behavior. Especially during a child's early and teenage years, a mother's role in reproducing these values in children is considered to be crucial.

Similarly, racism and economic inequality are key factors in creating high numbers of Black mothers raising teenage daughters who are also mothers and in limiting the financial and emotional support they receive from others (see Bell Kaplan forthcoming; Wilson 1987). The key to understanding the dynamics between the teen and adult mothers lies in the gender, race, and class inequities wherein poor, Black women are positioned at the bottom of the labor market. These inequalities are present in systems of discrimination wherein Black women, but not Black men, are punished, or expect to be punished, for stepping outside the traditionally assigned middle-class norms and values regarding teenage parenthood.

This study offers a sample of 22 teen mothers and 9 adult mothers of the teen mothers, using their perceptions of experiences to elucidate the complexities, contradictions, and conflicts arising within family relationships as the result of teenage pregnancy. The families in this study do not reveal a deviant culture. Nor are they the super-strong women who can cope without needing support (Myers 1980). Indeed, these teen mothers thought that motherhood would provide them with some kind of control over their lives. By contrast, the adult mothers thought their daughters' motherhood would further erode the little control adult mothers already had over their family life. The pivotal question is: What happens to family relationships when adolescent girls and their families have to deal with the pressures created by teenage motherhood?

I suggest the conflict between daughters and mothers can be traumatic for both if the daughters, as 15- or 16-year-old mothers, find themselves abandoned by the school system, their fathers, and the babies' fathers and feel that their mothers are their only source of support. What happens to these relationships when the mothers of teenage mothers themselves feel vulnerable, especially if they are young, single, have limited resources, and are in need of support themselves? These relationships may be further complicated if the adult mothers believe that their daughter's pregnancy is a reflection of lower-class behavior. These adult mothers may feel that they are also affected because the daughters' pregnancy is not their fault, but they will be perceived by others to be responsible for their daughters' situation. The adult mothers distance themselves from their daughters' behavior and align themselves with conventional expectations about teen mothers by linking themselves to traditional culture in unique ways (see Stokes and Hewitt 1976). In this study, when the daughters became pregnant, both daughters and mothers were angry and resentful of the other. That anger and resentment was debilitating and had long-term consequences on the mothers' relationships with their mothers.

Sample and Methodology

The interviews involved in this study are taken from a larger three-year study on Black teenage mothers who lived in Oakland and Richmond, California, between 1986 and 1989. This paper focuses on interviews with 22 teen mothers who lived in single-parent/mother only households. I also interviewed nine adult single-parent mothers of teenage mothers.

I met 12 of these teen mothers and 9 of their mothers through volunteer consulting work at a nonprofit teen parenting service agency in Oakland. The rest were drawn from a snowball sample in which the teen mothers provided me with names of other teen mothers. I gave the teen mothers written and verbal information on the research and asked their permission to interview their mothers. All mothers were interviewed for two to two-and-one-half hours, usually in their homes. (See Tables 1 and 2 for the demographic characteristics of the teen and adult mothers' samples.)

To gain the trust of the women in this study, I tried to create a nonhierarchical interview setting and a casual interview atmosphere. Also, being of the same race and gender, having my little boy accompany me on some visits, sharing with them my own similar family and class background, may have helped me establish rapport with the mothers (see Reinharz 1992).

Using Goffman's (1963) stigma analysis as a frame of reference, I suggest that discredited people will often act to cover whatever stigma they believe discredits them so that they can appear like others. With this in mind, I asked the teen and adult mothers about their attitudes and reactions to teenage motherhood. I wanted to know how they reorganized and redefined themselves within a context of difficult economic circumstances. Along with asking the teen mothers such questions as, "Who was the 'most' and 'least' supportive before, during, and after your pregnancy?", I asked adult mothers, "How did you respond to the news of your daughter's pregnancy?" and "Did your relationship with your daughter change after her pregnancy?" The interviews aptly illustrate both entrenched and emerging patterns in these daughter-mother relationships.

Black Teenage Mothers and Their Mothers

All of the teen and adult mothers lived in economically depressed inner-city areas of Oakland and Richmond in the midst of a visible drug and gang culture. Several of the teen mothers lived in neighborhoods where, "over 40 percent of the families were headed by single mothers and virtually all the single mothers received AFDC" (Oakland City Council Report 1988). Sixteen of the twenty-two teen mothers and their babies were living with their mothers. Two of these teen mothers were ineligible for welfare assistance because their mothers' annual income exceeded the family eligibility limits. The rest were receiving welfare assistance and living on their own.

Susan serves as an example of the teen mothers who were living with their mothers. Susan, a 16-year-old mother who dropped out of the ninth grade when she learned she was pregnant, lived with her mother and two sisters in a cramped two bedroom apartment in East Oakland. Her baby's father was serving a two-year term in a youth camp facility. Susan's father, who left the family when she was very young and moved to Oklahoma, refused to pay child support and seldom visited his children. To make matters worse, Susan said, her mothers' nurses' aide income of $11,000 disqualified Susan for welfare assistance.

According to Susan, her mother, Janet, was resentful and constantly complaining to Susan about the additional money it cost her to support her family since the baby's birth. Janet said she was indeed shocked when she learned that her daughter was pregnant. She thought that Susan (the first person in her family to become a teenage mother) was too young and had a too "irresponsible nature" to be a good mother. These

Table 1 Teenage Mothers' Demographic Characteristics

Name	Age	Age at Birth	Educational Background	Source of Income	Family Origin	Age of Mom at First Birth
Dana	21	15	D	AFDC	F	16
DeLesha	17	15	D	Emp.	2p.	20
Denise	25	18	HSG.	Emp.	F	15
DeVonya	17	15	11grd.	AFDC	F	16
Diane	20	17	S.C.	AFDC	F	22
Evie	43	17	C.Deg.	Disab.	2p.	23
Georgia	16	15	11grd.	AFDC	F	15
Irene	21	18	D	Unemp.	F	16
Jackie	17	15	11grd.	AFDC	F	15
Jasmine	17	16	10grd.	Pt. Emp.	F	17
Joanne	25	14	D	Emp.	F	21
Junie	15	14	9grd.	Mom	F	24
LaShana	17	15	D	AFDC	F	22
Lenora	20	15	D	Emp.	2p.	16
Lois	27	15	D	AFDC	2p.	15
Margaret	35	15	S.Col.	Emp.	F	22
Marnie	16	15	D	AFDC	2p.	20
Melanie	17	15	11grd.	AFDC	2p.	20
Terry	20	16	D	AFDC	F	16
Tracy	16	16	10grd.	AFDC	F	16
Shana	17	16	D	AFDC	F	15
Susan	16	15	D	Mom	F	21

Key: Education Level: D=high school dropout. HSG=high school graduate. C. Deg. = college degree. S. Col.=Some College. Income Source.: Disab.=Workers' Compensation Insurance. Family Origin Type: F=Female Headed Household. 2p.=Two parent household.

Table 2 Adult Mothers of Teenage Mothers' Demographic Characteristics

Name (Daughter)	Age	Marital Status	Educational Background	Source of Income	Annual** Income
Middle-Class Status Sliders					
Marie (Evie)	66	M	C.Deg.	Retired	$45,000
Alma (Diane)	42	W	C.Deg.	Emp.	32,000
Selma (Joanne)	46	M	C.Deg.	Emp.	25,000
Salina (Jackie)	32	S	HSG.	Emp.	23,000
Working-Class and Poor High Aspirers					
Martha (Margaret)	57	S	D.	Emp.	$13,000
Janet (Susan)	37	S	S.C.	Emp.	11,000
Jessie (Marnie)	36	S	D	AFDC	8,000
Mary (DeVonya)	54	S	D	Disab.	7,000
Ruth (Junie)	39	S	D	AFDC	6,500

Key: Education Level: D=high school dropout. HSG=high school graduate. C. Deg. = college degree. S. Col.=Some College. Income Source.: Disab.=Workers' Compensation Insurance. Family Origin Type: F=Female Headed Household. 2p=Two parent household. Marital Status: M=married. S=Single. W=widower.

**Approximation of income.

problems exacerbated the hostility between the mother and daughter, and their arguments escalated until they fell over tables and chairs trying to hit each other.

Twelve teen mothers qualified for welfare assistance. The rest were employed. Many thought they could resolve their problems by moving out of their mothers' homes. However, only a few of the older teenage mothers were able to establish stable households. Younger teen mothers had to count on friends to lend them sleeping space; sometimes, it was on the floor. Generally, the teen mothers couldn't stay longer than a week before they would have to look for new arrangements (see Elliott and Krivo 1991). For example, 16-year-old De Vonya, the youngest of six siblings, recalled moving into her friend's home after an argument with her mother when she told her she was pregnant. De Vonya did find her own apartment in a housing complex, a hangout for drug dealers. Within two weeks of moving in, faced with mounting expenses she couldn't afford, De Vonya moved out, leaving no forwarding address or telephone number.

De Vonya's mother, Mary, a single mother who depended on monthly Social Security checks, had trouble coping with De Vonya since the baby's birth. Mary said she wanted her daughter to do something with her life other than follow in her footsteps by being a teenage welfare mother. Mary was angry, hurt, and resentful that her youngest child, De Vonya, would repeat a family cycle of teenage pregnancy that began when her own mother gave birth to Mary at age sixteen. De Vonya's father, who stopped speaking to her for several months after he learned she was pregnant, refused to offer her much in the way of support. De Vonya's

reaction was: "Sometimes he gets on my nerves." Losing his support was extremely difficult for De Vonya, especially since her baby's father also broke off their relationship shortly after she became pregnant.

Most of the teen and adult mothers had poor educational skills, while some were educated and employed. But even those who were employed felt afraid that they could lose it all "in the wink of an eye," said 32-year-old Salina, mother of 16-year-old Jackie. As a result, they didn't see much of a future for themselves. When I asked the teen mothers (and adult mothers who had been teen mothers) why they became mothers so young, most responded like 16-year-old De Vonya: "Maybe I'll feel loved by having my own child." Being a mother was something she could do to feel good about herself, perhaps feeling she could be a mother even if she didn't have other options. All of the teen mothers agreed that they were only beginning to comprehend the impact of teenage motherhood on all aspects of their lives.

The Issue of Gender: Mothers' Obligations

First, teenage mothers reported that being teenage mothers placed great stress on their relations with their mothers, who strongly believed that their daughters had failed to adhere to the gendered norms about girls' sexual behavior. Second, these teen mothers were also adolescents, a period during which girls are often experiencing anxiety and confusion as they strive for maturity and are striving to develop trust and make connections with others.

Third, further complicating the challenges felt by these teen mothers is that, like all children,

they felt their mothers were obligated to care for them, regardless of the mothers' own problems. The teen and adult mothers' comments in this study underscore a crucial element of the norm concerning the mothering obligation: Mothers should be able to exert control over their daughters' sexual behavior. The teen mothers also reveal the daughters' expectations that their mothers be good mothers, offering unconditional love, understanding, and forgiveness. If mothers withdraw support, they are failing. These teen mothers idealized the concept of "a good mother" and became angry when their mothers didn't conform. These adult mothers are caught in an impossible dilemma. If a mother offers support, chances are others will pass on the stigma of her daughter's deviant status to her (see Goffman 1963): The family has "slipped" in its community standing. It was common, the adult mothers said, to hear neighbors say, "These girls have no guidance" in judging their mothers' maternal abilities.

Compounding these challenges were problems caused by the break-up of important relationships: the babies' fathers disappearing from their lives, "so-called" friends gossiping about them, as one teen mother put it—abandonments that caused the teen mothers to turn to their mothers for increased emotional and financial support, only to find both unavailable. At the same time, they were having to learn how to be mothers.

Fourth, the adult mothers, many of whom were barely making enough money to support their existing families, reported that teenage motherhood ran counter to their values about marriage and motherhood. The adult mothers, overwhelmed by their new situations, negatively evaluated their daughters' actions, fearing they would be held responsible for their grandchildren's welfare. Not only did the adult mothers not appreciate their daughters' pregnancies, they took adversarial positions, often failing to be supportive of their daughters. They also felt at risk both economically and morally.

The adult mothers developed impression management strategies that distanced them from their daughters' actions. These strategies are juxtaposed against the daughters' impression management strategies that linked them to their babies and motherhood. These critical feelings led to new tensions between mothers and daughters, or exacerbated old ones.

Negotiating the Status Transition

Mothers and daughters often mark transitions in their relationships by struggling to negotiate new ways of dealing with the changes in their status (Fischer 1986). In this regard, the teen mothers demonstrate how a disproportionate amount of negotiation occurs between daughters who are moving from nonmother to mother status and mothers who are moving on to being grandmothers—all of which is occurring at an inappropriate time in their lives.

These struggles emerge in the teen mothers' responses to the first research question, "Who was most or least supportive of you before, during, and after your pregnancy?" Before pregnancy, most of the teens had fights with their mothers over time allocated to television viewing, cleaning their rooms, and doing their homework—all typical family issues. Once pregnancy was established, 6 of the 22 teens had mothers who continued being supportive of them. Sixteen-year-old Georgia typified these mothers when she said her mother (who had also been a teen mother) helped her by sharing her own ex-

periences. Another teen mother, Terry, gave her mother credit for being emotionally supportive of her and for giving her helpful information about her own pregnancy. Her mother often told Terry how happy she was when Terry was born.

For 16 teen mothers, the family fights took on a new edge when pregnancy occurred. Only a third of these teenagers expected their mothers not to react negatively to the news of their pregnancies. Many anticipated a fight. Several said they were "scared" and feared their mothers' reactions when they were told the news, so they tried to hide their pregnancies from their mothers as long as possible. Seventeen-year-old Jasmine's story demonstrates this untenable strategy: "I didn't show until I was six months. I kept it in. Then I got sick. So my mother took me to the hospital for an examination and they told her."

The most compelling stories come from teen mothers responding to my question: "Who was the least supportive of you?" Sixteen teen mothers said that they left or were leaving their mothers' homes because of ongoing fights with their mothers. Seventeen-year-old De Vonya said:

She asked me whether I was going to keep it and who's the father and where were I going to stay. I told her, "Yeah, I'm going to stay." And she said, "How do you know that I want you here? I've already raised my kids."

De Vonya's expectations illustrate the norms and roles associated with the mothering obligation: Mothers should always be available and supportive of their children and never waver in that support regardless of their own problems. De Vonya expected her mother to mother her again and to continue previous levels of support, despite the extra demands an additional child would make on her mother. Her mother, who had

her own set of problems, worried that the responsibility for her grandchild would fall on her shoulders. Why was she worried? I suggest two reasons: First, she was the only parent available to care for her grandchild; second, she knew that her daughter expected her to offer all of her resources to help her grandchild.

Sixteen teen mothers associated the news of their pregnancies with a decline in their mothers' support. To Diane, from a middle-class family, her mother's feelings about status superceded her love for her daughter: "She looks down on people on AFDC, it's the same thing with teenage mothers." When Diane told her mother she had been pregnant for a month, her mother said she had to have an abortion right away, or she couldn't live in her house anymore. Diane was surprised by this strong reaction; until then, she and her mother had been fairly close. She moved out that night, stayed at a motel for a few days, and applied for emergency welfare aid. "This is not the life I had in mind," the young mother said.

Most teen mothers with unsupportive mothers said their mothers assailed their characters: "My mother called me a bitch and a whore." Their mothers' epithets apparently continued throughout the pregnancies, as illustrated by 15-year-old Junie, whose revelations about her mother's reactions are especially poignant:

When I was pregnant, she used to call me, "You're a whore, you're a tramp." I remember she was talking to a friend and calling me a whore and a tramp to her friends. I ran to my room and started crying. I left. When I got back, she said, "You big fat blimp, you don't need to be having this baby. You're too young."

Junie, like most teen mothers, was confused by her mother's negative labeling of her. These teen mothers, knowing other sexually active girls who were not pregnant, saw themselves as no different from those other girls. For the first time, many of the teenage mothers had to deal with a powerful negative label, one that was imbedded in the minds of others about Black girls who become mothers.

The Anti-Abortion Stand As an Affirmation of Motherhood

All but one of the adult mothers demanded that their daughters have abortions. While adult mothers demanded abortions, and an abortion could have resolved the issue of impending motherhood, the teens chose not to. A typical response by both sets of mothers came to light during these interviews. Junie said her mother called everyone in the family, including the teen's long-absent father, to garner support for her daughter having an abortion. In lieu of abortion, her mother wanted her to marry the baby's father. Junie said she wouldn't marry a man who refused to acknowledge his baby's existence.

Even mothers who themselves had been teen mothers wanted their daughters to have abortions. For example, Terry, whose mother was supportive of her, said she planned on having an abortion because her mother demanded it. Her plans fell through when the baby's father left town without giving her the agreed-upon half of the abortion fee. "Anyway," she justified her decision, "I'm glad I didn't. I wouldn't know what to do if I didn't have my baby."

When asked why they refused to have abortions, the teen mothers responded in "us against them" terms. Seventeen-year-old Melanie said with moral conviction: "My mother didn't get rid of me." Margaret, whose baby's father moved to a southern state shortly after she became pregnant, remembered thinking at the time, "I'm

going to have my baby. It's going to be rough but we'll make it."

At issue in this teen mother's statements about abortion and motherhood, is what C. Wright Mills (1956:5) would call, "Matters that transcend those local environments of the individuals and the range of [their] inner life." Melanie (like the others), did not consider herself particularly religious. But the moral convictions revealed in her comments may reflect the general religiosity of the Black community. Along with these moral beliefs, Melanie's and Margaret's comments also reveal that motherhood provided a coping strategy: a way to gain control over their lives and a way of fulfilling both social expectation and personal desire. Ironically, these teen mothers, who according to the popular view, do not have mainstream family values, were choosing a traditional model of women—motherhood. It didn't matter if their mothers approved or disapproved of their pregnancies, these teen mothers, who lived in depressed neighborhoods where there were few successful role models for girls, were driven by the desire to fit into the norms of the larger society.

Linking Gender and Race: The Limited Support of Extended Family

At one time, Black mothers could rely on their extended families as a resource when faced with a crisis (Stack 1974). Today, many of these Black families are too poor to help other family members (Staples 1994). De Vonya's interview provides a powerful example of a large Black family with little to offer in way of support to the teenage mother. Of De Vonya's five siblings, one brother was in jail, the other brother had disappeared years ago, and her three sisters

were all single parents on welfare. Her aunts and uncles worked at odd jobs or were unavailable to offer any support. Other mothers had similar stories, confirming that the extended Black family system has declined in recent years (Staples 1994).

I asked the teen mothers who else offered them support during and after they became pregnant. Fathers and other kin were virtually nonexistent in the teen mothers' assessments. Most teen mothers either did not know their fathers or know much about them. Two teen mothers said their fathers were "somewhat supportive." Twenty said that they counted primarily on one or two women friends for financial support. Only two of the teen mothers and adult mothers said they could rely on what Stack (1974) refers to as a mutual exchange system. Twenty-seven-year-old Lois, who became a mother at fifteen, lived with her grandmother and sister and considered her immediate family and a few women friends her family support system. But, the help she received from them was not consistent, since they had their own money problems. For two teen mothers, it was a matter of pride. As 16-year-old Tracy explained, "I was just too embarrassed to ask anyone [for help]."

Despite the lack of family support, these interviews illuminate the teens' expectations that nothing in the relationship with family, especially adult mother, should change—the norms and values associated with the way women mother would require that their mothers follow through with the needed support. The daughters perceived their mothers' refusals to be repudiations of this obligation rather than statements of economic powerlessness. The teens' ideas legitimize the wider society's view that mothering is women's essential nature.

Conforming to Cultural Norms

Before we discuss further specific aspects of the interviews with the adult mothers, we should consider why adult mothers in this study reacted so strongly to their daughters' pregnancies. Most adult mothers were deeply disappointed with their daughters; they all expected that their daughters would graduate from high school and go on to college. According to Furstenberg (1980), the mother who nurtures a teen girl in her early years could be the same person who, acting from her own needs, punishes the child she sees as immoral, especially when feeling challenged by someone whom she considers under her authority.

In this study, the mothers were reacting to the breaking of at least three strongly held gender expectations or norms about childbearing and sexuality. The mothers' negative labeling of their daughters reveals their adherence to the first of these norms: Young girls should not have babies before reaching adult status, and certainly not before marriage. In a study of Black mothers who have teenage daughters, Burton and Bengston (1985:34) find that, "The off-time accession to the lineage role creates," for many young mothers, conflicts in their view of themselves and in their families' systems of cohesion and social support.

For example, when 16-year-old Susan's baby was born, the tension between daughter and mother became unbearable, often dissolving into swinging matches. During one of my visits with Susan's mother, Janet—an attractive woman with two younger children who said she didn't think of herself as a grandmother—she threatened to put her daughter into a foster home. Susan fought back by warning her mother that she neglected her own children. Janet be-lieved her daughter to be a lazy mother whose baby should be taken away from her because, "She stays out late, leaves the baby with me all the time, doesn't do any work around the house, and sleeps late every day." Both mothers' comments reflect the increasing frustrations intrinsic in any relationship that has to adjust to sudden changes.

The second social norm aggravating the conflict between daughters and mothers is the cultural taboo against age inappropriate sexual behavior. Most of the adult mothers, including those who were themselves teen mothers, found it difficult to acknowledge that their 14-or-15-year-old daughters were sexually active. After the daughters' admissions, the mothers had to deal with the stigma (see Goffman 1963) and deviancy associated with Black teenage mothers:

I know she was only 14 when she got pregnant and some of my church friends couldn't stop blaming me for what happened to my daughter. Like I can follow her around everywhere to stop her from getting pregnant.

Forty-three-year-old Evie recalled her mother's reaction 25 years ago as if it just happened. With a trace of bitterness, she remembered:

The bigger I got during my pregnancy, the more my mother hated me. By the time I reached my seventh month she'd look at me, and close the door to my bedroom. So I finally left.

This vignette also illustrates the longevity of conflict between nine former teen mothers and their mothers. Evie's mother Marie said:

I wanted her to really be something, to go on and finish school, and I wanted to send her to Europe, to just be something other than a mother.

Despite Evie returning to school to earn a college degree in social work, her mother continued to imply she has failed: "My mother insinuates I could have done so much more, but I've ruined my chances for a good marriage and career." Evie believed her mother was concerned only about damage to her own reputation. Evie cried softly as she recalled old memories, "My mother hated me for it. I was just alone."

The third norm surfacing in these interviews is that "successful" mothering obligates one to pass on society's social values to children. Therefore, when a teen becomes pregnant, her mother's (but not her father's) abilities to socialize the daughter gain in significance. Mothers fear their daughters' failure may be linked to them: If the adult mother has been a teen mother herself her daughter's failure will be perceived as her own ongoing moral failure; if she is middle-class, others will think she doesn't properly control her daughter. By criticizing the daughter, the mother affirms her place in the world of convention: "Why am I being blamed? It's her fault," said one mother, distancing herself from the stigma of her daughter's sexual behavior.

The daughters' interviews bore out their mothers' concerns that friends were gossiping about them. Joanne, a 30-year-old former teen mother, provides an example. At the time of her teen pregnancy, she became estranged from her mother when church members threatened her mother's status in the community. Joanne's mother, Selma, carried herself as a model of moral virtues and taught her daughter to do the same. Joanne shared her mother's moral beliefs until she became pregnant, "I wanted to be married and to not have a baby at an early age."

Joanne describes how her mother's set of moral values affected her ability to grapple with Joanne's pregnancy. Her mother saw her family disgraced by ugly talk about her daughter:

My mother thought she had failed. She, as well as me, was being talked about.

That was the first sign in my family that all was not well.

Her mother grew increasingly concerned with the gossip, "My mother could not overcome her moral sense, and this had a tremendous impact on our relationship." Selma says Joanne's pregnancy was an indication that, "I didn't have control over her; she was irresponsible and didn't have control over herself."

Adult Mothers: Variations by Class

In considering the logic of the culture of poverty's perspective of the Black matriarchal family structure and the circumstances of the teens' adult mothers, what become significant are the meanings these adult mothers gave to their daughters' situations in concert with the daughters' perceptions of their mothers. The daughters' expectation that their mothers be available and approachable at all times (See Fischer 1986), collided with the mothers' expectation that their daughters would follow the traditional path to motherhood, by marrying first. Exacerbating the conflict was that the adult mothers were young themselves and still raising other children.

Adding weight to these meanings was the influence of the adult mothers' economic status: Three of the nine adult mothers had incomes of $6,500 to $8,000 a year; two working-class mothers earned yearly incomes of $11,000 to $13,000; four of the mothers were middle-class professionals with yearly incomes of $23,000 to $45,000. Neither class variation nor the mothers' status as former teen mothers illustrated marked differences in the problems they had with their teenage daughters. But, as we shall see, class variations and status did impact the meaning the adult mothers made of their daugh-ters' pregnancies, affecting the way they justified their coping strategies. Further, as we shall see, the adult mothers in this study shared certain common characteristics.

Before describing the adult mothers' perceptions of their daughters, I want to make an analytical contrast between sliders and aspirers. Both concepts refer to the aspirations people have regarding their dreams, abilities, and sense of place within the economic structure (see MacLeod 1987). Class sliders wanted to preserve their hard-won middle-class status for themselves (and their daughters). Class aspirers wanted their daughters to pull them up the class ladder by attaining a higher class status than they themselves had achieved.

Middle-Class Status "Sliders"

Four of the mothers were employed in middle-class professions: Two were school teachers, one was employed in a supervisory civil service occupation, and another worked as an insurance agent. Three were the first in their families to earn college degrees. I refer to this group as "class sliders." All of these mothers expressed concerns that their daughters' pregnancies would change their middle-class image for the worse; they linked teenage pregnancy to lower-class behavior, so they tried to distance themselves from their daughters. On the practical level, as the sole financial providers for their families, they had to be concerned about financially supporting another child, a burden that could spell downward economic mobility for them.

Alma, an elementary school teacher, said that teenage mothers have "ghettoized mentalities." Only low-class teenage girls, living in poor families where teenage pregnancy is a way of life, become pregnant. In line with this reason-ing, when her daughter Diane became the first teenage welfare mother in her family, Alma felt that Diane gave the family a "ghetto" image, thereby creating distance between the mother and daughter.

Evie's mother, a retired high school teacher, thought of her daughter's pregnancy as a "stigma." Evie's mother's inability to "forgive" Evie 25 years later demonstrates the long-term affect teenage motherhood can have on these mother-daughter relationships.

Another adult mother, Martha, a Deaconess in the church and moral authority in the family, demanded her 15-year-old pregnant daughter, Margaret, confess her "sin" to the church congregation, asking for forgiveness. Margaret did so but moved out of her mother's home. When Margaret, now 35 and a re-entry pre-law student, told her mother she had just registered for college, her mother didn't believe her; she doubted her daughter could do anything well.

Working-Class and Poor Adult Mother "Class Aspirers"

Unlike the middle-class mothers, four of the five "class aspirer" mothers had been teen-age mothers, two were still raising small children and on disability, welfare, or employed in low-wage service occupations. Notions of upward mobility echoed throughout these mothers' interviews, stressing their wish that their daughters lead the good life, climb the class ladder, and help the family do so as well. Sadly, the adult mothers tried to put their views across by putting themselves down: They felt that the only way to handle their experiences was to serve as negative role models for their daughters, as Ruth told me, of "what not to do." A 36-year-old mother of four, Ruth was disappointed with 15-year-old Junie: "She wanted to go to college. Now she be like me."

Ruth was afraid of being stigmatized as a "bad mother" who passed on "low moral standards" to her daughter. Often, this fear drove adult mothers like Ruth to act harshly toward their daughters. When 54-year-old Mary learned that De Vonya was pregnant, she refused to help her. Her own life had been "pure drudgery:" her daughters' pregnancy made it all the worse: "I wanted her to go to college, because this is what she keeps talking about."

Thirty-six-year-old Jessie, whose mother was fifteen when she was born, wanted her teenage daughter, Marnie, also pregnant at fifteen to "go to school and be a doctor or something." When her daughter became pregnant, she was "so hurt I can't describe it." Marnie, who expected compassion, was confused by her mother's lack of support, "After all, it happened to her. Instead of helping me she called me a bunch of names and still does."

Many of the daughters of "class aspirers" thought their mothers were punishing them. According to 17-year-old Shana, "She didn't really want me to have the baby, and she was given' me a hard time." Sixteen-year-old Marnie had a similar story:

[My mother] told me, "You do everything. No company, no telephone. The rest of the [children] can go out." She was punishing me for having my baby.

Was Marnie's mother punishing her daughter or merely assigning her daughter household tasks as many parents do? Each adult mother made different meanings of these experiences. Marnie's mother was afraid she would have to raise her grandchild, something she wasn't financially or emotionally prepared to do. The same was true for Mary, De Vonya's mother:

This is my daughter's responsibility. This is her mistake. It's not mine. It's not like I'm trying to punish her. But her baby days are over.

Mary saw her daughter's new motherhood as a signal of adult status (see Apfel and Seitz 1991). But whatever Mary's intentions, De Vonya, like Marnie, saw the housework assignments as a punishing strategy, creating friction between daughter and mother: "I can't stand her attitude and she can't stand mine," De Vonya declared. Shortly after the baby was born, De Vonya moved out of her mother's home. When 14-year-old Junie became pregnant, her mother, Ruthie, didn't know how to handle the news: "So I called her a bunch of names. I made her stay in her room for weeks at a time—I was so angry." As Stokes and Hewitt (1976:842) argue, when people confront a situation that seems "culturally inappropriate" they "organize their conduct, individually and jointly to get it back on track." One way the adult mothers could reorganize their lives was to develop impression management strategies that allowed them to cope with their daughters' "appalling" situation.

Impression Management Strategies

The adult mothers' interviews reveal the use of several impression management strategies in an effort to defend themselves against their daughters' "soiled identity" as Goffman (1963:65) would say, keeping the spotlight off themselves. According to Goffman's discussion of stigmatized people:

The issue is not that of managing tension generated during social contacts, but rather that of managing information about their failing: "To display or not to display; to tell or not to tell; to let on or not to let on; to lie or not to lie; and in each case, to whom, how, when, and where to disclose discrediting information about the self (1963:63).

A number of adult mothers used a "covering" strategy (Goffman 1963) as a way to distance themselves from the stigma associated with their daughters: adding a few years to their ages or to that of their daughters. Even now, one mother pretends that her 25-year-old daughter is older than her actual age. Evie, the daughter, said of her mother: "She didn't tell anybody she had a grandchild until he was three years old."

Another strategy most of the adult mothers used, I call "redirecting the gaze." Feeling the need to criticize a daughter during the interview, Alma, like other adult mothers, said she tried to raise her daughter well: "What can you do when she wants to hang out all day with those characters from the school? She's just like them." For this adult mother (as with most class sliders and aspirers), labeling her daughter worked as an impression management strategy. It allowed her to place, measure, and compare the obvious sign of her daughter's sexual behavior with other teenage girls' sexual and nonsexual involvements in explaining her daughter's pregnancy and to remove any issue of her responsibilities as a mother, detaching herself from her daughter's stigma.

In attempting to get their lives "back on track," the daughters developed their own impression management strategies. Most tried to shift the perception of themselves as problem daughters to that of good mothers. Tracy, a 16-year-old mother using this strategy, said she was a "regular old lady" who devoted all of her time to her baby, implying that the baby's birth gave her maturity and, in turn, made her a good mother. These young women also tended to deny they were having problems with their own lives. What they said about their home life, relations with their fathers and babies' fathers, along with my own observations of their living arrangements, tell another story. For example, Tracy, who was attending school, was inclined to say that everything was going well, despite having to study at the same time she was having to care for her child. She was failing in school. Another way to see the teen mothers' denial strategies is to understand that these are adolescent girls, and as such, they tend to want to fit in with others and appear as if they are in control of their situation.

Summary and Discussion
Consequences for Teen Mothers and Their Mothers

These interviews suggest the importance of understanding women's interactions with each other, along with how they confront a threatening situation, noting when these problems are structured by gender, race, and class. Affluent white middle-class mothers may find themselves encountering fewer severely critical events like their teenage daughter's motherhood. When they do, they usually have the children's fathers in the home who provide adequate financial resources (Fischer 1986). In this study, both teen and adult mothers made note of absent adult fathers and babies' fathers (see Wilson 1987). Mary, De Vonya's mother, compared her life with that of her husband's:

My husband, he leaves. Where would I find the money to leave? Where would I go? How would I live? And what would people say about me if I left like he did?

Mary's words convey a sense of being trapped by her daughter's (and her other children's) difficulties, touching on the real problems within these daughter-mother relations. Neither teen nor adult mother has others who can provide them with the resources they need to deal with serious problems such as teenage motherhood. Even

Alma, with a middle-class professional job, had to handle all of her daughter's problems alone. The absence of the fathers, or other supportive people, meant that these mother-daughter relationships became riddled with unresolvable dependency needs.

Health Problems

The friction and anger voiced by both teen and adult mothers must be understood on a deeper level than the typical struggle between mothers and daughters that ends when the daughters grow up. The lack of adequate support has serious consequences for adult mothers like Alma, Janet, and Mary. Studies of low income Black families (Allen and Britt 1984; Ladner and Gourdine 1984) find that they experience low levels of social support and high levels of acute stress. In this study, examples of such stress emerged as teen and adult mothers talked about their health problems. They experienced a disproportionate amount of anxiety and depression as indicated by a number of accidents, heart attacks (Evie had two), hypertension (six adult mothers), and back problems (two adult mothers). Many adult and teen mothers were involved in car accidents (five each), job-related injuries (seven adult mothers), and physical abuse (three teens/four adult mothers).

The adult mothers recognized the problems their daughters would bring to their already depleted lives. As Collins (1987) notes in her study of Black mothers, the mothering tasks can be so overwhelming for women who have so little that often they can't offer even motherly affection. The daughters in this study, angry and confused adolescents, looked at their mothers without understanding the socioeconomic problems forcing their mothers to take such a strong stance.

Conclusion: Debunking the Moral Value Argument

While this study is small and is limited to a particular region of the country, the findings do suggest that teenage motherhood stings as it stigmatizes both teenage and adult mothers, causing problems for them. To say that these adult mothers have deviant values they pass on to their daughters, thereby failing as mothers, ignores the obvious: Their capacity to be good mothers was tested by the severity of the problems they faced as Black mothers. But to suggest that Black mothers are superhuman—a common tendency in the literature—and can go it alone, is to suggest also that gender inequality, racism, and money problems do not affect them.

This study adds complexity to the structural perspective, providing rich evidence that Black mothers are not the "other," as the literature suggests. Rather, they are women with complex perceptions and problems. This research supports other findings (Bell Kaplan, forthcoming; Fischer 1986; Ladner and Gourdine 1984) that daughters and mothers may re-evaluate each other as daughters move into early motherhood. They tend to confront and negatively sanction each other when they have to deal with such realities. Therefore, this study refutes the current idea (McGrory 1994) that, "Illegitimacy has pretty much lost its sting in certain ghetto neighborhoods" (McGrory 1994:25), and, "We need to stigmatize it again" (p. 25).

We need to develop a more sophisticated understanding of the way in which gender relations and socioeconomic conditions transform daughter-mother relationships and the way society's beliefs about moral values influence the perception of these relationships.

The issue of moral values is an extremely important one for

these mothers, since the image of deviant mothers raising deviant daughters incites politicians to call for the end of welfare and other social policies. In the current political climate, welfare opponents argue that taxpayers should not support social policies for "immoral" Black mothers and their "immoral" teenage daughters. This study proposes that just such a need—the creation of family policies to assist teenage mothers and their adult mothers—is vital to the well-being of these mothers (and, ultimately, society), as evidenced by the number of health problems they report and by my findings that socioeconomic strains only multiply these problems.

These findings are also important because they indicate the need to place the causes of these family problems (and the causes of teenage pregnancies in the first place), within their historical, social, and economic context (Hardy and Zabin 1991; Ladner and Gourdine 1984). We need to understand that mothering as an ideology can and does exist apart from the practice of mothering. The Black mothers in this study adhered to the same ideology as white mothers in that they feel responsible for raising children, for the way children turn out, and for the values children espouse. Since these Black women, as compared to white women, are often raising teenage daughters alone, such mothering can become a daunting task.

Relational problems between daughters and mothers will persist, even increase, if politicians and social welfare agencies do not adequately address these mothers' social and economic problems. The adult mothers' needs are undercut by the stereotyped perceptions of them as failed mothers or as superstrong women who can cope with all kinds of hardship—a conservative ideology that assumes Black women have such unfailing personal character that they need little support from people in power. These mothers' economic realities, buttressed by wrongheaded sociological stereotypes, reinforce hostile conservative views and harmful political agendas.

As the teen mother interviews show, the real tragedy is that these teenagers have to expend energy on activities other than complex adolescent developmental issues. When adolescence is skipped, as it is for teenage mothers, girls may not learn how to develop their confidence and independence: to do as adolescents learn to do, move away from mothers, and then move back again as adults. Instead, much like sexually abused girls (see Musick 1987), they have problems making the leap across the developmental gap and become involved in defining themselves only in relation to the trauma inherent in being teenage mothers.

Older women's interviews, like Evie's for example, show that even women who find some measure of success in their adult lives find their success undermined by having been teenage mothers, especially when they have no way of understanding that experience other than from the moral perspective. The problem becomes more egregious when adult mothers are not able to offer them the kind of emotional and financial support they need to feel safe and secure as they handle teenage motherhood at the same time they must deal with adolescent issues.

Future Problems

Several candid teen mothers revealed another relationship problem. Terry, a 19-year-old mother with a three-year-old son, said she liked babies until they reached the age of two, when they became problems. When I asked 16-year-old De Vonya if she had any advice for other teenage girls, she yelled into the microphone, "Don't have no babies!" These teen mothers' reactions are more realistic than the "regular old lady" comment made earlier by 16-year-old Tracy. The dilemma for these mothers is that at this age and stage of adolescent development, a teen mother may not be able to push aside her own need to be mothered in order to adequately mother her child. Yet at the time these teenage daughters need "to become daughters again" (Fischer 1986), adult mothers can't afford to keep mothering their teenage daughters, economically, socially, or emotionally.

Negative messages about teenage and adult mothers' moral character also threaten the positive development of the teenage mothers' children, who need both mothers and grandmothers, since men are absent from their lives. Without financial resources and family policies providing support, without rebuilding the extended-family social support system, we may expect increased alienation within these families. The tragic consequence may be the further erosion of the already fragile social fabric of Black mother-headed families. As this study demonstrates, we can develop a complex and beneficial sociological framework if a comprehensive understanding incorporating a gender, race, and class perspective is used to find solutions to the problems experienced by young mothers, helping us discover preventative alternatives to teenage pregnancy.

References

Allen, Lind, and Darlene Britt. 1984. "Black women in American society." In *Social Psychological Problems of Women*, eds. A. G. Rickel, M. Gerrard, and I. Iscoe, 33–47. New York: Hemisphere.

Apfel, Nancy, H., and Victoria Seitz. 1991. "Four models of adolescent mother-grandmother relationships in Black inner-city families." *Family Relations* 40:421–429.

Bell Kaplan, Elaine. Forthcoming 'Not Our Kind of Girl:' Black Teenage Motherhood: Realities Hiding Behind the Myths. University of California Press, June 1997.

Brewer, Rose. 1995. "Gender, poverty, culture, and economy: Theorizing female-led families." In *African American Single Mothers*, ed. Bette J. Dickerson, 164–178. Beverly Hills, Calif.: Sage, Inc.

Burton, Linda M., and Vern L. Bengston. 1985. "Black grandmothers." In *Grand Parenthood*, eds. Vern Bengston and J. Roberston, 75–110. Beverly Hills, Calif.: Sage, Inc.

Collins, Patricia H. 1987. "The meaning of motherhood." *Sage* 2:32–46. 1990 *Black Feminist Thought*. New York: Routledge.

Elliott, Marta, and Lauren J. Krivo. 1991. "Structural determinants of homelessness in the United States." *Social Problems* 38:113–131.

Fischer, Lucy R. 1986. *Linked Lives*. New York: Harper & Row.

Furstenberg, Frank, Jr. 1980 "Burdens and benefits." *Journal of Social Issues* 36:64–87.

George, Susan M., and Bette J. Dickerson. 1995. "The role of the grandmother in poor single-mother families and households." In *African American Single Mothers*, ed. Bette I. Dickerson, 146–163. Beverly Hills, Calif.: Sage.

Geronimus, Arline T. 1990. "Teenage birth's new conceptions." *Insight* 30:11–13.

Gilligan, Carol. 1990. In *Making Connections*, eds. Carol Gilligan, Nona P. Lyons, and Trudy J. Hanmer, 6–29. Cambridge: Harvard University Press.

Goffman, Erving. 1963. *Stigma*. Englewood Cliffs, N.J.: Prentice-Hall, Inc.

Hardy, Janet B., and Laurie S. Zabin. 1991. *Adolescent Pregnancy in an Urban Environment*. Washington, D.C. The Urban Institute.

Ladner, Joyce, and Ruby M. Gourdine 1984 "Intergenerational teenage motherhood." *Sage* 1:22–24.

MacLeod, Jay. 1987. *Ain't No Makin' It*. Boulder, Colo.: Westview Press.

Mayfield, Lorraine P. 1994. "Early parenthood among low-income adolescent girls." In *Black Family*, 4th Edition. ed. Robert Staples, 230–242. Belmont, Calif.: Wadsworth Publishing Co.

McGrory, Mary. 1994. "What to do about parents of illegitimate children." *The Washington Post*, February 15:25.

Mills, C. Wright. 1956. *The Sociological Imagination*. New York: Oxford University Press.

Moynihan, Daniel P. 1965. "The negro family: The case for national action." U.S. Department of Labor: Washington, D.C.

Musick Judith S. 1987. "The high-stakes challenge of programs for adolescent mothers." A report for the Ounce of Prevention Fund, 1–4. Chicago, Ill.: Department of Children and Family Services.

Myers Wright, Lena. 1980. *Black Women: Do They Cope Better?* Englewood Cliffs, N.J.: Prentice-Hall.

Oakland City Council Report. 1988. "Women and children in Oakland, September, 1988." Unpublished report.

Reinharz, Shulamit. 1992. *Feminist Methods in Social Research*. New York: Oxford University Press.

Rich, Sharon. 1990. "Daughters' views of their relationships with their mothers." In *Making Connections*, eds. Carol Gilligan, Nona P. Lyons, and Trudy J. Hanmer, 258–273. Cambridge: Harvard University Press.

Rogers Earline, and Sally H. Lee. 1992. "A comparison of the perceptions of the mother-daughter relationship: Black pregnant and nonpregnant teenagers." *Adolescence* 107:554–564.

Russo, Nancy F. 1976. "The motherhood mandate." *Journal of Social Issues* 32:143–153.

Stack, Carol. 1974. *All Our Kin*. New York: Random House.

Staples, Robert. 1994. "The family." In *The Black Family*, ed. Robert Staples, 1–3. Belmont, Calif.: Wadworth.

Stokes, Randall, and John P. Hewitt. 1976. "Aligning actions." *American Sociological Review* 41:838–849.

Wilson, William J. 1987. *The Truly Disadvantaged*. Chicago: University of Chicago Press.

 Article Review Form at end of book.

WiseGuide Wrap-Up

- The meanings of dating, pregnancy, partnering, and parenting vary among racial, ethnic, and sexual groups.

- Intimate and familial relationships are affected by wider racialized social systems; they sometimes serve as important sites of cultural

contact and cultural struggle, though most intimates in this society come from the same racial and class backgrounds.

R.E.A.L. Sites

This list provides a print preview of typical **Coursewise** R.E.A.L. sites. (There are over 100 such sites at the **Courselinks**™ site.) The danger in printing URLs is that web sites can change overnight. As we went to press, these sites were functional using the URLs provided. If you come across one that isn't, please let us know via email to: webmaster@coursewise.com. Use your Passport to access the most current list of R.E.A.L. sites at the **Courselinks** site.

Site name: The Strength of Mixed-Race Relationships, by Erin Burnette

URL: http://www.apa.org/monitor/sep95/race.html

Why is it R.E.A.L.? Historical barriers to interracial dating, partnering, and child-rearing are slowly falling. This report from the American Psychological Association journal *The Monitor* examines the challenges and strengths of such relationships.

Key topics: interracial relationships, psychology

Try this: Racial homogamy in relationships reflects the social and racial stratification of our society. Write a brief paper analyzing how white people experience "racial privilege" when they are involved with other white people, and about how they lose racial privilege when they date people from other groups. Provide a sociological interpretation of how these experiences conspire to keep people of all races "in their places" in the United States.

Site name: Civil Rites: Arguments Against Same-Sex Marriage Mirror Those That Kept the Races Apart, by Deb Price

URL: http://www.eskimo.com/~demian/price-1.html

Why is it R.E.A.L.? This paper provides a good overview of the public policy decisions and the history of public sentiment related to interracial marriage. The history of interracial marriage is used as the basis for a discussion of public policy and public sentiment about same-sex marriage today.

Key topics: interracial marriage, public policy, popular sentiment, same-sex marriage

Try this: Make a list of historical arguments for and against marriage between people of different races and another list of arguments for and against people of the same sex. How similar are the lists? What are the implications of the lists for your own attitudes toward both kinds of "alternative" marriages?

section 7

Crime and Criminal Justice

Key Points

- Contrary to popular belief, the United States is not experiencing a dramatic upswing in violent crime—though its incarceration of young Black nonviolent offenders has reached unprecedented proportions.

- In a racially segregated society that affords the underprivileged too few opportunities, the possibilities for earning respect are limited to the culture of the streets.

- Within total institutions, such as the military, members of minority groups find fewer chances of seeing justice served.

- The crime of murdering abortion providers can be linked to the rhetoric and membership of white supremacist groups.

 **WiseGuide Intro**

What is crime? What is its relationship to race?

While there are a number of ways of defining crime, sociologists most commonly think of crime as the violation of the social norms that have been legitimized in the legal code. This definition recognizes that crime is socially constructed and that definitions of crime change with changes in society. For example, while it used to be illegal in many states for people of some races to marry people of others, this is no longer the case; while Jim Crow laws in the South made it illegal for Blacks to use "white" public accommodations, the abolishment of these laws made it legal for Blacks and whites to share public facilities, and the immigration of people of certain races and nationalities to the United States has sometimes been legal and sometimes illegal. In each case, the same activity is given a different legal definition at different times; sometimes these acts are criminal and sometimes they are not.

The history of race and racialization is closely connected to the history of theories of crime. Early criminological theories held that people who committed crimes (and were caught) were somehow biologically different from people who did not commit crimes (or were not caught). As you might imagine, these theories tied in nicely with theories that explained social differences between ethnic and racial groups as attributable to biological differences between them. In the United States, the dominant group of whites, however narrowly or broadly defined it might be in any given era, has often assigned responsibility for crime disproportionately to the ethnic and racial groups defined as nonwhite. While we might think that theories attributing criminality to biology are outmoded, in practice the criminal justice system often treats people of color very differently from whites in its administration of "justice." People of color are more likely to be arrested, referred to court, tried, convicted, and imprisoned; in addition, they are likely to receive longer sentences for the same crimes committed by whites. When the criminal act involves a victim, there is an amplification of this pattern: Blacks who harm whites receive much harsher sentences than whites who harm Blacks; Blacks who harm Blacks receive shorter sentences than Blacks who harm whites. These patterns suggest that, in the gaze of the law, Blacks' lives are worth less than those of whites. Such trends also suggest that the social pathology approach to explaining crime, which often centers on a deep belief in the biological bases for crime, is still alive and well as a sort of folk theory in American culture.

Americans also harbor some mistaken beliefs about the prevalence of crime and its association with race. The popular media often reinforce whites' fear of young Black males by giving the impression that whites are frequently victimized, are more frequently victimized than other groups, and are victimized only by people of color. In reality, the most common victims of violent crime are young Black males, and the people most likely to victimize them are people of the same race and sex. When it comes to interracial victimization, hate crimes committed by whites against people of color in the United States are the fastest growing form of bias crime. Despite what we see on television—or perhaps because of it, as some studies suggest—white people's violence against members of ethnic and racial minority groups is increasing annually.

Questions

Reading 21. What is institutionalized racism? How does the "war on crime" reflect cultural anxieties about race relations?

Reading 22. How might society change the "opportunity structure" available to young Black men? Who should assume responsibility for promoting such a change?

Reading 23. What evidence suggests that the Black man arrested in the Fort Bragg swastika case might have been falsely accused?

The readings in this section address some of the political, cultural, and social issues surrounding race and crime. In "Crime Control and Ethnic Minorities: Legitimizing Racial Oppression by Creating Moral Panics," criminologist William Chambliss traces the social history of the belief that crime rates are skyrocketing in the United States and demonstrates how this history reflects and promotes institutionalized racism. Anthropologist Elijah Anderson takes a closer look at the culture of Black communities in "The Code of the Streets." In "The Fort Bragg Swastika," journalist Larry Reibstein raises further questions about the complex ways in which white racism affects criminal charges against Blacks. This collection of readings should help you see how sociologists use understandings of culture, society, and power to look beyond simple crime statistics in an effort to answer the time-honored sociological question "What is *really* going on here?"

What is institutionalized racism? How does the "war on crime" reflect cultural anxieties about race relations?

Crime Control and Ethnic Minorities:

Legitimizing Racial Oppression by Creating Moral Panics

William J. Chambliss

On November 19, 1993, the U.S. Senate overwhelmingly passed a $23 billion crime bill, which authorizes $8.9 billion to hire 100,000 new police officers, $3 billion for high-security prisons, another $3 billion for boot camps for young offenders, $1.8 billion to combat violence against women, and $100 million for metal detectors for schools. In addition the bill makes being a member of certain types of gangs a federal offense, expands the death penalty to cover fifty-two additional offenses, and it permits the deportation of foreigners who are *suspected terrorists* without trial. Street crimes involving firearms would become a federal offense: continuing a long-time trend of expanding federal responsibilities for crime control. And the bill contains the infamous *three strikes and you're out* provision, providing mandatory sentences for persons convicted of three felonies. This provision, as it stands, would force judges to sentence a person convicted of three assaults to a mandatory life in prison.

The bill has created a furor in the press and has divided the law enforcement community. Philip Heymann, formerly the second highest person in the Justice Department, said simply that the bill "sounds terrific but doesn't make any sense" (*Washington Post*, Feb. 16. 1994: A1). He added, "It's become too easy to pretend we're going to solve this [the crime] problem with a set of remedies that look good for the first 15 seconds you look at them and very bad when you get to half a minute." Despite the divided opinion in the media and among judges, prosecutors and police, the bill has been hailed almost universally by politicians.

This bill, like a spate of anti-crime bills dating back to the late 1960s, is the culmination of the politicization of crime, a process that began when the Republican Party under the leadership of Barry Goldwater's presidential campaign in 1964 first raised *crime in the streets* as a major political issue (Chambliss and Sbarbaro, 1993). The end result of this process has many dire consequences, including that (1) the United States incarcer-

ates more of its citizens than any other country in the world (Figure 11.1), (2) federal and state budgets have shifted public expenditures from other, more important, social services to crime control, and (3) racism and the systematic oppression of minority groups, especially young African American men, has been legitimized and institutionalized in the criminal justice system.

Crime Control: The Nation's Growth Industry

Even before the Senate passed the 1993 crime bill, expenditures on criminal justice had increased more than fivefold between 1972 and 1988 (Table 11.1). The number of police officers in the U.S.A. doubled, and the number of people incarcerated increased by 150 percent (Maguire, Pastore, and Flanagan, 1992). Between 1969 and 1989 per capita spending on criminal justice in America's cities (municipal expenditures) rose from $34 to $120. County expenditures as a percentage of total budget rose from 10 to 15 percent between

Table 11.1	Federal and State Expenditures on Criminal Justice Selected Years: 1972–1988	
Year	State Expenditures	Federal Expenditures
1972	$3,026,000,000	$1,475,000,000
1976	5,194,000,000	2,356,000,000
1979	6,831,000,000	3,229,000,000
1985	15,697,000,000	5,546,000,000
1988	21,597,000,000	7,185,000,000

Source: Sourcebook of Criminal Justice Statistics, Washington, D.C., Bureau of Justice Statistics, 1984, 1988, 1992.

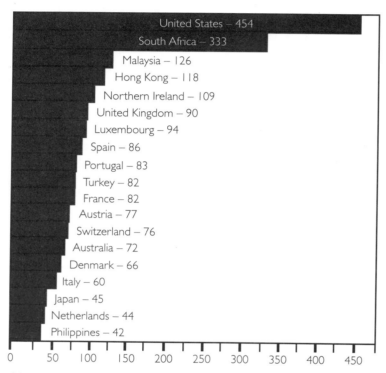

Figure 11.1 Incarceration rate per 100,000 population: 1990.

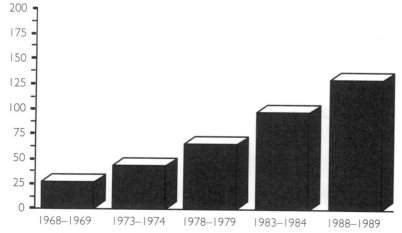

Figure 11.2 Per capita municipal expenditures on criminal justice, 1972–1988.

Source: U.S. Department of Commerce, Bureau of Census, State Government Finance, 1968–1969, 1973–1974, 1978–1979, 1983–1984, 1988–1989.

1973 and 1989 (Figures 11.2; 11.3). State expenditures showed even greater increases, rising tenfold from per capita expenditures on police and corrections of $8 in 1969 to $80 in 1989. State spending on prisons increased most dramatically, rising by a factor of twelve in this twenty-year period from $5 per capita to over $60 (Table 11.1). State government expenditure for building prisons increased 593% in actual dollars. Spending on corrections—prison building, maintenance, and parole—has more than doubled in the last ten years (Maguire and Flanagan, 1990; Maguire, Pastore, and Flanagan, 1992).

The target group most affected by increased incarceration are African Americans who account for almost fifty percent of the people in prison, even though they represent less than thirteen percent of the population (Table 11.2).

In times of budget deficits, public expenditures in one area mean a reduction of expenditures in others. The most significant shift in public expenditures is from expenditures on education to expenditures on crime control. The federal government halved its contribution to education between 1980 and 1990. County expenditures as a percent of the total budget devoted to education declined from 16 percent in 1974 to 14 percent in 1989. As a result, criminal justice expenditures have, for the first time in U.S. history, received more public funds from state, county, and municipal governments than has education (Figures 11.4 and 11.5).

The same trend is indicated by percentage increases in state expenditures on education and corrections between 1989 and 1990 (Tables 11.3 and 11.4).

Where state government's priorities are most clearly revealed is in the decision of where to allocate funds for facilities. Table 11.4 indicates that education is falling far be-

Table 11.2	Prisoners under Jurisdiction of State and Federal Correctional Authorities, by Race, 1991		
Total	**White**	**Black**	**Other**
824,133	365,347	395,245	63,541

Source: Sourcebook of Criminal Justice Statistics, 1992.

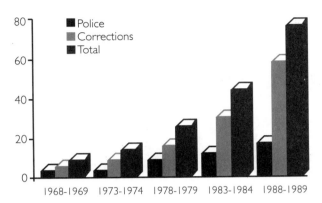

Figure 11.3 Per capita state expenditures on criminal justice, 1968–1989.

Source: U.S. Department of Commerce, Bureau of Census, *City Government Finances, 1968–1969, 1973–1974, 1978–1979, 1983–1984, 1988–1989.*

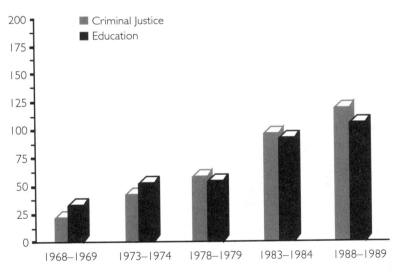

Figure 11.4 Comparison of per capita municipal expenditures on criminal justice and education, 1968–1989.

Source: U.S. Department of Commerce, Bureau of Census, *City Government Finance,: 1968–69, 1973–74, 1978–79, 1983–84, and 1988–89.*

hind corrections in the competition for these scarce resources despite widespread agreement that schools are generally in abominable physical condition.

The federal government increased its allocation of resources for criminal justice without a pause. The war on drugs, with a budget of $1 billion in 1981, received $13.4 billion in 1993. The government added seven hundred FBI agents in 1990, an increase of 25 percent. In Illinois in 1990 nearly two thousand teachers were laid off. Welfare for the poor was also severely cut. In real dollars the Aid to Dependent Children program's cash contribution to a mother with two children and no outside employment dropped from $7,836 in 1982 to $4,801 in 1991. The criminal justice system, by contrast, is virtually immune from the cuts experienced by other public services. On those rare occasions when a mayor or governor suggests cutting justice expenditures or even holding steady the number of police officers, politicking and arm-twisting by the police unions quickly reverse the decision. In Prince George's County, a suburb of Washington, D.C., for example, there was talk of layoffs and pay cuts for police. The police officer's union hired a public relations firm and ran television commercials citing increasing crime rates and accusing the county executive of hand-cuffing police officers with proposed budget cuts. The union spent over $10,000 in one week on television and newspaper advertisements. The correctional officers association of California is the second largest lobby in the state as measured by dollars spent in support of favored candidates for political office. The message is clear: you can increase the number of students in already overcrowded classrooms, fire teachers, cut head start and summer programs, but you dare not touch the police or prisons. One predictable result of the increase in expenditures and police officers is a doubling of the number of people in prison (Figure 11.6 and Table 11.5).

All these expenditures, arrests, and law enforcement policies are justified by an alleged increase in crime. The statistics and public statements generated and manipulated by the police and the FBI (particularly the Uniform Crime Reports) almost always paint the picture of an "alarming" increase in crime. These data are political, not factual, statements (Chambliss, 1993). The fact is

<table>
<tr><td colspan="2">**Table 11.3** Percent Increase in Elementary and Secondary Education Compared to Percent Increase in Expenditures for Corrections, 1989–1990</td></tr>
</table>

Percent Increase in Elementary and Secondary Education	Percent Increase in Corrections
7.3%	29%

Percent Increase in State Capital Expenditures for Higher Education and Corrections 1989–1990	
Percent Increase for Higher Education	**Percent Increase for Corrections**
46%	150.6%

Source: The National Association of State Budget Offices.

Table 11.4 Capital Expenditures by Selected States (in $ millions)

Eight states spent more money for capital expenditures on correctional facilities than for higher education facilities from 1988 through 1990, fiscal years. Leading this trend is Texas, which spent $0 on higher education facilities while spending $500 million on correctional facilities.

	Corrections	vs.	Higher Education	=	Difference
Texas	500		0		500
New York	612		314		298
Massachusetts	396		137		259
Connecticut	139		72		67
Ohio	30		0		30
New Jersey	199		166		30
New Hampshire	36		16		20
Maine	17		7		10
Total Difference					*1187*

In these eight states almost $1.2 billion more was spent for construction of prisons than on construction for higher education.

The state which spent the greatest amounts on capital expenditures for correctional construction was California. California spent $1.2 billion between 1988 and 1990, fiscal years. Its higher education capital expenditures for this period were $1.4 billion.

Source: The National Association of State Budget Offices.

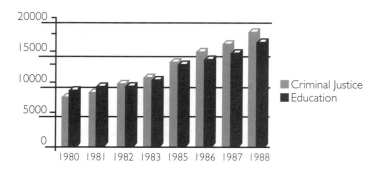

Figure 11.5 Per capital county expenditures on criminal justice and education, 1980–1988.

Source: U.S. Department Bureau of Census, *County Government Finances: 1983–84 and 1988–89.*

that, law enforcement, media, and political propaganda notwithstanding, the crime rate has not changed significantly since at least 1973 (Figure 11.7).

As Bogess and Bound have shown after systematically analyzing data provided by the FBI in the Uniform Crime Reports and data from the National Crime Victim Survey, "the large increase in the incarceration rate is attributable primarily to an increase in the likelihood of incarceration given arrest," not to an increase in the crime rate (Bogess and Bound, 1993). Bogess and Bound go on to point out that most of the increase in crime reported by the FBI in its annual Uniform Crime Reports (UCR) is attributable to *an increase in the reporting of crime by citizens,* not to an actual increase in crime. The FBI practice of manipulating the reports to justify increased expenditures on criminal justice by the use of misleading gimmicks, such as a *crime clock* that purports to depict how frequently different types of crime are committed, makes these data suspect. The UCR selects data as well to emphasize any increase in crime while ignoring decreases. In 1992, for example, the UCR reported an increase in the murder rate from 1988 to 1992 without noting that between 1980 and 1988 the murder rate had actually declined (Figure 11.8).

That the murder rate has shown no appreciable increase since the 1980s is particularly noteworthy, given the fact that the weapons in use today are more efficient than ever before. Pistols have been replaced with rapid-firing automatic weapons that leave a victim little chance of escaping with a wound. It follows that the victim survey findings of a decline in overall violence rates is reflected in a murder rate that is stable over a ten-year period, given that the likelihood of death from gun violence may actually have increased even

Table 11.5	Change in the State and Federal Prison Populations, 1980–92		
Year	Number of Inmates	Annual Percent Change	Total Percent Change Since 1980
1980	329,821	—	—
1981	369,930	12.2%	12.2%
1982	413,806	11.9	25.5
1983	436,855	5.6	32.5
1984	462,002	5.8	40.1
1985	502,752	8.8	52.4
1986	545,378	8.5	65.4
1987	585,292	7.3	77.5
1988	631,990	8.0	91.6
1989	712,967	12.8	116.2
1990	773,124	8.4	134.4
1991	824,133	6.6	149.9
1992	883,593	7.2	167.9

Note: All counts are for December 31 of each year and may reflect revisions of previously reported numbers.

—Not applicable.

Source: Bureau of Justice Statistics Bulletin, May 1993.

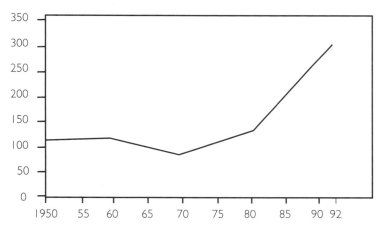

Figure 11.6 Prison population, U.S.A., 1950–1992 rate per 100,000 population.

Source: K. Maguire, A. Pastore, and T. Flanigan, *Sourcebook of Criminal Justice Statistics,* Washington, D.C., U.S. Dept. of Justice, Bureau of Justice Statistics, 1980, 1988, 1992.

Victimization trends, 1973–1992
Number of victimizations

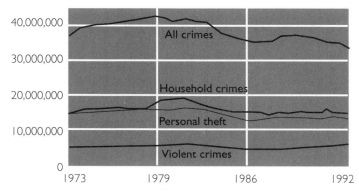

Figure 11.7 Respondents reporting being the victim of crime by type of crime.

Source: Bureau of Justice Statistics Bulletin, Criminal Victimization, 1992, Washington, D.C., U.S. Department of Justice, 1992.

though the number of violent acts has decreased.

It is important also to put in perspective the seriousness of the crimes reported by victims. For every type of crime reported, the least serious crime is the most common. Attempted crimes are reported twice as often as completed crimes. Larceny without contact occurs more than 20 times as often as larceny with contact. (Tables 11.6 and 11.7).

Furthermore, the fact that for every type of crime there is less than a fifty-fifty chance the victim will report the crime to the police is an indication of the crimes' seriousness. When asked why they do not report the crime, over half the victims say that the crime was "not important enough" or that "nothing could be done about it" (Bureau of Justice Statistics, 1993).

Finally, victim surveys show that it is very unlikely that anyone will be the victim of a crime in any given year. Over 90 percent of respondents report that neither they nor any member of their household was the victim of a criminal offense. Indeed, over a lifetime it is unlikely that most people will be the victim of a serious offense. Langan and Innes show that the risk of being a victim of a violent crime in any given year is less than 3 percent. Furthermore, 2.5 percent of this is accounted for by being a victim of an assault (Langan and Innes, 1984:185).

Creating Moral Panic

If actual crime rates have not been increasing, how did crime control come to take priority over almost every other social program? A review of the history of anticrime legislation from the 1960s suggests that it was a coalition of political, law enforcement, and mass media interests that, after thirty years of propaganda, created a moral panic about crime. That this moral panic derived from the manipulation of

Table 11.6	Estimated Number of Personal Victimization Rates per 1,000 Persons over Age 12, 1989: Completed and Attempted		
Crimes against the Person		**Completed**	**Attempted**
Aggravated assault		2.9	5.4
Simple assault		4.1	10.7
Larceny with contact		.6	.2

Table 11.7 Estimated Rate of Victimization per 100,000 Population by Seriousness of Offense, 1982

More Serious Offenses	**Less Serious Offenses**
Larceny with contact	Larceny without contact
306	7,945
Aggravated assault	Simple assault 1,708
931	1,700
Robbery with injury	Robbery without injury
220	310
Attempted robbery with injury	Attempted robbery without injury
708	2,638

From: Sourcebook of Criminal Justice Statistics. 1984. Washington, D.C.: U.S. Department of Justice, Bureau of Justice Statistics.

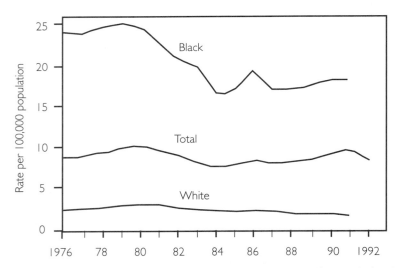

Figure 11.8 By race: U.S. murder rate, 1976–1992. Race-specific data is for single victim/single offender murders.

Source: Current Population Reports, P25–1095; Crime in the U.S. and Statistical Abstract of the U.S., various years.

public opinion is revealed by an analysis of criminal law legislation and political campaigns in the 1960s when *street crime* first was raised as a major political issue in America (Chambliss and Sbarbaro, 1993).

Crime became a national political issue for the first time in fifty years with the presidential campaign of 1964 when the Republican candidate, Barry Goldwater, sounded the alarm (Cronin et al., 1981:18):

Our wives, all women, feel unsafe on our streets. And in encouragement of even more abuse of the law, we have

the appalling spectacle of this country's Ambassador to the United Nations [Adlai Stevenson] actually telling an audience—this year, at Colby College—that, "in the great struggle to advance civil rights, even a jail sentence is no longer a dishonor but a proud achievement." Perhaps we are destined to see in this law-loving land people running for office not on their stainless records but on their prison record. (*New York Times*, September 4, 1964:13)

Goldwater's hue and cry did not strike a resonant chord in the American public. As *Newsweek* magazine editors observed: "Remarkably late in the campaign, Barry Goldwater was still a candidate in search of an issue that could score a voting breakthrough. . . . [He] did all he could to press the issue of law and order" (*Newsweek*, October, 19, 1964:27–34). Public opinion polls taken at the time confirmed the *Newsweek* analysis.

In the months preceding the election, the Gallup poll asked a sample of Americans what they thought were "the most important problems facing the nation." In spite of Goldwater's attempt to create moral panic, crime was not among them (Gallup, 1968).

The Gallup polls describe a public more concerned about war, civil rights, poverty, and unemployment than crime. Nonetheless, conservative Democrats, Republicans, and what Nils Christie aptly labels "the crime control industry" lobbied assiduously for harsher penalties and laws that gave more power to the police and fewer rights to the accused (Christie, 1993). Conservative legislators directed their attention primarily at Supreme Court decisions such as Miranda, Gideon, and Escobeda, which gave the accused the right to legal counsel, protection against coerced confessions, and the right to remain silent unless a lawyer was present.

Congressmen Ford and Senators McClellan, Stennis, Ervin, Hruska, Thurmond, Bible, and Lausche (a formidable conservative block of five Democrats and three Republicans) sponsored the Omnibus Crime Control and Safe Streets Act, which legalized wiretapping and "bugging" by federal agents and local police *without requiring a court order*. It authorized trial judges to admit confessions as voluntary after considering "all factors," thus emasculating the Miranda decision. The bill exempted law enforcement agencies from having to meet the requirements of the 1964 Civil Rights Act, which did not allow federal grants to agencies or organizations that discriminate.

In the 1968 presidential campaign (Nixon v. Humphrey), Richard Nixon and his running mate, Spiro Agnew (both later to be accused of serious crimes themselves), hammered away at the issue of "law and order." Nixon attacked the Johnson administration's focus on social conditions as the cause of crime:

By way of excuse, the present Administration places the blame on poverty. But poverty is just one contributing factor. During the Depression the crime rate was at an all-time low. The truth is that we will reduce crime and violence when we enforce our laws—when we make it less profitable, and a lot more risky to break them. (*New York Times,* October 25, 1968:34)

Nixon held the Supreme Court responsible for the crime problem. He assailed some of the court's decisions as having "tipped the balance against the peace forces and strengthened the criminal forces" (*New York Times,* September 30, 1968: 1). Nixon further stated:

The Supreme Court is not infallible. It is sometimes wrong. Many of the decisions break down 5 to 4, and I think that often in recent years the five-man majority has been wrong and the four-man minority right. We need more strict constructionists on the highest court of the United States. (*New York Times.* October 23, 1968:1)

Hubert Humphrey placed the blame for crime elsewhere:

Crime rates were highest among the poor and disadvantaged—who commit more crime but who also suffer more crime. In the long run we can only cut crime by getting at its cause; slums, unemployment, rundown schools and houses. This is where crime begins and that is where it must end. (*New York Times,* September 12, 1968:1)

In November, 1968 Richard Nixon was elected president. And in August 1968 a public opinion poll showed for the first time in twenty years that "crime, lawlessness, looting and rioting" was perceived by 29 percent of those asked as one of "the most important problems facing the nation." Fifty-two percent of those surveyed mentioned the Vietnam war as the most important problem facing the United States, and 20 percent still mentioned race relations as the most pressing issue facing the nation (Gallup Poll, 1972:2107).

The campaign of conservative politicians supported by media coverage of crime and the law enforcement establishment's nonstop propaganda campaign succeeded in raising crime as a major issue for the American people. It must be noted, however, that this was at a time when riots in the cities and violent demonstrations were taking place throughout the country and "crime" was only mentioned by a significant number of respondents when it was collected together with lawlessness, riots, and looting. The public's concern also was short-lived, for crime is not mentioned again until 1980 when "drugs" is seen as one of the nations' most important problems (Table 11.8).

On January 15, 1969, Senator John McClellan, along with Senators Ervin and Hruska, the ranking members of the Senate judiciary subcommittee on criminal law and procedures, introduced the Organized Crime Control Act (OCCA) in the Senate. McClellan took the opportunity to comment on his vision of future law enforcement under Nixon and to reprimand the Supreme Court: his speech made clear the fact that the concern was not only with organized crime but with overturning "liberal" Supreme Court decisions (Senate Hearings, 1969:512). Despite the fact that the bill was severely criticized as being unconstitutional by the ACLU, some members of congress and the New York Lawyers Association, the bill was passed into law. It contained measures that substantially increased police powers especially vis-à-vis poor defendants, thus reducing the civil liberties protections of earlier Supreme Court decision such as Miranda, Escobeda, and Gideon.

On October 15, 1970, President Nixon signed the OCCA into law at the Justice Department. The bill contained some revolutionary changes in the administration of criminal law: it changed the evidence-gathering process, created new federal sanctions and punishments, created a powerful investigative grand jury, established the special grand jury with increased powers, including the ability to write reports, and for the first time, compelled witnesses to testify if they were granted limited immunity. The bill allowed district courts to incarcerate uncooperative witnesses for as long as the grand jury was in session, and, finally, it expanded the conditions under which witnesses could be charged with perjury.

The years following the Nixon presidency have witnessed a continued assault on civil liberties and an expansion of federal authority in crime control. The Reagan and Bush administrations hammered away at the issue of crime and created the "war on drugs," complete with a "drug czar" and the expenditure of billions of dollars for crime control. Although the public was slow to respond to the barrage, it gradually came around.

Crime and Public Opinion

Politicians, law enforcement officials, and the media made crime a national issue in the 1960s, 70s, and

Table 11.8	The Most Important Problem Mentioned in Gallup Polls from 1935 to 1990		
1935	Unemployment	1963	Keeping peace, race relations
1936	Unemployment	1964	Vietnam, race relations
1937	Unemployment	1965	Vietnam, race relations
1938	Keeping out of war	1966	Vietnam
1939	Keeping out of war	1967	Vietnam, high cost of living
1940	Keeping out of war	1968	Vietnam
1941	Keeping out of war, winning war	1969	Vietnam
1942	Winning war	1970	Vietnam
1943	Winning war	1971	Vietnam, high cost of living
1944	Winning war	1972	Vietnam
1945	Winning war	1973	High cost of living, Watergate
1946	High cost of living	1974	High cost of living, Watergate, energy crisis
1947	High cost of living, labor unrest	1975	High cost of living, unemployment
1948	Keeping peace	1976	High cost of living, unemployment
1949	Labor unrest	1977	High cost of living, unemployment
1950	Labor unrest	1978	High cost of living, energy problem
1951	Korean war	1979	High cost of living, energy problem
1952	Korean war	1980	High cost of living, unemployment
1953	Keeping peace	1981	High cost of living, unemployment
1954	Keeping peace	1982	Unemployment, high cost of living
1955	Keeping peace	1983	Unemployment, high cost of living
1956	Keeping peace	1984	Unemployment, fear of war
1957	Race relations, keeping peace	1985	Fear of war, unemployment
1958	Unemployment, keeping peace	1986	Unemployment, fear of war
1959	Keeping peace	1987	Fear of war, unemployment
1960	Keeping peace	1988	Budget deficit, drug abuse
1961	Keeping peace	1989	Drugs, poverty, homelessness
1962	Keeping peace	1990	Budget deficit, drugs

80s, and thereby *legitimized* the passage of laws and the allocation of major resources to the problem. They claimed to be responding to "public opinion." The political scientist James Q. Wilson, citing the Gallup polls, supported the conservative assault:

In May 1965 the Gallup Poll reported that for the first time "crime" (along with education) was viewed by Americans as the most important problem facing the nation. In the months leading up to the Democratic National Convention in 1968—specifically in February, May and August—Gallup continued to report crime as the most important issue. (Wilson, 1985: 65–66)

There is no evidence to support these claims. Indeed, Wilson's statements are pure fiction, made up, apparently, to support his and conservative politicians' ideological bias. Crime was *not* reported in the Gallup poll of May 1965, as Wilson claims. In May 1965 the Gallup poll

did not even ask what respondents thought was the most important problem facing the nation. But in June 1965 the question was asked and the responses were as follows: Vietnam: 23 percent; civil rights: 23 percent; threat of war: 16 percent; prestige abroad: 9 percent; spread of world communism: 9 percent; juvenile delinquency: 2 percent (Gallup Poll, 1965).

It is a gross distortion of fact to say, as Wilson does, that the 1968 polls "in February, May and August Gallup continued to report crime as the most important issue." Gallup did not ask the question in February. In May 1968 the question was asked and only 15 percent of the respondents named crime including riots, looting, and juvenile delinquency as the most important problem, but 42 percent named Vietnam and 25 percent race relations. In August crime is mentioned by 29 percent as the most important

problem, but the Vietnam war was seen as the most important problem by 52 percent (Gallup Poll, 1968).

These findings suggest the possibility that rather than responding to public concerns about crime, the crime issue was used by politicians as a smoke screen behind which they could carry out unpopular public policies, such as the Vietnam war, and pass laws that could be used to suppress public opposition and political dissent. But the long-term consequences have been even more sinister. For the end result of the law and order campaign begun in 1964 has been to criminalize an entire population of young black males and to fuel racism in America.

Young Black Men and Crime Control

Although laws are in theory applied to all violators, they are in fact applied in a discriminatory fashion against minorities. While constituting less than 13 percent of the population, African Americans make up almost 50 percent of the inmates in prison and an even higher proportion of those in jail (Table 11.2). So ubiquitous is the pattern of discriminatory law enforcement that the effect has been to criminalize an entire population. Studies in Washington. D.C., and Baltimore, Maryland, have revealed that nearly 50 percent of the African American male population between the ages of 18 and 35 is at any given time either in prison, on probation, parole, or a warrant is out for their arrest (Miller, 1992).

Observations of the routine practices of police departments and prosecutorial practices expose the institutionalized racism resulting from the expansion of the crime control industry (Skolnick and Fyfe, 1993). Police departments across the nation police the urban underclass ghetto with a vigilance that would create political revolution were the same tactics and policies implemented in white middle-class communities. In Washington, D.C., for example, the police have established, a rapid deployment unit (RDU: originally designed for riot control), which routinely patrols the black ghetto in search of law violators (Chambliss, 1993). Members of the RDU drive in patrol cars through the ghetto on nightly vigils looking for suspects. "Suspects" include all young black males between the ages of twelve and thirty who are visible: driving in cars, standing on street corners, or in a group observed through a window in an apartment.

To do their job, which members of the RDU see as "getting the shit off the streets," RDU officers express disdain for the constitutional rights of suspects or the department's guidelines for proper search, arrest, or use of force. The operational procedures followed in

moving from seeing young black males to actually confronting them consists mainly of finding an excuse rather than a legal reason for stopping a suspect. For young black males driving in a car, the best excuse is some minor infraction: a broken taillight, at ornament hanging from the mirror, a license plate light that is not working. On occasion if the RDU officer has a "strong feeling" or a "solid hunch" that someone he sees driving around may be in possession of drugs or weapons, the officer may have to stop the car and create the broken taillight with a quick slap of his pistol butt.

Once the excuse to stop is found or created, the RDU officer calls in other cruising officers in the area. Each RDU cruiser has two officers. The call will usually bring two more cars, always at least one more car: four to six officers in all. In the case of stopping a car (which is how RDU does most of its business), the RDU cruiser siren is blasted like a bombshell through the night, the two or three police cars screech to a halt around the suspects' car, and the officers exit their cruisers with guns drawn. Keep in mind that this is because, except for the officers "hunch" based on the age and skin color of the occupants of the car, the only "crime" being committed here is that the car being stopped had a broken taillight or some ornament hanging from the mirror. The occupants of the car are instructed at gun point to get out of their car with their hands up. Racial slurs usually accompany the commands: "Get out of the car motherfucker and don't reach for nothing or you'll be eating this gun for dinner."

Next comes the officers' superficial adherence to legality: "We're gonna search your car, OK?" An affirmative answer is assumed by either silence or any bodily gesture such as a shrug or a nod. Failing to get either a shrug a nod or if the suspect says no, which

in my observation happened only once, the officers look for some reason to enter the car: a piece of paper in the back seat that could appear to be a marijuana paper in poor light, something white on the floor mat that might be cocaine. While two or three officers search the car, the other two or three have instructed the suspects to empty their pockets—slowly—all the while at gunpoint.

By these measures and other quasi-legal or undeniably illegal ones, the police in Washington arrest and incarcerate a higher proportion of the city's population than any other city in the world. For what? The majority of the arrests are for the possession of small amounts of crack, cocaine, or marijuana. A defendant's sentence, which in 90 percent of the cases, follows from a negotiated guilty plea is effected by *priors*: previous arrests for, usually, the same kind of offense.

Through such measures the prisons of America are overflowing with minor offenders. A study by the Department of Justice found that over 35 percent of all federal prisoners are "low-level drug offenders with no current or prior violent offenses on their records, no involvement in sophisticated criminal activity and no previous prison time (Bureau of Justice Statistics, 1994). Austin and Irwin in a study of inmates in federal and state prisons found that the majority of inmates were sentenced to prison for crimes which respondents to public opinion surveys described as "not serious" (Austin and Irwin, 1991). The authors conclude: "The vast majority of inmates are sentenced for petty crimes that pose little danger to public safety or significant economic loss to victims." (Figure 11.9.)

A 1989 survey of the arrest reports of a sample of inmates held in a jail housing over two-thousand prisoners found that trespassing

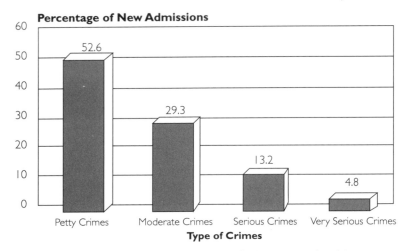

Percentage of New Admissions

52.6

29.3

13.2

4.8

Petty Crimes | Moderate Crimes | Serious Crimes | Very Serious Crimes

Type of Crimes

Figure 11.9 National estimate of the severity of crimes committed by persons admitted to state and federal prisons.

Source: James Austin and John Irwin, *Who Goes to Prison?* Copyright © 1991. Used by permission of the National Council on Crime and Delinquency.

and possession of small amounts of cocaine accounted for the majority of arrests. Trespassing was typically a crime committed by homeless black men seeking food in fast-food restaurants and possession of narcotics consisted of the possession of small amounts (under $40 worth) of marijuana, crack, cocaine, or "drug paraphernalia" (a pipe or even cigarette paper) (Holman and Chambliss, 1991).

Only a few miles from where the RDU and the narcs are active, lies "Foggy Bottom," home of George Washington University. On any night of the week one finds students at George Washington University enjoying leisurely evenings in their dormitory, fraternity, or sorority, underage students drink, use false ID's to go to bars and nightclubs, and in the presence of a "cool" professor they roll their marijuana cigarettes or stuff white powder up their noses. Not infrequently at fraternity parties or while out on a date these students commit rape and various other sexual assaults. Not all of them; but if the RDU paid half as much attention to the crimes of students at the universities as they do to young black males, the arrest and incar-

ceration rate for young white males would certainly approach that of young black males. And if procedures that are followed routinely in the ghetto were followed here, the students would be violently shoved against a wall, called names, threatened with death, hand cuffed, banged around, shoved into a police car, and taken off to jail for booking. This does not happen at George Washington University or at any of the other Washington, D.C., campuses; not even at the predominantly black universities: Howard and the University of the District of Columbia. On those rare occasions when a student is found with drugs, is accused of "date rape," or of the crime of purposely getting a woman drunk in order to have sex with her, they are given counseling, not a jail sentence (Schreiber, 1993).

As a result of the treatment of young black males by the criminal justice system from arrest to incarceration, the poor black community is a community of ex-convicts. Men hardened by the experience of jail and prison; women with husbands, lovers, their children's father, brothers, uncles, and nephews with criminal records; men stigmatized and unable to break the stigma;

men used to being brutalized by police, prosecutors, jailers, and other inmates. Men return with experiences of being raped, threatened, and assaulted by police and inmates. Some return to the community with AIDS and other diseases contracted while in jail or prison.

Most of the men arrested have children. The children know where their daddy is. For many children in the ghetto a visit to prison is more common than a visit to the zoo. In this way the children share the experience of prison. Prison becomes a normal part of the life of young people in the black ghetto. Virtually everyone has a close relative and over 50 percent have a parent in prison, on probation, parole, in jail, or in hiding because there is a warrant out for their arrest (Miller, 1992).

In prison African Americans are vastly overrepresented in the most severe conditions of incarceration. They comprise a disproportionate number of people in maximum security compared to their numbers in the prison population. In Maryland, for example, there are over eighteen-thousand prison inmates; 288 of these inmates are in "supermax": the Maryland Correctional Adjustment Center. These inmates are confined to their cells from twenty-two to twenty-four hours a day. Their cell is an 8 by 12, cement block room with a cement bed on which is a thin mattress. There is an aluminum toilet (with no toilet seat), a washbowl, and two bookshelves. There are two windows about four inches in width and twelve inches long. The windows are covered by a thick steel mesh. The door to the cell is solid, except for a small window three inches by six inches. When these men leave their cells they must first strip down and hand their clothes to a guard through a small slot in the wall, which the guards can open but the inmates cannot. While the guard examines the clothing the inmate stands naked and must make a 360 degree circle so that the guard can see that he has no weapon on his body. After inspecting the clothing, the guard returns it and watches the inmate dress. The inmate then stands with his back to the slot in the wall; he places his arms through the slot and the guard attaches handcuffs.

Inmates are sent to this prison from other prisons where they have been defined as dangerous to either other inmates or to prison guards. They are given a minimum thirteen-month sentence from which there is no possible reduction. Their sentence to this prison may be increased, but it cannot be reduced. For the first four months they are confined to their cell *twenty-three hours a day*. If they do not act up, or in the words of the prison wardens, if they "get with the program," they are then moved to the next level where they are confined for twenty-two and a half-hours a day. After three months at this level, assuming they have not been written up by a guard or prison official, they are confined to their cell for twenty-two hours a day. In each instance they are permitted recreation and a shower during the one to two hours they are out of their cell. Recreation consists of being allowed to play basketball or run around in an enclosed cage approximately twenty by twenty feet.

If an inmate is found guilty of committing an infraction of any of the rules—speaking to guards in unapproved ways, throwing feces or urine at the guards, being disruptive—he begins his thirteen-month confinement again. At the end of thirteen months, a board of three prison officials determines whether the inmate is ready to be returned to the prison population.

Of the 288 inmates in this "supermax" prison, *five* are white. That is, year in and year out, over 95 percent of the inmates confined to "supermax" are African Americans, whereas only 75 percent of the general prison population is African Americans.

The violence, anger, and message of revolt articulated so dramatically in the rap music of the current generation of young African Americans speaks volumes about the impact of the present criminal justice system on the attitudes of young black men. The songs encourage striking out at the police and the courts, not as symbols of white power but tools of the white man's oppression. When Rodney King was tried in a white suburban court by four white men, six white women, one Hispanic and one Filipino woman, but no black jurors, the consequences were apparent to everyone as angry black citizens rioted in the most costly and deadliest riot in American history. The riots left 54 people dead, over two-thousand injured, and five-thousand buildings destroyed or damaged. There were seventeen-thousand arrests, and property destroyed of more than $1 billion. Forty thousand jobs were lost as a consequence of the destruction. Although poorly publicized by the media reluctant to be accused of contributing to the spread of riots, there were outbreaks in Atlanta, Seattle, Washington, and Madison, Wisconsin, as well.

Reducing Crime

The official justification for the unprecedented expansion of the crime control industry is, of course, that it will reduce crime. Increased police surveillance, mandatory prison sentences, and more severe penalties have never effectively reduced crime. The criminal justice system is demonstrably the least effective and arguably the most counterproductive of all social policies designed to reduce crime. People whose lifestyle incorporates criminality into it, professional thieves, drug addicts, and drug dealers, accept the possibility of jail or prison as "the cost of doing business." As David Dragna, a heroin addict remarked after being sentenced to prison for the tenth time, "It's just getting easier. It doesn't bother me." As Harry King, a professional safecracker (at the other extreme of the criminal type from David Dragna) put it: "I don't like to go to prison any more than an office worker likes to punch the clock. It's just one of the bad parts of my profession. I live with it" (King and Chambliss, 1984).

The recidivism rate of ex-prisoners should be adequate evidence against the efficacy of imprisonment as a solution to crime. According to a study of recidivism conducted by the National Institute of Justice, "of the 108,580 persons released from prisons in 11 states in 1983 . . . an estimated 62.5% were rearrested for a felony or serious misdemeanor within 3 years." These findings are consistent with research dating back to the nineteenth century.

The criminal justice system as a means of coping with the problem of crime is an utter failure. It is the one institution that receives more public funding the more it fails. It is as though a university managed to take literate students in as freshman and graduated illiterates four years later, but was able to convince a gullible public that this was because it did not have enough money.

To be sure, we do not possess sufficient knowledge to confidently advocate alternative social policies that would be effective. Research on the impact of education suggests that early childhood education may effectively reduce the likelihood of being arrested as a teenager (Geiger, 1992). Prison education programs have been shown to substantially reduce recidivism (New York Department of Correctional Services, 1991; Littlefield, 1989; Holloway and Moke, 1986). And sociological theories of crime causation all suggest the importance of education. At the very least it is safe to conclude on the basis of extant knowledge that the massive expenditures on crime control would be more effective in reducing crime were they allocated instead to repairing the dismal condition of our public schools, especially those that serve the poor and minorities. But current policies have little to do with what works, but everything to do with politics, the creation of moral panics, racism, and the mobilization of bias (Chambliss and Zatz, 1994).

Summary and Conclusion

Between 1964 and 1990 a coalition of interests including conservative legislators, the crime control industry, and the media created a moral panic about crime in the United States. As a result, public expenditures at every level of government have been transferred from other social programs into crime control. Police powers have been substantially increased both by increases in numbers of police officers and laws giving the police a virtual carte blanche in dealing with suspects. The nature of policing in a class-society inevitably leads to policing the poor and minorities rather than those in social classes capable of creating problems if they are heavily policed. As a consequence. we have seen a dramatic increase in the number of arrests, convictions, and prison sentences meted out to the poor and especially the minority poor.

For the young black male population overpoliced and overincarcerated whose lives are a torment of poverty and policing, current policies have created a hostile and divided society. Racism is justified by the self-fulfilling prophesy of policing the ghetto and pointing the finger at ghetto crime rates as a justification for institutionalizing racism.

References

Austin, James, and John Irwin. 1991. *Who Goes to Prison?* San Francisco: National Council on Crime and Delinquency.

Bogess, Scott, and John Bound. "Did Criminal Activities Increase During the 1980's? Comparisons Across Data Sources." 1993. *Research Report No. 93–280.* Ann Arbor, Mich. Population Studies Center.

Broderick, Vincent. 1969. "The Proposed Organized Crime Control Act of 1969." House Hearings, 1969:291.

Bureau of Justice Statistics. 1993. *Highlights from 20 Years of Surveying Crime Victims.* Washington, D.C. U.S. Department of Justice.

Bureau of Justice Statistics. 1994. "Drug Offenders in Federal Prison." U.S. Department of Justice, Washington, D.C. (February).

Chambliss, William J. 1991. *Trading Textbooks for Prison Cells.* Alexandria, Va.: National Center on Institutions and Alternatives.

Chambliss, William J., and Edward Sbarbaro. 1993 "Moral Panics, Repression, and Racism: The Drug War in America." *Socio-Legal Bulletin.* Summer 4–11.

Chambliss, William J., and Marjorie Zatz. 1994. *Making Law: The Law, State and Structural Contradictions.* Bloomington: Indiana University Press.

Chambliss, William J., 1994 "Policing the Ghetto Underclass." *Social Problems,* May. (in Press)

Christie, Nils. 1993. *Crime Control as Industry.* London: Routledge.

Congressional Quarterly. 1965–1972.

Congressional Quarterly Almanac. 1965.

Cronin, Thomas E., Tania Z. Cronin, and Michael E. Milakovich. 1981. *United States Crime in the Streets.* Bloomington: Indiana University Press.

Gallup Polls. 1951–1992.

Geiger, Kent, 1992. "Education and Delinquency." Washington. D.C. National Education Association.

House Reports. U.S. House of Representatives. 1965–1975.

Holloway, Jerry, and Paul Moke. "Post Secondary Correctional Education: An Evaluation of Parolee Performance," 1986. Unpublished MS, Wilmington, Ohio.

Holman, Barry, and William J. Chambliss. 1991. "Residents in the Crossbar Jail." Paper delivered at the American Society of Criminology, San Francisco.

King, Harry, and William J. Chambliss. 1984. *Harry King: A Professional Thief's Journey.* New York: John Wiley.

Langan and Innes, eds. 1984. *Sourcebook of Criminal Justice Statistics.* U.S. Department of Justice. Bureau of Justice Statistics. Washington, D.C.: U.S. Government Printing Office.

Littlefield, John F. 1989. "Characteristics of the Ohio Inmate Intake Population and the Implications for Correctional Education Programming." Paper presented at International Conference of Prison Education, Milton Keynes, U.K.

Maguire, Kathleen, and Timothy J. Flanagan, eds. 1990; 1991. *Sourcebook of Criminal Justice Statistics 1990.* Washington, D.C.: Bureau of Justice Statistics.

Maguire, Kathleen, Anne L. Pastore, and Timothy J. Flanagan. 1992. *Sourcebook of Criminal Justice Statistics.* Washington, D.C. Bureau of Justice Statistics.

Miller, Jerome M. 1992. *Search and Destroy: The Plight of African American Males in the Criminal Justice System.* Alexandria, Va: National Center on Institutions and Alternatives.

Newsweek, 10/19/1964. "The Curious Campaign—Point by Point."

New York Department of Correctional Services, 1991 "Analysis of Return Rates of the Inmate College Program Participants." Albany. Division of Program Planning, Research, and Evaluation.

New York Times. January 6, 1991; Sept. 4, 1964; Sept. 12, 1968; Sept 30, 1968; Oct. 23, 1968; Oct. 25, 1968.

New York Times Magazine. 1964–1970.

Schreiber, Leslie. 1993. "Alcohol and Rape on College Campuses." PhD. dissertation. Washington, D.C. George Washington University.

Senate Hearings. U.S. Senate. 1965–1975.

Skolnick, Jerome H., and James J. Fyfe. 1993. *Above the Law.* New York: Free Press.

Uniform Crime Reports. 1980; 1984; 1988; 1992. "Crime in the United States." Washington, D.C.: U.S. Department of Justice.

Washington Post. Feb. 16, 1994.

Wilson, James Q. 1985. *Thinking about Crime.* New York: Vintage.

Wolfe, Alan. 1977. *The Limits of Legitimacy.* New York: Free Press.

 Article Review Form at end of book.

How might society change the "opportunity structure" available to young Black men? Who should assume responsibility for promoting such a change?

The Code of the Streets

In this essay on urban anthropology a social scientist takes us inside a world most of us glimpse only in grisly headlines—"Teen Killed in Drive-By Shooting"—to show us how a desperate search for respect governs social relations among many African-American young men.

Elijah Anderson

Of all the problems besetting the poor inner-city black community, none is more pressing than that of interpersonal violence and aggression. It wreaks havoc daily with the lives of community residents and increasingly spills over into downtown and residential middle-class areas. Muggings, burglaries, carjackings, and drug-related shootings, all of which may leave their victims or innocent bystanders dead, are now common enough to concern all urban and many suburban residents. The inclination to violence springs from the circumstances of life among the ghetto poor—the lack of jobs that pay a living wage, the stigma of race, the fallout from rampant drug use and drug trafficking, and the resulting alienation and lack of hope for the future.

Simply living in such an environment places young people at special risk of falling victim to aggressive behavior. Although there are often forces in the community which can counteract the negative influences, by far the most powerful being a strong, loving, "decent" (as inner-city residents put it) family committed to middle-class values, the despair is pervasive enough to have spawned an oppositional culture, that of "the streets," whose norms are often consciously opposed to those of mainstream society. These two orientations—decent and street—socially organize the community, and their coexistence has important consequences for residents, particularly children growing up in the inner city. Above all, this environment means that even youngsters whose home lives reflect mainstream values—and the majority of homes in the community do—must be able to handle themselves in a street-oriented environment.

This is because the street culture has evolved what may be called a code of the streets, which amounts to a set of informal rules governing interpersonal public behavior, including violence. The rules prescribe both a proper comportment and a proper way to respond if challenged. They regulate the use of violence and so allow those who are inclined to aggression to precipitate violent encounters in an approved way. The rules have been established and are enforced mainly by the street-oriented, but on the streets the distinction between street and decent is often irrelevant; everybody knows that if the rules are violated, there are penalties. Knowledge of the code is thus largely defensive; it is literally necessary for operating in public. Therefore, even though families with a decency orientation are usually opposed to the values of the code, they often reluctantly encourage their children's familiarity with it to enable them to negotiate the inner-city environment.

At the heart of the code is the issue of respect—loosely defined as being treated "right," or granted the deference one deserves. However, in the troublesome public environment of the inner city, as people increasingly feel buffeted by forces beyond their control, what one deserves in the way of respect becomes more and more problematic and uncertain. This in turn further opens the issue of respect to sometimes intense interpersonal negotiation. In the street culture, especially among young people, respect is viewed as almost an external entity that is hard-won but easily lost, and so must constantly be guarded. The rules of the code in fact provide a framework for negotiating respect. The person whose very appearance—including his clothing, demeanor, and way of moving—deters transgressions feels that he possesses, and may be considered by others to possess, a measure of respect. With the right amount of respect, for instance, he can avoid "being bothered" in public. If he is bothered, not only may he be in physical danger but he has been disgraced or "dissed" (disrespected). Many of the forms that dissing can take might seem petty to middle-class people (maintaining eye contact for too long, for example), but to those invested in the street code, these actions become serious indications of the other person's intentions. Consequently, such people become very sensitive to advances and slights, which could well serve as warnings of imminent physical confrontation.

This hard reality can be traced to the profound sense of alienation from mainstream society and its institutions felt by many poor inner-city black people, particularly the young. The code of the streets is actually a cultural adaptation to a profound lack of faith in the police and the judicial system. The police are most often seen as representing the dominant white society and not caring to protect inner-city residents. When called, they may not respond, which is one reason many residents feel they must be prepared to take extraordinary measures to defend themselves and their loved ones against those who are inclined to aggression. Lack of police accountability has in fact been incorporated into the status system: the person who is believed capable of "taking care of himself" is accorded a certain deference, which translates into a sense of

physical and psychological control. Thus the street code emerges where the influence of the police ends and personal responsibility for one's safety is felt to begin. Exacerbated by the proliferation of drugs and easy access to guns, this volatile situation results in the ability of the street-oriented minority (or those who effectively "go for bad") to dominate the public spaces.

Decent and Street Families

Although almost everyone in poor inner-city neighborhoods is struggling financially and therefore feels a certain distance from the rest of America, the decent and the street family in a real sense represent two poles of value orientation, two contrasting conceptual categories. The labels "decent" and "street," which the residents themselves use, amount to evaluative judgments that confer status on local residents. The labeling is often the result of a social contest among individuals and families of the neighborhood. Individuals of the two orientations often coexist in the same extended family. Decent residents judge themselves to be so while judging others to be of the street, and street individuals often present themselves as decent, drawing distinctions between themselves and other people. In addition, there is quite a bit of circumstantial behavior—that is, one person may at different times exhibit both decent and street orientations, depending on the circumstances. Although these designations result from so much social jockeying, there do exist concrete features that define each conceptual category.

Generally, so-called decent families tend to accept mainstream values more fully and attempt to instill them in their children. Whether married couples with children or single-parent (usually female) households, they are gener-

ally "working poor" and so tend to be better off financially than their street-oriented neighbors. They value hard work and self-reliance and are willing to sacrifice for their children. Because they have a certain amount of faith in mainstream society, they harbor hopes for a better future for their children, if not for themselves. Many of them go to church and take a strong interest in their children's schooling. Rather than dwelling on the real hardships and inequities facing them, many such decent people, particularly the increasing number of grandmothers raising grandchildren, see their difficult situation as a test from God and derive great support from their faith and from the church community.

Extremely aware of the problematic and often dangerous environment in which they reside, decent parents tend to be strict in their child-rearing practices, encouraging children to respect authority and walk a straight moral line. They have an almost obsessive concern about trouble of any kind and remind their children to be on the lookout for people and situations that might lead to it. At the same time, they are themselves polite and considerate of others, and teach their children to be the same way. At home, at work, and in church, they strive hard to maintain a positive mental attitude and a spirit of cooperation.

So-called street parents, in contrast, often show a lack of consideration for other people and have a rather superficial sense of family and community. Though they may love their children, many of them are unable to cope with the physical and emotional demands of parenthood, and find it difficult to reconcile their needs with those of their children. These families, who are more fully invested in the code of the streets than the decent people are, may aggressively socialize their children into it in a normative way. They believe in the code and judge themselves and others according to its values.

In fact the overwhelming majority of families in the inner-city community try to approximate the decent-family model, but there are many others who clearly represent the worst fears of the decent family. Not only are their financial resources extremely limited, but what little they have may easily be misused. The lives of the street-oriented are often marked by disorganization. In the most desperate circumstances people frequently have a limited understanding of priorities and consequences, and so frustrations mount over bills, food, and, at times, drink, cigarettes, and drugs. Some tend toward self-destructive behavior, many street-oriented women are crack-addicted ("on the pipe"), alcoholic, or involved in complicated relationships with men who abuse them. In addition, the seeming intractability of their situation, caused in large part by the lack of well-paying jobs and the persistence of racial discrimination, has engendered deep-seated bitterness and anger in many of the most desperate and poorest blacks, especially young people. The need both to exercise a measure of control and to lash out at somebody is often reflected in the adults' relations with their children. At the least, the frustrations of persistent poverty shorten the fuse in such people—contributing to a lack of patience with anyone, child or adult, who irritates them.

In these circumstances a woman—or a man, although men are less consistently present in children's lives—can be quite aggressive with children, yelling at and striking them for the least little infraction of the rules she has set down. Often little if any serious explanation follows the verbal and physical punishment. This response teaches children a particular lesson. They learn that to solve any kind of interpersonal problem one must quickly resort to hitting or other violent behavior. Actual peace and quiet, and also the appearance of calm, respectful children conveyed to her neighbors and friends, are often what the young mother most desires, but at times she will be very aggressive in trying to get them. Thus she may be quick to beat her children, especially if they defy her law, not because she hates them but because this is the way she knows to control them. In fact, many street-oriented women love their children dearly. Many mothers in the community subscribe to the notion that there is a "devil in the boy" that must be beaten out of him or that socially "fast girls need to be whupped." Thus much of what borders on child abuse in the view of social authorities is acceptable parental punishment in the view of these mothers.

Many street-oriented women are sporadic mothers whose children learn to fend for themselves when necessary, foraging for food and money any way they can get it. The children are sometimes employed by drug dealers or become addicted themselves. These children of the street, growing up with little supervision, are said to "come up hard." They often learn to fight at an early age, sometimes using short-tempered adults around them as role models. The street-oriented home may be fraught with anger, verbal disputes, physical aggression, and even mayhem. The children observe these goings-on, learning the lesson that might makes right. They quickly learn to hit those who cross them, and the dog-eat-dog mentality prevails. In order to survive, to protect oneself, it is necessary to marshal inner resources and be ready to deal with adversity in a hands-on way. In these circumstances physical prowess takes on great significance.

In some of the most desperate cases, a street-oriented mother may simply leave her young children alone and unattended while she goes out. The most irresponsible women can be found at local bars and crack houses, getting high and socializing with other adults. Sometimes a troubled woman will leave very young children alone for days at a time. Reports of crack addicts abandoning their children have become common in drug-infested inner-city communities. Neighbors or relatives discover the abandoned children, often hungry and distraught over the absence of their mother. After repeated absences, a friend or relative, particularly a grandmother, will often step in to care for the young children, sometimes petitioning the authorities to send her, as guardian of the children, the mother's welfare check, if the mother gets one. By this time, however, the children may well have learned the first lesson of the streets: survival itself, let alone respect, cannot be taken for granted; you have to fight for your place in the world.

Campaigning for Respect

These realities of inner-city life are largely absorbed on the streets. At an early age, often even before they start school, children from street-oriented homes gravitate to the streets, where they "hang"—socialize with their peers. Children from these generally permissive homes have a great deal of latitude and are allowed to "rip and run" up and down the street. They often come home from school, put their books down, and go right back out the door. On school nights eight- and nine-year-olds remain out until nine or ten o'clock (and teenagers typically come in whenever they want to). On the streets they play in groups that often become the source of their primary social bonds. Children from decent homes tend to be more carefully supervised and are thus likely to have curfews and to be taught how to stay out of trouble.

When decent and street kids come together, a kind of social shuffle occurs in which children have a chance to go either way. Tension builds as a child comes to realize that he must choose an orientation. The kind of home he comes from influences but does not determine the way he will ultimately turn out—although it is unlikely that a child from a thoroughly street-oriented family will easily absorb decent values on the streets. Youths who emerge from street-oriented families but develop a decency orientation almost always learn those values in another setting—in school, in a youth group, in church. Often it is the result of their involvement with a caring "old head" (adult role model).

In the street, through their play, children pour their individual life experiences into a common knowledge pool, affirming, confirming, and elaborating on what they have observed in the home and matching their skills against those of others. And they learn to fight. Even small children test one another, pushing and shoving, and are ready to hit other children over circumstances not to their liking. In turn, they are readily hit by other children, and the child who is toughest prevails. Thus the violent resolution of disputes, the hitting and cursing, gains social reinforcement. The child in effect is initiated into a system that is really a way of campaigning for respect.

In addition, younger children witness the disputes of older children, which are often resolved through cursing and abusive talk, if not aggression or outright violence. They see that one child succumbs to the greater physical and mental abilities of the other. They are also alert and attentive witnesses to the verbal and physical fights of adults, after which they compare notes and share their interpretations of the event. In almost every case the victor is the person who physically won the altercation, and this person often enjoys the esteem and respect of onlookers. These experiences reinforce the lessons the children have learned at home: might makes right, and toughness is a virtue, while humility is not. In effect they learn the social meaning of fighting. When it is left virtually unchallenged, this understanding becomes an ever more important part of the child's working conception of the world. Over time the code of the streets becomes refined.

Those street-oriented adults with whom children come in contact—including mothers, fathers, brothers, sisters, boyfriends, cousins, neighbors, and friends—help them along in forming this understanding by verbalizing the messages they are getting through experience: "Watch your back." "Protect yourself." "Don't punk out." "If somebody messes with you, you got to pay them back." "If someone disses you, you got to straighten them out." Many parents actually impose sanctions if a child is not sufficiently aggressive. For example, if a child loses a fight and comes home upset, the parent might respond, "Don't you come in here crying that somebody beat you up; you better get back out there and whup his ass. I didn't raise no punks! Get back out there and whup his ass. If you don't whup his ass, I'll whup your ass when you come home." Thus the child obtains reinforcement for being tough and showing nerve.

While fighting, some children cry as though they are doing something they are ambivalent about. The fight may be against their wishes, yet they may feel constrained to fight or face the consequences—not just from peers but also from caretakers or parents, who may administer another beating if they back down. Some adults recall receiving such lessons from their own parents and justify repeating them to their children as a way to toughen them up. Looking capable of taking care of oneself as a form of self-defense is a dominant theme among both street-oriented and decent adults who worry about the safety of their children. There is thus at times a convergence in their child-rearing practices, although the rationales behind them may differ.

Self-Image Based on "Juice"

By the time they are teenagers, most youths have either internalized the code of the streets or at least learned the need to comport themselves in accordance with its rules, which chiefly have to do with interpersonal communication. The code revolves around the presentation of self. Its basic requirement is the display of a certain predisposition to violence. Accordingly, one's bearing must send the unmistakable if sometimes subtle message to "the next person" in public that one is capable of violence and mayhem when the situation requires it, that one can take care of oneself. The nature of this communication is largely determined by the demands of the circumstances but can include facial expressions, gait, and verbal expressions—all of which are geared mainly to deterring aggression. Physical appearance, including clothes, jewelry, and grooming, also plays an important part in how a person is viewed; to be respected, it is important to have the right look.

Even so, there are no guarantees against challenges, because there are always people around looking for a fight to increase their share of respect—or "juice," as it is sometimes called on the street. Moreover, if a person is assaulted, it is important, not only in the eyes of his opponent but also in the eyes of his "running buddies," for him to avenge himself. Otherwise he risks being "tried" (challenged) or "moved on" by any number of others. To maintain his honor he must show he is not someone to be "messed with" or "dissed." In general, the person must "keep himself straight" by managing his position of respect among others; this involves in part his self-image, which is shaped by what he thinks others are thinking of him in relation to his peers.

Objects play an important and complicated role in establishing self-image. Jackets, sneakers, gold jewelry, reflect not just a person's taste, which tends to be tightly regulated among adolescents of all social classes, but also a willingness to possess things that may require defending. A boy wearing a fashionable, expensive jacket, for example, is vulnerable to attack by another who covets the jacket and either cannot afford to buy one or wants the added satisfaction of depriving someone else of his. However, if the boy forgoes the desirable jacket and wears one that isn't "hip," he runs the risk of being teased and possibly even assaulted as an unworthy person. To be allowed to hang with certain prestigious crowds, a boy must wear a different set of expensive clothes—sneakers and athletic suit—every day. Not to be able to do so might make him appear socially deficient. The youth comes to covet such items—especially when he sees easy prey wearing them.

In acquiring valued things, therefore, a person shores up his identity—but since it is an identity based on having things, it is highly precarious. This very precariousness gives a heightened sense of urgency to staying even with peers, with whom the person is actually competing. Young men and women who are able to command respect through their presentation of self— by allowing their possessions and

their body language to speak for them—may not have to campaign for regard but may, rather, gain it by the force of their manner. Those who are unable to command respect in this way must actively campaign for it—and are thus particularly alive to slights.

One way of campaigning for status is by taking the possessions of others. In this context, seemingly ordinary objects can become trophies embedded with symbolic value that far exceeds their monetary worth. Possession of the trophy can symbolize the ability to violate somebody—to "get in his face," to take something of value from him, to "dis" him, and thus to enhance one's own worth by stealing someone else's. The trophy does not have to be something material. It can be another person's sense of honor, snatched away with a derogatory remark. It can be the outcome of a fight. It can be the imposition of a certain standard, such as a girl's getting herself recognized as the most beautiful. Material things, however, fit easily into the pattern. Sneakers, a pistol, even somebody else's girlfriend, can become a trophy. When a person can take something from another and then flaunt it, he gains a certain regard by being the owner, or the controller, of that thing. But this display of ownership can then provoke other people to challenge him. This game of who controls what is thus constantly being played out on inner-city streets, and the trophy—extrinsic or intrinsic, tangible or intangible—identifies the current winner.

An important aspect of this often violent give-and-take is its zero-sum quality. That is, the extent to which one person can raise himself up depends on his ability to put another person down. This underscores the alienation that permeates the inner-city ghetto community. There is a generalized sense that very little respect is to be

had, and therefore everyone competes to get what affirmation he can of the little that is available. The craving for respect that results gives people thin skins. Shows of deference by others can be highly soothing, contributing to a sense of security, comfort, self-confidence, and self-respect. Transgressions by others which go unanswered diminish these feelings and are believed to encourage further transgressions. Hence one must be ever vigilant against the transgressions of others or even *appearing* as if transgressions will be tolerated. Among young people, whose sense of self-esteem is particularly vulnerable, there is an especially heightened concern with being disrespected. Many inner-city young men in particular crave respect to such a degree that they will risk their lives to attain and maintain it.

The issue of respect is thus closely tied to whether a person has an inclination to be violent, even as a victim. In the wider society people may not feel required to retaliate physically after an attack, even though they are aware that they have been degraded or taken advantage of. They may feel a great need to defend themselves *during* an attack, or to behave in such a way as to deter aggression (middle-class people certainly can and do become victims of street-oriented youths), but they are much more likely than street-oriented people to feel that they can walk away from a possible altercation with their self-esteem intact. Some people may even have the strength of character to flee, without any thought that their self-respect or esteem will be diminished.

In impoverished inner-city black communities, however, particularly among young males and perhaps increasingly among females, such flight would be extremely difficult. To run away would likely leave one's self-esteem in tatters. Hence people often feel constrained not only to stand up and at least attempt to resist during an assault but also to "pay back"—to seek revenge—after a successful assault on their person. This may include going to get a weapon or even getting relatives involved. Their very identity and self-respect, their honor, is often intricately tied up with the way they perform on the streets during and after such encounters. This outlook reflects the circumscribed opportunities of the innercity poor. Generally people outside the ghetto have other ways of gaining status and regard, and thus do not feel so dependent on such physical displays.

By Trial of Manhood

On the street, among males these concerns about things and identity have come to be expressed in the concept of "manhood." Manhood in the inner city means taking the prerogatives of men with respect to strangers, other men, and women—being distinguished as a man. It implies physicality and a certain ruthlessness. Regard and respect are associated with this concept in large part because of its practical application: if others have little or no regard for a person's manhood, his very life and those of his loved ones could be in jeopardy. But there is a chicken-and-egg aspect to this situation: one's physical safety is more likely to be jeopardized in public *because* manhood is associated with respect. In other words, an existential link has been created between the idea of manhood and one's self-esteem, so that it has become hard to say which is primary. For many inner-city youths, manhood and respect are flip sides of the same coin: physical and psychological well-being are inseparable, and both require a sense of control, of being in charge.

The operating assumption is that a man, especially a real man,

knows what other men know—the code of the streets. And if one is not a real man, one is somehow diminished as a person, and there are certain valued things one simply does not deserve. There is thus believed to be a certain justice to the code, since it is considered that everyone has the opportunity to know it. Implicit in this is that everybody is held responsible for being familiar with the code. If the victim of a mugging, for example, does not know the code and so responds "wrong," the perpetrator may feel justified even in killing him and may feel no remorse. He may think, "Too bad, but it's his fault. He should have known better."

So when a person ventures outside, he must adopt the code—a kind of shield, really—to prevent others from "messing with" him. In these circumstances it is easy for people to think they are being tried or tested by others even when this is not the case. For it is sensed that something extremely valuable is at stake in every interaction, and people are encouraged to rise to the occasion, particularly with strangers. For people who are unfamiliar with the code—generally people who live outside the inner city—the concern with respect in the most ordinary interactions can be frightening and incomprehensible. But for those who are invested in the code, the clear object of their demeanor is to discourage strangers from even thinking about testing their manhood. And the sense of power that attends the ability to deter others can be alluring even to those who know the code without being heavily invested in it—the decent inner-city youths. Thus a boy who has been leading a basically decent life can, in trying circumstances, suddenly resort to deadly force.

Central to the issue of manhood is the widespread belief that one of the most effective ways of gaining respect is to manifest "nerve." Nerve is shown when one

takes another person's possessions (the more valuable the better), "messes with" someone's woman, throws the first punch, "gets in someone's face," or pulls a trigger. Its proper display helps on the spot to check others who would violate one's person and also helps to build a reputation that works to prevent future challenges. But since such a show of nerve is a forceful expression of disrespect toward the person on the receiving end, the victim may be greatly offended and seek to retaliate with equal or greater force. A display of nerve, therefore, can easily provoke a life-threatening response, and the background knowledge of that possibility has often been incorporated into the concept of nerve.

True nerve exposes a lack of fear of dying. Many feel that it is acceptable to risk dying over the principle of respect. In fact, among the hard-core street-oriented, the clear risk of violent death may be preferable to being "dissed" by another. The youths who have internalized this attitude and convincingly display it in their public bearing are among the most threatening people of all, for it is commonly assumed that they fear no man. As the people of the community say, "They are the baddest dudes on the street." They often lead an existential life that may acquire meaning only when they are faced with the possibility of imminent death. Not to be afraid to die is by implication to have few compunctions about taking another's life. Not to be afraid to die is the quid pro quo of being able to take somebody else's life—for the right reasons, if the situation demands it. When others believe this is one's position, it gives one a real sense of power on the streets. Such credibility is what many inner-city youths strive to achieve, whether they are decent or street-oriented, both because of its practical defensive value and because of the positive way it makes them feel about themselves. The difference between the decent and the street-oriented youth is often that the decent youth makes a conscious decision to appear tough and manly; in another setting—with teachers, say, or at his part-time job—he can be polite and deferential. The street-oriented youth, on the other hand, has made the concept of manhood a part of his very identity; he has difficulty manipulating it—it often controls him.

Girls and Boys

Increasingly, teenage girls are mimicking the boys and trying to have their own version of "manhood." Their goal is the same—to get respect, to be recognized as capable of setting or maintaining a certain standard. They try to achieve this end in the ways that have been established by the boys, including posturing, abusive language, and the use of violence to resolve disputes, but the issues for the girls are different. Although conflicts over turf and status exist among the girls, the majority of disputes seem rooted in assessments of beauty (which girl in a group is "the cutest"), competition over boyfriends, and attempts to regulate other people's knowledge of and opinions about a girl's behavior or that of someone close to her, especially her mother.

A major cause of conflicts among girls is "he say, she say." This practice begins in the early school years and continues through high school. It occurs when "people," particularly girls, talk about others, thus putting their "business in the streets." Usually one girl will say something negative about another in the group, most often behind the person's back. The remark will then get back to the person talked about. She may retaliate or her friends may feel required to "take up for" her. In essence this is a form of group gossiping in which individuals are negatively assessed and evaluated. As with much gossip, the things said may or may not be true, but the point is that such imputations can cast aspersions on a person's good name. The accused is required to defend herself against the slander, which can result in arguments and fights, often over little of real substance. Here again is the problem of low self-esteem, which encourages youngsters to be highly sensitive to slights and to be vulnerable to feeling easily "dissed." To avenge the dissing, a fight is usually necessary.

Because boys are believed to control violence, girls tend to defer to them in situations of conflict. Often if a girl is attacked or feels slighted, she will get a brother, uncle, or cousin to do her fighting for her. Increasingly, however, girls are doing their own fighting and are even asking their male relatives to teach them how to fight. Some girls form groups that attack other girls or take things from them. A hard-core segment of inner-city girls inclined toward violence seems to be developing. As one thirteen-year-old girl in a detention center for youths who have committed violent acts told me, "To get people to leave you alone, you gotta fight. Talking don't always get you out of stuff." One major difference between girls and boys: girls rarely use guns. Their fights are therefore not life-or-death struggles. Girls are not often willing to put their lives on the line for "manhood." The ultimate form of respect on the male-dominated inner-city street is thus reserved for men.

"Going for Bad"

In the most fearsome youths such a cavalier attitude toward death grows out of a very limited view of life. Many are uncertain about how long they are going to live and believe they could die violently at any time. They accept this fate; they live on the edge. Their manner conveys the message that nothing intimidates them; whatever turn the encounter takes, they maintain their attack—rather like a pit bull, whose spirit many such boys admire. The demonstration of such tenacity "shows heart" and earns their respect.

This fearlessness has implications for law enforcement. Many street-oriented boys are much more concerned about the threat of "justice" at the hands of a peer than at the hands of the police. Moreover, many feel not only that they have little to lose by going to prison but that they have something to gain. The toughening-up one experiences in prison can actually enhance one's reputation on the streets. Hence the system loses influence over the hard core who are without jobs, with little perceptible stake in the system. If mainstream society has done nothing *for* them, they counter by making sure it can do nothing *to* them.

At the same time, however, a competing view maintains that true nerve consists in backing down, walking away from a fight, and going on with one's business. One fights only in self-defense. This view emerges from the decent philosophy that life is precious, and it is an important part of the socialization process common in decent homes. It discourages violence as the primary means of resolving disputes and encourages youngsters to accept nonviolence and talk as confrontational strategies. But "if the deal goes down," self-defense is greatly encouraged. When there is enough positive support for this orientation, either in the home or among one's peers, then nonviolence has a chance to prevail. But it prevails at the cost of relinquishing a claim to being bad and tough, and therefore sets a young person up as at the very least alienated from street-oriented peers and quite possibly a target of derision or even violence.

Although the nonviolent orientation rarely overcomes the impulse to strike back in an encounter, it does introduce a certain confusion and so can prompt a measure of soul-searching, or even profound ambivalence. Did the person back down with his respect intact or did he back down only to be judged a "punk"—a person lacking manhood? Should he or she have acted? Should he or she have hit the other person in the mouth? These questions beset many young men and women during public confrontations. What is the "right" thing to do? In the quest for honor, respect, and local status—which few young people are uninterested in—common sense most often prevails, which leads many to opt for the tough approach, enacting their own particular versions of the display of nerve. The presentation of oneself as rough and tough is very often quite acceptable until one is tested. And then that presentation may help the person pass the test, because it will cause fewer questions to be asked about what he did and why. It is hard for a person to explain why he lost the fight or why he backed down. Hence many will strive to appear to "go for bad," while hoping they will never be tested. But when they are tested, the outcome of the situation may quickly be out of their hands, as they become wrapped up in circumstances of the moment.

An Oppositional Culture

The attitudes of the wider society are deeply implicated in the code of the streets. Most people in inner-city communities are not totally invested in the code, but the significant minority of hard-core street youths who are have to maintain the code in order to establish reputations, because they have—or feel they have—few other ways to assert themselves. For these young people the standards of the street code are the only game in town. The extent to which some children—particularly those who through upbringing have become most alienated and those lacking in strong and conventional social support—experience, feel, and internalize racist rejection and contempt from mainstream society may strongly encourage them to express contempt for the more conventional society in turn. In dealing with this contempt and rejection, some youngsters will consciously invest themselves and their considerable mental resources in what amounts to an oppositional culture to preserve themselves and their self-respect. Once they do, any respect they might be able to garner in the wider system pales in comparison with the respect available in the local system; thus they often lose interest in even attempting to negotiate the mainstream system.

At the same time, many less alienated young blacks have assumed a street-oriented demeanor as a way of expressing their black-ness while really embracing a much more moderate way of life; they, too, want a nonviolent setting in which to live and raise a family. These decent people are trying hard to be part of the mainstream culture, but the racism, real and perceived, that they encounter helps to legitimate the oppositional culture. And so on occasion they adopt street behavior. In fact, depending on the demands of the situation, many people in the community slip back and forth between decent and street behavior.

A vicious cycle has thus been formed. The hopelessness and alienation many young inner-city black men and women feel, largely as a result of endemic joblessness and persistent racism, fuels the violence they engage in. This violence serves to confirm the negative feelings many whites and some middle-class blacks harbor toward the ghetto poor, further legitimating the oppositional culture and the code of the streets in the eyes of many poor young blacks. Unless this cycle is broken, attitudes on both sides will become increasingly entrenched, and the violence, which claims victims black and white, poor and affluent, will only escalate.

 Article Review Form at end of book.

What evidence suggests that the Black man arrested in the Fort Bragg swastika case might have been falsely accused?

The Fort Bragg Swastika

Did the army blame the wrong man for racism?

Larry Reibstein

When Nazi Swastikas were painted on the barracks doors of six black Special Forces soldiers at Fort Bragg, N.C., last July, the army knew it faced another explosive racial incident. Seven months earlier, three soldiers—two with ties to neo-Nazi skinhead groups—were charged in connection with the murders of two black Fayetteville residents. The incident reinforced suspicions of links between white supremacist groups and base soldiers. At the Democratic convention, President Clinton kept the issue in the spotlight, saying Special Forces soldiers "do not deserve to have swastikas on their doors."

So there was some relief, and surprise, when the army quietly disclosed a few weeks later that an African-American soldier was suspected of spray-painting the doors, including his own. The army suggested the two-foot-high swastikas were not racially motivated but merely the work of a disgruntled soldier, whom it didn't name. Members of the Special Forces said they felt vindicated, and leaders of the local black community accepted the explanation.

But now it seems that neat picture was far too simple. Last week, after *Newsweek* began making inquiries, the army filed a less serious charge against the black soldier, Sgt. Robert L. Washington, and, according to his lawyer, signaled plea negotiations. Washington's civilian lawyer, James A. Martin, said he was told by army prosecutors that the "evidence was falling apart and was very, very weak." Washington and Martin go further, contending that the army's evidence—paint found on the soldier's shoes and pants—is so suspect it may very well have been planted. Nearly as disturbing is Washington's contention he was singled out because he was considered a troublemaker—he had several times in his career filed charges of racial harassment—and this was payback time.

In response to questions, the Special Forces command asserted in a statement that it had conducted a "thorough and exhaustive investigation" and was treating Washington fairly. It declined to discuss specific evidence but said it was continuing with administrative proceedings against Washington.

On paper Washington, 31, doesn't fit the image of a mischief maker. Documents show a nearly spotless record and lavish praise for his work analyzing intelligence reports for the Special Forces. A native of Tifton, Ga., he joined the army in 1990 after getting a bachelor's degree in sociology from the University of Georgia.

Yet a review of the investigative files shows that army probers strangely zeroed in on Washington within hours of the incident in the early morning of July 16. After searching his barracks room and finding nothing, investigators bluntly told him they knew he did it, Washington said. According to the army records, a former commander, with whom Washington had tangled on a racial complaint a year before, had suggested that prosecutors home in on the soldier. Washington also said an investigator told him that he knew a black person had done it because "95 percent of the time a black person complains about vandalism, the black is doing it to himself."

Investigators immediately took clippings of his fingernails and the clothes he slept in. Subsequent tests revealed no evidence of paint on those items, documents show. A few days later investigators asked him to spray-paint more than 80 swastikas on barracks doors in some sort of a test. A few days after that, now a week and a half after the actual incident, investigators removed seven pairs of his shoes for testing.

Forensic tests of those items constitute the heart of the army's case. A report from the army's Criminal Investigation Laboratory in Fort Gillem, Ga., concludes that the red paint from the doors was "consistent with" paint marks found on Washington's shoes and pants. But the report goes on to say that the spherical paint particles had not adhered to the clothing—like a stain—but instead "were found laying on the surface" of the items. This indicated, the report said, that the paint was "dry prior to contacting the surface." Martin, who only recently left the army, where he served as a lawyer, contends that spray paint would not dry from the time it left the can until it hit the clothing. He suggests one way dried paint chips would get on the clothing: if someone placed them there. He doesn't rule out contamination from another source, such as, bizarrely enough, Washington's paint test.

If the army has a problem with the evidence, it's not quite willing to clear Washington. The army originally was seeking an "other than honorable" discharge, a severe sanction that would deny him military benefits for life. Under the new offer, according to Martin, he would receive a more favorable discharge but have to leave the army for a totally unrelated reason —he recently failed a physical-fitness test. Washington, rejecting his lawyer's advice, says he's not taking the deal. "These guys were out to slander my name, so why should I leave quietly?" he says. He also says leaving now won't help answer the question, just who did paint the swastikas? The army seems to be wondering, too: it's left a $10,000 reward on the table until December.

 Article Review Form at end of book.

WiseGuide Wrap-Up

- Structural inequalities in wealth and power promote criminal behavior, as do arrest and sentencing rates

- stunningly differentiated along the lines of race.

- The struggle for respect in the context of limited opportunities for

legitimate achievement may account for street crime within Black inner-city communities.

R.E.A.L. Sites

This list provides a print preview of typical **Coursewise** R.E.A.L. sites. (There are over 100 such sites at the **Courselinks**™ site.) The danger in printing URLs is that web sites can change overnight. As we went to press, these sites were functional using the URLs provided. If you come across one that isn't, please let us know via email to: webmaster@coursewise.com. Use your Passport to access the most current list of R.E.A.L. sites at the **Courselinks** site.

Site name: Survey Confirms Police Racism

URL: http://news2.thdo.bbc.co.uk/hi/english/uk/newsid%5F292000/292599.stm

Why is it R.E.A.L.? The legal system constitutes one of the strongest forces of social control in modern societies, and on the front lines of that system are police officers and the departments for which they work. This report describes police racism in the United Kingdom.

Key topics: institutionalized racism, criminal justice

Try this: Read the report and think about its generalizability to the United States. Search the World Wide Web for sources on racism in police departments in this country. How might both countries address their problems with institutionalized racism in police departments?

Site name: Fighting Hate Across the Nation

URL: http://www.civilrights.org/lcef/hat.html

Why is it R.E.A.L.? Hate crimes have captured public attention more often in the past decade, and the federal government has responded with a number of legislative initiatives to address the problem. States and municipalities have also responded, often prodded into action by grassroots organizations. This site provides a wealth of information about hate crimes, federal and state policies, and statistics about victims and victimizers.

Key topics: hate crime, racial bias crime, statistics, public policy

Try this: Follow the links to "Hate Crime Statistics" and then to "Offenses by Motivation and Suspected Offenders' Race." Print out the statistics you find there. Which racial, religious, and sexual groups are most likely to be victimized by hate-motivated violence? Which groups are most likely to commit such acts? Conceptualize a sociological explanation for the patterns you see.

section 8

Key Points

- The British government and the antiracism group Anti-Racist Action have both developed ad campaigns against racism, but their strategies for reaching white audiences vary.

- Law professor Patricia Williams criticizes the findings of the Clinton advisory panel on race.

- Police brutality appears to be on the upswing, but some communities are developing strategies to curb the trend.

- One philosopher compares whites to "the receivers of stolen goods," because they have benefited from the racism their ancestors practiced and must, therefore, assume responsibility for making amends.

- After watching his small children mimic his racist posturing, one man decided to try to save himself—and them.

Challenging Racism

 **WiseGuide Intro**

Early in this century, W.E.B. DuBois, a prominent African-American sociologist, wrote that "the problem of the 20th Century is the problem of the color line." At the end of the twentieth century, this formulation appears nearly as simple as it is enduringly true. At the end of the twentieth century, we recognize that there are many color lines and that, in order to resist racism, we must also resist class stratification and gender hierarchies, because the problem of the "color line" cannot be solved without eliminating these mutually reinforcing systems of domination. Still, were DuBois writing today, he would likely reassert that the most compelling problem facing the United States is that of the color line: the system of social inequalities organized around the cultural significance we attach to arbitrarily selected biological characteristics.

The endurance of racism and the subtleties of its late-twentieth-century forms sometimes discourage students from believing that racism can end and that each of us can play a part in its demise. European-American students often feel defensive about racism, knowing both that they didn't create the system of racial privilege in this country and that they have likely benefitted from it. The white students who recognize racism as a problem and hope to resist it are often confused about what they might do to build a more egalitarian society. Forgetting that they, too, "have a race," they often feel unauthorized to speak out about issues of racial discrimination. Students of color, who sometimes experience their very survival in white-dominated society as an important means of challenging racism, often face conflicts over whether to spend their time investing in their own educational progress or organizing to challenge the racism of white-dominated institutions. In addition, they face the question of whether to take on the responsibility of educating well-meaning whites about racism and its effects or to demand that white students educate themselves about the history of race in the United States. For both students of color and concerned white students, challenging racism can be confusing, frustrating, and exhausting.

Nonetheless, it is important to recognize the incredible impact of concerned individuals on race relations in U.S. society. For example, abolition, the movement to end lynching, the legalizing of citizenship for nonnative-born Chinese and Japanese people, the end of Jim Crow laws, the *Brown v. Board of Education* and *Loving v. Virginia* decisions, school desegregation, the Civil Rights Act, Affirmative Action programs, and the marked increase in minority literacy and high school graduation rates have all come about as a result of the efforts of concerned people of many races who have exercised the courage and commitment to voice objections to racial stratification. Anthropologist Margaret Mead said that we should "never underestimate the ability of a small band of committed individuals to change the world; indeed it is the only thing that ever has." The history of racial and ethnic relations has proven her right.

The first step toward addressing any social problem, of course, is educating ourselves about its origins and its consequences. In this reader, you have had the opportunity to learn about racial and ethnic stratification and its connections to the social hierarchies that reinforce it. With luck, this brief introduction has encouraged your curiosity and will inspire you to seek out other resources in order to deepen your understanding of race and ethnicity. Once we have educated ourselves about the issues, we can begin to determine how to position ourselves relative to them. Will we decide that race is not "our issue"? Will we feel comfortable perpetuating the system we inherited from our society? Will we feel comfortable if we do not work to make the world a place in which, as Dr. Martin Luther King hoped, we "will be judged by the content of [our] character, instead of the color of [our] skin"?

Business writer Vikram Dodd explores applied antiracist strategies in advertising in the article "Anti-Racist Ad Fuels Debate on Strategy: Advertisement Sponsored by the Anti-Racist Alliance." While Dodd's article explores the work of the British Commission for Racial Equality (CRE), law professor Patricia Williams' "An American Litany: Diary of a Mad Law Professor," comments on President Clinton's advisory panel on race in the context of recent events. In "When Justice Kills: After Years of Decline, Police Brutality Is on the Rise, Sparking a Reform Movement," journalist Bruce Shapiro writes about the events leading up to the unjustified police shooting of twenty-one-year-old Malik Jones and about interventions that communities and police departments are developing for eliminating such tragedies. Philosopher Gordon Marino's essay, "Apologize for Slavery? Facing Up to the Living Past," analyzes popular sentiment about the possibility of President Clinton apologizing for slavery, as well as the resistance of white people to the prospect of taking responsibility for challenging racism. Finally, in "Confessions of a Skinhead," journalist James Willwerth recounts the transformation of T. J. Leyden, Jr., as he "renounces life as a white supremacist, neo-Nazi brawler." As you read these articles, think about your own place in the racialized structure of our society and about the role you might play in making a positive contribution toward resisting racism.

? ? Questions ? ?

Reading 24. Which of the ad campaigns do you believe are more likely to make a difference? Why? How would you design an ad against racism?

Reading 25. How does Patricia Williams resist racism? How does she conceptualize the relationships between racism and other egregious forms of social control?

Reading 26. What are Black children taught about how to deal with white police officers? What sorts of institutional strategies might be used to eliminate police brutality?

Reading 27. Should whites apologize for slavery? Should whites take responsibility for racism? If so, what might that look like, in practical terms? If not, what are some alternative strategies for promoting racial equality?

Reading 28. What does T. J. Leyden's story suggest about the possibilities for white activism against racism?

Which of the ad campaigns do you believe are more likely to make a difference? Why? How would you design an ad against racism?

Anti-Racist Ad Fuels Debate on Strategy:

Advertisement Sponsored by the Anti-Racist Alliance

Vikram Dodd

A war of words has broken out over the latest anti-racism ad, due to break this month in cinemas across the U.K. The hard-hitting commercial, which shows a black man's life flashing before him as he lies dying after being stabbed by a racist gang, has been commissioned by the Anti-Racist Alliance.

The pressure group is looking for a more controversial and provocative campaign than it believes the government's Commission for Racial Equality has so far managed to put together.

The advertising agencies responsible for the separate campaigns have also entered the fray. The ARA commercial is going for the audience's heartstrings and empathy. Its star, Patrick Robinson, better known to more than 13 million viewers as Martin Ashford in BBCl's Casualty, plays a black professional.

The black and white commercial opens on the actor's flickering eyes and is followed by a Citizen Kane-inspired flashback of key events in the character's life, such as graduation and getting married. The three-minute ad is underscored by Louis Armstrong's "What a Wonderful World," which was donated free by the musician's estate. But as the ad comes to the end it abruptly changes tone, as the commercial reveals that the man is dying after a racist attack.

Maher Bird Associates' Mark Tomblin explains that the ad targets middle-class whites who regard themselves as unprejudiced. The aim is to get them to identify with the character, realize the magnitude of the racist problem and the 140,000 racial attacks a year, and prod them into doing something about it.

Tomblin says: "The message we're trying to get across is that racism destroys lives, it destroys life chances."

But Tomblin's support of his own agency's work comes with criticism of the campaigns against racism put together in the past. His strongest words are reserved for ad agency Saatchi & Saatchi, which produced the campaign for the Commission for Racial Equality, the statutory body which is charged with enforcing the Race Relations Act.

Tomblin brands the Saatchi output as "counter productive." One of its latest ads says that racists have smaller brains than other people, another shows adults shouting racial abuse while young children from different races are shown playing happily together.

"The commercials are hectoring. They put racists in boxes. The brains ad may have been creatively clever, but was strategically dumb," he asserts.

Tomblin claims the people in focus groups said they did not identify with the ads, as the examples of racism within them were aggressive and brutal. The aim of the new campaign is to make people identify with the victim.

But Saatchi & Saatchi's Ajab Singh, who headed the CRE campaign, says Tomblin is missing the point, as the two commercials he mentions were strands in a three-year campaign. Singh says Saatchis was the first-ever campaign to tackle racism, and more than pounds lm worth of free advertising space was donated by media owners, including cinema, press, and posters.

Singh says the lack of money to spend was overcome by generating column inches in newspaper coverage about the campaign, and he rejects claims that it has failed to target racists. "If you are a racist, the ads won't stop you being one but make it more socially unacceptable for you to be one.

"Magazines like *Marketing* are always quantifying campaigns via things such as recall. An area such as racism is completely different. If our ad means there is one less racist attack all the effort and money will be justified."

Louise Ansari, spokeswoman for the CRE, also defends the government-backed campaign, and what it has achieved. "A year before this campaign started, 70% of the public had no idea what the CRE did. A year after it begun that the figure was down to 50%."

 Article Review Form at end of book.

How does Patricia Williams resist racism? How does she conceptualize the relationships between racism and other egregious forms of social control?

An American Litany:

Diary of a Mad Law Professor

Patricia J. Williams

After more than a year's worth of labor, the President's advisory panel on race has come back with what by all accounts is a series of "modest" recommendations aimed at promoting "harmony," "dialogue" and "reconciliation." What times, I think. It took fifteen months just to agree that we should speak nicely to one another.

Consider the swampy dialogic territory faced by New Yorkers these days. The airwaves crackle with stories about the carryings-on of Khallid Muhammad *aka* "the black Hitler"; the NYPD *aka* "the new Gestapo"; and Mayor Rudolph Giulianai *aka* "Il Duce," "Kaiser Rudolph," "Bull Connor" and "El Toro Feroz."

Khallid Muhammad, organizer of the Way-Under-A-Million Youth March, begins his sentences with "We came in peace . . . we came in love," and finishes them with descriptions of Jews as "bloodsuckers" and of Harlem's black leaders as "bootlicking" sissies. Joseph Locurto, a policeman suspended for participating in a Labor Day parade float that mocked the vicious murder of a black man, defends himself by asserting that *lots* of police officers use insulting racial slurs all the

time, yet no one's ever been fired for it. In Broad Channel, Queens, described as an all-white neighborhood, where the parade took place, citizens rush to denounce all forms of bias with painfully revealing innocence: "Whether it's a black float or a Jew float, it's all in fun. They may call it prejudice, but it isn't."

Meanwhile Mayor Guiliani courts peace by insuring that all the trains and rallies run on time, threatens the arrest of organizers of the Million Youth March for inciting riot-control police to riot; and, over the opposition of most parents and the schools chancellor, formally assigns the oversight of discipline in the public schools to . . . the police department.

Not that there isn't some spiritual unity abroad in the Big Apple. Norman Siegel, head of the NYCLU, supports, on First Amendment grounds, both Khallid Muhammad and Joseph Locurto in their claims against the city. Residents of Broad Channel find themselves in sudden agreement with "that Al Sharpton" because, as one man put it, "he always accuses Giuliani of overreaching." And both Sharpton and Giuliani remain heroes unto their own constituencies, each buoyed by separate-but-equal vows never to back down or say they're sorry.

If these events were not contorted enough, sorting out the lesson to be learned is thornier still. People shiver at the crudities of the parade in Broad Channel. (The float, called "Black to the Future," was, according to a lawyer for the men involved, just a little joke about what would happen to the "all-white" area if blacks moved in.) But few of us feel implicated in any larger sense—even though statistics indicate that most Americans live in just as profoundly segregated communities. In the same vein, it is easy to expend all one's outrage on Khallid Muhammad when he quotes Hitler. It is harder perhaps to decipher and acknowledge the shadowy legacy of Hitler's dehumanization of Jewish women in the morally frenzied shock-jock and talk-show portrayals of Monica Lewinsky as a mall-crazed, fleshy and licentious "princess." It's a no-brainer to condemn Broad Channel parade participants for mocking the Hasidic community (as they did in an earlier parade), but there's much less wrath for the well-heeled East Side denizen who, when reminded of an upcoming Jewish holiday, let drop a surly but elegantly spoken "You can tell who has all the money."

There is also a subtle tendency to treat bias among blacks as

Patricia J. Williams, "An American Litany." Reprinted with permission from the October 12, 1998 issue of *The Nation*.

though it were intrinsically more fearsome than bias among whites. Let me be clear. I do think of prejudice among blacks as a disappointment, a betrayal of the sensibility that, perhaps *naïvely*, one might suppose comes from a history of oppression. But I also think that one must be careful not to allow that disappointment to crystallize into a kind of skewed moral resentment in which white prejudices are weighted as somehow less mean-spirited, ignorant or dangerous. Some time ago, for example, I heard some clerks in a clothing store chatting calmly in a remarkably anti-Semitic fashion. Equally remarkable was their total unself-consciousness in allowing me to overhear them. I wrote about it in *Alchemy of Race and Rights,* wondering at their presumptuousness—either in assuming I would not take offense or in treating me as though I were invisible. I failed, however, to mention the race of the clerks—

they were white, as it happens—an omission that genuinely disturbed a number of commentators on the book. Seventh Circuit Court Judge Richard Posner summarized their concern:

> If the clerks were black, the issue is black anti-Semitism, itself emblematic of the pathologies, none of which she discusses, of black America. If they were white, the issue is reconciling the willingness of whites to treat a black as one of themselves in opposition to other whites with William's unrelievedly bleak view of American race relations.

So if black, the clerks were "emblematically" and inherently pathological. If white, "the issue" suddenly becomes the failure to acknowledge the ever-so-generous "willingness" of white anti-Semites to "treat a black as one of themselves"; and only an "unrelievedly bleak view of American race relations" stands in the way of full participation in the moment of liberatory, equal-opportunity anti-Semitism.

I rehash all this because I am intensely curious as to why the parade in Broad Channel making fun of Hasidic Jews, and an earlier one lampooning gay people, apparently went unremarked until now. What do we hide from ourselves by such unbalanced and misplaced complacence?

Good people of all persuasions like to think of Khallid Muhammad and "Black to the Future" either as wild aberrations or as mere commonplace pranks that got a "little out of hand." It is as American as apple pie, the passionately sincere denials that almost always follow the disclosures of behavior like this. When caught, then I, you, we, they, never, ever really meant a word of it.

But the hard stuff still awaits: What, exactly, *do* we mean?

 Article Review Form at end of book.

What are Black children taught about how to deal with white police officers? What sorts of institutional strategies might be used to eliminate police brutality?

When Justice Kills:

After Years of Decline, Police Brutality Is on the Rise, Sparking a Reform Movement

Bruce Shapiro

Two young men not long out of high school are chased in their car by police, who completely surround them. They have no weapons, no drugs. Their offense is an ill-considered run after being pulled over for speeding. In a panic, the driver shifts into reverse. Suddenly two police officers shatter the car's windows with their revolver butts. Then the officer on the driver's side shifts the gun in his hand, sticks it inside the window and fires—one, two, three, four times—at the upper body of the young man at the wheel, who throws himself over his friend in a gesture of protection and whispers, with bewildered, dying breath, "Sam, they're shooting at us."

My heart sank when I read the name of the dead driver, Malik Jones, in the next day's New Haven Register. Malik's father, Jimmy Jones, is a Muslim cleric in New Haven and a professor at Manhattanville College, passionately dedicated to racial reconciliation. Malik's mother, Emma Jones, is a lawyer and an activist in New Haven's African-American community. I first met her nearly fifteen years ago, when I co-hosted a weekly radio show and she was a guest, arriving at the station with Malik in tow. I don't think I had seen Malik since he was small. But the same mild face now stared mutely out from the newspaper.

Most of the facts are straightforward. At dusk on April 14, 21-year-old Malik and his friend Samuel Cruz were driving along a main drag in East Haven, a quiet suburban town. East Haven is famously hostile to people with dark skin: Though adjacent to 40-percent-minority New Haven, the town does not have a single black police officer or firefighter, which has provoked a suit by the N.A.A.C.P. After a couple of years working as a probate court clerk, Malik had recently had some minor run-ins with the law—motor-vehicle offenses and probation for drug possession. A few weeks earlier he'd been arrested again on a drug-sale charge.

At 6:15 p.m., an East Haven police van driven by Officer Robert Flodquist tried to pull Jones and Cruz over. (The East Haven police claim a motorist had complained that Jones's car was speeding, though it may also have been a case of "D.W.B."—Driving While Black.) Malik made a U-turn and raced onto Interstate 95 back over the city line, followed within moments by a high-speed convoy of East Haven and state police. The frightened young man was apparently trying to get home: After ten minutes the chase ended with Jones and Cruz cornered just a few blocks from Jones's mother's house. Officer Flodquist leapt from his van. Later he claimed Jones tried to back into him; Cruz says Jones was trying to avoid colliding with a cruiser ahead. Whatever the reason, it was Flodquist who broke Jones's window and shot him. Cruz, drenched in blood, was first dragged handcuffed back and forth between squad car and ambulance as police officers and E.M.Ts argued over who should have custody; then he spent the night in the lockup, still in his bloody clothing, because of a motor-vehicle warrant.

Even taking the suburban police account at face value, the

Bruce Shapiro, "When Justice Kills." Reprinted with permission from the June 9, 1997 issue of *The Nation*.

shooting of young Malik Jones has all the incendiary elements of the Rodney King case: a black driver pulled over by a white officer, adrenaline-powered cops, an unarmed and outnumbered victim. But in its particulars it also opens a window into political and legal nuances of police brutality, which after years of decline is on the rise again around the country.

It's not just famously thuggish police departments like L.A.'s. In Prince George's County, Maryland, outside Washington, 24-year-old Archie Elliot was shot fourteen times while handcuffed in police custody, after being pulled over for drunk driving. In a Pittsburgh suburb, 31-year-old Jonny Gammage, cousin of a Steelers defensive lineman, was pulled over for repeatedly touching his brakes and somehow ended up strangled. And in New York City, once a laboratory for police reform, civilian complaints of excessive force have risen 41 percent since Mayor Giuliani introduced his "zero tolerance" policies—widespread arrests for minor violations. Three-quarters of those complaints are filed by black or Latino citizens, against a police department that remains 75 percent white. Amnesty International last year reported that court settlements and judgments paid out by New York for police abuse rose from $13.5 million in 1992 to more than $24 million in 1994. Amnesty charges that many cases of police violence in New York violate basic international human rights standards.

The re-emergence of police brutality is hard to document precisely, since most figures rely on wildly variable municipal complaint policies. The "public order" philosophy and neighborhood crackdowns now in vogue in some cities, however, seem to make violent police-civilian conflict more likely, and contribute to a sense that cops should take the gloves off. The bible of the public-order policing philosophy, George Kelling and Catherine Coles's recent book Fixing Broken Windows, doesn't even mention police brutality as a policy issue, although it attacks civil libertarians for trying to restrict police conduct. In one telling omission, Kelling and Coles elaborately praise the public-private campaign that "took back" New York's Grand Central Station and environs from the homeless, without even a footnote acknowledging that beatings by a brutal goon squad (documented by The New York Times) achieved much of the taking back.

Whatever its sources, the rise in police brutality is in turn slowly generating new efforts to curb the violence. This emerging campaign—if a recent conference on police brutality at Hunter College sponsored by New York's Center for Constitutional Rights (C.C.R.) is any indication—differs both philosophically and strategically from the reform efforts of years past. For one thing, current scholarship has clarified the underlying dynamic of much police violence. Malik Jones's killing displayed typical warning signs. The East Haven officers' motor-vehicle stop and particularly the high-speed chase were high-risk triggers for violent attack by police. A study commissioned in 1994 by the National Institute of Justice found complaints of excessive force filed after nearly half of high-speed chases. Some departments—including that of New Haven, though not its suburban neighbor—now ban them in all but life-threatening circumstances. It's known, too, that police assault is likely as not to begin with a casual defiance of authority—an insult or flight from a traffic stop—rather than a serious crime.

On a practical level this means looking at training and departmental discipline. "In most departments it is just a core of officers who commit acts of brutality," argues C.C.R. legal director Michael Deutsch. "There is widespread failure to train, failure to supervise and failure to discipline." If East Haven had an intelligent hot-pursuit policy and better-trained officers, Malik Jones might still be alive.

Today's anti-brutality campaigners rely little on the courts: Lawyers know the Supreme Court has spent most of the past fifteen years broadening police power. On April 28, for instance, in an opinion by Justice Sandra Day O'Connor, the Court held that a police department that knowingly hires an officer with a record of assault need not be liable if that officer injures civilians.

And getting accountability through state laws and courts is even more difficult—for reasons well illuminated by the Jones case. Two days after the killing, Roger Vann, the president of the New Haven N.A.A.C.P., called for Officer Flodquist's arrest. But that's not likely. Because it involved a crosstown chase, the case is being investigated not by New Haven's department (which was not involved in the chase) but by the Connecticut state police—who had their own trooper on the scene and thus have a stake in the outcome. A decision to indict Flodquist must come from the State's Attorney, who relies on his close working relationship with police. And finally, Connecticut law specifically gives police officers wide latitude if they act in the belief they are protecting others—no matter how murderous their judgment.

That leaves the possibility of a federal civil rights charge, as with Rodney King—and there was talk, at that New York conference, of making such prosecutions a priority. Mauri Saalakhan of the Washington, D.C., Peace and Justice Foundation said he was glad a Pittsburgh judge had just dismissed charges against Jonny Gammage's killer, "because now the Justice Department has no excuse not to move forward." As Deutsch of the C.C.R. pointed out, the Justice Department has the power to seek injunctions against police departments with systematic brutality problems. But while Justice has occasionally filed suit in egregious cases like that of the Philadelphia Police Department, even Congress might not be able to rouse it to systematic monitoring. In 1995 Congress ordered Janet Reno to compile national police brutality statistics; she has yet to do so.

With legal recourse so limited, much of the emphasis of the new police-brutality reformers is political—aimed at creating stronger independent review authorities and even special prosecutors. "We recognize that the police department and the entire system is going to advocate for the police officer," says Hector Soto, a former commissioner on New York City's Civilian Complaint Review Board. "So you need a place in every municipality where the civilian is going to be believed in the first instance." In San Francisco, the Bay Area PoliceWatch Project has run a community organizing campaign on the issue. Similar drives are under way in Los Angeles, Phoenix and Pittsburgh. This year Connecticut's state legislature killed a proposed review board because of police union opposition.

In a sharp departure from "off the pigs" rhetoric of the past, there are also widespread efforts to establish links with responsible police officers. "When you find those officers who agree with you," East Orange, New Jersey, cop DeLacey Davis told the New York conference to much applause, "you've got to support them. When cops cross that threshold they are marked

people." He should know. Davis was ostracized for years after he refused to remain silent when another cop assaulted a citizen in front of him.

Many of today's anti-brutality campaigners have thrown in their lot with the community-policing movement. This is not sentimentality about beat cops. It is an attempt to establish a counterweight to the famous "blue wall of silence" that protects police violence as well as corruption; to encourage officers to feel as accountable to neighborhoods as they are to fellow cops. "As long as we are going to have police in our communities, we need to control them," argued Officer Davis.

The culture of policing, though, takes its cue from the culture at large. In the days after Malik Jones's killing the New Haven Register ran dozens of comments from readers to its call-in line; with few exceptions, the remarks from suburban readers were vicious and hostile. "The officer was completely justified in what he did. He was dealing with criminals." "The police cannot properly do their job because they always have to worry about racism and brutality. As soon as someone gets shot they say it's racism." Officer Flodquist himself had to beg East Haveners not to stage a support rally sure to raise tensions.

Similarly, many of New Haven's African-American leaders were doing everything they could to step back from "playing the race card." The tone was set first by Malik Jones's parents. "The family does not want Malik's death to cause division," they said. The evening after he was buried I sat in on a meeting of the N.A.A.C.P. at St. Luke's Church, down Dixwell Avenue from the funeral home. In the room were mostly middle-aged professionals. I have known some

of them for years and have never seen them so shaken, while at the same time so determined to act with gravity and restraint. It was as if Jones's shooting had torn aside a veil of middle-class security. The whole room intimately understood Malik's impulse to flee, an understanding bitterly confirmed by the young man's fate. Shirley Ellis-West, the chapter's secretary, recalled the advice she often gave her own children: "If you are ever pulled over in East Haven, keep going and don't stop until you get home." Chuck Allen, a former state legislator, spoke quietly of his mother's injunction to keep his hands on the wheel and visible if he is ever pulled over, advice he had followed only a few nights before on a drive back from Hartford. While those suburban newspaper readers were complaining about blacks crying racism, the owner of an African-American bookshop was counseling that the community "not just 'talk black' at a time like this."

Malik Jones's death may not have had a racially motivated component; not all such cases do. And he was buried that afternoon by a diverse honor guard of his schoolmates and friends, white, black and Latino, dressed in baggy jeans, sweatshirts and baseball caps. "It was Malik's thought that there was one race, one human race," his mother, Emma, said in her soft Alabama accent. But his killing, and the growing epidemic of police violence of which it is part, reveals a deep racial chasm in the basic experience and perception of law and whom it serves. "All the family wants is justice," Jones's survivors said. Yet how to trust in justice when justice itself does the killing?

 **Article Review Form at end of book.**

Should whites apologize for slavery? Should whites take responsibility for racism? If so, what might that look like, in practical terms? If not, what are some alternative strategies for promoting racial equality?

Apologize for Slavery?

Facing Up to the Living Past

Gordon Marino

Gordon Marino is associate professor of philosophy and director of the Howard V. and Edna H. Hong Kierkegaard Library at Saint Olaf College in Northfield, Minnesota.

For reasons that would be interesting to explore, gestures of collective repentance have recently become quite popular. In 1994, the pope offered an apology for past sins committed by the church against non-Catholics. In the summer of 1995, the Southern Baptists, who number over 15 million, voted to express a resolution of repentance which read in part, "We lament and repudiate historic acts of evil such as slavery from which we continue to reap a bitter harvest." British Prime Minister Tony Blair has apologized for England's indifference to the plight of the Irish during the Potato Famine, and in January the Canadian government formally apologized for its historic mistreatment of indigenous peoples. Last year, President Bill Clinton apologized on behalf of We the People to the African-Americans who were the unwitting subjects in the infamous Tuskegee study on syphilis,

and seriously considered the possibility of apologizing for slavery in general. The president subsequently called for a "national conversation" about race, and appointed a commission to promote such a conversation.

Reactions to Clinton's initial proposed mea culpa varied. Senate Majority Leader Trent Lott (R-Miss.) said he probably would not favor an official apology, "because I think we should be looking to the future, talking about things we need to do to work together." Ward Connerly, an African-American entrepreneur, regent of the University of California, and architect of the California anti-affirmative action referendum, Proposition 209, pronounced this verdict on the idea: "Apologizing for slavery is probably one of the dumbest things anyone could do." Offering a more muted criticism, the Reverend Jesse Jackson remarked that an apology would have "no substantive value." He then went on to warn that such gestures could "divert attention away from our ability to, in fact, close the gap [between whites and African-Americans] with real structure and investment." On the

other hand, the civil rights leader Julian Bond maintained that an apology for slavery would be a good and important symbolic gesture. And the recent release of Steven Speilberg's *Amistad* has made the history and moral legacy of slavery a vibrant issue yet again.

Last summer, in between Little League baseball games in a largely white Minnesota town, I did some informal polling of my own. Though none of the people I talked to took the president's proposed apology to be an urgent matter, about half expressed mild support for the idea. Others scoffed at repenting for what they took to be ancient history. The wife of a professor commented, "Why should I apologize for something done to blacks more than a hundred years ago?" A fair question which might be restated: "Why should I apologize for a crime that I had nothing to do with?" Or more to the point, "By what authority can I apologize for someone else's actions?" It would, after all, be hubristic for me to think that I could repent for a mugging in which I did not participate. Likewise, it would be absurd to

"Apologize for Slavery?" by Gordon Marino, *Commonweal*, February 13, 1998, Vol. 125, No. 3. Reprinted by permission of the author.

pretend that I could repent for slaveholders and traders who themselves refused to repent.

As a professor of philosophy, over the years I have encountered many white students who accurately or paranoically believe that they are constantly being asked to feel guilty and repent for racist institutions and actions in which they themselves had no hand. When it comes to race and repentance, these students are of the Aristotelian opinion that we should be praised or blamed only for our own voluntary actions. Here it should be observed that, oddly enough, many of them feel no qualms about taking pride in the accomplishments of the various communities with which they identify, such as their college, fellow countrymen, townsfolk, church brethren, or for that matter, members of their local major league baseball team. And yet, the logic of their claim that responsibility only extends as far as one's own free will would seem to militate against the idea of any form of ego-enhancement derived from the accomplishments of others.

This minor inconsistency aside, many who sneer or snarl at the suggestion of apologizing for deeds from the deep past need to consider the possibility that we may bear a moral connection to actions that we did not ourselves commit. In this regard, it would be useful to distinguish between actions that one neither commits nor profits from and actions not committed but profited from. Suppose, for example, that unbeknownst to me, a friend of mine robs a bank and makes off with $7 million. Clearly, I am neither responsible for the robbery nor am I in a position to apologize for it. However, if after telling me about the theft, I accept a million dollars of the stolen loot, then I am no longer innocent of the robbery, despite the fact that I had nothing at all do to with the heist.

It could, I think, be argued that white people have profited from our racist past and thus, relative to slavery, we are more akin to receivers of stolen goods than we are to innocent bystanders who just happen to bear a physical likeness to slave owners.

No doubt some will reply that they are unaware of drawing any benefits from slavery and racism. This lack of awareness would be exculpatory if in fact slavery and discrimination did not serve the interests of whites. However, if ignorance of being privileged is an ignorance we ourselves are responsible for producing, then we become morally reproachable receivers of stolen goods. And to be psychologically realistic, whites have a strong investment in blinking at their assessment of the broad effects of racism. To return to my earlier example, let us assume that when I accepted the gift of a million dollars, I had no reason to think that the money had been stolen, but that years later I came to understand that the funds upon which I had built a comfortable and respectable life had been pilfered from the accounts of your great-grandparents. Would the fact that many years had gone by cover the sin to such a degree that I would not bear any responsibility to the descendants of my great-grandparents' victims who, thanks to my ancestors, now led a distinctively unprivileged existence?

Individuals who benefit from a crime are mistaken in thinking that they have nothing to do with the crime. If responsibility does not extend from the robber baron to his children, then so long as the perpetrator of a crime can escape indictment by his immediate victim when he is alive, then the material benefits of his wrongdoing can be passed along with impunity to future generations.

Once again, it is essential to distinguish between cases in which

one generation is entirely innocent of a transgression committed by an earlier generation, and those in which the sins of the father continue to bear fruits of advantage for his descendants. Although I am not sure that a presidential apology would have the healing effects that some anticipate, I do know that white Americans have profited from slavery and discrimination. In a competitive society we have always had a leg up on African-Americans, whether it be in hunting for a job, loan, house, or advancement in a corporate firm. If you do not believe me on the last count then consider the Texaco scandal in 1996 where unsuspecting white corporate executives were caught on tape espousing racist sentiments. Or consider a story that a friend shared with me. My friend, who is about thirty-five, recently returned to his hometown in a Detroit suburb for a class reunion at his richly integrated public high school. After the reunion, four of his old school chums persuaded him to go out and play a few golf holes. All were corporate executives and registered Democrats. And yet when the issue of race came up, all of them swore that they would never "take the risk" of hiring an African-American to fill a leadership role in their respective companies. In other words, any white applicants who sought employment in one of their firms would have a decisive advantage over all African-American applicants.

I was not involved in the civil rights struggle of the sixties. While I have huffed and puffed and shaken my head about racial injustice, I have made no significant sacrifices for the cause of racial justice. I have no special authority to preach on the matter, and yet I have lived long enough to recognize by whose sweat and on whose back this country has been built and why. Because of slavery and

CommonWealth One
Federal Credit Union

Your savings federally insured to $100,000

NCUA
National Credit Union Administration, a U.S. Government Agency

NO. 351264

DATE	TELLER	G.L. NO.	TRANSACTION DESCRIPTION	DATE	DESCRIPTION	ACCOUNT NUMBER	PREVIOUS BAL.	PAYEE	TRANSACTION AMT.	NEW BALANCE	AMOUNT

DATE	TELLER	G.L. NO.	TRANSACTION DESCRIPTION	ACCOUNT NUMBER	PREVIOUS BAL.	PAYEE	TRANSACTION AMT.	NEW BALANCE
02OCT00	7786–276		Share Withdrawal	319566–0	924.09		85.00	839.09

MINIMUM PERIODIC PAYMENT	PAYMENT DUE DATE	FREQUENCY OF PAYMENT	DAILY PERIODIC RATE	ANNUAL PERCENTAGE RATE
				%

TRANSACTION PROCESSED BY:

JULIE HARPER

Payable to: ANDREW R LUMB AND HARRISONBURG ELECTRIC COMMISSION

Service Offices:

Main Branch
4875 Eisenhower Avenue
Alexandria, VA

Northwest Branch, lobby level
1111 16th Street, NW
Washington, DC

AMC Branch, lobby level
5001 Eisenhower Avenue
Alexandria, VA

Humphreys Engineer Center Branch
Kingman Building, Room G7
Telegraph and Leaf Road
Fort Belvoir, VA

Pulaski Branch, lobby level
20 Massachusetts Avenue, NW
Washington, DC

James Madison University Branch
Gibbons Hall
Harrisonburg, VA

VERIFY NO.   351264

21

discrimination, African-Americans have provided an endless supply of cheap labor. They still work the fields, wash white babies and white octogenarians, shake drinks in country clubs, and mop floors in the classrooms in which white folks debate about race. It was no mistake that a black woman closed my dead father's eyes. It was no accident that a black woman was there when my child first opened his blue eyes. As a result of institutionalized racism, African-Americans have been cornered into doing more than their fair share of protecting, building, and preserving this land. For that reason, I suggest that even white Americans who have cursed racism have unwillingly and perhaps unwittingly benefitted from it. Thus, whites are in no position to slough off the call for an apology by insisting that they have no connection to slavery.

The Hebrew Scriptures ring with intimations that blessings and blandishments can be passed on from generation to generation. For one of myriad examples, the children of Abraham are blessed because of Abraham's faith. On the other side of the ledger, there was clearly a point in time when the Israelites believed that the sins of the father would be punishable unto the fourth generation. The revolutionary prophet Ezekiel inveighs against the notion of cross-generational responsibility. Attempting to focus his people's attention on their individual actions, Ezekiel proclaims that if a man has a son "who has seen all the sins that his father has done, considers and does not do likewise . . . he shall not die from his father's sin" (Ezekiel: 18:14–17). When we refuse to acknowledge the harm that our community has inflicted upon others, when we the unoppressed refuse to acknowledge that, at least for a time, oppression benefits those who are not forced to walk on the other side of the street, then we fail to turn away from the sin of oppression. By turning a blind eye, the sins of the father become the sins of the more passive son. By refusing to acknowledge who has been doing what for the last four hundred years, we fail to turn away from the grievous sins of our forefathers.

Some have argued that the president should not offer an apology for slavery because such an apology would have either no impact or a negative effect. Those who worry about the negative impact of a mea culpa are afraid that a proclamation of regret might distract us from the task of closing the divide in opportunities that exists today between African-Americans and whites. Some fear that African-Americans will clutch onto the prize of an apology and become less persistent in their demands for initiatives intended to redress the destruction wrought by slavery and racism.

I suspect that an apology for slavery would resonate in many different ways in the African-American community. While I would be unwilling to predict the political effects of a statement of regret, there is, I think, little reason to worry about people being lulled to sleep by it. Either way, if the president is still considering offering such a gesture, he ought not to put too much weight on the potential impact of the apology.

If acts of collective repentance make any sense at all it is on the basis of their kinship to individual expressions of repentance. When an individual repents, he acknowledges culpability and regret for harms that he has visited upon someone else. In the Judeo-Christian tradition it is believed that once an apology is offered, it is the moral responsibility of the person transgressed against to decide whether or not to accept that apology. (Apropos of this point, legal scholar Patricia Williams offered a powerful argument to the conclusion that if an apology is tendered, blacks ought to politely refuse to accept it [*The Nation,* July 14, 1997].) Nowhere in either the Hebrew Scriptures or the New Testament is there counsel to the effect that asking for forgiveness is conditioned on our expression of repentance falling on welcoming ears.

 Article Review Form at end of book.

What does T. J. Leyden's story suggest about the possibilities for white activism against racism?

Confessions of a Skinhead:

After 15 Years in the Movement, T. J. Leyden Jr. Renounces Life As White-Supremacist, Neo-Nazi Brawler

James Willwerth

Los Angeles

Watching cartoons with his two children one Saturday morning last year, Thomas James Leyden Jr. was startled when his elder son, then 3, abruptly turned off the television. "Mom says we can't watch shows with niggers on them," the boy explained. The ugly word—and the sentiment behind it—did not exactly spring unsolicited from the preschooler's head; his dad sports enough neo-Nazi tattoos and credentials to explain the boy's action. But hearing his son talk that way, says Leyden, 30, "hit me like a ton of bricks. I knew I was taking him down a path where he'd end up in jail or dead, remembered for something horrible like the Oklahoma bombing. All of a sudden I didn't want him to be like me."

Until his change of heart, Leyden had given 15 years of his life to brawling and recruiting for neo-Nazi causes. His activities had even landed him on the Klanwatch list compiled by the Southern Poverty Law Center. But in June, Leyden walked into the Simon Wiesenthal Center's Museum of Tolerance in Los Angeles and renounced his former life. It was not an easy thing to do: Klanwatch analyst Laurie Wood says Leyden is "asking for trouble" from his former associates.

Those engaged in the fight against bigotry cannot believe their good fortune in finding someone who can shed some light on the shadowy world of neo-Nazis. Wisenthal staff members, who have held several long debriefing sessions with Leyden, have big plans for him: they have made arrangements for a laser surgeon to remove his tattoos, and this fall they hope to take him on a lecture tour at U.S. military bases, where Defense Department rules permit local commanders to decide whether to tolerate "passive" extremists in uniform. He has also offered to counsel troubled teenagers. "No one like this has ever walked through our doors," says the center's founder and dean, Rabbi Marvin Hier. "He's the real McCoy."

Leyden's journey from normal kid to thug and back again, began when he was a teenager in the blue-collar town of Fontana, California. His parents divorced when he was 15, and he became angry, lonely and, most important to skinhead recruiters, vulnerable. "I needed to lash out," he explains. "They look for young, angry kids who need a family." He dropped out of school and began meeting skinheads hanging around the punk-rock scene. The trappings—bomber jacket, shaved head and steel-toed Dr. Martens boots—and hard-line beliefs soon followed. "These were good guys, I thought," he says now. "I thought I was being patriotic. We would drink and fight, try to clean up America that way." At one party he attacked a white youth who was dating a black girl and who had objected to his neo-Nazi ranting. "I kicked him bloody until somebody pulled me off, then grabbed a beer and joked about it," Leyden recalls. Over the years, he says, hundreds of such fights followed.

His parents, Sharon and Thomas Leyden Sr., who say they raised their son to abhor racism, were horrified by his transformation. But when Sharon confronted him, she says, "it didn't work at all." They finally agreed he would not talk about "those things" at her house or bring his thuggish friends through her door. "He would just be my son," Sharon says. "I told him I believed people always come back to what they really are inside. And I knew what he was inside, and that he would be back."

First, though, she had to watch him go still farther away. When he was 21, Leyden joined the Marines. According to Leyden, for the first two years of his service at the Kaneohe Bay Marine Corps Air Station in Hawaii, his supervisors chose to overlook his extracurricular activities. "Off duty, I'd walk around in a tank top so people could see my tattoos," he says. "I wore my Dr. Martens, kept my hair as short as possible and tucked in my pants the way Nazis used to do. I had a Third Reich battle flag in my locker and the Confederate Stars and Bars on my wall."

And Leyden was doing more than just collecting paraphernalia; he was developing into a sophisticated neo-Nazi activist. Through a fellow skinhead he came to the attention of Tom Metzger, founder of the White Aryan Resistance, based in California. "Tom wanted more military recruiters," Leyden recalls. "They started sending me literature." And he worked hard for his cause, recruiting at least four fellow travelers, who then went off to other bases. The Marines finally reacted when he had Nazi storm-trooper lightning bolts tattooed on his neck. In a 1990 evaluation his superior officer wrote, "Loyalty is questionable, as he willingly admits to belonging to a radical group called 'skinheads.'" Leyden then received an "other than honorable" discharge, for what the military dubbed "alcohol-related" misbehavior.

Once he returned to the civilian world, the "movement" embraced him. His racist friends even helped him find a wife. "They wrote and asked if I was meeting skinhead girls," Leyden remembers. "When I said it was hard in Hawaii, white-power girls on the mainland started to write." Leyden clicked with Nicole Rodman, who met him at the airport when he returned to California. They had an Aryan wedding two weeks after meeting and were legally married in 1992.

By day Leyden worked as a telephone installer. By night, he claims, Nicole was pulling him deeper into the skinhead world. She introduced him to such key characters as Metzger, his son John and skinhead martyr Geremi Rineman, who was paralyzed during a racial gunfight. Neo-Nazis generally agree that the Metzgers set the standard for inventive recruiting when John insulted Roy Innis of the Congress of Racial Equality during a 1988 Geraldo Rivera show and started a slugfest. Rivera got a broken nose in the ensuing brawl, and White Aryan Resistance's telephone lines lit up with new members. "After that," notes Leyden, "when somebody said he joined in 1988, we knew he was a Geraldo skin."

Leyden took similar tactics to southern California schools, papering junior high campuses with hate material to provoke fighting between white and nonwhite kids. Days after a fight, he would ask white students, "Shouldn't there be a group for you?" Affectionately known as "Grandpa" because of his advanced age, Leyden led younger skinheads on recruiting drives, tossing White Aryan Resistance leaflets on doorsteps and giving racial comics to young teenagers on their way home from school.

Beneath the energy and drama of his extremist life, though, discomfort began to gnaw at Leyden. For starters he was finding his social life to be cloyingly ingrown. "We usually stayed home to avoid contact with other races," Leyden explains. And as discontent seeped in, so did conflict. Leyden's brother is a policeman, and skinhead jokes about killing cops started to seem less than funny. His mother, who had polio as a child, has a slight limp, while Leyden's closest friends were busy calling disabled people "surplus whites."

But as he grew away from the movement, his wife remained loyal, Leyden says, spending more and more time with hard-core skinheads, some of whom Leyden thought were involved with guns and drugs. Following Nicole's wishes, the couple had left California for the "whiter" environment of St. George, Utah, and when he lost his job there, to Hailey, Idaho. (Nicole declined to comment for this story.) The marriage began to fall apart, and Leyden says he reached a torturous emotional crossroad: he even contemplated striking out to locate remnants of the Order, the near extinct racist commando units smashed by federal authorities more than a decade ago.

In the end, though, his two boys, now 2 and 4, kept him from the edge. "We have a saying in the movement that you don't want the weekend patriot—you want his kid," he observes. "I took a long look at my two sons. If my oldest is that radical now, he and his brother might be Order members some day. They'll murder people because of their skin color, religion or sexual preference. They'll go to jail, maybe die. My kids will be sacrificed. The idea hurt." Last fall he left Nicole, with whom he is now engaged in a bitter custody battle, and returned to California to live with his mother. It took some time, but with Sharon Leyden's encouragement he found the courage to contact the people at the Wiesenthal Center, a place his mother had heard about on TV news. "I'd spent years praying that hate would be removed from this family," she said recently. "I'm proud of my son." He had finally come home.

 Article Review Form at end of book.

- Although much legislative progress has been made toward racial equality, serious social inequalities along the lines of race persist.

- Members of society from all races can find ways to participate in challenging racism—through education, public protest, community organizing, and the taking of responsibility for ending racism. Because European-Americans especially benefit from American racial stratification, they have a crucial role to play in abolishing racism.

R.E.A.L. Sites

This list provides a print preview of typical **Coursewise** R.E.A.L. sites. (There are over 100 such sites at the **Courselinks**™ site.) The danger in printing URLs is that web sites can change overnight. As we went to press, these sites were functional using the URLs provided. If you come across one that isn't, please let us know via email to: webmaster@coursewise.com. Use your Passport to access the most current list of R.E.A.L. sites at the **Courselinks** site.

Site name: Race Traitor—Abolish the White Race by Any Means Necessary

URL: http://www.postfun.com/racetraitor/features/abolish.html

Why is it R.E.A.L.? This online journal addresses racism by declaring that the way to end it is by abolishing the white race—not through genocide but through education that critically examines the social construction of whiteness and the benefits attached to it.

Key topics: whiteness, antiracism, abolition of whiteness

Try this: Read this introductory page from "Race Traitor." Outline the logic of the argument in the paper. Do you agree with the argument or not? Write a reaction paper explicating why you support or do not support the conclusions "Race Traitor" draws. What are the implications of your position for your personal actions?

Site name: Anti-Racist Community Work: A Radical Approach, by Professor Rowena Arshad

URL: http://curry.edschool.virginia.edu/go/multicultural/papers/malcolm1.html

Why is it R.E.A.L.? This paper, written from the perspective of a scholar focused on ending racism in Scotland, offers additional ideas about conducting antiracist community work.

Key topics: racism, antiracism, community organizing

Try this: Read the paper. Consider how generalizable Dr. Arshad's recommendations are to the U.S. context. Outline how we might take a "radical approach" to antiracist community work in the United States.

Site name: Will We Ever Get Rid of Racism? Your Reaction

URL: http://news2.thdo.bbc.co.uk/hi/english/talking%5Fpoint/ newsid%5F285000/285352.asp

Why is it R.E.A.L.? This site, managed by the BBC, allows anyone with web access to state an opinion about whether racism can be or will be eradicated. Interesting comments from people from many countries address this important question.

Key topics: racism, public opinion

Try this: Read the comments posted on the list and analyze them sociologically. Do some groups of people take particular perspectives on the issue? For example, do people from wealthy countries see the issue differently from how people from poor countries see it? Do men and women differ in any systematic ways in their attitudes or predictions? Offer an interpretation of the patterns you find.

Index

Note: Names and page numbers in **bold** type indicate authors and their articles; page numbers in *italics* indicate illustrations; page numbers followed by *t* indicate tables; page numbers followed by *n* indicate notes.

Putting it in *Perspectives*
-Review Form-

Your name:_____   Date: _____

Reading title: _____

Summarize: Provide a one-sentence summary of this reading: _____

_____

_____

_____

Follow the Thinking: How does the author back the main premise of the reading? Are the facts/opinions appropriately supported by research or available data? Is the author's thinking logical?

_____

_____

_____

_____

_____

_____

Develop a Context (answer one or both questions): How does this reading contrast or complement your professor's lecture treatment of the subject matter? How does this reading compare to your textbook's coverage?

_____

_____

_____

_____

_____

_____

_____

Question Authority: Explain why you agree/disagree with the author's main premise.

_____

_____

_____

_____

_____

_____

_____

COPY ME! Copy this form as needed. This form is also available at http://www.coursewise.com
Click on: *Perspectives*.